A HISTORY OF THE
FIRST WORLD WAR IN
100
OBJECTS

This book is dedicated to the memory of
Professor and Brigadier Richard Holmes, CBE, TD
scholar, gentleman and soldier
patron and founder of the Guild of Battlefield Guides

A HISTORY OF THE
FIRST WORLD WAR IN
100
OBJECTS

John Hughes-Wilson

IWM Consultant, Nigel Steel
Editor, Mark Hawkins-Dady

CONTENTS

CONTENTS

Without a doubt, the First World War changed everything. The years 1914–18 stand as a Rubicon over which all those who were involved in the war, directly and indirectly, were forced to cross. What seemed a gilded way of life of the late Edwardian era, imbued with wealth and empire and majesty, was lost as irretrievably as if a giant pair of iron gates had slammed shut across it.

Moreover, the seeds of so much discontent were sown in the war's immediate aftermath that they bore poisoned fruit over succeeding decades. The disillusionment that set in during the late 1920s led to appeasement in the face of aggressive dictators in the 1930s, and to yet another world war in the 1940s as – in the view of many – the First World War's unfinished business exploded again. Later, Communist Russia, born in the chaos of 1917, provided one side in a Cold War that framed world events from the 1950s to the 1980s, and which saw proxy "hot" wars in the Middle East, Africa and Asia. In the 1990s and 2000s even renewed worries about Germany's power and the outbreak of Balkan violence returned, so familiar from 1914. In short, so much of what defines us and our world in the early 21st century can be traced back to "The Great War for Civilization".

The story of that war has been told many times, but this book offers a fresh approach. As its starting point it takes the material legacy of the war. Thousands of different objects and artefacts dating back to 1914–18 survive, ranging from the mundane to the extraordinary, from the terrifying to the humorous. Each has its own story to tell. Here, 100 of these micro-stories form a spine around which has been woven a comprehensive narrative relating what happened in the run up to the war, during the war itself and in its immediate aftermath.

As a result, this book offers a multi-track approach. For a straightforward, full narrative, readers can start at the beginning and move forward, following developments on a broadly chronological basis. They can trace events as they played out over several continents – events which led to the demise of four empires (German, Austro-Hungarian, Russian and Ottoman) and casualties in their millions, confirming that it was truly a war like no other ever experienced before.

Alternatively, readers can take a more thematic approach and, via the chapter headings and cross-references, pursue particular strands – for example, the Western Front year by year, or changes in the way of life for civilians back home; the arrival of aerial warfare, or the development of submarine warfare; the advent of poison gas and the tank, or the emergence of modern propaganda.

At the heart of the book lies the fundamental relationship between the "big picture" and the intimate insights offered by the 100 objects, the majority taken from the unparalleled collections of Britain's Imperial War Museum – an institution itself inaugurated in 1917 as a direct response to the war. Looking at history via objects is not a new idea. But rather than 100 purely generic or symbolic objects, those chosen here invariably have particular stories to tell – of their makers, of their users and of how they were discovered or preserved. By appreciating these dimensions, we are brought more starkly face to face with the human angle – the individuals connected with the objects. To really understand the First World War, it is as important to listen to the thoughts of an individual Tommy about his rations, or his wife's disgruntlement at food queues back home, as it is to grasp the grand strategy of battles or the horrifying statistics of casualties.

We live daily with the consequences of the First World War. Truly, it still shapes the world in which we live. Its bloody history sounds out as a warning to us all, and each one of these 100 objects echoes like a bell across the intervening passage of time.

John Hughes-Wilson
Nigel Steel

Warships of the Imperial German Navy's 2nd Battle Squadron make a stately progress into the North Sea, prior to 1914. The most visible flexing of German military muscle in the years before the war was the expansion of her navy. To British eyes it suggested that German ambitions went well beyond continental Europe, threatening the British Empire itself. The stage was being set for a global war, fought on land, at sea and in the air.

INTRODUCTION

IMPERIALISM, NATIONALISM & THE ROAD TO WAR

1

01

KING GEORGE'S IMPERIAL CROWN
THE HEYDAY OF THE BRITISH EMPIRE

BEFORE 1914

In the early years of the 20th century, the British Empire was arguably at its zenith. Britain did not just rule the waves, but also administered vast swathes of land – accounting for a quarter of the globe. It was a situation that, as the great Victorian statesman Lord Salisbury observed, encouraged the sentiment that "the sun never sets on our Empire".

Such an empire was not achieved by brute force and bayonets – which is not to say that force had not played a part in the building and policing of empire. From Henry Morgan's first piratical looting of the Spanish West Indies in the late 1600s to the annexation of the gold and diamonds of South Africa in 1899, Britons had never flinched from using arms to seize valuable assets. And when the future Earl Kitchener of Khartoum marched into the Sudan in 1898 he brought with him a modern army and several Maxim machine guns, both of which proved extremely efficient in slaughtering the native opposition.

However, Kitchener illustrates the counterbalancing dimension, too. He – and Britons generally – saw his imperial mission not as crude conquest but as enlightening liberation, in this case to crush the Islamic fundamentalism of the day. From a Victorian perspective, the British Empire brought the benefits of civilization, law, commerce and Christianity to less-favoured peoples; it was a kind of duty, in Kipling's poetic phrase the "White man's burden". In a post-imperial age it is unacceptable to espouse such ideas and values. But by the standards of the time they were a reflection of noble ideals, and for Britons of all classes – from the great aristocratic houses to

> "THE SUN NEVER SETS ON OUR EMPIRE."
>
> *Lord Salisbury*

> "THAT'S BECAUSE GOD DOES NOT TRUST THE BRITISH IN THE DARK!"
>
> *Colvin R. De Silva*

British imperial majesty was encapsulated in the Imperial Crown of India. It was created by royal jewellers Garrard & Co. in 1911, to be worn by George V at the spectacle of the Delhi Durbar to mark his accession as "King Emperor". The combined weight of its emeralds, rubies, sapphires and 6,100 diamonds prompted him to note: "Rather tired after wearing the Crown for 3 ½ hours, it hurt my head, as it is pretty heavy." The band at its base is set with 16 jewelled clusters of emeralds, sapphires and diamonds, and above this four cross-*pattées*, containing rubies, alternate with four fleurs-de-lys containing emeralds. Out of each of these a half-arch rises up to the *monde* (or globe), topped by another emerald set in a cross-*pattée*. Not actually part of the Crown Jewels, the Imperial Crown is nevertheless today kept with them in the Tower of London. No Durbars were held for the accessions of Edward VIII and George VI, so the Delhi Durbar of December 1911 represented the only occasion on which this majestic symbol was used.

the grimiest slums – the empire represented something solid, something proud and a force for good. Its showcase was the (generally efficient and honest) administration of what was long regarded as the empire's "jewel in the crown", India, by a mere 1,000 civil servants.

The truth is that the rationale of the British Empire was complex and many-faceted. It was part global commerce, economics and trade; part military and naval bases worldwide to protect those interests; and part the bringing of civilization, "true religion" and progress.

There were, of course, critics of empire even then. In southern Africa, the Anglo-Boer War (1899–1902) was a defining moment, seen by British radicals as little more than a greedy war of conquest. The herding of Boer wives and children into "concentration camps" and their subsequent deaths from poor sanitation and disease created an outcry that rattled many of the Victorian Establishment's complacent certainties. In the House of Commons, the Welsh MP David Lloyd George denounced what he called a "naked war of annexation" in ringing terms as one in which "the savagery which must necessarily follow will stain the name of this country". Anti-imperialist thinkers also saw – quite correctly – that Britain's armed forces served overseas primarily to protect the flow of money back to London. They also observed – equally correctly – that this money did not go to benefit the British taxpayer, who had subsidized those armed forces, nor to Britons in general, but to a tiny handful of plutocrats, bankers and speculators such as Cecil Rhodes, with his grandiose dream of a British railway from the Cape to Cairo, and the great banking houses like Rothschilds. Well might J.A. Hobson argue, in his 1902 study *Imperialism*, that "Finance is the governor of the Imperial engine, directing the energy and determining the work." Many politicians, including the former prime ministers Gladstone and Disraeli, had made large sums from imperial finance. While riches appeared to accrue to the few, the costs of maintaining and defending the empire, and the drain of some of the best brains to run it, arguably constituted an enormous burden on the motherland.

To the man or woman in the street none of this was apparent. They saw only the shop-front glories of empire: the Diamond Jubilee of the old Queen in 1897 or the ever-spreading tide of red across the map of the world. To even the poorest members of society this demonstration of Britain's imperial pomp and reach was living proof that the British were somehow a superior race, that Britain's achievements were unsurpassed and that Britain really was a great power.

One exotic occasion, captured on early film, says it all. In December 1911, British imperial majesty demonstrated its potency on the dusty plains outside Delhi. There, "King Emperor" George V received his Indian subjects' homage in a magnificent traditional ceremony known as a Durbar, combining pomp, demonstrations of allegiance and opulence. Hundreds of thousands of visitors flocked to the Durbar, with a great tented city built to house them. Foremost were more than 560 Indian princes and rulers, each of whom was to pledge allegiance and bow three times before the king emperor and queen empress as they sat on silver thrones beneath the rich canopy of the Royal Pavilion. Although the Durbar marked George's accession, it was not a coronation; nevertheless, a crown was needed to complete the ceremony. Yet, as the Old Royal Law of Britain forbade the Crown Jewels from being taken abroad, a new one was needed. There could scarcely have been a more dazzling embodiment of the empire's glory in the years leading up to 1914 than the Imperial Crown of India, its thousands of gemstones set within a frame of silver, laminated with gold. It cost £60,000, a princely sum paid for by the exchequers of India.

Such a spirit of imperial self-confidence and cohesion stretched well beyond India, too, and ensured that the "British lion's cubs" of the great White Dominions also lined up behind British interests. In 1914, the British government regarded Canada, Australia, New Zealand and South Africa as virtual extensions of metropolitan Britain herself. Fortunately, so did the Dominions. If the empire was a hidden burden to Britain in peacetime, in war it would suddenly become a major asset.

Thus, when Britain did declare war in August 1914, the government automatically committed the colonies and Dominions, who gave solid military, financial and material support over the next four years. Over 2.5 million men would serve in the Dominions' armies, as well as many volunteers from the Crown Colonies, including hundreds of thousands from India. In 1917 this contribution was recognized by Lloyd George, by then British prime minister, when he invited the Dominions' prime ministers to join the Imperial War Cabinet and help coordinate Britain's global policy.

The British Empire survived the war, of course, and even expanded in its aftermath. But it is salutary to remember that in 1914 imperial glory and maritime reach were no guarantees of victory in a scenario that Britain had managed to avoid for a century: full-scale conflict with the massed armies of powerful European rivals.

King Emperor George V and Queen Empress Mary glance towards the camera during the affirmation of Britain's imperial control over India that was the Delhi Durbar (12 December 1911). In the war of empires that followed in 1914, Indian troops would play a full part, on the Western Front, in Mesopotamia, in East Africa, in Palestine and at Gallipoli.

02

THE PEN THAT SIGNED THE ULSTER COVENANT
BRITISH TROUBLES & IRISH TENSIONS

1909 TO 1914

There is a view that the high summer of 1914 represented a brief golden age, when the country bathed in its imperial glow and the British Isles stood strong, prosperous and united. Pride in empire there was, but as for the domestic situation nothing could be further from the truth. From the time that Herbert Asquith became prime minister in April 1908 until the outbreak of war in August 1914, Britain was rocked by crises and spasms of increasingly violent confrontation. Industry, already being economically outstripped by foreign rivals, was beset with strikes; the government battled with the House of Lords in a constitutional crisis; and there was an increasingly militant movement to win votes for women.

By far the greatest threat was of Irish civil war. The prospect of granting Home Rule for Ireland, with a Parliament in Dublin, provoked the threat of a violent backlash from Protestants in Ulster – and even mutiny in the British Army. Nothing offers a clearer window onto the troubled times than the pages of the popular magazine *Punch*. Its headline cartoon for 1 July 1914 portrayed Britannia gazing nervously from her ramparts across the Irish Sea to the dark clouds on the horizon, where a storm whips up the words "civil war".

> **"THE ARMY WILL HEAR NOTHING OF POLITICS FROM ME, AND IN RETURN I EXPECT TO HEAR NOTHING OF POLITICS FROM THE ARMY."**
>
> *Prime Minister Herbert Asquith*

This pen was used by Colonel Fred Crawford at the signing – reputedly in blood – of the Ulster Covenant, one of the totemic occasions of modern Irish history. A leader of the Protestant resistance to the introduction of Irish Home Rule, it was Crawford who organized the illegal landing, in April 1914, of rifles and ammunition for use by the new paramilitary Ulster Volunteer Force. Eighteen months earlier, on 28 September 1912, he used this pen to put his name to the Ulster Covenant, the solemn pledge eventually signed by more than 470,000 men and women in Ulster stating their loyalty to the United Kingdom and their determination to resist the establishment of an independent Irish Parliament. The tradition that Crawford signed in blood persisted, but a forensic analysis of the bright red signature in 2012 revealed no residual traces of blood. It appears more likely that the claim was simply part of the heightened emotions of this pivotal day. The pen is now kept in the Ulster Museum.

The years 1909–14 witnessed widespread industrial unrest, as many working people experienced rising prices and stagnant incomes. Wage cuts, poor working conditions and steady inflation left many of the lower paid increasingly disgruntled and militant. Trades union membership rose by half, and organized labour began to flex its muscles with greater confidence, resulting in strikes, some of them violent. Troops were sent to reinforce police at Tonypandy in South Wales in November 1910, when striking miners rioted through the streets, and to Liverpool in the following, hot, summer, when dock strikes fuelled months of virtual anarchy. The army shot two rioters, the Cabinet ordered a battleship to the Mersey, and Liverpool's lord mayor even warned that "a revolution was in progress".

Inevitably, productivity was affected. In 1913, over 11 million days were lost to strikes and related actions. By 1914 the nation that had proudly proclaimed herself the "Workshop of the World" at the Great Exhibition of 1851 was beginning to lag behind. Manufacturing enterprises built up half a century before were being challenged by the more modern processes of the United States and, more seriously, Germany.

In politics, the Liberal government's welfare reforms – non-contributory old age pensions and a national insurance scheme – drove up taxes, as did the naval expansion to counter German ambitions (*see* Chapter 4). The House of Lords voted down the budget, and a constitutional crisis was only avoided by the king threatening to create enough new Liberal peers to curtail the power of the Lords as the government pushed through a new Parliament Act (1911).

All this was taking place against a vociferous and highly visible campaign of direct action by Emmeline Pankhurst's "Suffragettes", the Women's Social and Political Union, who represented the more radical element of the suffragist campaign for women's voting rights. The Suffragettes recognized the oxygen of publicity that a spell in jail generated and moved from chaining themselves to railings to violent protest. From 1912 an arson campaign began, artworks were slashed and golf courses sprayed with acid. While their actions at no time imperilled the state, they contributed to a national mood of instability.

Amid this sea of troubles, it was in Ireland, though, that Britain faced her most acute crisis. Since 1801, Ireland had been constitutionally part of the United Kingdom, and a vociferous and determined Protestant minority in the northern counties ("Ulster") had seen off previous attempts to reach a Home Rule settlement, fearing Catholic domination.

When, in April 1912, Asquith introduced a third Parliamentary Bill that offered Ireland a separate Parliament and limited self-government, many of Ireland's Protestants were outraged. They were supported at Westminster by other Unionists, including the bulk of the Conservative Party Opposition. The previous September, Sir Edward Carson, leader of the Ulster Unionist Party, had told a rally outside Belfast that Unionists might soon have to form their *own* government in Ulster if Home Rule were granted, and he ordered a draft constitution be drawn up for it. A week after the introduction of Asquith's Bill, Carson addressed another massed rally, at which his supporters agreed to sign a solemn pledge of unwavering opposition to Home Rule.

Thus, on 28 September 1912 – Ulster Day – in a well-organized ceremony combining religious fervour with political defiance, 80,000 people gathered in Belfast to sign the Ulster Covenant. After attending church, Carson headed a march to Belfast City Hall, guarded by 2,500 men armed with wooden staves and commanded by Fred Crawford. Using a special silver pen, Carson was the first to sign the Covenant, on a table draped with the Union flag.

Protestant resistance now moved up a gear with the establishment of the paramilitary Ulster Volunteer Force (UVF), many of its members Covenant-signers. In the south the Catholic nationalists, too, were beginning to mobilize, by way of the Irish Volunteers. They lacked the organization of the UVF, but they contributed to the overall sense of an inexorable slide towards direct confrontation.

As the Home Rule Bill progressed through Parliament, tensions continued to rise and now began to permeate the army. In March 1914, the army commander in Ireland, Lieutenant General Sir Arthur Paget, was warned to prepare for the securing of key buildings. But he was concerned that many of his officers came from Ulster families and faced divided loyalties. His advice from the War Office was that "officers whose homes are actually in the province of Ulster ... may apply for permission to be absent from duty during the period of operations, and will be 'allowed to disappear'

"A LIFE OF SECURITY; A LIFE OF SEDENTARY OCCUPATION; A LIFE OF RESPECTABILITY: THESE THREE QUALITIES GIVE THE KEY TO [ENGLAND'S] SPECIAL CHARACTERISTICS ... AND ASPIRATIONS."

C.F.G. Masterman, The Condition of England, *1909*

from Ireland". But those without this close connection, and who simply found the prospect of firing on other British citizens distasteful, would "at once be dismissed from the service". Many of his officers regarded it as an ultimatum.

Matters reached a head when, at the Curragh barracks in central Ireland, Brigadier General Hubert Gough, whose home was in Ulster, warned that 57 of his 70 officers would resign on the spot rather than enforce Home Rule. The government was shocked by the so-called "Curragh Mutiny" and the realization that the army could not be relied on. In the end, Gough was given a Cabinet guarantee that his troops "would not be called upon" to enforce Home Rule.

Despite every effort to find a political solution, there appeared to be no way out of the deadlock. The paramilitaries were openly arming and preparing for a bloody confrontation. At the end of April 1914, the UVF landed a shipment of 30,000 foreign rifles and 3 million rounds of ammunition in Ulster and swiftly spirited them into hiding. At the beginning of July, the Irish Volunteers landed its own cache of arms in the south. This time British soldiers blocked the way, but the guns got through nonetheless. Across Ireland, two armed militia were now drilling and preparing for a civil war. Meanwhile, far away in the Balkans an international crisis of ever greater proportions was forcing Whitehall's attention onto mainland Europe.

Irish Home Rule *did* come into effect a few weeks after the outbreak of the First World War, but it was then suspended for the duration of the conflict. Yet it is worth remembering that in July 1914 the shooting war expected by many Britons looked more likely to begin on their own doorsteps than in some far-off foreign field.

Workers gather to hear speeches outside the Woolwich Arsenal, London, during their strike of July 1914. Around 8,000 of them downed tools following a dispute over the use of non-union labour, which the Spectator *described as "one of the very gravest incidents in the recent history of labour unrest". In summer 1914, the British Isles was a volatile place.*

03

A PRUSSIAN *PICKELHAUBE*
PRUSSIAN MILITARISM & GERMANY'S RISE

18TH TO EARLY 20TH CENTURIES

The crisis that enveloped Europe in summer 1914 involved decisions taken by a newly emergent power – a nation that 50 years previously did not even exist. A united Germany was only born in 1871, when her patchwork of independent kingdoms, grand-duchies and other states (and statelets) finally came together in a political union. They did so not as equals but around Prussia, which in less than a decade had demonstrated her strength through defeats of Denmark (1864), Austria (1866) and France (1871). The King of Prussia now became the new "Kaiser", or Emperor, of the German imperial state, and Prussian attitudes and ways of doing things were embedded in the new country.

Prussian pre-eminence was in one sense surprising: because of her poor soil and relative poverty, Prussia was known as the "Sandbox of the Holy Roman Empire". But over the centuries, the challenge of life beyond the southern Baltic coast had bred a tough and hardy people, as well as a system of economic and military obligation. Prussian landowners – the aristocratic class of *Junkers* – ruled over a peasant population of serfs tied to the land. This rule by an elite was reinforced by the Prussian kings' adoption, from the 1730s, of universal military service through regional recruiting districts called "cantons". Each was tied to a local regiment, and a list was kept of all men of military age, who were enrolled automatically into the regiment for one year's training before being sent home on indefinite unpaid leave to work the land. Legally, every man remained an enlisted soldier. This was the system that was credited with creating Prussia's unique military-based society.

The distinctive helmet known as the *Pickelhaube* came to represent Germany's military tradition and became one of the best-remembered objects of the First World War. Its compact, rounded body of shiny leather was topped by a tall metal spear-like spike, designed to fend off a blow from a sword. Developed by the Prussian army, it was subsequently used across the whole of Germany's new Imperial Army (albeit reluctantly in Bavaria where it was seen to be *too* Prussian), and in 1914 German soldiers went to war in a design first introduced in 1895. The still-cherished identities of pre-unification Germany were conveyed in the coats of arms adorning the front of the helmet, the most common being that of Prussia. For Allied soldiers, the helmets became much-prized souvenirs; this particular Prussian one was picked up by Private Farndon Groom, who went to France with the 7th Battalion, London Regiment, in March 1915. He kept it for the rest of his life. By 1916, with leather in short supply and a move, across the Western Front, towards adopting metal helmets, the *Pickelhaube* gave way to the spike-less *Stahlhelm*.

> "A WAR... IS BUT THE HIGHEST EXPRESSION OF TRUE CIVILIZATION ... WAR IS A POLITICAL NECESSITY AND THAT IT IS FOUGHT IN THE INTEREST OF BIOLOGICAL, SOCIAL AND MORAL PROGRESS."
>
> *General Friedrich von Bernhardi, 1912*

Because most officer appointments were restricted to the nobility and landowners, this meant that many *Junkers* were simultaneously army captain and landlord over their serf-conscripts. Military discipline reinforced feudal jurisdiction and frequently encroached into strictly civil affairs. Thus, if a man wanted to leave the country without permission, he could be charged with desertion – for every man was either a trained soldier or a potential recruit. It is not for nothing that the French thinker and politician Mirabeau observed, following the exploits of Frederick the Great (1712–86), that: "Prussia is not a state with an army, but an army with a state." The serfs were emancipated in 1807, but the country remained essentially a "military-agrarian complex", controlled by the interlocking interests of the monarchy, the army and a feudal aristocracy.

The combination of Prussia's stunning victories and Minister-President Prince Otto von Bismarck's considerable diplomatic skills proved powerful arguments for persuading Berlin's neighbours to unite under Prussia. However, despite recognizing the practical advantages of unification, they remained wary of an inevitable Prussian dominance and its potential dangers. For one thing, the appointment of the imperial chancellor – Bismarck – lay in the hands of the new Kaiser, and as such effectively became a Prussian choice. Not directly linked to the elected Parliament (*Reichstag*), the German chancellor was nevertheless responsible for devising and instituting national policy. With the appointment in his gift, the Kaiser was able to exert a much stronger degree of direct political control over his chancellor than, for example, the British monarch could do over his prime minister, particularly in areas such as defence and foreign policy.

Between 1871 and 1914, the united Germany underwent a massive transformation. Socially and politically, there remained tensions between Prussia and the other regions, between the aristocratic landowning elite and the emerging middle classes, whose prosperity was linked to rising urban industries, and above all between liberal civilians and the military cabal that lay at the heart of the state. The liberals steadily sought to limit the power of the military and win control over the army, but failed.

Possibly the greatest change in Germany's first 40 years was her emergence as a major global economic power. With great dynamism, she set about introducing the latest, most efficient industrial practices. The result was a rapid increase in manufacturing capability. In 1870 British industry dominated the world, meeting almost one-third of the world's industrial demands. By 1910, Britain's share of the global manufacturing market had fallen to less than 15 per cent, now supplanted by the United States which had over one-third. But the real surprise lay in the upstart Germany, now – albeit narrowly – besting Britain with a market share of almost 16 per cent. Not only in specialist areas, such as chemicals and optics, was Britain falling behind, but her capacity even lagged in traditional materials like steel. British output may have almost doubled in two decades to reach 6.4 million tons by 1910, but in the same period, German output more than quintupled to reach 13.5 million tons.

This rapid rise unsurprisingly worried many of Germany's neighbours. Initially, Bismarck pursued the diplomacy of peaceful coexistence, while projecting the new Germany as a mature and responsible nation. But in June 1888 this situation was radically altered by the accession of a thrusting new Kaiser, Wilhelm II, who harboured ambitions for Germany's growing political strength to be more widely recognized across the world. Dismissing Bismarck within two years, Wilhelm began to lead Germany on a "new course", most notably in international affairs.

As the balance of power now shifted, Germany deepened ties with her cultural and linguistic compatriots in Austria-Hungary. But relations with the powers that flanked Germany to east and west – Russia and France – deteriorated, and in 1894 a Franco-Russian *entente* was signed. It was intended to provide both countries with mutual support, but it contributed to a German sense of containment and encirclement. Increasingly feeling herself under threat, Germany's overconfident military now became a political factor. The Prussian-dominated General Staff in Berlin was determined to avoid a war on two fronts. Its head, Count Alfred von Schlieffen, outlined a plan that would come to bear his name, by which Germany could strike a swift knockout blow to eliminate France from any war and then tackle Russia. Through its close links to the Kaiser, and with little concern for the feelings of the *Reichstag*, the General Staff effectively became a political force in its own right, encouraging and even setting the nation's European foreign policy agenda. Guided by the rigid parameters of the railway timetables that would need to be followed in the event of mobilization, the army began to set in train – literally – operational plans as precise as a jeweller's watch movement that were effectively outside civil political control and diplomatic restraints.

The army thus played a powerful role in Germany in the years leading up to the First World War, and German society became increasingly dominated by what was seen by many observers as rampant militarism. But while the army may have been *the* dominating influence, it was not the only service flexing its muscles. At the very end of the 1890s the Imperial German Navy began to emerge from the shadow of the army. While the navy's influence in society as a whole may have been slight, its hold over the imagination of the Kaiser was great and, through this, its impact on Germany's fate between 1900 and 1914 eclipsed even that of the army.

A display of Pickelhauben *and other headgear, as a confident Kaiser Wilhelm II of Germany* (foreground, left), *flanked by his six sons, leads a parade through Berlin in 1913. It was a year that witnessed patriotic celebrations of the centenary of Prussia's Wars of Liberation against Napoleonic France, as well as the Kaiser's 25th year on the throne.*

04

SERGEANT MILLER'S RECRUITMENT SIGN
ANGLO-GERMAN NAVAL RIVALRY

1898 TO 1914

For over 100 years following Nelson's victory at Trafalgar (1805), Britain's Royal Navy had undisputed command of the world's oceans. This situation was a natural adjunct to protecting maritime commerce and projecting imperial power. Periodically waves ruffled the waters, such as when the French launched the world's first ironclad battleship, *La Gloire*, in 1859. But by 1861 Britain had her own iron-hulled battleship, HMS *Warrior*, prompting Lord Palmerston's satisfied observation that it looked like "a black snake among rabbits". Supremacy bred a certain complacency. Yet, as the century closed, Britain still possessed more battleships in service than the combined strength of Germany, France, Russia, the United States and Japan.

The picture was beginning to change, however, most acutely through the emergence of the new German *Kaiserliche Marine* (Imperial Navy), aggressively expanded from 1898 under Kaiser Wilhelm II and his naval secretary of state, Admiral Alfred von Tirpitz. The consequences for European security would be immense, as Berlin's naval ambitions ratcheted up tensions, reconfigured diplomatic relations and strained resources.

> The reign of Edward VII (1901–10) marked a period of resurgence for Britain's Royal Navy. A renewed vigour imbued its ranks in response to the alarming German efforts, from 1898, to create their own world-class navy. From 1904, Admiral Sir John ("Jackie") Fisher introduced sweeping changes and the frenetic Anglo-German naval arms race was turned on its head. As a vast shipbuilding programme progressed, recruitment continued to deliver the sailors and Marines to man the vessels. This unembellished, enamelled Edwardian recruitment sign was posted by Sergeant Major John Miller, Royal Marines, outside his house in Norwich. The "Admiralty recruiting office" was, in this case, his own front room. In King Edward's name, Sergeant Major Miller invited men to join the world's greatest navy and carry the essence of the British way of life across the empire. In a few years they would be doing considerably more than that.

The new Kaiser's ambitions reflected his personal admiration – and resentment – of the history, power and prestige of the Royal Navy. Germany possessed a small coastal fleet, mostly based in the Baltic, and had no real need for a wider "blue water" navy. But the Kaiser increasingly saw the size and strength of his fleet as a determinant of German aspirations and a symbol of Germany's right to a "place in the sun". Capricious and impulsive, Wilhelm wanted a navy big enough to challenge Britain's, and in Tirpitz he found an only too-willing partner. Both men absorbed US Captain

> **"THE NAVY IS THE MOST IMPORTANT DEFENCE OF THE COUNTRY, IN WHICH EVERY SUBJECT OF THE QUEEN HAS AN INTEREST OF THE DEEPEST CHARACTER."**
>
> *Justice Willes, Henwood versus Harrison (1872)*

Alfred Mahan's *Influence of Sea Power Upon History* (1890), including its emphasis on maritime control to encourage and protect commerce, and they thought that by building a navy to challenge British dominance they might convert the German *Reich* from a land-based *Grossmacht* into a global *Weltmacht* – from a great power into a world power.

They were well aware how provocative this move could be, and they also realized they could not create a larger fleet than the Royal Navy. But had not Mahan written that even an inferior fleet, simply through its existence, could influence the policy and actions of a larger one by maintaining the threat of a "fleet in being"? With sufficient strength, Tirpitz believed, they could inflict enough damage in a confrontation to eliminate Britain's fleet as a *world* power. In fact, he believed that to avert such a risk Britain would avoid battle, in which case her navy would be emasculated anyway. Moreover, such was the extent of the Royal Navy's global responsibilities that Tirpitz did not believe Britain would be able to concentrate enough ships in the waters around Germany to fight with the full weight of her theoretical power.

Tirpitz called this his *Risikogedanke*, or "risk theory", and risky it certainly was. The problem was that it cut both ways: Britain might back away, fearing potentially catastrophic losses, or she might rise to the challenge, solidifying British hostility to Germany. Thus, Tirpitz initially favoured a stealthy "brick by brick" approach, and his navy bills of 1898, 1900 and 1906 were designed to *discreetly* transform German naval might.

It was a dire miscalculation. Both Tirpitz and Wilhelm failed to appreciate just how sensitive the British were to any naval challenge, however disguised. The incipient German threat was a major factor in forcing Britain to re-examine strategic priorities, and effectively signalled the end of the century-long *Pax Britannica* and Britain's years of "splendid isolation". In 1902, an alliance was signed with Japan, which allowed Britain to reduce the strength of her fleet in the Far East (*see* Chapter 19). Two years later, with earlier colonial squabbles neatly shelved, Britain and her traditional rival France signed the Entente Cordiale. Among other things, this began a long process of redistributing Britain's naval strength from the Mediterranean to its home waters in the North Sea and the Channel. In exchange, the French navy began to take responsibility for the Mediterranean. By 1907 Britain had concluded a second *entente*, with Russia. Ironically, Germany's provocative naval expansion had actually precipitated an increased sense of German encirclement and helped create the Triple Entente in Europe against which it would fight in 1914.

Within the Royal Navy, profound changes were also at work. In October 1904, Admiral Sir John Fisher was appointed First Sea Lord, the navy's professional head. Eccentric and energetic, he was exactly the man to revitalize the Senior Service. He organized a major overhaul, scrapping old ships held in dockyard reserves ("a miser's hoard of useless junk" was his description of obsolescent cruisers) and embarking on a new strategy based on a large fleet concentrated in home waters – yet again, calling Tirpitz's bluff. Most importantly, he began a major shipbuilding programme based on an innovative design of battleship, HMS *Dreadnought*, which stunned the world at her launch in February 1906. She was the first all big-gun battleship, clad with heavy armour, boasting 12-inch guns and propelled by powerful steam turbines. She was a fast, formidable – and expensive – addition to the Royal Navy. At a stroke Fisher made all other battleships obsolete, including his own.

Tirpitz responded by openly demanding funds from a compliant *Reichstag* "to meet the British challenge". What followed was a naval arms race to rival the later Cold War in its relative cost and intensity. Between 1906 and 1912 Britain launched 29 capital ships (battleships and battlecruisers) compared to Germany's 17; Germany's naval budget doubled and Britain's shot up by 40 per cent. As costs heated up, relations between the two countries cooled.

By 1909 it was clear that Germany was building warships on an unprecedented scale. The Royal Navy's slender margin of superiority risked falling to just four dreadnoughts, and something like panic ensued. The "great naval scare" mobilized

British people and politicians into throwing funds behind a rapid construction programme: as politicians debated over whether to build four or six more dreadnoughts, in the end, as Winston Churchill wittily put it in 1909, "we compromised on eight". In fact, the government was responding to popular pressure under the slogan "We want eight, and we won't wait!" It made all the difference, when war came. By 1912 the Royal Navy's battle fleet had mushroomed to over 30 capital ships, consolidating what was now a solid margin over Germany.

The wisdom, albeit expensively bought, of ploughing money into Britain's strategic naval defence was demonstrated by the so-called Agadir Incident of 1911, concerning colonial rivalry in Morocco. France unilaterally sent troops, ostensibly to help put down a revolt against the sultan, but in the process defying an earlier agreement with Germany. So the Kaiser ordered the German gunboat SMS *Panther* to the coastal city of Agadir, on the pretext of protecting German citizens and business interests. It was a naked act of gunboat diplomacy and generated a crisis defused only by intense diplomacy and a run against German banks. It also demonstrated two realities: that German naval power was now a major factor in international disputes; and that relations between Berlin and the Entente allies were highly volatile.

By 1913, while the British continued to build battleships and battlecruisers as fast as they could, Germany discreetly switched to a policy of launching submarines. For both countries, the naval arms race was a massive drain on resources and fuelled pre-war suspicions. For Britain, it was, at least, a logical move to protect her security, her commerce and her empire. In 1918, as in 1914, Britannia still ruled the waves. As for the Kaiser, he suffered the indignity that, in 1918, sailors of his precious High Seas Fleet were in the forefront of the revolution that overthrew him.

A drawing, based on a photograph, of HMS Dreadnought after her launch by King Edward VII at Portsmouth (17 February 1906). This warship, the world's most powerful, lent her name to a whole new class of battleship, and Germany and Britain vied with each other to build more of them. In the subsequent war, both sides took great care to protect such naval assets.

05

A MAP OF EUROPEAN RIVALRY
EUROPE'S ALLIANCES & ANIMOSITIES

1870 TO 1914

The radical changes that swept through the Royal Navy in the decade before 1914 responded to the particular challenge of Germany's growing naval strength. But they also reflected Britain's more pragmatic strategic repositioning in an increasingly polarized world, as old rivals formed new pacts and dangerous threats emerged, creating a complex and – ultimately – too fragile Europe.

Perhaps the starting point for this European realignment was the bitter Franco-Prussian War of 1870–71, in which Prussian success spurred the unification of the German nation on the back of French defeat and humiliation. Indeed, it was on French soil, at Versailles, that German unity was proclaimed on 18 January 1871, and a month later the Prussian army marched through the Arc de Triomphe and down the Champs Elysées to underscore the sense of triumph. The concurrent loss of the French territories of Alsace and Lorraine to Germany fed an enduring French national desire for *la Revanche*: "revenge".

As a consequence, it could be said that France both expected and indeed wanted another war. And if renewed war was going to be inevitable, France needed allies when it came. Initially, Britain stood aloof, while Russia was kept sweet by Germany's Bismarck – at least until the new Kaiser, Wilhelm II, ditched his wily chancellor and abandoned this pragmatic friendship. Thus, when France and Russia signed a formal alliance in January 1894, Germany found herself sandwiched between them. The balance of power seemed to be shifting.

The polarization of Europe in 1914 is clearly reflected by this British poster, originally printed in London a few weeks after war began with a sardonic English caption. Each country is represented by national stereotypes, with the main belligerents as "Dogs of War" now let "loose in Europe". To the northwest stands a British bulldog, protected by a stocky Jack Tar restraining warships on leads. Aligned alongside a French poodle, the bulldog bites the nose of a German dachshund "thought to have gone mad". The dachshund is yoked to an "Austrian Mongrel" intent on bullying little Serbia. But Serbia is being protected by a Russian bear, exactly as the dachshund had hoped as this should allow it to "steal a bone or two through the fighting". Beyond the Balkans, a crouching Turk with a fez-wearing dachshund stretches out one hand to close the Dardanelles, while in the other he holds two German warships on a leash in the Black Sea. This clear piece of anti-German propaganda was actually reprinted in Hamburg and sold for 50 pfennigs, with the English title and text translated to lay the blame for war on aggressive, untrustworthy Britain. This is one of those German copies.

The new scenario increased the importance of Germany's already deepening relationship with Austria-Hungary. Prussia had fought and defeated Austria in 1866, and usurped from Austria the moral leadership of Europe's ethnic Germans. But Bismarck had been careful to nurture relations, and the two powers moved closer together in the years that followed. This process was fortunate for the Habsburg monarchs of Austria, as it disguised a steady decline in power for their multilingual, multinational patchwork empire of ethnic Germans, Magyars, Slavs, Czechs, Poles, Slovaks, Serbians and Italians. In 1867, recognition of the special position of the Magyars of Hungary created the Dual Monarchy, in which the Emperor of Austria became simultaneously King of Hungary.

Closer links produced a formal alliance (1879) between Germany and Austria-Hungary, which became a Triple Alliance when joined by Italy in 1882. Austria-Hungary, though, remained most threatened by the turbulent region of the Balkans. Here, as the Ottoman Empire contracted towards the edge of mainland Europe, local and nationalist rivalries filled the vacuum. In 1878, three new independent countries emerged – Serbia, Montenegro and Romania – and Bulgaria and Greece grew larger. These were dynamic nation-states, whose ethnic groups overlapped with those of Austria-Hungary's southern provinces.

Of particular concern, the emergence of Serbia created a new nation of Slavs. Vienna looked on, alarmed, at growing Serbian ambitions to unite all of the region's Slavs. Moreover, the changes in the political complexion of the Balkans exacerbated Austro-Hungarian tensions with Russia, who saw herself as protector of all the Balkans' Slavs. Conscious that such tensions could precipitate war, the two powers signed a ten-year pact (1897) agreeing not to intervene directly in the affairs of the Balkan nations. However, in 1908, Austria-Hungary stoked Balkan tensions when the old Ottoman region of Bosnia-Herzegovina declared unilateral independence. Instead Austria, given responsibility for Bosnia-Herzegovina at the Congress of Vienna that year, seized the opportunity to formally annex it, but in doing so, the empire acquired a million more Slavs, most of whom had no desire to fall under Habsburg rule.

Neither the Russian nor Austro-Hungarian empires were directly involved, though, in the vicious Balkan Wars of 1912 and 1913. In the First Balkan War, Bulgaria, Greece, Montenegro and Serbia united and successfully fought the Ottoman Empire for her residual territory in Europe. In the internecine Second Balkan War, Bulgaria fought Greece and Serbia over some of the spoils (Macedonia), with the Ottoman forces (and Romania) taking the opportunity to attack Bulgaria and regain territory. Almost 230,000 casualties died from the fighting or from disease.

Austria-Hungary itched to use the First Balkan War to resolve the issues that had long threatened her own internal stability, but fear of Russia's response kept her out. In Berlin's eyes, however, the war was perceived as one fought *by* Russia at arm's length, and Chancellor Theobold von Bethmann Hollweg made it clear that Germany would fully support Austria-Hungary if the fighting spilled out of the Balkans and Russia became involved. In return, London signalled that if a German attack on Russia pulled in the French, under the terms of the Franco-Russian alliance, then Britain would not be prepared to see the French defeated. These uncompromising diplomatic statements provided a chilling preview of the scenario that would play out only 18 months later.

By now, Britain's repositioning from her years of "splendid isolation" was complete. Indeed, the 1904 Entente Cordiale with France, underscored by the charm of Edward VII, had the effect of turning the politics of Europe upside down. It was a fact most clearly highlighted by the Agadir crisis in 1911 (*see* Chapter 4), where German hopes that Britain would criticize French actions came to nought – and, in fact, Germany's gunboat diplomacy simply moved the British and French closer together. After Agadir, the Franco-British redeployment of ships to protect the Mediterranean and the northern waters around the Channel was completed, and secret military discussions laid down clear plans for the despatch of an expeditionary force to France in the event of war.

Britain's deepening friendship with France was mirrored by her relationship with Russia. Never quite as close, it nevertheless moderated strategic threats to the security of the British Empire. Russia no longer cast quite such a shadow over India, or over Britain's position in the Middle East, allowing the British to reconsider the risks they faced and see ever more clearly where the primary threat lay – in Germany's increasingly aggressive policies.

In truth, the emergence of a new, enlarged and unified Germany – complete with a booming economy, a growing population of 68 million by 1914 and a large and efficient army – was always likely to destabilize the balance of power in Europe. For nearly 20 years this threat had been kept at bay by Bismarck's pragmatic diplomacy, but after his dismissal by Wilhelm II there is little doubt that Germany became a bellicose and ambitious state, whose world-power aspirations were ill-concealed. In October 1908, the Kaiser gave an alarming interview to the London *Daily Telegraph*, in which he boasted that his General Staff had planned British strategy during the Anglo-Boer War, warned that the majority of Germans were openly hostile to Britain and stated that "the legitimate ambition of patriotic Germans refuses to assign any bounds". British popular sentiment reflected Germany's challenge, with children cheekily claiming that the German product trademark "DRGM" really stood for "Dirty Rotten German Make".

With hindsight, it is clear that by the summer of 1914 the European nations stood on the verge of a geo-strategic earthquake. Like the subterranean shifts of vast tectonic plates, the European balance of power had changed in such a way that dangerous fault lines had built up, storing up enormous pressures. Whole nations, as well as individual citizens, stood waiting for an eruption. Both Germany and France were expecting and preparing for a showdown. But no-one knew when that would be or where it would occur.

In the end, it was to be in the Balkan city of Sarajevo in June 1914.

THE BOILING POINT.

The Balkan pot threatens to boil over in this 1912 Punch *cartoon by Leonard Raven-Hill. Attempting to keep a lid on the simmering tensions are some familiar national stereotypes of the Great Powers: Britain's John Bull and a French general (*back row*) along with a bearded Russian, a* Pickelhaube-*wearing Prussian and an amply moustached Austro-Hungarian (*perhaps the emperor*).*

06

THE ARCHDUKE'S BLOODSTAINED TUNIC
ASSASSINATION & THE ROAD TO WAR

SUMMER 1914

The original "shot heard 'round the world" was poet Walt Whitman's description of the opening salvo that led to American independence. But the phrase found a truly global context in the single shot that ended the life of the heir-presumptive to the Austro-Hungarian throne on 28 June 1914. The conspirators who set out to murder Archduke Franz Ferdinand had no clue that they would spark a cataclysm. They calculated that the worst that might happen would be another localized Balkan war, from which a Greater Serbia could emerge having "liberated" the remaining Serbs of the Austro-Hungarian Empire. Their miscalculation, soon to be compounded by the mis-steps of political and military leaders, meant that within six weeks the power blocs of Europe were lined up against one another in war across the continent. The archduke's cut and bloodstained military tunic remains as mute testimony to a deed that would result in the deaths of an estimated 16 million people.

Franz Ferdinand and his wife Sophie met their end in Sarajevo. This was the capital of the former Ottoman province of Bosnia-Herzegovina, whose annexation by Austria-Hungary in 1908 caused alarm in neighbouring Serbia. Serbia's military successes in the two Balkan Wars of 1912 and 1913 had emboldened elements within her army, and government, to stir up Serb nationalism within Austria's Balkan territories, including among the many ethnic Serbs of Bosnia.

> Unusually for Archduke Franz Ferdinand, on his visit to Sarajevo he was accompanied by his wife, Duchess Sophie of Hohenberg. It was rare for the couple to be seen together in public. The duchess was not of royal birth, and the marriage was considered to be "morganatic" – she could never have the same status as her husband, nor could her children inherit the Austro-Hungarian throne. On that day she shared her husband's fate, though, when one of the assassin's bullets hit her in the stomach; she collapsed onto the floor of their car, dying soon afterwards. The other bullet hit the archduke in the neck, and blood instantly spurted across the front of his blue high-collared ceremonial tunic, where the dark stains remain today. The archduke's aides tried to undo the jacket, but soon realized it would be quicker to cut through it. These cuts are also still clearly visible. Franz Ferdinand's tunic has traditionally been displayed in Vienna's *Heeresgeschichtliches Museum* (Military History Museum), in its Sarajevo Gallery, alongside the Graf & Stift car in which the royal couple were travelling, the gun used by killer Gavrilo Prinćip – and even the sofa on which the archduke died back at the town hall. The macabre, blood-spattered garment provides a visceral link with one of the most momentous events of the 20th century.

On Sunday 28 June 1914, the archduke and his wife were driven together into the Bosnian capital. His presence in Bosnia was officially as Inspector General of the Army; more symbolically, his presence demonstrated Austrian sway over the province. Unbeknown to him and his entourage, distributed along the route were six assassins from the Young Bosnia nationalist movement. They were sponsored by the Black Hand, a secret Serb society, and ultimately directed by the chief of Serbian military intelligence, Colonel Dragutin Dimitrjević, known as "Apis". Many Black Hand members held important Serbian army and government positions. The organization trained guerrillas and saboteurs, and had been responsible for a range of political murders (and attempted murders) and atrocities since the Balkan Wars. The Serbian Prime Minister Nikola Pašić may have known about some Black Hand operations, but seems to have been afraid at this stage to intervene with its operations. On 28 June, though, it was less the murderous professionalism of the Black Hand's proxies that delivered Franz Ferdinand to his fate, and more a series of bungles and confusions, by all parties.

At Sarajevo station, the royal couple were greeted by a motorcade of open-topped cars. From the start there was a security blunder as three local police officers got into the first security car and sped off, leaving the archduke's special security detail behind. Franz Ferdinand, Duchess Sophie, the local governor and the archduke's military aide got into the third car and followed on to inspect a local barracks.

At shortly after 10 a.m. the motorcade passed two of the would-be assassins on the route, but they seem to have frozen when they had a chance, and ten minutes later it was left to a third, Nedeljko Cabrinović, to throw a bomb, which bounced off the folded roof of the archduke's car to explode under the vehicle behind, seriously wounding its passengers. Cabrinović's own attempt at instant martyrdom failed when he vomited up his suicide pill and was unable to drown himself in the shallow River Miljacka. Dragged out by the police, he was beaten by an enraged crowd before being led off under arrest. The motorcade sped off at high speed to its destination, the town hall, giving other conspirators no chance to get at the archduke.

A shaken Franz Ferdinand read out his planned speech from bloodstained notes – the papers had been in the damaged car – before discussing changes to the planned programme. Finally it was decided to visit the wounded in hospital. At about 10.45 a.m. the royal visitors boarded the third car in the motorcade and drove off. Unfortunately, no-one had advised the driver of the new route, and he took a wrong turning, bringing his royal passengers directly outside a delicatessen where one assassin had retreated from the fray, convinced the plot had failed. As the car attempted to back out, and stalled, Gavrilo Prinćip took his unexpected opportunity: two 0.38-calibre shots, at point-blank range hit home, mortally wounding the couple. The archduke's jugular was severed, and in his last words to his wife he supposedly begged her to live for the sake of their children. In the event, her death, from a stomach wound, preceded his as she slumped to the floor of the car. The archduke was rushed back to the town hall where he reportedly said of his wound "it is nothing", before expiring.

Prinćip was arrested on the spot and anti-Serbian rioting broke out in Sarajevo. Indeed, all the conspirators were rounded up and put on trial: several were hanged, but both Prinćip and Cabrinović, being underage, were imprisoned – to die of tuberculosis in 1918 and 1916 respectively. A year later, Serbia clamped down on

Black Hand members, and Apis and two of his associates were charged over different allegations and executed by firing squad. On his way to execution he admitted his guilt and acknowledged that he'd become a political embarrassment: "I am to be killed today by Serbian rifles solely because I organized the outrage at Sarajevo."

By then, of course, the tensions that had been brought to a height by the intelligence chief's squalid Balkan conspiracy had set Europe ablaze – with incalculable consequences. In the immediate aftermath, as news of the assassination spread, a wave of revulsion swept the chancelleries of Europe. Clearly, some sort of confrontation appeared imminent between Serbia and Austria-Hungary and a third Balkan war seemed inevitable. Less clear was how the crisis would propel the wider geo-politics of alliances towards catastrophe. In the face-offs that now ensued, behind Austria-Hungary stood Germany, while behind Serbia stood Russia – and behind Russia stood France, technically committed to aid Russia in the event of war. But the polarized alliances of Europe needed some further ingredients before the peace would catastrophically fail.

In Germany, the General Staff's operational plans had come to dominate any planning for transition to war at the expense of flexible diplomacy. That Germany's military elite, and Kaiser Wilhelm too, was hot for war is no great secret. Chief of the General Staff Helmuth von Moltke had recorded in 1913 that the chance for a showdown and a war with Russia had been missed; a few days after Franz Ferdinand's fatal day, the Kaiser convened a secret war council on 5 July at Potsdam, bringing together politicians, generals, diplomats, industrialists and bankers, asking them if they were ready for war. Only the bankers demurred, explaining that they needed at least two weeks to convert their stocks into cash.

A photograph, partially retouched, captures the moment when assassin Gavrilo Prinćip is taken out of the reach of the baying crowds and into custody at Sarajevo's police headquarters, on 28 June 1914. His assassination of Archduke Franz Ferdinand well and truly made the Balkan pot boil over.

The Kaiser then ordered all the participants to disperse and give an appearance of normality in order to buy time for the Austrian ultimatum to Serbia, issued just over two weeks later. Having effectively offered at Potsdam what has been described as a "blank cheque" of unconditional German support for Austria-Hungary in any dispute with Serbia or Russia – and expecting a limited war in the Balkans – the Kaiser then embarked on the imperial yacht for his annual Scandinavian summer cruise. After the humiliation of Russian defeat at the hands of the Japanese in 1905, the German military was mistakenly convinced that the Russian army could be no immediate or credible threat.

If Berlin's policy was rife with misjudgments that summer, Vienna had its fair share, too. Fully emboldened by German support, Austria-Hungary had two options to punish Serbia for the assassination: a diplomatic ultimatum that would force Serbia to heel once and for all; and, should that fail, a military strike. To Vienna's surprise, Serbia agreed within three days to nearly all of the Austrian demands in her ultimatum of 23 July, wrongfooting the Austrian-German axis and garnering international support. As the Kaiser commented, the decision provided "a great moral victory for Vienna, but with it, every reason for war disappears". Unfortunately, Wilhelm's accurate observation took no notice of the wider diplomatic realities.

A German crowd seems largely untroubled at the news of the country's mobilization (1 August 1914), except for one pensive face turned towards the camera. Perhaps she had an inkling of what was to come. But over the previous 100 years Prussians and Germans had enjoyed success in the wars they had fought, large and small.

By now the widely shared fears of being caught unprepared in the event of war were becoming a self-fulfilling prophecy. Russia warned that she would support Serbia if Austria-Hungary dared to attack. France affirmed that she would support Russia if the latter were attacked. Serbia had already appealed to Russia, and on 25 July, Russia, fearing a German pre-emptive strike, secretly issued orders for partial mobilization. The same day, Serbia began to mobilize, and Emperor Franz Josef ordered Austrian mobilization against Serbia.

On 28 July 1914, Austria-Hungary declared war on Serbia, following it up with a bombardment of the capital, Belgrade, on the 29th. Almost immediately there was a sense of events being out of control. Germany insisted that Russia's general mobilization, beginning on 30 July, be stopped immediately and warned France that she should remain neutral in the event of a German–Russian war. Russia ignored Berlin's ultimatum and the French refused to give any assurances, resulting in German and French orders to mobilize. The powder train fizzled rapidly towards detonation.

For the military machine of Germany, mobilization and war were effectively synonymous, with even the Kaiser now unable, or unwilling, to order his generals to step back from the brink. On 1 August, Germany declared war on Russia. From then on, war with France became inevitable, Germany's declaration coming on 3 August. German strategy to avoid a long war on two fronts rested on crushing France as quickly as possible, and so on 2 August Germany delivered an ultimatum to neutral Belgium demanding right of way through the country to attack northern France.

While the Entente with France predisposed Britain to come to the former's aid, it was the Belgian situation that tipped the scales for Whitehall. As a guarantor power for the 1839 Treaty of London, which had established Belgium's neutrality, Britain felt obliged to uphold that guarantee. British Foreign Secretary Sir Edward Grey announced in Parliament on 3 August that Britain would fight to defend Belgium should this become necessary. When the Belgians refused to agree to the German ultimatum, the British responded with two carefully worded notes. The first was delivered on the morning of 4 August and sought – in Grey's typically elliptical diplomatic language – belated assurances that Germany would not violate Belgium's neutrality. Later in the day, when he had confirmation that Germany had definitely invaded, Grey sent a second note, warning that as a signatory to the Treaty of London, Britain needed to receive "a satisfactory reply" by midnight of Germany's withdrawal from Belgium or she would commence hostilities.

When the British ambassador delivered this message in Berlin on the evening of 4 August, German astonishment was genuine. A very agitated Chancellor von Bethmann Hollweg declared, in a phrase that has found its way into the history books, "War? And all for just a word – neutrality – just for a scrap of paper?" (*see* Chapter 31). As the midnight deadline passed, with Germany's bluff called, Britain, too, was at war.

It was but the last in a series of disastrous miscalculations by Germany and Austria-Hungary, for whom any idea of pursuing a containable regional conflict had now been shattered. The assassination of an archduke had ensured that a combustible mix – of alliance blocs, political suspicion and fear, territorial ambition, nationalism, and rigid military pre-planning – had been stoked with human error to set the Continent ablaze, sending Europe, as Lloyd George put it, "slithering over the brink into the boiling cauldron of war". Now, in Grey's sad and enduringly poignant phrase, doom seemed to beckon: "The lights are going out all over Europe; we will not see them lit again in our lifetime."

THE SHOCK OF THE NEW

07

THE NEW PAPER MONEY
BRITISH WAR MEASURES & "DORA"

FROM 1914

British reactions to the prospect of war evolved rapidly as August 1914 opened. King George privately believed, as late as 1 August, that his people wanted nothing to do with a continental war, a view echoed among pressmen and politicians. But the German ultimatum to Belgium significantly swayed the mood. On the two days before 4 August, patriotic crowds thronged Trafalgar Square and the Mall in front of Buckingham Palace. In the weeks that followed, the view that hostilities would be "over by Christmas" came to the fore, and some voices now enthused over war as a form of welcome moral scourge following lax times, or as a chance for glory.

At a less heady level, there were signs of anxiety and apprehension. There were surges in spending, as people stocked up with food and other necessities for whatever was to come. Government ministers and some business leaders appeared sanguine, proclaiming "business as usual". But if this suggested an inactive government, waiting for events to take their course, it was very far from the truth. While few anticipated a conflict lasting years, both Westminster and Whitehall appreciated that it was not just the military forces that needed mobilizing – British society and industry would need to be placed on a war footing as soon as possible.

Changes began almost immediately, some of them to last decades, and one or two persisting to this day. On 6 August, the Currency and Banknotes Act replaced gold sovereigns with some new and purely symbolic paper money. The 10-shilling and £1 note were born, as a measure to preserve the nation's gold reserves.

In 1914, certain sums of money were still paid in gold coins. A sovereign was worth £1 (or 20 shillings), and a half-sovereign was therefore 10 shillings. The government realized it would need all its gold reserves to pay for the war, so in order to remove as much gold as possible from domestic circulation, on 7 August the Treasury issued its first paper £1 and 10-shilling notes. Higher-denomination paper money (£5 and above) had existed for many years, and lower values (£1 and £2) had occasionally circulated as notes, but the war made £1 and 10-shilling notes common currency for the first time. By the end of 1915 gold coins had virtually disappeared. The first notes were hastily produced, and their design was basic. They were printed in a single colour (black for £1, red for 10 shillings) on the front side of special paper normally used for making stamps. Signed by the Permanent Secretary to the Treasury, Sir John Bradbury, the £1 note became known as a "Bradbury". In 1928, the manufacture of banknotes passed to the Bank of England, and the £1 note remained a staple of British life until its withdrawal in 1988.

> **"I THINK THE WHOLE OF THE DEFENCE OF THE REALM ACT IS BASED, NOT ON THE IMPOSITION OF MARTIAL LAW, BUT ON THE EXTENSION OF MILITARY LAW TO CIVILIANS, AND IT IS AGAINST THAT EXTENSION THAT I AM PROTESTING."**
>
> *Lord Parmoor, House of Lords, 4 February 1915*

These Notes are a Legal Tender
for a payment of any amount.
Issued by the Lords Commissioners
of His Majesty's Treasury
under Authority of Act of Parliament.

Ten Shillings

10'

N⁰ A/3 215859

John Bradbury

SECRETARY TO THE TREASURY

These Notes are a Legal Tender
for a payment of any amount.
Issued by the Lords Commissioners
of His Majesty's Treasury
under Authority of Act of Parliament.

One Pound

R 11 N⁰ 97050

John Bradbury

SECRETARY TO THE TREASURY

Beyond such monetary measures, Whitehall moved swiftly to control a large swathe of national life, much of it in an unprecedented way, clamping down to censor communications, muzzle dissent, seize property, control labour and direct vital industries and transport mechanisms for the duration of the war.

The key instrument was the Defence of the Realm Act (DORA), which was rushed through Parliament and became law on 8 August 1914. The Act – extended on 28 August and 27 November, and supplemented in 1915 and 1916 (and indeed throughout the war) – was to influence British life long after the First World War. The original Act was unusually short, but that belied its potency, for it started with a blanket preamble that gave great power not only to the government but also to many other authorities: "His Majesty in Council has power during the continuance of the present war to issue regulations as to the powers and duties of the Admiralty and Army Council, and of the members of His Majesty's forces, and other persons acting on His behalf, for securing the public safety and the defence of the realm."

Security fears were uppermost, and the original Act threatened court martial for any soldier and, tellingly, any civilian who communicated information to the enemy that would jeopardize "the success of the operations of any of His Majesty's forces or the forces of his allies or to assist the enemy".

As the Act was revised and supplemented, its reach extended across the nation's communications and industrial base. By November 1914 all factories linked to army and navy needs had to be placed at official disposal, giving government control over such industries as shell production and shipbuilding. The government took control of coal mines, and though it did not nationalize the railway companies they had to be run as the authorities ordained. Whitehall now effectively directed labour, while the production of coal and the movement of trains could be prioritized for the war effort. From 1915, engineering firms could be commanded to produce only the products the government ordered.

Security, communications and war *matériel* were obvious targets. But the laws went into other areas of life, and explicitly removed age-old British liberties in the name of wartime security. The population relied on the printed word for information, and now newspapers were censored (and self-censored), with access to military information controlled by the authorities; indeed, initially no war correspondents were allowed anywhere near the frontlines.

It can be argued that such measures were merely prudent precautions, but other sacrificial lambs of pre-1914 British life were quietly led to the slaughter. In an age when Temperance movements flourished but beer flowed freely, DORA now allowed publicans to dilute beer and began to force pubs to tighten their opening hours under the new licensing laws, until by late spring 1915 most were limited to two daily sessions, from noon to 2.40 p.m. and 6.30 p.m. to 9.30 p.m. The theory was that the enforced abstinence would make workers in the vital industries fitter for their tasks. It also became illegal to buy a round for anyone.

Although the precise hours would change, like the paper money the licensing of alcohol sales was one very long-lasting legacy of the "temporary" wartime measures. But perhaps the most enduring piece of national engineering introduced under the umbrella of DORA was the adoption, from May 1916, of British Summer Time (BST). In ordering clocks to move forward by an hour in the summer, the government ensured that factories, especially, had maximum daylight and could work for longer.

DEFENCE OF THE REALM ACT, 1914.

Evacuation Orders.

Section VIII.   GREEN SECTION.

Sub-Section   *Sub-Marshal* Mr F J H Budds

Address 28 Penshurst Rd

Place of Assembly: DUMPTON PARK.
Alarm Signal will be TWO MAROONS.

On the Alarm Signal take Two Days' Provisions, Lock-up your House and proceed to the Place of Assembly. All Special Constables for your Section will wear a Green Scarf round their Left Arm and you must Obey their Orders.

TAKE NO HOUSEHOLD GOODS WITH YOU.
The Police will look after your House.

NOTE.—There is no immediate likelihood of any attack, but precautions must be taken for such an event in time of war.

BY ORDER OF THE MAYOR,
For the Naval and Military Authorities.

A proliferation of paperwork was one result of the Defence of the Realm Act. This Evacuation Order (c.1914) gives instructions on where to assemble and what to take in case of an emergency such as invasion, and optimistically reassures civilians that the police will take care of their houses. Emerging threats such as aerial bombardment would change the nature of the domestic threats, too.

Public clocks themselves were banned from chiming during the day – indeed, a whole raft of measures stipulated times when things could, or could not, be done. Theatres and other entertainment venues had to close by 10.30 p.m., and from August 1916 woe betides anyone whistling for a taxi after 10 p.m. As the war progressed, more and more regulation was introduced under the blanket of DORA. The ones that would make the biggest difference to ordinary people's lives would be the gradual introduction of food rationing, from January 1918 (*see* Chapter 80), and the extension of income tax to lower-middle and lower class earners.

Inevitably, there was some opposition to the successive Acts, which intensified with the introduction of conscription in 1916 (*see* Chapter 34). Pre-war Britain had experienced considerable industrial unrest, and the industrial needs of war now bolstered workers' bargaining power – to the worry of managers and government alike. The imposition of controls on labour were seized on by some trade union activists as a pretext for strikes. In March 1915, the Treasury reached pay agreements with 35 unions, but pockets of militancy remained, a prime example being at the shipyards on Clydeside. In official eyes, a small group of near-revolutionaries was openly fomenting dissent and looking for a confrontation. After the Clyde Workers' Committee journal, *The Worker*, was prosecuted for an article criticizing the war, leading agitators Willie Gallacher and John Muir were convicted and imprisoned under the provisions of DORA. Other left-wing activists were dealt with similarly. A better-remembered victim of DORA is the philosopher Bertrand Russell, kicked out of his Cambridge college for his pacifist activities and finally jailed in 1918 for six months.

DORA undoubtedly succeeded in giving the British government immense power over the population during the war. Overall, the Acts were significant for three main reasons: they made Britain better equipped to wage a long and industrial-scale war; they pushed government control into areas that had hitherto never been considered as the business of the state; and, just as the £1 note endured, Whitehall would continue to cling to some of those powers long after their original purpose was long forgotten.

08

"YOUR COUNTRY NEEDS YOU"
LORD KITCHENER & THE RECRUITMENT DRIVE

1914 TO 1915

The adjective "iconic", outside its strict religious context, refers to an image that is instantly recognizable and appears to encapsulate an era, a brand, an idea – or even a nation. If ever there was an iconic figure of the British war effort it was the imperial celebrity Kitchener – or, more fully, Horatio Herbert, Earl Kitchener of Khartoum. It is Kitchener's sternly commanding face and implacably stabbing finger that has come to symbolize the uniquely British recruiting campaign of 1914–15, and which left an image that was much replicated and adapted, imitated and subverted, to become one of the most familiar and influential of the 20th century.

Since the resignation of the Secretary of State for War following the Curragh Mutiny earlier in 1914 (*see* Chapter 2), the War Office had been run by the prime minister, Herbert Asquith. On the outbreak of war, he realized a new military figurehead was essential and, responding to public demand, hoisted Kitchener into the Cabinet as the new secretary of state.

> The 1914 poster in which Lord Kitchener summoned Britons to military service achieved subsequent fame as *the* graphic image of the First World War. It is even falsely claimed that the poster alone inspired a million men to join up. The real story, though, is more complex. For a start, the now famous poster was only published on a very small scale, and almost certainly not outside London. It never formed part of the official recruiting campaign orchestrated by the Parliamentary Recruiting Committee, and so few were printed that today the only known surviving poster is in the Imperial War Museum (and was acquired only in the 1950s). The original version, which is shown here, was not even drawn as a poster, but rather for the cover of the 5 September edition of the magazine *London Opinion*. Cartoonist Alfred Leete created it. In the subsequent poster versions, reprinted some weeks later, a revised wording was adopted, while the original design found itself on another locally produced poster, surrounded by the flags of Britain's Allies. It is one of the great ironies of the First World War that, through the sheer strength of Kitchener's personality and his intimate connection with the uniquely British voluntary recruiting programme of 1914–15, a simple magazine cover has come to be remembered as one of the most influential posters of the 20th century.

Kitchener's career as imperial warrior and administrator seemed entirely fitting for his new role. Born in 1850, he was a classically Victorian figure of a soldier: sober, serious and heavily moustached. Towering over his contemporaries in every way – he

"WELL, IF KITCHENER WAS NOT A GREAT MAN, HE WAS, AT LEAST, A GREAT POSTER."

Attributed to Margot Asquith or her daughter

"YOUR COUNTRY NEEDS
YOU"

ALFRED
LEETE

was 6 feet 2 inches in height – he struck an imposing figure from the start and enjoyed a remarkable career. By 1892 he was *Sirdar*, or Commander, of the British-controlled Egyptian army. While there he led the British expedition up the Nile to the Sudan to defeat the Khalifah's Dervish army at the Battle of Omdurman (1898) and went on to rule the Sudan as an enlightened and reforming governor-general, by the standards of the day.

By contrast, as commander-in-chief in South Africa during the latter part of the Second Anglo-Boer War (1899–1902), Kitchener's methods were not pretty. Farms were burned, and Boer women and children rounded up into concentration camps where bad sanitation and lack of care killed one-third of them and caused a public outcry in Britain. This was the ruthless, hard-headed soldier who became the face of Britain's early contribution to the First World War.

Purely by chance, in the summer of 1914 Kitchener was on leave in Britain, thus prompting Asquith's unexpected offer. He immediately issued a stark warning to his fellow ministers that this would be a long and bloody war lasting at least three years, and that the effort to defeat Germany would need huge new armies, requiring Britain's manpower "to the last million". His Cabinet colleagues looked at one another in disbelief.

But Kitchener was right. He had only to look at the German army – with its 98 mobilizable divisions, 850,000 soldiers and 2.9 million reservists – to realize that this was going to be no lightning war. By contrast, on 4 August 1914, the British Army, consisting of the Regular Army, the Reserves and Special Reserves, and the newly formed part-time Territorial Force, could muster immediately just 235,000 professional soldiers, of whom about half were serving overseas, mainly in India. Unlike its continental neighbours, Britain had always eschewed national service or conscription, and traditionally relied on volunteers. The British Expeditionary Force that crossed the Channel in the first weeks of war was a mere 150,000 strong. So the need to build up a bigger army was obvious, and on 6 August the Cabinet agreed to Kitchener's request to recruit half a million more men.

Kitchener's aim, to be precise, was to raise and equip a completely *new* force, separate from the existing organization within the War Office (such as the Territorial Force, which he distrusted), to become what was effectively a New Model Army of citizens. On 11 August, he initiated a massive recruiting campaign. At first the poster appeals were very plain, using only printed words. But, with the formation of the Parliamentary Recruiting Committee (PRC) later that month, they became more sophisticated in their emotional reach. Gradually the PRC took on responsibility for maintaining the momentum of recruitment and continued this relentlessly into 1915. As a result hundreds of thousands of young men flocked to volunteer for the colours every week: 462,000 in September and more than a million by Christmas 1914. Recruiting offices were swamped with men impelled by patriotism, by a sense of adventure and, very often, by a desire to escape – from the drudgery of mill, mine, factory, field or office, from a domestic difficulty or even a pregnant girlfriend.

To say that the army and the War Office's slender resources were overwhelmed by the speed and enthusiasm of the Kitchener recruits is an understatement. Britain lacked the uniforms, weapons, tents and trainers to administer this new horde of recruits, certainly in the early months. With an intake of more men in a weekend than a regimental depot might normally take in a year, the system was jammed. As a result many would-be soldiers spent the autumn and winter of 1914 in their civilian clothes, drilling with broom handles and living in lodgings. They were often trained by "dug outs" from the Anglo-Boer War, elderly NCOs and, very occasionally, a lightly wounded survivor returned from the trenches.

By the spring of 1915 things had improved. Uniforms, rifles, newly built camps – even field guns – had begun to equip Kitchener's "New Armies". Each normally consisted of six divisions, drawn from all over the country, and the "First Hundred Thousand" (K1) was soon followed by a Second (K2), Third (K3) and even a Fourth (K4). In all, nearly 2 million men would respond to Kitchener's call to arms. More men volunteered between August and November 1914 (900,000) than were in the entire army at the outbreak of war. It was a stunning achievement, for which Maurice Hankey, War Cabinet Secretary from 1916, gave due credit: "He had conceived and brought into being, ... a national army capable of holding its own against the armies of the greatest military power the world had ever seen."

Kitchener's star waned subsequently. In 1915, the inability to produce enough shells – the great "shell scandal" – was laid at his door (rather than at the failings of British industry), and he was implicated in the failure of that year's Gallipoli campaign. Autocratic and secretive by nature, and growing ever more weary of the gossip and intrigues of his Cabinet colleagues, he withdrew further into himself. There was relief in the Cabinet when it was decided that Kitchener should make a diplomatic mission to Russia, and so it was that on 5 June 1916 he sailed from Scapa Flow aboard HMS *Hampshire*. Battling against a Force 9 gale off the Orkney Islands, the cruiser struck a German mine laid just the week before. Kitchener died of exposure with over 600 others in the freezing, mountainous seas, his body never to be recovered.

News of Kitchener's death produced mixed emotions. The verdict recorded by Asquith's wife, the acid-tongued Lady Margot Asquith, was reputedly that "if Kitchener was not a great man, he was, at least, a great poster". The judgement did not reflect his achievements; but it did sum up his popular image for later generations.

09

THE NEWCASTLE COMMERCIALS' DRUM
PALS BATTALIONS

1914 TO 1916

One of the most remarkable, yet salutory, outcomes of Lord Kitchener's successful recruiting campaign was the phenomenon of the Pals battalions. A fortnight after war began, Lieutenant General Sir Henry Rawlinson observed to Kitchener that men would be more willing to enlist if they could serve with their friends. He suggested a battalion be formed from men who worked in the City of London, and within six days the "Stockbrokers' Battalion" had recruited 1,600 volunteers – nearly enough for two battalions. The Earl of Derby also discussed a similar idea with Kitchener, and at a meeting in Liverpool on 28 August, attended by 1,500 men, he spoke about forming a "battalion of pals" – and the term stuck.

Across Britain, local authorities, industrialists and committees of private citizens now took up the idea with enthusiasm; by the end of September over 50 towns in Britain had formed Pals battalions, with the major cities raising more than one. Glasgow formed battalions from the city's Tramways Department and Boys' Brigade; Manchester raised no less than seven battalions. Even little Barnsley raised two. There were cyclists' battalions, sportsmen's battalions and even public schools' battalions. Altogether, 643 of the 994 volunteer battalions raised by June 1916 came about through local initiatives, and many were inevitably placed in the same divisions.

In August and September 1914, as patriotic enthusiasm gripped Britain, Newcastle-upon-Tyne was prominent among the many towns and cities that formed Pals battalions. On 2 September, George Renwick MP suggested to the Newcastle and Gateshead Chamber of Commerce that they offer to the War Office a battalion of men from local businesses. Accepted on 8 September, within eight days the Newcastle Commercials were at full strength. They were formally established as the 16th Battalion, Northumberland Fusiliers, and later formed their own band using a set of drums, bugles and fifes given to them by Mrs Renwick. This surviving drum, still brightly painted, shows the battalion's name and regimental crest. On 1 July 1916, the battalion attacked Thiepval at the opening of the Somme campaign. Of those Commercials who proudly enlisted early in the war as a symbol of Newcastle's civic pride over 350 were killed.

It was the crucible of modern war that revealed the scheme's great drawback. When units suffered casualties, these losses – and the sense of loss back home – were concentrated. At Serre on 1 July 1916, the first day of the Somme campaign, the Pals battalions of the 31st Division – prominently the Accrington, Sheffield, Leeds and

"I HAVE PLEDGED ... TO PROVIDE FOR BARNSLEY AND DISTRICT A BATTALION TO FORM A PART OF OUR OWN REGIMENT OF THE YORK AND LANCASTERS. THIS OFFER HAS BEEN ACCEPTED BY LORD KITCHENER AND I KNOW WHEN ASKED ... YOU WILL RESPOND, AS BARNSLEY AND DISTRICT HAS ALWAYS RESPONDED – WITH ONE VOICE."

*William Goodworth England,
Mayor of Barnsley*

Barnsley pals – went into attack. By nightfall they were almost wiped out for no gains. At Montauban, the Manchester and Liverpool Pals of the 30th Division also attacked. They captured all their objectives, but at high cost. Whole towns in the North of England went into mourning. The impact of casualties like these, multiplied across Britain, can be said to have marked the point in the war when hope turned to grief. The idea of too closely knit Pals battalions would never again be repeated.

10

HMS *LANCE*'S 4-INCH GUN
THE OPENING OF NAVAL HOSTILITIES

AUGUST AND SEPTEMBER 1914

Given the intense naval rivalry preceding the war, it was appropriate that the first actual Anglo-German hostilities occurred at sea.

Mid-July 1914 had heralded a long-planned royal review of Britain's vast fleet off Portsmouth. When the Austrian rejection of Serbia's reply to her ultimatum became known, the First Sea Lord (Admiral Prince Louis of Battenberg) suspended the review and ordered full mobilization, approved by Churchill. On 28 July, as the European crisis worsened, the lion's share of the fleet was ordered to its secure war station at Scapa Flow in the Orkney Islands, there to be renamed the "Grand Fleet". An 18-mile-long column of warships, without lights, steamed through the narrow Straits of Dover and headed north. Other ships were directed to Portland to guard the exits from the Channel into the Atlantic, and to Harwich to watch over the southern reaches of the North Sea. Whatever happened, the Royal Navy was prepared for war – which came soon enough. Only hours after Britain entered the war the destroyer HMS *Lance* fired the very first British shot.

Early on 5 August 1914, with the reality of war sinking in, the Royal Navy's 3rd Flotilla, based at Harwich, left to patrol the Thames Estuary. Its ships received reports of a strange vessel dropping objects overboard, and two destroyers, HMS *Lance* and HMS *Landrail*, went to investigate. They found a ship that appeared to be a Great Eastern Railway North Sea ferry, but it suspiciously raced off as they approached. Another destroyer signalled by lamp that the ship appeared to be laying mines. HMS *Lance* opened fire with this weapon, one of its 4-inch Quick-Firing Mark IV Guns. It was the first British shell fired in the war – but it missed. *Landrail* now also started to fire, along with the flotilla leader, the light cruiser HMS *Amphion*. Their target turned out to be a disguised German auxiliary minelayer, SMS *Königin Luise*. Under heavy fire, the ship sank shortly after midday – the first German naval casualty. Nevertheless, the German minelayer had a posthumous revenge. As the British returned to Harwich next day, HMS *Amphion* hit one of *Königin Luise*'s mines and it, too, sank, to create another "first" of the war – the first British naval casualty. Three years later, the Royal Navy was determined to match the British Army in securing powerful objects for the nation's new war museum, and the Director of Naval Ordnance suggested "the first gun that was fired after the commencement of hostilities". It was presented to the Imperial War Museum in 1919 and remains a constant reminder of the first of millions of shots fired in anger by British forces over the next four years.

The previous day the Grand Fleet had been rocked by a change of leadership. Its ageing commander-in-chief, Admiral Sir George Callaghan, was nearing retirement but nevertheless was peremptorily relieved of command to be replaced by a reluctant Admiral Sir John Jellicoe, who protested to Churchill: "You court disaster ... Fleet is imbued with loyalty for C-in-C." Jellicoe had other reasons to be worried. He was only too well aware of the modern dangers from mines and torpedoes, and the submarine threat to Scapa Flow soon became clear. On 15 August, HMS *Birmingham*

rammed and sank a U-boat off Fair Isle; three months later, on 23 November, another was trapped and beached in the approaches to Scapa Flow itself. Jellicoe was forced to keep his ships at sea over the winter of 1914–15, moving to Loch Ewe on the west coast of Scotland and then Lough Swilly in Ireland. At one point, with 2 battlecruisers detached to the Falklands, 6 dreadnought-type battleships in the dockyard and the battleship HMS *Audacious* sunk by a mine in October, he had no numerical advantage over the 16 battleships and 5 battlecruisers of the German High Seas Fleet. Only when Scapa's defences were complete in the New Year could the Grand Fleet concentrate its ships again in the Orkneys.

Despite a nervous Jellicoe's concerns, the Royal Navy quickly began a maritime blockade of Germany, including patrols and minefields. And it seized the initiative in the first engagement of any size, drawing blood on 28 August 1914. Noting that the Germans sent regular destroyer patrols into the coastal waters around the island of Heligoland, about 30 miles off the German coast, the British set up an ambush. The plan was that a force of submarines would lie in wait for the German patrols, backed by a covering force of light cruisers and 30 destroyers. They in turn would be supported over the horizon by six heavier cruisers and five battlecruisers.

After first contact the German light craft fled, drawing the British onto the guns of German cruisers emerging from harbour. In their turn, the British destroyers retreated, bringing the German ships onto the heavier British cruisers. The battle degenerated into a confused mêlée in the mist until Vice-Admiral Sir David Beatty ordered his 1st Battlecruiser Squadron to intervene. In the words of one British officer, "There straight ahead of us in lovely procession, like elephants walking through a pack of pye [wild] dogs came *Lion*, *Queen Mary*, *Princess Royal*, *Invincible* and *New Zealand*. How solid they looked, how utterly earthquaking." At full speed and with guns blazing they blew three German cruisers apart.

Altogether, Germany lost three light cruisers and one destroyer sunk, with four other light cruisers damaged. The Battle of Heligoland Bight was a decisive British victory and had the effect of making an already cautious High Seas Fleet even more so. The battle shook the Kaiser's confidence badly. He ordered his fleet to "hold itself back and avoid actions which can lead to greater losses".

A month later the *Kaiserliche Marine* got its revenge. The old cruisers HMS *Aboukir*, *Hogue* and *Cressy* were part of the 7th Cruiser Squadron, tasked with a highly exposed North Sea patrol in the shallow waters off the Dutch coast. On 22 September, a single U-boat, *U-9*, torpedoed and sank all three. *Aboukir* went down first. Her consorts, thinking she had hit a mine, stopped in the water and lowered rescue boats – a decision described by Churchill as "an act of chivalrous simplicity" – and were in turn fatally holed for their pains. The Royal Navy lost over 1,400 sailors, and as a result of the disaster abandoned forward-patrolling by cruisers, intended to enforce the blockade. Warships were now ordered never to heave to in dangerous waters and henceforth to manoeuvre on a zigzag course. It had been a brutal lesson in the new dangers of submarine warfare.

Such losses confirmed, in the final months of 1914, that the only viable strategy for blockading Germany – both to contain the High Seas Fleet and strangle German maritime trade – was to operate at a distance. Attempting a traditional close blockade, off the enemy's coast and harbours, was merely presenting the defenders with targets on their doorstep – ever more vulnerable in an age of submarines and mines. The policy of a distant blockade therefore developed as the only realistic option for

Royal Navy seamen watch the stricken German cruiser SMS Mainz, *at the Battle of Heligoland Bight (28 August 1914).* Mainz *sank shortly after 2 p.m., though the majority of her crew, including Oberleutnant* Wolfgang von Tirpitz, *son of the German naval supremo, were rescued by German and British ships.*

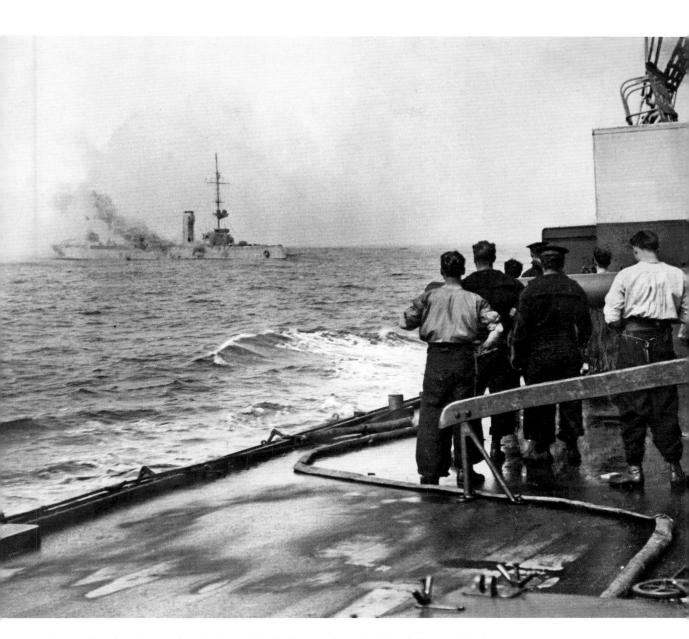

the naval authorities, and it reinforced the decision to base the Grand Fleet at the northerly location of Scapa Flow. The thinking was that with the Channel blocked from Portland, and the Norwegian Sea from Scapa and by British minefields, the Germans would remain bottled up in their own waters. It was a sound concept strategically – with the exception that it did allow the High Seas Fleet the tactical freedom to sally forth from its base at Wilhelmshaven into the North Sea.

Before the year was out the German fleet would use that remaining freedom to add a new dimension to the naval war, by attacking England's northeast coast itself – and her unsuspecting civilian population (*see* Chapter 16).

11

GERMAN JACKBOOTS
THE SCHLIEFFEN PLAN & GERMAN INVASION

AUGUST 1914

That the First World War developed into a titanic four-year-long struggle could well be blamed on the failure of the German General Staff's audacious opening gambit. A plan conceived as a means to knock out France within six weeks, allowing Germany then to turn unhindered on Russia, became one of the biggest politico-military mistakes in history.

The plan in question has become known as the Schlieffen plan, having originally been formulated by Count Alfred von Schlieffen, Chief of the General Staff of the German army between 1891 and 1906. Once France and Russia became allies in 1894, the dangers of a two-front war were obvious to Berlin, and Schlieffen sought to tackle this problem – but as a purely military challenge. This Prussian military technocrat appears to have totally ignored the political implications of his proposed solution, and his political contemporaries were too weak to overrule him.

German thinking was governed by three main factors. First, since her defeat in the Franco-Prussian War, France had constructed strong lines of defensive forts along her border with Germany. Second, while France was expected to mobilize within a month, the conventional wisdom was that Russian mobilization would be much slower. Last, thanks to Belgium's neutrality, the Franco-Belgian border was wide open and unfortified. For Schlieffen, this last point made the solution obvious: invade France quickly, with a huge sweep through Holland and Belgium.

The German plan for 1914 depended on speed. But there would come a point when the soldiers would have to rely on the oldest means of movement – on foot. In the first month of the war the Germans on the right wing of their attack marched over 300 miles and were soon over 60 miles beyond their nearest railhead. Since the Prussian victory over Austria in 1866, one of the key components in the Prussian uniform had been a pair of tough, knee-length field boots. With only minor changes, what were formally known as the M1866 *Marschstiefel* ("marching boots") remained one of the iconic symbols of German soldiers thereafter. Often referred to as "jackboots" because of their similarity to the much taller, strongly reinforced (or "jacked") cavalry riding boots, in 1914 *Marschstiefel* were made in natural light brown leather, and they were unpolished, with the rough side facing out – as the pair depicted here. It was only in 1915 that orders were issued for the boots to be blackened and polished. To make the boots more durable their soles were embedded with around 40 hobnails and the heels with curved strips of iron. Such well-made and rugged boots equipped the Germans soldiers well for the rigours ahead.

Schlieffen had initially addressed the challenge of a two-front war as early as 1897, when he drafted his first formal memorandum on the subject. The "Schlieffen plan" was never a single operational order; it was really an ongoing series of memoranda by whoever was head of the German army, and it evolved over several years. Key modifications included weakening the German defences in Alsace-Lorraine in order to suck the French deep into German territory and extending the attack's right wing so that it could sweep right round and take Paris from the west. Indeed, "Strengthen the right" are supposed to have been Schlieffen's last words when he died in 1913, never to see his plan enacted.

It was assumed that further south the French would likely be distracted by the yearning for *la Revanche* (revenge) for the disastrous Franco-Prussian War of 1870–71, and therefore by the temptation of trying to regain the territory they had lost in Alsace and Lorraine. As a result, the thinking went, German forces could outflank the French line of defensive forts and sweep down behind the French army from the north, destroying it within six weeks.

It was a conception of Napoleonic boldness; but times and technology had changed since the 19th century. By confronting France in a huge semicircle from the Channel to the Alps, the Germans were ceding the advantage of interior lines of communication and supply to the defenders. And by 1914 that meant railways: the French would be able to use their own well-developed system to switch troops quickly to meet developing threats. Germany's railway network was vital, of course, in getting troops to the Belgian border; and it was to secure the surrounding Belgian rail network that Liège had to be captured so quickly. But inevitably, millions of German troops would still then have to proceed on foot through potentially hostile Belgian countryside to northern France. In having to deal with the likelihood of blown-up bridges and destroyed communications (including railways) – as indeed turned out to be the case – they would face an ever-lengthening supply chain stretching back to the German border. The second fundamental flaw in Schlieffen's plan was that it took no political account of the consequences of invading neutral Holland and Belgium to get at France. In the end, it was this factor that guaranteed British involvement in the war.

Fundamentally, Schlieffen's ideas relied for success on the triumph of audacity, wide movement and shock. The plan, at root, was little more than a gambler's throw on a huge strategic scale, resting too much on the mechanistic schedules of the German railway staff's timetables. Even in purely military terms, it took no real account of the problems of logistics, and it disregarded what the great 19th-century theorist of conflict, Clausewitz, called the "friction of war": things always go wrong, things always take longer, the unexpected always happens.

Schlieffen's successor, Helmuth von Moltke ("the Younger", to distinguish him from his celebrated military uncle), had more political sense and more scruples than his predecessor. He rejected the notion of invading Holland, pointing out that in a major war Germany would be better off respecting Dutch neutrality to maintain trading links through Holland with the rest of the world. Concerned about the vulnerability of German defences to a French attack, he also allocated new units to his left flank in Alsace-Lorraine and refused to push more units to the right wing in the north; he suggested, reasonably enough, that it was pointless to multiply numbers if they could not be properly supplied with ammunition and fodder. Therefore, relative to the strength of his left flank, he reduced the strength of the right – the hammer blow, which had been intended to smash through Belgium. It was no longer realistically strong enough to do this, and through his refinements Moltke realized Schlieffen's dying fears. Put simply, in the end German forces proved insufficiently numerous.

The final manifestation of Schlieffen's original plan, complete with Moltke's modifications and changes, received its baptism of fire in the first week of August 1914. From the start, the Belgians refused to conform to German expectations, resisting strongly and forcing the invaders for nearly a month to divert troops to protect their lengthening supply lines. The Germans had to bombard Belgian fortresses along the River Meuse into surrender, the final one (at Namur) falling on 24 August. Although the Belgian countryside was now theoretically wide open for the Germans' westwards advance, the Belgian army's retreat to its fastness around Antwerp required a diversion of German forces to keep it holed up there. And as the Germans moved west, their logistics became ever more difficult; hundreds of undernourished horses were dying by the day, while the troops, on foot, were exhausted.

Despite the fact that along the Franco-German border the French army's counter-stroke had been repulsed with terrible losses (*see* Chapter 12), the German timetable for its great ambition of envelopment was looking increasingly under threat. The Schlieffen plan was confirming an old military truth, articulated by Moltke's uncle: "no plan survives contact with the enemy".

By the first week in September, it had collapsed, and Schlieffen's bold roll of the dice slowly turned into Germany's long nightmare of war on two fronts.

A well-known photograph shows German troops advancing in their Marschstiefel *(marching boots), possibly through Belgian fields in August 1914 – but more likely in pre-war manouevres. The Schlieffen plan demanded rapidity of movement, but the truth was that much of it would have to be on foot. The infantry were not much different from Caesar's legions.*

12

PANTALONS ROUGES – "A NATIONAL AFFAIR!" THE BATTLE OF THE FRONTIERS

AUGUST 1914

An observer in a balloon looking down on France's eastern border in mid-August 1914 may have seen an unusual line of red rolling towards Germany. He would have glimpsed the massed ranks of the French infantry as they launched their long-cherished bid to regain Alsace and Lorraine from Germany. These men were still kitted out in their traditional 19th-century uniforms, including the famous *pantalons rouges*, or red trousers, considered by traditionalists as representing the "martial soul of France".

Once war in the West began, there was little doubt as to exactly where France would mount her offensive against Germany. Regaining the territories of Alsace and Lorraine, lost almost half a century before to Prussia, drew the French like moths to a candle flame and represented the overriding aim of the French General Staff's planners. Accordingly, over the years they had built up a fortified zone from Verdun south to Toul and Nancy, and they planned to use this as the springboard for mass attacks further south. As a result, by 1914 this stretch of Franco-German border appeared too well defended for any German offensive.

To the north of Verdun, France's defence relied on the difficult terrain of the central Ardennes forest, with its lack of good roads, and the promise of Belgian neutrality beyond (not to mention the circuitousness of any German attack through Belgium). It also seemed logical to the French that any major German attack in the north would have to sap German defences elsewhere, to French benefit.

> A desire to restore a sense of French martial glory fuelled the French national psyche on the eve of war. It partially explains the French military emphasis on personal courage and will power, virtues summed up in the idea of "*élan*". And the intensity of this belief was reflected in the deep, rich red of the *pantalons rouges*. In the Franco-Prussian War, French infantrymen had marched to war effectively wearing the colours of their national flag: red trousers, white gaiters and a long blue coat. By the end of the 19th century, the red trousers and blue coat still formed the standard French infantry uniform. As other armies modernized their field dress, adopting neutral, less conspicuous colours, French politicians resisted all attempts to update theirs, rejecting the recommendations of the French military. The *pantalons rouges* in particular were seen as sacrosanct, French parliamentarian Étienne Clémentel declaring them resolutely in 1911 to be "a national affair!" The result was that in 1914, when the French armies charged across the frontiers into Germany they were dressed much as they had been over 40 years before – and were highly visible targets against the landscape.

> **"ABOLISH RED TROUSERS? NEVER! RED TROUSERS ARE FRANCE."**
>
> *Eugène Étienne, French politician*

The key to what became collectively known as the Battle of the Frontiers lay in the most recent French operational plan, known as Plan XVII. It reflected the fact that the French General Staff had begun to emphasize offensive operations as the only real battle-winning option. Lieutenant General Ferdinand Foch, one of France's most influential military thinkers, had, when he was a lecturer at the French Staff College, pointed out that defensive battles would be unable to bring about a decisive result, and final victory would always require decisive, offensive action. But some disciples had promoted Foch's doctrine as *"attaque à l'outrance"* – attack to excess – and promulgated the idea that the best method involved troops hurling themselves at the enemy and relying on *élan*, raw courage and the power of the bayonet to sweep the enemy away. In an age when tactics and technology were bolstering the effectiveness of the defence, these were dangerous thoughts. Plan XVII was to spawn the most costly French campaign of the whole war.

However, its concept was simple enough. On completion of French mobilization (which turned out to be 14 August), France attacked straight across the frontier into Lorraine, with the First Army heading towards Sarrebourg and the Second Army towards Morhange. Opposing them was the army of Crown Prince Rupprecht of Bavaria, with strict orders from the German High Command to make a fighting retreat and suck the French into a trap. The victorious French obligingly surged ever deeper into the occupied territories. Foch's XX Corps reached the outskirts of Morhange on 17 August and General Auguste Dubail's army entered Sarrebourg in triumph the next day, marking the high water mark of Plan XVII.

The problem was that 200 miles to the north, a worried General Charles Lanrezac, tasked with covering the French left flank with his Fifth Army, was examining reports of huge German forces massing to his north, advancing through Belgium and threatening to outflank him. He begged the French commander-in-chief, General Joseph Joffre, to allow him to realign his forces accordingly.

Joffre reluctantly agreed to some minor adjustments. But he, too, had reasons to be worried. To the south, Rupprecht's army had turned the tables at Sarrebourg and Morhange and shot the impetuous French attacks to ribbons. On 20 August, the Germans were counterattacking, sending the French reeling back to the fortifications of the Grande Couronné around Nancy. It was a major French defeat. To the north, against the inexorable German progression through Belgium, Lanrezac was hastily repositioning around Charleroi, aiming to hold bridges over the Meuse and Sambre – as he faced the numerically far superior German Second and Third armies.

Despite all this, Joffre remained intent that the French should continue with the second phase of Plan XVII – their own offensive, eastwards, into the Ardennes. He was not alone in supposing that if the Germans were strong in the north and south, they must logically be weak in the centre. Thus, from Verdun north to Neufchâteau, the French Third and Fourth armies advanced into the misty hills and forests of the Ardennes. Expecting weaker forces, they instead collided with two German armies advancing west with orders to act as a hinge for the main German attacks to the north and the south. The resulting encounter battles, between 21 and 22 August, were every bit as catastrophic for the French as the defeats at Morhange and Sarrebourg, as the infantry yet again hurled themselves forwards in the attack to be mown down by machine guns and well-directed artillery fire. A future French president, Charles de Gaulle, then a young lieutenant in the French 33rd Regiment, wrote movingly of the futility and carnage of the scene:

"IN THE NORTH, OUR ARMY ... APPEARS TO HAVE SUFFERED CHECKS OF WHICH I STILL DO NOT KNOW THE FULL EXTENT, BUT WHICH HAVE FORCED IT TO RETIRE ... ONE MUST FACE FACTS ... OUR ARMY CORPS HAVE NOT SHOWN ON THE BATTLEFIELD THOSE OFFENSIVE QUALITIES FOR WHICH WE HAD HOPED."

General Joseph Joffre, 24 August 1914

Suddenly the enemy's fire became precise and concentrated. Second by second the hail of bullets and the thunder of the shells grew stronger. Those who survived lay flat on the ground, amid the screaming wounded and the humble corpses. With affected calm, the officers let themselves be killed standing upright, some obstinate platoons stuck their bayonets in their rifles, bugles sounded the charge, isolated heroes made fantastic leaps, but all to no purpose. In an instant it had become clear that all the courage in the world could not withstand this fire.

In 1914, French North African regiments of Zouaves normally wore summer uniforms of white trousers and blue tunics, but for the rest of the year they too donned the patriotic pantalons rouges. *Here, Zouaves go on the attack in Lorraine during the Battle of the Frontiers.*

By 23 August Plan XVII lay in ruins. The idea that moral courage and an attacking spirit alone could prevail over modern firepower had been exposed as a massive error. Despite it being only three weeks since the start of the war, France had already suffered 140,000 casualties, including over 4,000 officers – 10 per cent of her officer corps – and everywhere the French armies were in retreat. In the north, only the arrival of the British Expeditionary Force at Mons had saved Lanrezac's Fifth Army from being completely outflanked to the west.

Joffre gradually became aware of the magnitude of the defeat. As his battered armies began to pull back he took two decisive steps. First, he blamed his subordinates ("grand shortcomings on the part of commanders"), sacking dozens of them and replacing them with younger, more dynamic men. And on 25 August he ordered a great retreat and the formation of a new army to counterattack on the River Marne. These were difficult decisions, but they stabilized and restored balance to the French position.

The first month of the war cost the French a staggering 260,000 casualties, including 75,000 dead, 27,000 of whom were killed on 22 August alone – a third more than the numbers of British killed on the first day of the Somme in 1916. Despite the undoubted bravery of the ordinary French soldiers – the *poilus* – everywhere *pantalons rouges* now carpeted the fields and forests of eastern France, sometimes literally stacked up; those men who had survived were shuffling back, exhausted.

The Battle of the Frontiers was over. It had been, quite literally, a bloody disaster for the French.

13

AN ATROCITY POSTER
GERMAN ATROCITIES & *SCHRECKLICHKEIT*

FROM AUGUST 1914

As the invading German forces marched through Belgium in August 1914, stories of atrocities against civilians quickly began to spread. They were to be seized on and exaggerated by Allied propaganda, but they had clear roots in the acts that were summed up in the word *Schrecklichkeit* – "frightfulness" or "terror".

To make matters worse, many of these actions were not the kind of casual brutalities committed against a conquered population by an ill-disciplined soldiery. They were deliberate operations ordered by the General Staff. The aim was to cow the civilian population and to prevent them from attacking the occupying troops – while punishing those who did. Clausewitz, the high priest of German military theory and doctrine, had written that "terror" could shorten wars. But more than that the German army was drawing on memories of an earlier war.

During the Franco-Prussian War, the Prussians had been harassed in France by civilian snipers known as *franc-tireurs* (literally "free shooters"), who then faded back into the population. The morale of the invaders was sapped by this often unseen enemy, and the Prussians regarded such acts as cowardly, unethical and against the laws and customs of war. Thus, in 1914 the Germans were almost pathologically determined to contain, even extinguish, any acts of civilian resistance from the outset. With the policy of *Schrecklichkeit*, they visited instant reprisals on the occupied population, as well as shelling and burning buildings.

This vibrant poster was produced in Dublin in May 1915, and it exploited a general sense of moral outrage at German killing and destruction beyond the battlefields of Belgium and northern France. It formed part of an ongoing programme to reinvigorate Irish enlistment, which, after initial enthusiam, was waning. Over the rousing exhortation "Irishmen Do your Duty!", it highlighted one of the last, but most infamous, instances of German *Schrecklichkeit*: the burning of Rheims cathedral. This historic building – where in earlier times French kings were crowned – was intermittently shelled by German artillery for ten days from 20 September 1914. The Germans claimed it was a legitimate target, because the tower was being used for observation and French guns were positioned nearby, but the French denied it and the world believed them. Images of flames engulfing this architectural masterpiece proved deeply damaging to Germany's reputation and did much to sway international opinion against her, compounding the earlier reports of Belgian atrocities. This poster was also able to appeal to a sense of shared Catholic outrage at religious "desecration". Here, in plain sight, was the very essence of what everyone was fighting against.

Belgian women make their way gingerly through rubble, passing German guards, outside what is left of the Hôtel de Ville (town hall) of Louvain, Belgium (August 1914). The result of retribution, rather than of battle, the destruction of this centre of culture outraged neutral opinion and simplified the Allies' propaganda battle.

Executions of Belgian civilians began as early as 4 August. From the first week of the German invasion, reports gained currency of potshots being taken at the invading army, and the Belgian newspapers boasted of the fact. Soon the occupied areas began to pay a terrible price, with stories of massacres and mass killings appearing in the international press. By 21 August rumours were circulating that the little town of Andenne on the Meuse had been sacked. Two days later, General Karl von Bülow's Second Army posted notices warning the civilian population of the recently captured Liège that "the general commanding these troops has burned the town [Andenne] to ashes and has had 110 persons shot". As the Germans advanced further into Belgium and the policy of retribution deepened, the list of atrocities lengthened. At Seilles 50 civilians were executed; at Tamines more than 380 died, with many herded into the town square and systematically shot and bayoneted. The epitaph on their gravestones says it all: "*1914 – Fusillée par les Allemands*".

Visé was said to have been sacked completely, with hundreds of inhabitants shot. The survivors fled over the border into Holland carrying their tales of horror. When the US Minister to Belgium and Holland later visited the town he reported it completely empty and described it as "a vista of ruins that might have been Pompei". German *Kultur* (culture), which embraced the glories of Beethoven and Goethe, was beginning to be seen as something rather different by a shocked world.

At Dinant, also on the Meuse, German troops from Saxony appear to have run amok. They herded several hundred civilians into the square, including the congregation of a church, and lined them up against the sides. They then marched two firing squads into the middle and opened fire. Six hundred and thirty-two men, women and children were murdered, including little Felix Fivet, five weeks old. Astonishingly, but tellingly, the German commander, General von Hausen, insisted that the real responsibility for the killings lay not with his soldiers but with the Belgian government, as it had "approved this perfidious street fighting contrary to international law".

Disbelief that Belgians had the temerity to oppose the German invasion was one factor stoking such retribution; the genuine fear that civilians might start a guerrilla campaign, egged on by the Belgian government, was another. Belgian posters warning civilians *not* to snipe at Germans were even regarded by some German commanders as a cunning means to implant the idea of attacking the invaders.

Major General Erich Ludendorff, who before the war had been Chief of Operations to Moltke, the Chief of the German General Staff, had led the successful assault on Liège. He believed that the Belgian government had "systematically organized civilian warfare" and expressed his personal disgust at the methods of the alleged *franc-tireurs*. Ordinary German soldiers, too, appear to have been genuinely terrified of falling out on the march, one recording that "the thought of falling into the hands of the Walloons was worse than sore feet". To keep them alert, German propaganda made ludicrous claims about Belgian priests leading armed bands of civilians against isolated German sentries and cutting up their bodies. Back in Berlin, Princess Blücher, an English-born aristocrat and diarist, recorded her belief that there were 30 German officers lying in Aachen hospital with their eyes put out by Belgian women. It was simply not true.

In contrast with such wild allegations, the most notorious German atrocity of all was well documented and witnessed by hundreds. It began on 25 August, when German forces moved into the ancient Belgian university city of Louvain. At first the nervous townsfolk went about their business, with their invaders paying for souvenirs and even having their boots shined and hair cut. Things began to go wrong the next day. When stories began to circulate of a German soldier shot in the leg by a Belgian civilian, the *Burgomaster* (mayor) and his staff were arrested as hostages. That night, a riderless horse bolted through the town square, overturning wagons and panicking the German soldiers, who later claimed that they had been fired on by civilians. The citizens said that the Germans had fired on each other in the dark.

The next morning, the Germans decided to act. General von Lüttwitz, the new military governor of Brussels, solemnly told the astonished US and Spanish representatives that the Germans proposed to destroy Louvain because, he (mistakenly) claimed, "our general has been shot by the son of the Burgomaster", and that "the population has fired on our troops". True to their word, the Germans set fire to the city and started killing its inhabitants and looting. American journalists confirmed the stories, reporting flames rising from burning rows of houses and drunken German soldiers on the rampage.

Louvain University's world-renowned library of medieval books and manuscripts, housed in the Clothworkers Hall, was deliberately set alight: 230,000 books and an irreplaceable collection of tapestries were destroyed. Across the square in the church of St Pierre were priceless medieval painted altar panels and statues. In a six-day orgy of destruction, the occupying forces burned the lot. Louvain was comprehensively sacked, its stories of death and destruction disseminated by the thousands of distraught refugees fleeing from the city.

A storm of international protest burst over the Germans, but to little avail. To make sure that there was no misunderstanding, Berlin announced that its "reprisals" were deliberate and measured and that war on non-combatants was a policy designed to punish those who dared to oppose the occupying German army.

The atrocities, real or alleged, merely united opinion around the world in the belief that the German forces were akin to a new barbarian horde and added weight to a growing feeling that the defeat of Germany was a truly just cause. This sense of shared outrage soon cemented the Allies' relations and encouraged them to issue a declaration in September, promising that none of them would agree a separate peace with Germany. And *Schrecklichkeit* delivered an enduring propaganda tool to the Allies, to be exploited throughout the war (*see* Chapter 31).

14

PATTERN 1908 WEB EQUIPMENT
THE BRITISH EXPEDITIONARY FORCE
JOINS BATTLE

AUGUST TO SEPTEMBER 1914

In August 1914, the British Army began its own contribution to the land war across the English Channel. The British Expeditionary Force (BEF) that crossed to the Continent eventually consisted of six infantry divisions and five brigades of cavalry; at just over 150,000 men, all professionals, they were a tiny force compared to the mass conscript armies of France and Germany.

Despite the deficiency in size, the BEF was arguably the best-trained and best-equipped army Britain had ever fielded. It was shaped under two main influences: the impact of the Boer farmers, who had inflicted embarrassing defeats and serious casualties on Britain's Imperial Forces in South Africa at the turn of the century; and the reforms introduced by Richard Haldane, Secretary of State for War (until 1912), which had modernized and revitalized the service. The results were striking. New organizations, new tactics and new training had all placed the army on a fresh footing, and a new General Staff ensured that when war came the BEF could be efficiently run. The BEF that set out to France in 1914 truly was a well-trained, highly mobile and tightly knit "band of brothers", confident of victory.

An infantryman must carry all he needs – food, tools and ammunition – as comfortably as possible. During the Anglo-Boer War, British soldiers still wore their traditional white leather equipment, but its colour and gleaming brass buckles picked them out on the veldt. Ammunition sweated in the equipment's pouches and easily fell out, and something new was clearly needed. In 1908, an innovative new set of personal equipment was introduced, made of flexible, woven cotton webbing. Put together from more than 12 individual pieces, it formed a single unit that could be taken on and off by undoing just one buckle on the main belt. Attached to the shoulder straps was a large pack, containing a change of clothes and a sewing kit. Strapped to the belt was a smaller haversack holding rations, a knife and fork and the means to clean the owner's rifle. Fixing the shoulder straps to the main belt were two sets of ammunition pouches, holding a total of 150 bullets in strips of 5 for easy loading. A 17-inch sword bayonet hung at the back, along with a water bottle and the components to make an entrenching tool. Despite its complexity, the equipment was carefully balanced and comfortable to wear, and in 1914 it outclassed the comparable equipment of other armies in the field. Indeed, this "Pattern 1908 Web Equipment" – as it was formally known – proved so popular that it changed little over the next 30 years.

> "THE ANGEL OF THE LORD, ON THE TRADITIONAL WHITE HORSE AND CLAD ALL IN WHITE WITH A FLAMING SWORD, FACED THE ADVANCING GERMANS AT MONS AND FORBADE THEIR FURTHER PROGRESS."

> Brigadier John Charteris, describing the mythical "Angel of Mons" that troops claimed to see, 1914

After landing in France early in August, the BEF moved to the left of the French General Lanrezac's Fifth Army, at Maubeuge on the River Sambre, before marching over the Belgian border. Neither the British nor the rapidly advancing German First Army, under General Alexander von Kluck, knew of the other's presence until they collided, at Mons, on 23 August. For the first time since Waterloo, the British Army was fighting in continental Europe. When the news of the Kaiser's instruction to "exterminate" this "contemptibly small army" reached the regiments of the BEF they adopted the insult proudly, responding in kind in their marching songs – not always "It's a Long Way to Tipperary" and more likely to be "Oh we don't give a f***, For old von Kluck, And all his barmy army" (to the tune of "The Girl I Left Behind Me").

Germans, but especially the French, had been dying in their thousands across the whole Front during the Battle of the Frontiers (*see* Chapter 12). Now the fighting at Mons confronted the British with the stark reality of modern war. German infantry attacks over open ground were cut to ribbons by the massed firepower of the British regulars, trained to fire 15 aimed rounds a minute from their Lee-Enfield rifles. The very first Victoria Cross of the war was earned on the canal, by Private Sidney Godley of the Royal Fusiliers. At the Nimy Bridge he fired his Vickers machine gun to the last despite being badly wounded, while all around were killed. In their turn the British were stunned by the weight and volume of German artillery and the sight of their mates being blown into chunks of meat by the enemy's 600 guns. Although the casualties were relatively light compared with the later industrialized battles, the 1,600 killed, wounded and missing shook the BEF.

Mons was a small battle in the wider strategic context, but by chance the BEF stood at a crucial place in the German strategic plan. Kluck's army was supposed to sweep down and surround Paris, but now the BEF blocked its way. To their puzzlement – for they thought Mons represented a great victory – the grumbling Tommies now donned their equipment to obey orders to retreat, in order to conform with the French, who were falling back rapidly around them.

Three days later, and 22 miles to the south at Le Cateau, the Germans caught up with the British II Corps, one of the two that comprised the BEF. At dawn on 26 August, its commander, General Sir Horace Smith-Dorrien, ordered his men to deliver what he called a "stopping blow". After a day's hard fighting, II Corps disengaged and slipped away, having lost 38 guns and 7,800 more men killed, wounded and taken prisoner. (This proved the last time that the Royal Artillery deliberately placed its field guns forward in the frontline.) Despite these heavy casualties, Smith-Dorrien's stand at Le Cateau had succeeded in its aim, allowing the BEF to gain two days' march on the enemy as the great retreat headed south for the River Marne.

As the tired and footsore soldiers struggled on, wrong conclusions were drawn by all sides. The BEF's resourceful quartermasters dumped piles of food and ammunition by the roadside so that units could help themselves as they marched past. The Germans mistook this as evidence that the BEF was a broken and defeated force *abandoning* its supplies. And the BEF could still pack a punch. At dawn on 1 September an attack by elements of the German 4th Cavalry Division wrought havoc on the exposed "L" Battery of the Royal Horse Artillery outside the village of Néry (*see* Chapter 98), but despite crippling losses it was repulsed by a spirited counterattack.

Little of this penetrated the mind of the BEF's commander, Field Marshal Sir John French. He was shocked by what he incorrectly saw as the collapse of his army, mistaking the inevitable chaos and losses of a 200-mile fighting retreat for disintegration and potential defeat. Impulsive as ever, he decided to remove the BEF from the firing line and take it away from the battle to regroup and rest. The horrified French commander-in-chief, Joffre, and an equally appalled Cabinet in London rushed to stop Sir John pulling the BEF out at the very crisis of the battle. Joffre needed the BEF for his planned counterattack on the Marne, and the British Cabinet was determined to be seen to be backing its French ally. Secretary of State for War Field Marshal Lord Kitchener hurried to Paris in full uniform and in a frosty exchange behind closed doors (for which no written record exists) appears to have bluntly ordered a sulky Sir John to get on with it – or else.

On 5 September, a French counterattack from Paris forced Kluck's right wing to face west, opening up a 30-mile gap between his troops and the adjacent German Second Army. This was the chance for which Joffre had been waiting. He implored Sir John to join him in an advance north across the Marne, banging his fist on the table and thundering: "*Monsieur le Maréchal*, the honour of England is at stake!" Moved – and startled – an emotional Sir John promised: "We'll do all that our fellows can do." To their intense relief, the men of the BEF were finally ordered to turn and advance.

On 6 September, the BEF crossed the Marne and moved cautiously north into the gap between the German First and Second armies, forcing both to recoil. The Germans were left with no alternative but to retreat. The BEF and French armies followed up slowly, only to be stopped in the middle of September as they ran up against dug-in German defences 50 miles to the north, along the River Aisne. The seeds of trench warfare were sown as the opening phase of the war in the West came to an end.

The days between Mons and the Aisne had cost the old regulars of the BEF dear. But worse was to come. Many of the original BEF would not survive to sport their "Mons Star" service medals.

15

B43 – A LONDON BUS AT THE FRONT
THE B.E.F. & THE FIRST BATTLE OF YPRES

OCTOBER TO NOVEMBER 1914

In mid-September 1914, as the weary British survivors of Mons, Le Cateau and the Marne threw themselves against the first German trenches along the River Aisne, it became clear that frontal assaults were unlikely to succeed. The BEF had now suffered three weeks of steady casualties, and it needed to regroup, re-equip and absorb new drafts.

With overextended supply lines and communications, it made strategic and logistic sense for the BEF to shorten its links to the Channel ports. During the last two weeks of September, with minimum fuss, the BEF moved north in stages, returning to its original position on the left flank of the French armies. In fact, with stalemate on the Aisne, *both* sides began manoeuvring to the north, looking to turn the other's flank in what became known as "the race to the sea". It ended when the Belgian army opened the sluice gates to flood the low-lying plains by the coast, and neither side could go any further. Opposing lines of trenches started to spread, reaching down as far as the Swiss border.

One of the key problems exposed by the frenetic pace of events in these weeks had been transport. Large troop movements could be carried out by the French rail network, but as the fighting slowed and began to coalesce around smaller areas of intense confrontation, the shifting of men between these places proved more difficult and required a different solution. It was provided, in part, by the introduction of London buses.

Bus B43 was one of the first batch (1910) of B-type vehicles built for the London General Omnibus Company. Before the war it worked routes 8 (Willesden–Old Ford) and 25 (Victoria–Seven Kings), and it carried up to 34 passengers. But in October 1914 it became one of the first buses requisitioned for service at the Front, seeing service during the First Battle of Ypres. It survived the conflict, returning to its civilian role, and in 1920 it was selected to parade with a group of veteran drivers before King George V at Buckingham Palace – said to be the only time the king ever boarded a bus.

Bus B43 was withdrawn from service in 1924 and given to the drivers' Old Comrades' Association. Decorated with a brass radiator cap in the image of Bruce Bairnsfather's famous wartime cartoon character "Old Bill", it became a feature of special events, parades and even old comrades' funerals, until on 30 April 1970 members of the Association handed it over to the Imperial War Museum for safekeeping. Bus B43 remains a unique object – a pioneering piece of mechanical engineering, unexpectedly drawn into the turmoil of war.

ANCRE SOMME

RAL

B43

LN 4743

Although the BEF was well equipped with transport, this largely consisted of horse-drawn vehicles. In August 1914, the British Army went to war with 165,000 horses, but it possessed only 1,200 mechanized vehicles. More motor transport was always going to be needed, and in October 1914 the War Office requisitioned 300 B-type buses from the London General Omnibus Company, along with their civilian drivers. Indeed, they had been built under subsidy to be adaptable for military use. They were driven straight off the streets of London and ferried across to the trenches of Flanders, the first to arrive still boasting their red livery and their London destination boards.

The buses would soon prove their utility, and over the next four years they became an integral part of the military transport system. In time the civilian drivers were replaced, along with the glass windows, and the buses, now painted green, were configured to carry 25 fully laden soldiers. Working along the length of the British Front, they would carry thousands of weary men, and it is a testament to their overall efficiency that the wartime record for moving off a brigade of around 3,500 troops eventually stood at an impressive 4½ minutes.

In October 1914, the first of the buses encountered the BEF straggling south from the medieval city of Ypres, the last city in unoccupied Belgium, positioned at the crossroads of several strategic routes across ancient Flanders. There, between mid-October and November 1914, the old professional British Army once again confronted the full might of the Kaiser's forces and paid a heavy price. Ypres was to become the graveyard of the BEF.

The new German Chief of the General Staff, Erich von Falkenhayn, ordered a massive offensive to seize the Channel ports. No fewer than six army corps, more than 250,000 men, were set to surge forward in intensive fighting around Ypres, intent on breaking through weakened Allied defences. For three weeks the fighting was bitter, and it was only with the arrival of French reinforcements that the line eventually held.

The increasingly desperate Germans rushed mass formations of hastily assembled reserve corps, many including untrained student volunteers, into the attack. Lacking even basic military skills, they were mown down by relentless British rifle fire in what German propaganda played up as the murder of innocents. The climax came between 29 October and 12 November. Eleven Allied divisions around Ypres, many of them mere husks of their former selves, were attacked by 24 German divisions supported by 700 guns. Kaiser Wilhelm himself came forward to witness the final assaults and the capture of Ypres.

At times, the outcome hung in the air. On 31 October, at Gheluvelt, on the Menin Road, the Germans broke through; they were only repulsed by a desperate counter-attack from the depleted 2nd Battalion, Worcestershire Regiment, the very last British reserve unit. On the same day, to the south at Messines, Britain's first non-professional soldiers entered the fight.

The 14th Battalion, London Regiment, known as the "London Scottish", were so-called "week-end" soldiers of the new Territorial Force. Arriving by bus at Ypres two days earlier, they were ferried by these same vehicles down to Messines Ridge to join battle. Their fight on Halloween 1914 was a traumatic affair. The enemy attacked in the dark and, in confused hand-to-hand fighting illuminated by a burning mill and hayricks, nearly broke through before being repulsed by the inexperienced part-timers. In the end the London Scottish was cut off and had to pull back

Men of the 2nd Battalion, Royal Warwickshire Regiment, are transported in convoys of buses (6 November 1914) to the First Battle of Ypres, during the last days before the Western Front solidified into trench lines. The buses still sport their "LGOC" designation – London General Omnibus Company.

in confusion. Casualties were horrific: of the regiment's 700 men in action, only 300, including many wounded, answered roll call the next day.

On 11 November German forces made a last major assault, heralded by a heavy-artillery bombardment. The densely packed attacking troops again offered easy targets to the British infantry; yet, despite the terrible losses, the Prussian Guards began to break through near Nonne Bosschen Wood and along the Menin Road itself. They were only stopped by artillery blazing away over open sights at 500 yards' range, and by a mixture of Royal Engineers and headquarters clerks deployed as infantry.

By 14 November the weather had broken and the German attacks petered out. Yet these events made a lasting impression on at least one soldier, at that time commander of the British I Corps. For the rest of the war, General Sir Douglas Haig believed that, with just one more push, the Germans would have flooded through, after which there would have been nothing to stop them seizing the Channel ports. There is little doubt that this experience of just how close the Germans had been to breaking through at Ypres coloured his tactical stubbornness for the rest of the war.

The First Battle of Ypres cost the BEF another 8,000 men killed, 30,000 wounded and an astonishing 18,000 completely disappeared. It is no exaggeration to say that the original BEF of August 1914 was now gone forever, and with it the unique character of the Edwardian British Army. From now on, Britain's part in the war would be fought increasingly by the part-timers of the Territorial Force, the citizen volunteers of Kitchener's "New Armies", men from around the empire (and in particular the Dominions of Australia, Canada and New Zealand, and Britain's Indian Empire) – and from the end of 1916 by conscripts. But only the selfless dedication of the original professional soldiers of the BEF, the "Old Contemptibles", had bought the time for these new British armies to build up their strength.

16

AN IRON CROSS FOR "BABY-KILLERS"
GERMAN BOMBARDMENT & THE BATTLE
OF DOGGER BANK

DECEMBER 1914 TO JANUARY 1915

By October 1914, British naval strategy had consolidated around conducting a "distant" blockade against Germany, converting the North Sea into a watery no-man's land. With an inferior number of capital ships – battleships and battlecrusisers – the Imperial German Navy could only respond by attempting to lure small groups of Royal Navy warships into a chase and then onto freshly laid minefields or the guns of its main High Seas Fleet. This was the thinking behind Admiral Franz von Hipper's audacious bombardment of Great Yarmouth on the Norfolk coast on 3 November 1914. Little damage was done, but it demonstrated that the British northeast coast was open and vulnerable to attack. Encouraged by that success (and the realization that two of Britain's most modern warships were far away, off the Falkland Islands: *see* Chapter 22), Hipper's "Scouting Group" of battlecruisers mounted another, more ambitious operation. Emerging from the mist, at dawn on 16 December 1914, they opened fire on the coastal towns of Old (East) Hartlepool, West Hartlepool, Whitby and Scarborough.

West Hartlepool was, it could be argued, a legitimate military target. It was the base of the 9th Destroyer Flotilla, had three munitions factories and was defended by a battery of three guns. But Scarborough and Whitby were different; they were not military targets, and thus specifically excluded from attack by the terms of the Geneva and Hague Conventions.

For the Germans, the attack on Britain's northeast coast may have had the clear strategic purpose of drawing out the British ships, but to the British public the bombardment represented nothing more than a brutal, unprovoked attack on innocent civilians in their own homes – another German atrocity. That widespread view was clearly, and sardonically, expressed through the production and sale of this rough copy of a Prussian Iron Cross. Embossed on the front were the names HARTLEPOOLS (reflecting the distinct East and West Hartlepool, which were only combined into one decades later), SCARBORO' and WHITBY, with the date 1914. On the back were three more names, from France and Belgium: RHEIMS, LOUVAIN and AMIENS. The implication of this twinning was clear: that the Germans were now meting out the same kind of *Schrecklichkeit*, or "terror", on British civilians as they had visited on those continental cities.

From the earliest days of the war, a specialist intelligence unit in the Admiralty, known as Room 40, had been able to read German naval wireless signals. Using

a series of captured enemy codebooks, Room 40 could now provide advance warning of many intended German operations, and in mid-December the Admiralty was made aware of Hipper's planned raid. But it did not know that the main High Seas Fleet intended to shadow Hipper's battlecruisers across the North Sea.

A squadron of battlecruisers and destroyers under Vice-Admiral Beatty had set out from Cromarty on 15 December to rendezvous with the 2nd Battle Squadron (of dreadnought-type battleships) from Scapa Flow, under Vice-Admiral Sir George Warrender, and the combined group headed south.

At 07.55 the German battlecruisers *Derfflinger* and *Von der Tann* appeared off Scarborough and opened fire with their 11-inch guns. Seventeen civilians were killed and several hundred wounded. Further north, at Hartlepool, the battlecruisers *Seydlitz*, *Moltke* and *Blücher* began to bombard the town. Although there were Royal Navy ships (and a submarine) in harbour at Hartlepool, a lack of steam and other factors prevented any effective response from them. In all, the Germans fired 1,150 rounds leaving 102 killed and 467 wounded – including 424 civilians. They did not have it entirely their own way, though; the Heugh Coastal Defence Battery returned 123 rounds and damaged *Blücher*'s upper works and turrets.

At sea, the outlying ships of both fleets met and a running battle began. Afraid that the full might of the Grand Fleet might be bearing down upon it, the High Seas Fleet turned tail and headed for home – losing an opportunity to destroy Beatty's battlecruisers. The British now searched for Hipper's battlecruisers as the latter pulled away from the northeast coast, but they were hampered by, among other things, bad weather, poor visibility and confused communications. Hipper's ships were able to evade interception and return successfully to port.

The attacks were hailed as a triumph in Germany, which justified the targets by describing them as "fortified towns". The Kaiser even awarded (a reluctant) Hipper the Iron Cross and German newspapers crowed over the "heroism of our sailors". In Britain there was universal denunciation of "the baby-killers of Scarborough", as Winston Churchill described the raiders. Indeed, the most important effect of the raids on the larger British war effort was in galvanizing public support, as outraged British men, rallied by the cry "Remember Scarborough!", rushed to the colours.

As for the Royal Navy, Jellicoe now began to deploy elements of his Grand Fleet further south, moving Beatty and his battlecruisers to Rosyth. For Hipper, the ease with which his ships had eluded any British pursuit emboldened him, as 1915 opened, into planning a sweep into the shallow waters of Dogger Bank to investigate British trawlers suspected of relaying intelligence to London. However, the British advantage of access to German signals and intentions paid off again, and the tables were turned. Beatty's battlecruisers sailed to intercept. In this engagement it was the Germans who were ambushed, at dawn on 24 January 1915, and who had to flee. Despite serious mistakes – by both sides – the battle was a definite British victory. Ironically, its legacy was good for the Germans but disastrous for the Royal Navy.

It was a clear day and the faster British ships gradually overhauled the strung-out, fleeing German squadron. In the rapid long-range exchange of gunfire two notable events were to alter the course of the battle. SMS *Seydlitz* was hit by a 13.5-inch shell, which penetrated a gun turret. The explosion caused a flash fire in the ready-use ammunition, which set fire to the magazine. A brave sailor opened the red hot valves with his bare hands and flooded the magazine, saving the ship.

The damaged German cruiser SMS Blücher *lists dramatically during the Battle of Dogger Bank, her crew clinging desperately to the side – or already in the water. Owing to a Royal Naval signalling mix-up, British warships concentrated on finishing her off rather than pursuing other enemy ships. As many as 1,000 of* Blücher's *crew met a watery end.*

The second event was the 14 hits on Beatty's flagship, HMS *Lion*, which slowed her to half speed. Beatty could only fume impotently as his battlecruisers began to disappear ahead of him. As he transferred his flag to a destroyer he attempted to keep his ships in pursuit of Hipper by way of two simultaneous flag signals – "steer northeast" and "engage the enemy's rear" – on the same flag hoist. They were misunderstood. The curse of over-tight Victorian Royal Navy discipline then struck as, schooled to obey senior officers' orders or be court-martialled, the British ships left the fleeing German battlecruisers and turned northeast to concentrate instead on the already damaged heavy cruiser SMS *Blücher*. Under a hail of fire, *Blücher* rolled over and sank. Beatty attempted to correct the mix-up with a new flag signal, but by now the distance between him and the other ships was too great. Meanwhile, the battered German battle squadron made good its escape.

In terms of what it might have achieved, Dogger Bank was, for the Royal Navy, a classic case of a golden opportunity lost. But British public opinion celebrated a victory, and the Germans rightly regarded the battle as a major reverse. SMS *Seydlitz* remained in dry dock for four months, while a worried Kaiser once again ordered that no risks were to be taken by his High Seas Fleet and replaced Friedrich von Ingenohl as its commander-in-chief with Hugo von Pohl.

As with all early battles in any war, Dogger Bank provided some vital lessons. It highlighted the need for safer ammunition handling, better communications, well-practised damage-control drills and tighter control of the distribution of fire to targets. But while the chastened Germans learned those lessons, the victorious British did not. At Jutland in 1916 they would learn them the hard way (*see* Chapter 61).

17

ERIC ROWDEN'S CHRISTMAS BUTTON
THE CHRISTMAS TRUCE

DECEMBER 1914

War is one of humanity's oldest social activities, and soldiers have always found ways and pretexts to fraternize with the enemy. The Christmas Truce of 25 December 1914 is the best known among many "live and let live" instances that, perhaps surprisingly, pervaded trench warfare. Informal truces and agreed ceasefires to rescue wounded men were not uncommon, and trench routine appears to have included a tacit early morning truce, as the cold and tired soldiers on both sides got on with cooking their breakfasts. But Christmas 1914 was something different in scale.

On 24 December, Germans put out small Christmas trees on their parapet and sang carols. British soldiers joined in, and then shouted conversations began where the lines were close. As Christmas Day dawned, the sense of goodwill spread. Private Frank Richards of the 2nd Battalion, Royal Welsh Fusiliers, recorded that both sides put up boards saying "Merry Christmas", and then a few brave souls walked, with their hands up, towards the Germans, who responded in kind, met and shook hands. Richards' company commander tried to stop it all, but was too late.

Elsewhere, Captain Sir Edward Hulse of the Scots Guards agreed a truce with a German officer. What followed was an exchange of gifts, as German beer, sausages and spiked helmets were swapped for bully beef, biscuits, tunic buttons and regimental badges. Someone even organized an impromptu hare coursing.

On Christmas Day 1914, Eric Rowden was a 19-year-old corporal with the Queen's Westminster Rifles (1/16th Battalion, London Regiment). It was one of the first Territorial battalions to go to France, arriving on 1 November 1914, and some weeks later, on 23 December, it entered the trenches east of Armentières for its second tour in the frontline. The next day was Christmas Eve, and Rowden and his fellow soldiers could hear the Germans opposite begin singing. That night not a shot was fired. Christmas Day itself began frostily and with a heavy mist. There was some contact with the Germans but it was not until after Christmas lunch, when the mist had cleared, that large numbers of the "enemy" were seen standing in no-man's land. In his diary, Rowden noted: "I went out and found a German who spoke English a little and we exchanged buttons and cigarettes and I had 2 or 3 cigars given me and we laughed and joked together, having forgotten war altogether." He got the soldier with whom he exchanged buttons to write down his name, "Werner Keil", and added his regiment, "179th Saxon", on a postcard. The button still remains firmly attached to the same postcard a hundred years on, a testament to that extraordinary day.

"SHOOT 'IM? WHY SIR? 'E AIN'T DONE NO 'ARM TO ME!"

British frontline sentry, as quoted in the diary of a brigadier general

In Richards' sector, the Germans brought two barrels of beer, and further afield an informal football match took place, one of several. The cartoonist Bruce Bairnsfather even recorded one of his machine gunners cutting a German's "unnaturally long hair". In fact, all nine British divisions reported verbally arranged truces on Christmas Day. It was not an exclusively Anglo-German phenomenon either; in the villages of the Vosges, for example, French and Germans exchanged presents in disused trench tunnels.

Newspapers printed stories and photographs of German and British soldiers celebrating Christmas together in no-man's land, and soldiers wrote home about their extraordinary experiences. But "Authority" took a dim view. An angry General Smith-Dorrien ordered an investigation and insisted that the spontaneous truce not be repeated. To make sure, it was bombardments, rather than carols, that accompanied Christmas the following year.

18

AUSTRIAN COMMEMORATIVE RIBBONS
TANNENBERG & THE EASTERN FRONT

1914 TO 1915

If, as 1914 wore on, the war in the West developed into a static affair of trench lines and stalemate, the same could not be said of the long Eastern Front. From the moment the Russians marched across the border into East Prussia, the fighting ranged back and forth across Central Europe, with frequent changes of fortune. The vast chessboard of the terrain from the Baltic coast to the Bulgarian border lent itself to a war of movement, and nowhere was that more true than in one of the German army's most spectacular victories: at Tannenberg, in the last week of August 1914.

German strategic thinking held that Russian mobilization, though inevitably large, would be slow. But the government in St Petersburg managed to mobilize two whole armies within three weeks and on 15 August invaded East Prussia, much to the consternation of Kaiser Wilhelm and his nervous Chief of the General Staff, Moltke. East Prussia – part of the sacred heartland of the ruling Hohenzollern dynasty – was Germany's Achilles' heel. Its coastal capital, Königsberg, was only 75 miles from the Russian border, while only 100 miles to the south a salient of Russia's Polish territory bulged westwards, south of the East Prussian border defences. The Russian invasion caused dismay in Berlin, as newspapers spread stories of terrified German refugees fleeing Cossack hordes. Alarmed reports from General Maximilian von Prittwitz, the commander of the German Eighth Army, warned that he was badly outnumbered. Berlin now redirected eastwards two army corps that had been intended for the Western Front.

Since the 18th century it had been a Germanic tradition to produce decorative silk ribbons as commemorative souvenirs. Known as *Vivat Bänder* (from the Latin epithet *fama semper vivat* – "may his fame last forever" – and *Bänder*, the German for "ribbons"), they were often designed by notable artists, and blended symbolic illustrations with heraldic devices and ornate lettering. The souvenirs were usually sold for charity, and after the outbreak of war in 1914 one of the most popular was the German *Rote Kreuz* (Red Cross). A range of *Bänder* was also produced, mostly in Berlin and Vienna, to celebrate popular heroes, major victories such as occurred at Tannenberg and other important events. The two *Bänder* shown here were both produced in Vienna in 1915. *Vivat unsere glorreiche Armee* ("Long Live our Glorious Army") was designed by the artist Alfred Offner and highlights the five key branches of the Austro-Hungarian army. *Vivat das befreite Galizien* ("Long Live Liberated Galicia") celebrates the German and Austro-Hungarian recapture of Galicia in May 1915 from the Russians. Both are testament to a confident belief in the war effort at this time.

On 20 August, the Russian First Army pushed the Germans back from the German–Russian border at the Battle of Gumbinnen, and a worried Prittwitz ordered a retreat, with half his force falling back to the north to defend Königsberg. The rest of his Eighth Army was ordered to make a general retreat behind the line of the River Vistula, 140 miles to the west, thus abandoning most of East Prussia to the advancing Russians. Prittwitz was promptly sacked for his troubles.

Berlin replaced him with General Paul von Hindenburg, together with Erich Ludendorff as his chief of staff, who was fresh from his early conquest of the Belgian fortress complex at Liège. On arrival at their new HQ they were met by the Chief of Eighth Army's Operations Branch, Colonel Max Hoffmann. The intelligent and articulate Hoffmann was the General Staff's Russian expert: he spoke the language, he had served in Russia and, most important of all, he had produced a plan. Rather than concede East Prussia to the Russians, Hoffmann advocated attacking the Russian Second Army in the south while leaving Königsberg to defend itself in the north.

This was risky, but Hoffmann had a trump card up his sleeve. The Germans were able to read all the Russian signals. The poorly educated Russian signallers seemed unable to master codes and ciphers, and to avoid delays they were often transmitting "in clear" – verbatim. The result was a windfall of intelligence: Russian troop strengths, movement schedules and operational orders were now an open book, and messages between the First and Second armies showed how poorly the two Russian generals were cooperating: General Paul von Rennenkampf, commander of the First Army, and General Alexander Samsonov of the Second had allegedly even come to blows a decade before, after the Russian defeat by the Japanese in 1905.

Rennenkampf refused to move south and assist the Second Army, signalling that he needed at least three days before his men could march. His units had outrun their supplies. Another signals intercept provided a complete order of battle of Samsonov's dispositions as well as his army's planned route of attack. Faced with this gift of opportunity, Hindenburg and Ludendorff agreed Hoffmann's plan and promptly authorized the immediate movement of one army corps to the south via the excellent East Prussian railway system. The German dispositions were completed with the march south of two further corps to face Samsonov's right flank, while a fourth was moved by rail over 100 miles against the Russian left flank.

On 27 August, General Hermann von Francois's I Corps commenced battle by attacking Samsonov's exposed left flank. Samsonov attempted to push through in the centre, but thereby exacerbated the vulnerability of his flanks. German signallers began to intercept desperate pleas for assistance from Samsonov. But they knew from intercepted orders from the Russian High Command, *Stavka*, that Rennenkampf's First Army was to continue northwest towards Königsberg and thus even further away from the embattled Second Army. Aerial reconnaissance confirmed that a huge gap was opening up between the two Russian armies. By 29 August the Germans had completed their encirclement. As the pincers closed and Samsonov's army collapsed, the general and his staff fled through the forests in the dark. Somewhere in the fastness of the night Samsonov blew his brains out.

By contrast, Hindenburg became a national hero overnight and Germany's saviour. He took up Hoffmann's idea to name the battle "Tannenberg" to redress the defeat, in 1410, of the Teutonic knights, from whom he claimed descent. The contribution of Colonel Hoffmann – the originator and coordinator of the brilliant plan – was overlooked in the euphoria of victory. Of the 150,000 Russian soldiers who fought at Tannenberg, about 50,000 were killed or wounded and around 95,000 captured. The Germans had destroyed a complete Russian army, captured more than 500 guns and gained an historic victory.

Tannenberg stands as one of the most decisive battles of the First World War. It was to have two related and enduring effects: first, the defeat demoralized the Russians to such an extent that many Russian generals thereafter acquired a serious inferiority complex and never really believed that they could beat the German army; second, it brought the "Duo" – Hindenburg and Ludendorff – to national prominence and power as Germany's virtual warlords.

More immediately, Hindenburg and Ludendorff, once reinforced by the two corps transferred from the Western Front, quickly moved north against the Russian First Army around the Masurian Lakes. Rennenkampf was lucky to escape being surrounded and pulled back hastily to the border. That second German victory, in the second week of September 1914, effectively destroyed Russia's capacity for carrying out offensive operations against northeastern Germany.

However, the advantages of this strategic victory for the Central Powers were threatened by the defeat of the Austro-Hungarian armies far to the south, along the Carpathian Mountains, where Russian fortunes were better and quantities of troops much more numerous. The grand strategy favoured by Franz Conrad von Hötzendorf, the Austrian chief of staff, had been for a pincer movement with German forces to swallow much of Russian Poland. But, in a confused mobilization, Austria-Hungary had split her forces ineptly across two fronts, south against Serbia and northeast against Russia. Initial success in the latter had dissipated, and now Russian armies had advanced deep into the Austro-Hungarian province of Galicia and up to the Carpathian Mountains, while also threatening, to the west, the vital industries of German Silesia. The Russians had scored major victories, isolating the massive

Some of the nearly 100,000 Russian PoWs from the ill-fated Second Army (30 August 1914), after the comprehensive German victory at the Battle of Tannenberg. At this stage, Germany was both an invading power and an invaded nation, but victories at Tannenberg and, shortly afterwards, the Masurian Lakes pushed the fighting back over her borders.

A hand-coloured lantern slide (1915) shows the battering suffered by the strategically significant Austro-Hungarian fortress of Przemysl during its two sieges by the Russians and its recapture in June 1915. One of the largest forts in Europe, it had been recently bolstered to withstand the effects of modern artillery. It was certainly tested in 1914–15.

defensive fortress of Przemysl, on the River San, and driving back the Austro-Hungarians for hundreds of miles, with as many as 350,000 casualties. To counter this crisis the Germans were now forced to rush reinforcements to help their ally and, with a new Ninth Army, they counterattacked from Silesia in October along the River Vistula and towards Warsaw in an effort to stop the Russian advance. But the Germans were rebuffed, narrowly escaping envelopment.

The Russian *Stavka* now planned to make good on its successes with offensives west into Germany and southwest further into Austria-Hungary. But they were pre-empted by Hindenburg and Ludendorff's renewed drive, with the Ninth Army, towards Warsaw and Lodz in November 1914. Yet again, the Germans had the advantage of accurate signals intelligence and planned to attack the Russians' flank as they advanced into Silesia; but this time the Russians had the advantage of vastly superior numbers and very nearly trapped the Germans in their turn.

As winter set in, and amid dreadful weather conditions, both sides tried to manoeuvre for advantage around Lodz without any marked success, although the city itself fell to the Germans after they were reinforced by troops transferred east, after the fighting at Ypres. The result was a stalemate; and by early December a combination of exhaustion, bad weather and, on the Russian side, lack of ammunition – which was an increasing Russian military problem – had forced the battle to an inconclusive end, and Germans and Russians alike dug trenches to consolidate their positions. Further south, as 1914 drew to a close, a joint Austro-Hungarian and German force managed to take advantage of a gap near Limanova, in the Carpathians, to at least stymie the potential Russian threats to Budapest and southern Germany.

Among the Central Powers, Austria-Hungary's losses and setbacks were confirming her role as the junior partner, with strategic direction increasingly a German affair. By early 1915, Hindenburg was effectively commander of the whole Eastern Front. He now planned a series of rolling offensives with the aim of pushing the Russians well away from Silesia and, ideally, knocking them out of the war altogether. Falkenhayn reluctantly agreed to the plans, probably because a knockout blow in the East would allow a concentration on the Western Front.

The most northerly German onslaught came on 7 February 1915 around the Masurian Lakes, when the German Eighth Army attacked in the middle of a snowstorm and drove the Russians back 70 miles in a week. The Russians retreated in disorder and a complete corps was surrounded and surrendered on 21 February. However, the very next day a whole Russian army counterattacked and forced the Germans to dig in. The battle achieved little at a cost of 56,000 Russian casualties and 100,000 prisoners. In the south, on 22 March 1915, the beleaguered fortress of Przemysl, which had been besieged for a second time, was finally forced to surrender having exhausted its food and its defenders. Since 1914 it had tied up a Russian army of nearly 300,000 men and blocked the gateway to the Carpathian Mountains. The Russians captured as many as 126,000 prisoners and 700 pieces of artillery.

Meanwhile, the Germans and Austro-Hungarians quietly massed two armies under General August von Mackensen around Gorlice and Tarnow, southeast of Cracow. On 2 May 1915, they attacked, catching the Russian defenders by surprise. A rout ensued, with Russian units fleeing amid scenes of confusion. Disaster now threatened the whole Russian Southwestern Front when, albeit with heavy casualties, the Austro-Hungarians stormed Tarnow. Within 24 hours the German Eleventh Army had blown a gap 15 miles wide in the Russian lines and continued advancing towards the Vistula, barely slowing to mop up thousands of bewildered prisoners. Every Russian effort to counterattack was beaten back by overwhelming German artillery fire. By 10 May *Stavka* recognized the disaster and ordered a general retreat.

The Germans kept the pressure up all through June as the Russians now fell back across a 300-mile front, broken in arms and spirit. One Russian general wrote: "The spring of 1915 I shall remember all my life ... no cartridges, no shells. Bloody fighting and difficult marches day after day. No end to weariness, both physical and moral." The final thrust was a combined German and Austro-Hungarian offensive towards Przemysl. On 3 June, it was recaptured. Austro-Hungarian forces were back where they had started ten months earlier.

By September 1915 the Central Powers' advance was consolidated with the capture of Warsaw and its forts (with the loss of 1,300 guns and 900,000 Russian shells) as well as Vilna (Vilnius) to the north. The Russians pulled back over 300 miles in the centre during their "Great Retreat", trading space for survival. All their gains of 1914 were lost, although ironically they now were in a better strategic position with a much shorter, more defensible front, running from Riga on the Baltic to Ternopil in western Ukraine, and better lines of communication. The Germans and their Austro-Hungarian allies were triumphant at their "colossal" victory. But Russia had not been knocked out of the war and, despite the German High Command's best efforts, *Stavka* had managed to extricate its forces from the clutches of the Central Powers' sweeping offensives designed to trap and annihilate whole armies.

The cost of these Eastern Front battles – largely unknown or written about in the West – was horrific. The casualties of 1914–15 cannot be recorded with accuracy, but best estimates are that the Central Powers lost 620,000 (mainly Austro-Hungarians) and the Russians over 3 million men, including prisoners, dwarfing the statistics on the Western Front for the period.

The Russian débâcle of 1915 was to have far-reaching political consequences. On 21 August 1915, Tsar Nicholas II dismissed Grand Duke Nicholas Nikolaevich as commander-in-chief and took direct control of the army.

Russian military leadership could only get worse.

19

BARNARDISTON'S SAMURAI SWORD
JAPAN ENTERS THE WAR

AUGUST TO DECEMBER 1914

It was the entry of Japan into the war, on 23 August 1914, that turned the conflict from a clash of European powers into a war of global belligerents. In 1902, Japan, a burgeoning sea power, had entered into an alliance with the world's greatest maritime power, Britain. The outbreak of European war now gave competing factions in Japanese politics – the army, the navy and ambitious imperialist politicians – an opportunity to build an imperial presence in the Pacific and to make inroads into China.

When Germany declared war on France, Tokyo – encouraged by London – issued a warning to the German Empire to withdraw German troops from Tsingtao (Qingdao), the German navy's East Asia Squadron base in China. (This was the base that German troops had seized in 1897, after which China had formally ceded it to Germany.) Berlin did not respond. Now, with a British request for help in hunting down any German armed merchantmen at sea providing a welcome catalyst for Japanese ambitions, Japan declared war.

The German East Asia Squadron was commanded by Admiral Maximilian Graf von Spee, and it consisted of the heavy armoured cruisers *Scharnhorst* and *Gneisenau* together with escorting light cruisers. They could have posed a serious threat to the Royal Navy's warships based at Hong Kong and merchantmen all over the South Seas. Spee, mindful of orders that his ships "retain their freedom of movement for as long as possible", had no intention of waiting to be trapped in port and he set sail immediately from Tsingtao. Maintaining radio silence, the German squadron headed into the central Pacific, avoiding the more powerful ships of the Imperial Japanese Navy, notably the British-built *Kongō* – possibly the finest warship of the age.

The North China Field Force was hastily assembled for the siege of Tsingtao under Brigadier General Nathaniel Barnardiston, a widely experienced officer. He successfully kept his small British and Indian contingent at the forefront of operations alongside the much larger Japanese force. When Tsingtao was finally seized, Barnardiston was showered with letters and telegrams of congratulation from towns and cities across Japan; some municipalities went further, and the Mayor of Yokohama sent a gift in the form of a *katana*, a samurai sword. He explained that this particular sword had been "made some three hundred and fifty years ago by Fijiwara Shigetaka, a famous artist". Given the symbolic resonance of such swords within Japan, this was indeed an impressive way for the mayor to express his appreciation of, as he put it, British "co-operation with our army in the capture of the German stronghold in the Far East".

Kongō and her sister ships did not pursue the Germans as they slipped away and instead laid siege to Tsingtao in support of 60,000 Japanese troops, who were aided by two British-led battalions of the North China Field Force. When Tsingtao finally surrendered on 7 November, the Japanese fleet sailed on to seize German island possessions in the western Pacific, in an agreed division of spoils with Britain and her Dominions. (British, Australian and New Zealand landing parties had already scooped up other former German Pacific islands.)

By Christmas 1914 Japan's brief war was effectively over, and victorious soldiers and sailors paraded to celebrate their victory. It had allowed Tokyo to create a mini-empire at virtually no cost; it bolstered Japanese demands for commercial and military rights in China of the kind that European powers enjoyed; and it guaranteed Japan a seat at the top table in any peace conference. For the Far East, Japan's brief involvement in the First World War would cast a long shadow.

20

THE IMPERIAL EAGLE IN AFRICA
THE WAR IN AFRICA

1914 TO 1918

In one sense, the war was always likely to be a form of *world* war, because Britain, Germany and France were imperial powers whose writ extended well beyond Europe. The campaign in Africa, though, turned out to be a genuine sideshow to events that determined the outcome of the war. It was a limited colonial campaign within a global war. In East Africa it did, however, witness an extraordinarily tenacious German resistance, where tens of thousands of Allied soldiers, supported by larger numbers of porters, chased at the very most 3,000 German and 15,000 *Askari* (African) soldiers for four years.

At the time of the European carving up of Africa, the 1885 Congo Act had stipulated that overseas colonies would remain neutral in the event of a European war. For one thing, European powers were fearful of the consequences of arming their own colonized Africans. Despite this high-minded peacetime diplomatic aspiration, that neutrality was swiftly broken by the British; they attacked German river outposts near Lake Victoria, on the border of British and German East Africa, on 5 August 1914, within 24 hours of the outbreak of war. Three days later, to ram the point home, the port of Dar es Salaam was bombarded by two Royal Navy warships, while in West Africa Allied forces were invading the German colonies of Kamerun and Togoland. The war was global.

> Before the war, wireless communications from Germany's African colonies and from her warships around the coast were channelled through a powerful radio transmitter at Kamina in Togoland. Capturing it represented a principal strategic objective for the Allies, and forces from the neighbouring British Gold Coast and French Dahomey quickly took action. On 7 August, the Gold Coast Regiment took control of Togoland's capital, Lome, and three weeks later German technicians at Kamina destroyed the transmitter, quickly ending the war in Togoland. In 1916, the visiting British governor of the Gold Coast saw this great mosaic Imperial German eagle above the porch of the former Government House in Lome and ordered it to be shipped to his own residence in Accra. There it was built into the floor of a new dining room, where apparently it gave "many people a gratifying practical means of expressing their feelings towards the late German dynasty". But when peace was about to be signed at Versailles, the governor appeared to have second thoughts. The mosaic was lifted and shipped to the new War Museum in London, where it arrived in August 1919. Still resplendent and proud, the eagle remains a symbol of the Kaiser's desperate need to spread the German wings around the world in the years before 1914.

"WE ARE THE PORTERS, / CARRYING THE FOOD FOR THE PORTERS CARRYING THE FOOD FOR MORE PORTERS, / CARRYING MORE FOOD FOR THE PORTERS, / WHO ARE CARRYING THE AMMUNITION"

African porters' chant, 1917

Lieutenant Colonel Paul von Lettow-Vorbeck, commander of the forces in German East Africa, ignored his civilian governor's protestations and began to prepare his initial 260 German soldiers and 2,472 *Askari Schutztruppen* (literally "protection troops") for action. His overall strategy was to make tactical retreats in the face of superior forces, but still to try to bog down as much Allied manpower and ordnance as possible in order to prevent their deployment to the Western Front. This remarkable leader was to succeed tactically but fail strategically. The Allies never caught him; yet none of the forces engaged in their fruitless pursuit of him were ever destined for the European war.

In September 1914, Lettow-Vorbeck raided British outposts, but the British gained control of Lake Victoria. At sea, Germany's one major Indian Ocean warship, the light cruiser SMS *Königsberg*, surprised and sank HMS *Pegasus* off Zanzibar on 20 September, but in July 1915 the German ship was in turn trapped inshore and disabled.

The British also launched military strikes against German East Africa and on 2 November landed an Indian Army Expeditionary Force at Tanga on the coast. It was a disaster. The invading troops panicked and fled despite outnumbering the German forces by a ratio of eight to one. Amid confusion, a general retreat to the boats was followed by evacuation on 5 November. The rout had also left Lettow-Vorbeck 600,000 rounds of ammunition, rifles, machine guns and food supplies.

A year-long long pause in East African hostilities was broken only in December 1915 by the sinking of a German lake steamer. However, in July 1915 after a six-month campaign, South African troops had finally conquered German South West Africa (modern Namibia). With aspirations to extend South African borders, by way of trading conquered territory with the Portuguese, the South African General Jan Christian Smuts now took over leadership of a new East African offensive. He mustered an Imperial force of around 20,000 troops – South Africans, Rhodesians and British, but also including 7,000 Indians and native Africans. With the collapse of German resistance in Kamerun in February 1916, Lettow-Vorbeck represented the one remaining obstacle to Allied control in the continent.

Smuts's strategy was to attack from several directions with the promise of Belgian and some Portuguese support (Portugal declared war on Germany in March 1916). His forces attacked from British East Africa, taking Arusha and the German HQ at Moshi. From the Congo, Belgian forces advanced east in April 1916 and occupied Ruanda-Urundi (modern Rwanda and Burundi), in the northwest of German East Africa, by June, but not without interruption from a series of sharp actions by Lettow-Vorbeck. The British then attacked south across Lake Victoria and took Tabora, the administrative centre of central German East Africa, also suffering casualties from Lettow-Vorbeck's men who, typically, then melted away into the bush.

The Germans, though, were rarely the main problem. The campaign degenerated into a debilitating chase through largely unmapped terrain at the height of the rainy season. Smuts favoured mounted infantry, but horses died in droves from the depredations of the tsetse fly, and men from malaria, with some units down to an effective 10 per cent strength. Illness, poor nutrition and exhaustion drastically reduced the European units, and it was no wonder that by the later stages of the war the vast majority of Britain's fighting men were the native Africans of the Kings African Rifles. Logistics became a nightmare, too, as more and more supplies had to be carried forward – mainly to feed the hundreds of thousands of porters necessary.

Nevertheless, by the year's end Smuts's forces controlled large tracts of German East Africa. The Germans remained invisible, except when they ambushed and attacked Allied columns.

In early 1917, Smuts left for London, to join the Imperial War Cabinet. In July, another South African, Major General J.L. van Deventer, launched a major offensive to trap the elusive Germans once and for all. By October 1917 Lettow-Vorbeck had been forced to retreat south, albeit still able to tie down large numbers of the enemy and even defeat them on occasion. At Mahiwa (in modern Tanzania) in October 1917, the Germans turned on their pursuers, inflicting 2,700 casualties. But it was effectively the *Schutztruppe*'s last stand, as it lost an irreplaceable 519 men and vital ammunition. Berlin promoted Lettow-Vorbeck to the rank of major general and even tried, abortively, to send supplies by Zeppelin. But the dwindling numbers of *Schutztruppen* were on their own.

At the turn of the year, Lettow-Vorbeck crossed south into Portuguese East Africa (modern Mozambique) to raid and capture fresh supplies. For the next nine months his dwindling retinue of Germans and *Askaris*, with wives and children, evaded its pursuers. He divided it into three columns, one of which ran out of food and ammunition and was finally forced to surrender. In desperation, in August 1918 he turned north and managed to cross German East Africa under the noses of the enemy to invade Northern Rhodesia (modern Zambia). Two days after the Armistice was signed in Europe, the Germans captured Kasama, looking for food and ammunition. It was there on 14 November 1918, at a spot now marked by the Lettow-Vorbeck Memorial, that the German commander received news of the Armistice. He marched the remnants of his army to Abercorn and formally surrendered on 23 November 1918.

A self-contained theatre it may have been, a long way from the attentions of London and Berlin, but for those involved, the East African campaign was long and costly. Disease killed or incapacitated 30 people for every one killed in battle. Overall, British Imperial forces lost over 10,000 men, most of them from disease, and the Germans about 2,000. By far the most numerous victims of the campaign, though, were native Africans on all sides, perhaps numbering a hundred thousand dead. And for British and French colonial authorities, conscription of native Africans prompted rebellions.

As for Lettow-Vorbeck, he was hailed as a conqueror when he finally returned to Germany. Mounted on a black charger, he led 120 survivors of the *Schutztruppe* through Berlin's Brandenburg Gate in March 1919 to a hero's welcome, the leader of the only undefeated part of the German army in the First World War.

Men of the 4th Battalion, King's African Rifles, watch over a wounded Askari who has been fighting for Lettow-Vorbeck in the last days of the war (November 1918). As with the exercising of colonial power in general, the war in Africa was often a proxy affair, conducted largely by Africans against Africans under the direction of relatively few Europeans.

21

ADMIRAL SOUCHON'S MEDALS
THE OTTOMAN EMPIRE ENTERS THE WAR

4 AUGUST TO 4 NOVEMBER 1914

By the end of 1914, Germany and Austria-Hungary had a significant new ally in the shape of the Ottoman Empire, the vast sprawling territory that covered much of the Middle East. It was a development that created new fronts – in the Eastern Mediterranean, in the Black Sea, and in the Caucasus and Middle East. In due course it would witness the final collapse of the empire long regarded as the "sick man of Europe". But the immediate events that determined the Ottoman alignment with the Central Powers owed much to the adventures of two fleeing German warships and their feisty commander, Admiral Wilhelm Souchon.

Few individuals get the chance to change the course of world history, but the bold and determined Admiral Souchon is a contender. As commander of the Imperial German Navy's Mediterranean Division, he literally followed a course that, in August 1914, not only secured the Ottoman Empire as a German ally, but also set in train massive global political repercussions. The shape of the modern Middle East and even the turbulent history of the Soviet Union can both be traced back to his actions in evading the British to bring his two ships in triumph to the Ottoman capital. With great pageantry, the vessels were symbolically handed over to the Ottoman government, though they remained firmly in German hands. Souchon's status as a contemporary hero in both nations is clearly reflected in his war medals, acquired by the Imperial War Museum in 1988. On the left are a string of German decorations (including the Iron Cross 2nd Class and the Order of the Red Eagle). At the opposite end are two versions of the Ottoman Silver Imtiaz (Medal of Merit), the first inscribed to "Admiral Souchon Pasha". Today, despite the unforeseen consequences of what he did, he remains an admired figure, regarded as an archetypal man of action.

The story started in the Mediterranean, hours prior to Britain's entry into the war. On 4 August 1914, Admiral Sir Archibald Berkeley Milne watched in disbelief as the German Mediterranean Division – consisting of the battlecruiser SMS *Goeben* and her light cruiser escort SMS *Breslau* – sailed at full speed past his flagship. The British squadron was heading west, to close off the entrance to the Mediterranean at Gibraltar, while the German ships were fresh from bombarding the French colonial ports of Phillipeville and Bône on the North African coast. As the German ships passed, at a distance of 8,000 yards, they were sitting ducks for the three British battlecruisers' twenty-four 12-inch guns. But Milne could not open fire, as Britain's ultimatum to Germany over Belgium had until midnight (German time) to expire.

Milne therefore took what practical action he could. He immediately reversed course and set off to pursue the German ships. But the Germans were quicker. Admiral Souchon sped off as fast as he could, heading for Italy, at the expense of bursting one water pipe – and killing four stokers. The desperate chase went on all day as the British fell further behind and, as night fell, the Germans vanished into the darkness and contact was lost.

For two days the frustrated British ships patrolled the seas off southern Italy, while Souchon sheltered at Messina, piling vital coal into *Goeben* and *Breslau*'s bunkers. But the German admiral had soon overextended the limits of his stay in neutral Italy and now faced a difficult choice. His orders from Berlin had been to take his ships to the Ottoman capital, Constantinople (modern Istanbul). But beyond Messina, he knew the British ships were waiting. And if he sought safety at Pola (Pula) instead, on Austria-Hungary's Croatian coast, he risked being bottled up in the Adriatic for the duration of the war, which was unthinkable. Thus, fully coaled, Souchon took up the challenge and ordered his ships to head full steam eastwards across the Mediterranean for the Dardanelles, boldly running the British gauntlet. For Souchon and the world, it was to prove a fateful decision.

British ships spotted the *Goeben* immediately. The cruiser *Gloucester* followed, but at a safe distance, as the German battlecruiser's heavy guns raised shell splashes around her, to the amazement of the passengers on a passing Italian cruise ship. Belatedly, a British squadron of four elderly cruisers tried to chase the fleeing German vessels but could only watch them disappear into the Aegean. *Goeben* had escaped. The British thought that Souchon was now trapped, since by international treaty the Dardanelles were closed to the ships of belligerent nations; they did not know that Souchon had been told to sail right through. Greeted by a Turkish destroyer that appeared flying the signal "Follow Me", the Germans ships were eventually led through the minefields to Chanak. Souchon was determined to make a decisive contribution to Ottoman–German relations and, in his later words, "to force the Turks, even against their will, to spread the war to ... Russia".

For years the Ottoman Empire had sought the support of one or more of Europe's leading powers. But Russia had been its fiercest rival for almost 100 years, while the French (and British) held ambitions of one day taking control of the Levant, particularly Syria, and the British were otherwise lukewarm, despite sending a naval mission in 1908 to help rebuild the Ottoman navy. By contrast, Germany had assiduously courted the Ottoman Empire for many years, and its bankers and engineers had invested time and technology in what became known as the Berlin-to-Baghdad Railway. The young and conceited Kaiser Wilhelm II had visited Constantinople twice as the guest of the sultan, the second time (1898) bringing gifts of weapons, travelling to Jerusalem and Damascus, praising Islam and even decorating Saladin's tomb (*see* Chapter 89) – all giving rise to the myth of 'Hajji Wilhelm', the supposedly Muslim Kaiser of Germany. Now, the prospect of levering Constantinople into war on Russia and fostering *Jihad*, a Muslim rebellion in British India and Egypt, were tempting goals.

Outwardly, the Ottoman Empire remained neutral. However, a secret Ottoman–German treaty signed on 2 August 1914 in theory pledged the Empire to support the Austro-German cause against Russia. Chief among the "pro-war" faction were Enver Pasha, Djemal Pasha and Talaat Pasha, the Ottoman ministers of War, the Navy and the Interior respectively. They led the nationalist Young Turk movement, with sufficient power to shape events.

At the same time, Britain's stock with Ottoman opinion fell sharply. Prior to the war two dreadnought-type battleships had been under construction for the Ottomans in British shipyards but, with war imminent, the First Lord of the Admiralty, Winston Churchill, had cancelled the contracts and – quite legally – on 28 July, seized both ships for the Royal Navy, with a paltry offer of compensation. The more than £6 million cost of commissioning the two ships, the *Sultan Osman I* and the *Reshadieh*, had been raised from millions of individual donations throughout Ottoman territories. Turkish pride was outraged and nationalist sentiment was stoked.

In Constantinople, the German ambassador sensed an exploitable opportunity. For two days *Goeben* and *Breslau* waited just inside the Dardanelles Straits. Souchon sailed to Constantinople on his own and persuaded the Ottoman government that the time had come. On 15 August, he returned to his ships and next day led them

"THOSE WARSHIPS' ACTIONS BROUGHT MORE SLAUGHTER, MORE MISERY AND MORE RUIN THAN HAS EVER BEFORE BEEN BORNE WITHIN THE COMPASS OF A SHIP."

Winston Churchill, referring to Goeben *and* Breslau

in line across the Sea of Marmara to Constantinople, where they won a rapturous welcome. The German ambassador promptly offered both ships to the Ottoman navy, lock, stock and barrel, in recompense for the two battleships that had been – in Turkish eyes – "stolen" by the British. The offer was accepted, and *Goeben* and *Breslau* were renamed *Yavuz Sultan Selim* and *Midilli*, though they retained their German crews. Admiral Souchon was even proclaimed the new commander-in–chief of the Ottoman navy. To ram the point home, he and his men were photographed sporting the naval-issue Ottoman fez instead of the German naval cap.

It was a masterstroke of diplomatic opportunism, which suited Enver Pasha and the other pro-war leaders. Although the Ottoman Empire remained *technically* neutral, its sympathies were forced into the open. For several months all was quiet, as the *Goeben* and *Breslau* sat at anchor and Souchon worked up the rest of the Ottoman fleet. But in late October, and despite the misgivings of many ministers, Enver Pasha despatched the two German ships into the Black Sea where they bombarded the Russian ports of Odessa and Sebastopol. This was an open act of war, and, on 4 November 1914, Russia declared war on the Ottoman Empire, to be followed by British and French declarations a day later.

Constantinople was now irrevocably locked into the war as Berlin's ally. Eventually, a different Middle East would emerge – but not before the Ottoman Empire had suffered humiliating defeat, disintegration, millions of dead and economic ruin.

3

THEATRES OF WAR

22

A PIG CALLED TIRPITZ
WAR IN THE PACIFIC & SOUTH ATLANTIC

AUGUST 1914 TO MARCH 1915

When Japan (with British help) moved against Tsingtao (*see* Chapter 19), the German East Asia Squadron under Admiral von Spee was left without a home port and base. The question now arose: should he disperse his ships and cause mayhem on the high seas for as long as he could, or should he keep his little fleet together? The principles of cruiser warfare dictated that he should split his forces and harry enemy shipping wherever he could, and for as long as possible, while trying to avoid full-scale battle. One of his captains, Karl Friedrich Max von Müller of the SMS *Emden*, argued forcefully for just such a plan. Spee detached *Emden* to act as a single independent raider in the Indian Ocean, but kept the rest of his ships together.

Müller fully justified Spee's decision. During a two-month rampage, he sank a Russian cruiser, raided and bombarded Madras and Penang, and captured or sank around 30 merchant vessels. His exploits disrupted British shipping and diverted no less than 60 warships to hunt him down. It was a bravura performance, but such success could not continue indefinitely.

> By March 1915, only one of Spee's squadron remained: SMS *Dresden*. She was short of ammunition and fuel, and arranged to rendezvous with a German collier off the Chilean island of Más a Tierra (now Robinson Crusoe Island). But the signal was intercepted by the British light cruiser HMS *Glasgow,* which, together with HMS *Kent*, surprised *Dresden* on 14 March. The German ship sought to parley, but during negotiations its crew scuttled her. Amid the floating debris, *Glasgow*'s sailors noticed something unusual: a large pig swimming as fast as its trotters would allow. One man jumped in, was nearly drowned by the struggling animal, but managed to haul it back to the ship – where it was christened "Dennis, the pig PoW". In 1916, *Glasgow* returned to Britain, and Dennis – by now renamed "Tirpitz" (in "honour" of Germany's naval supremo) – was sent to Whale Island gunnery school in Portsmouth. The following year, Tirpitz was sold at the first of three charity auctions, on each occasion being bought by the Duke of Portland, whose payments totalled £1,785 (roughly £68,000 today). Tirpitz's death in 1919 was not the final chapter in the porcine saga. His head, seen here, was stuffed and mounted in Piccadilly and his trotters became the handles of a carving set – an enduring, unusual legacy of the East Asia Squadron's dramatic exploits across two oceans.

On 9 November, *Emden*'s luck ran out. She was finally caught by the Australian cruiser HMAS *Sydney* as Müller was raiding the radio station in the Cocos Islands.

"I AM QUITE HOMELESS. I CANNOT REACH GERMANY. WE POSSESS NO OTHER SECURE HARBOUR. I MUST PLOUGH THE SEAS OF THE WORLD, DOING AS MUCH MISCHIEF AS I CAN UNTIL MY AMMUNITION IS EXHAUSTED, OR A FOE FAR SUPERIOR IN POWER CATCHES ME."

Admiral von Spee

Emden was trapped while her landing party was ashore, and outgunned in a hopeless contest. With over 130 of his crew dead, his guns out of action and his ship on fire, Müller beached *Emden* and hauled down his flag. His enemies were generous in victory, and Müller was hailed as a hero by the British press. The *Daily Telegraph* wrote: "von Muller has been enterprising, cool and daring in making war on our shipping, and has revealed a nice sense of humour. He has moreover shown every consideration to the crews of his prizes. There is not a survivor who does not speak well of him."

While *Emden* was creating havoc off India, Spee sailed his squadron east across the Pacific towards Chile, which was neutral but traditionally friendly to Germany. Here he hoped to collect intelligence and coal prior to a hazardous dash around Cape Horn to reach Germany and safety. But he stopped to bombard the French island of Papeete on 22 September, thus broadcasting his location to the world. The British Admiralty correctly deduced that Spee must be heading for South America and thence Cape Horn, and Rear Admiral Sir Christopher Cradock's Western Atlantic Squadron was ordered to deploy south to intercept.

This put Cradock, now in the Falkland Islands, in a quandary. His only big-gun ship was the obsolescent battleship HMS *Canopus*. She had been sent to join his regular squadron, but Cradock was told (incorrectly) that she could only manage 12 knots. So he decided to leave *Canopus* behind and split his force into two squadrons for the Pacific and Atlantic coasts of South America. He sailed west around the Horn into the Pacific, heading towards German radio signals at Coronel, off the coast of Chile, and meeting the German squadron on 1 November 1914. Cradock's squadron consisted of the outdated armoured cruisers HMS *Monmouth* and his flagship HMS *Good Hope*, plus some escorting light cruisers. They were substantially outgunned and outmatched by Spee's squadron, added to which *Good Hope*'s reservist crew had only performed one main armament practice shoot in three months.

As the battle lines closed at the Battle of Coronel, the British initially had the advantage of the setting sun behind them, which dazzled their opponents. But the 8.2-inch guns of the German armoured cruisers *Scharnhorst* and *Gneisenau* outranged the elderly British cruisers and as the sun sank below the horizon the British ships were silhouetted against the afterglow. Cradock's flagship was hit before she could even open fire and within half an hour was pounded into a blazing ruin by accurate German fire from the winners of the Kaiser's prize for fleet gunnery. Within an hour *Good Hope* sank with all hands, including Cradock. *Monmouth* was badly hit too. An hour later the German light cruiser *Leipzig* found the stricken cruiser in the dark, listing and on fire, with gun turrets blown away. Opening fire at 1,000 yards – effectively point-blank range – she blew *Monmouth* apart. Heavy seas prevented any attempt at rescue, and there were no survivors.

Spee's victory was a shattering defeat for the Royal Navy, which, since Nelson's day, had an expectation of nothing less than victory. The words of a German commentator, claiming that "Germany had dealt the most severe blow that British prestige had suffered in a century", stung the Admiralty into action. Vice-Admiral Sir Doveton Sturdee with two of the Grand Fleet's fast battlecruisers was sent to the South Atlantic. Spee remained all too aware of his true vulnerability, alone in a hostile ocean with dwindling ammunition. Two days later he reached Chile and put in to Valparaiso Roads to coal and gather up-to-date intelligence. A friendly Chilean lady pressed a bouquet of flowers into his hand. "They will do nicely for my grave", he responded.

The following month, after Spee had rounded Cape Horn into the South Atlantic, the British finally got their revenge. On 8 December 1914, Spee decided to bombard the Falkland Islands; its capital, Port Stanley, was the main British coaling base and wireless relay station covering Cape Horn. He was surprised to discover two battlecruisers in the harbour that could both outrun and outgun him, for Sturdee had already arrived there to refuel. The German squadron fled, but by mid-afternoon was overhauled by the British and brought under fire by the battlecruisers' 12-inch guns. Realizing that he could not hope to outpace the faster British ships, Spee decided to engage them with his two armoured cruisers alone, to give his light cruisers a chance to escape.

The result was inevitable. *Scharnhorst* and *Gneisenau* were both battered into submission and sunk: 2,200 German sailors were killed or drowned in the freezing South Atlantic, including Spee and his two sons. The British mopped up the other fleeing German light cruisers, and only *Dresden* escaped, to survive for another three months.

Admiral Lord Fisher, the First Sea Lord, who had despatched the two battlecruisers to the South Atlantic, recognized the significance of the Battle of the Falkland Islands immediately. He wrote to Churchill: "The consequences ... have affected our position in every part of the globe." Not only was the morale and prestige of the Royal Navy restored, but now no German warship threat remained beyond the North Sea to threaten British merchant shipping and its imperial communications. The elimination of Spee's cruisers allowed dozens of British warships from around the world to return to home waters – one carrying a captured pig.

Admiral von Spee's flagship SMS Scharnhorst, *pictured in November 1914, during the time when it was taking on coal and supplies off the Chilean coast. Just a few days earlier, the* Scharnhorst's *guns had helped despatch Rear Admiral Cradock's HMS* Good Hope *and HMS* Monmouth. *A month later, Spee and his ship would also go to the bottom.*

23

MAJOR ANDERSON'S STICK
THE MESOPOTAMIAN CAMPAIGN

NOVEMBER 1914 TO NOVEMBER 1918

In cultivating the Ottoman Empire's entry into war (*see* Chapter 21), Germany, and especially the Kaiser, had ambitions to unleash the furies of Islam against the British, including fomenting rebellion in India and Egypt. German diplomatic pressure culminated in the Ottoman *Fatwa* of 14 November 1914, when the sultan, as "Caliph of all Islam", proclaimed *Jihad* (holy war) against infidels – excepting, of course, Germans, Austro-Hungarians or neutral Americans.

In the event, nothing like a mass rising of India's 100 million Muslims took place. And by then, Britain had already taken action to secure her regional interests. Forces moved immediately on the outbreak of war to protect the Suez Canal, and an Indian Army Expeditionary Force (IEF "D") went to Ottoman Mesopotamia (modern Iraq) to secure the partly British-owned oilfields at Abadan in neighbouring Persia. The government of India, and particularly the Viceroy, Lord Hardinge, had long wanted to establish British control over southern Mesopotamia and to bring a region only loosely ruled by the Ottomans under Anglo-Indian influence. A three-year campaign would witness early success, and eventual victory. But it also saw misery – not least from the often appalling conditions of temperature extremes, flies, disease (and inept medical arrangements) and, for some, the ravages of forced marches into captivity.

In August 1914, Alexander Anderson was managing the Bombay Burmah Trading Corporation Ltd in Rangoon. Following the outbreak of war, the government of India appealed for recruits, and in Rangoon a company of gunners was mustered to join a larger Volunteer Artillery Battery in Bombay. Anderson led just under 50 men to Bombay where, to their surprise, they were immediately sent to Basra in Mesopotamia. From there, he followed earlier Indian Army contingents, leading his men up the Tigris to Amarah and (by November 1915) to Kut. The next month, Anderson's guns were in the thick of the action as Kut was besieged by Ottoman forces, and by April 1916 things were looking grim. When the garrison finally surrendered, he noted in his diary: "So ended the long period of fighting, waiting and hoping, suspense and anxiety, and starving. The impossible and unthinkable had happened and one felt stunned." With as much dignity as their tired, emaciated frames allowed, the men marched out of Kut. But after the squalor and deprivation of the siege, worse awaited them in captivity. Anderson took only this gnarled, knotted wooden walking stick. He had it in Kut, he carried it throughout the terrible march to the camps, and he kept it with him for the next two years in Turkey. It was, like Anderson himself, a great survivor.

"THERE IS A DRY WIND BLOWING THROUGH THE EAST, AND THE PARCHED GRASSES WAIT THE SPARK. AND THAT WIND IS BLOWING TOWARDS THE INDIAN BORDER. WHENCE COMES THAT WIND, THINK YOU?"

John Buchan, in his 1916 novel of Ottoman intrigue, Greenmantle

As Anglo-Indian troops had been ready for some days, the Mesopotamian campaign began on 6 November 1914, the day war was declared. A naval bombardment of Ottoman forts at the Shatt el Arab, where the Tigris and Euphrates run into the Persian Gulf, was followed by the IEF's landing and seizure of Basra. Ottoman forces fled north, while the British quickly secured the pipeline at Abadan and consolidated their position around the Gulf. For imperial planners, wider horizons now beckoned.

By April 1915 the IEF had moved slowly northwards from Basra with apparent ease, but temptations lured the victorious British into biting off more than they could chew. GHQ in Delhi now regarded the security of the Abadan pipeline as secondary to a successful advance up the Tigris, ultimately all the way to Baghdad. However, back in London British ministers were divided between, on the one hand, guarding the pipeline and limiting the deployment of more British forces to the region and, on the other, encouraging the push to Baghdad, if only for propaganda reasons. A compromise was agreed. The ambitious new IEF commander, Lieutenant General Sir John Nixon, would make a limited upriver advance as far as Kut-al-Amara, about 120 miles south of Baghdad. But in the muddle of divided command, conflicting orders and slow communications, Nixon tried to do *everything*. He split his force, moving to secure the pipeline with 9,000 men and ordered Major General Sir Charles Townsend to advance up the Tigris with a division and drive the Turks back.

Townsend was successful – at first. In a series of sharp actions, supported by gunboats on the river, he drove the enemy back to Kut by September. There, after further debate in London and Delhi, he was ordered on to Baghdad. Less than 20 miles short of his goal, Townsend reached the ancient city of Ctesiphon, where his increasingly overstretched forces were halted in a tactically indecisive battle on 22 November 1915. Townsend pulled his exhausted division back to Kut, where he entrenched in early December and waited for reinforcements. But Kut was isolated. It could be defended, but it could not be resupplied. The Ottomans encircled the defences and sent fresh forces downriver to prevent any British relief. Townsend's offers to break out were initially rejected by Nixon, who eventually did send a relief force, but its three attempts to break the siege failed. Come spring 1916, Townsend's men were still hopelessly trapped. By 21 April all normal rations had gone. With food supplies running low and disease rife, Townsend surrendered on 29 April 1916. Over 13,000 soldiers became Ottoman prisoners, and about 4,000 of those would perish,

Fascinated locals look on, while others help a British gunnery team, kitted out in solar topees, as they haul a 6-inch howitzer up a Baghdad slope (1917). The terrain and climate of Mesopotamia, and the nature of its logistical problems, made the campaign a punishing experience for all those who took part.

many on the forced march north into Anatolia. Townsend, though, was housed comfortably on an island in the Bosphorus for the duration of the war.

Knives were sharpened in Whitehall and India at what was seen as a humiliating reverse. Townsend and Nixon were inevitably the principal scapegoats, but, if nothing else, the disaster forced a complete reorganization of the force in Mesopotamia. Defeat brought the very reinforcements and improvements that should have been committed earlier, and responsibility for the campaign passed from the Indian government to London. There, the War Committee authorized a renewed offensive under a new commander, Lieutenant General Sir Stanley Maude. Logistics remained a problem: at first, supplies were mostly loaded up at Basra and sent north in special shallow-draught steamers along the Tigris. Over the next year thousands of lorries were sent out and a road was built north to Baghdad, along with a light railway. From May to November 1916, as these vital logistic issues were being addressed, four new British divisions arrived to beef up the existing force.

British fortunes now improved greatly. When Russian troops moved into northern Persia towards the end of 1916 and threatened any retreat by the Ottomans (and their German advisors), Maude also struck in Mesopotamia, advancing methodically up both banks of the Tigris, bypassing the enemy at Kut and sweeping around to Baghdad, where he defeated a weakened Turkish defence. On 11 March 1917, the IEF finally entered Baghdad to be greeted as liberators. Both sides then paused the fighting during the intense seasonal heat, which allowed British supplies and reinforcements to catch up, and the battered remnants of the Ottoman Sixth Army to withdrew north to Mosul, to regroup.

Beginning again in early autumn 1917, Maude's forces resumed their advance. But on 18 November, Maude died of cholera in Baghdad. He was replaced by Lieutenant General Sir William Marshall, and though operations continued they were on a reduced scale. British and Russian forces advancing from the north and east were closing in on the Ottomans by the spring of 1918. But, after the 1918 hot season, Marshall slackened his pace: he was constrained by the demands from other Ottoman theatres (*see* chapters 78 and 89) and the need to support the mobile "Dunsterforce" campaign being carried out by Major General Lionel Dunsterville in Persia and Azerbaijan. One later critic, historian Cyril Falls, was less understanding, describing Marshall as "astonishingly inactive, not only in the hot season but through most of the cold".

By October 1918, as an armistice with the Ottoman forces began to look a real possibility, Marshall was directed by Whitehall that "every effort was to be made to score as heavily as possible on the Tigris before the whistle blew". A British force from Baghdad advanced a remarkable 80 miles in two days to the Little Zab River, where it defeated the Ottoman Sixth Army at the Battle of Sharqut. The Ottoman commander İsmail Hakkı Bey knew of the concurrent peace talks, and to spare his men unnecessary losses he surrendered on 30 October, as the Armistice of Mudros was signed.

The Mesopotamian campaign was over. It left some sobering statistics for the IEF: 11,012 killed, 3,985 dead from wounds, 12,678 dead from sickness, 13,492 missing and prisoners, and 51,836 wounded. There was also a final act. In blatant contravention of the Armistice, the British continued their advance north to seize the oilfields of Mosul on 2 November. Control and the ownership of them would become an internationally contentious issue for years to come.

"OUR ARMIES DO NOT COME INTO YOUR CITIES AND LANDS AS CONQUERORS OR ENEMIES, BUT AS LIBERATORS."

General Sir Stanley Maude, in the "Proclamation of Baghdad", March 1917

24

AN AUSTRALIAN BATTALION'S FLAG
THE GALLIPOLI CAMPAIGN

FEBRUARY 1915 TO JANUARY 1916

The Gallipoli campaign of 1915 was a major geo-strategic defeat for the Allies and a disastrous reverse for Britain. By contrast, it reinvigorated the Ottoman Empire, spreading a sense of national pride that continues to this day. For Australia and New Zealand, too, the skill and tenacity of the Australian and New Zealand Army Corps – the ANZACs – stoked an emerging sense of nationhood. All together the campaign killed and maimed hundreds of thousands of men and consumed scarce resources. For Britain, it changed the face of domestic politics in the middle of an increasingly intensive war, while globally it helped condemn Tsarist Russia to ultimate defeat and revolution. Without any doubt, Gallipoli and its consequences were one of the key episodes of the war.

The first Australians to land at Gallipoli on 25 April 1915 did not come from the more developed, earlier colonized New South Wales or Victoria, but the less-populated outer states of Queensland, South Australia, Tasmania and Western Australia. Together, the men formed the 3rd Brigade of the 1st Australian Division. This careworn flag belonged to the 12th Battalion, which went ashore on the beaches around the headland of Ari Burnu in the first assault. Apparently extemporized during the months of training in Egypt, it is made of coarse cloth with crudely sewn details ("12 Bn" on top, "III Bde" underneath). It was essentially a giant version of the battalion's colour patch – the unique coloured identification symbol worn by every Australian unit. The 12th Battalion's patch was a rectangle of white above an identical one of light blue, exactly like the flag before it faded with age. Landing part of the 12th Battalion from his destroyer HMS *Ribble*, Lieutenant Commander Ralph Wilkinson RN told his wife: "The Australians were fine. I felt proud that I was a Briton. They pulled in singing a song, 'Australia will be there!' and I could see them scaling the cliffs waving their sword bayonets, and hear them 'cooeeing' like mad." The Gallipoli landing now stands at the heart of Australian and New Zealand national identity. The qualities of endurance, initiative and "mateship" that the ANZACs showed throughout the campaign are now held to epitomize the pioneering roots of both nations – strengths somehow engrained in this rudimentary flag.

In August 1914, the First Lord of the Admiralty, Winston Churchill, resurrected a long-standing idea for an attack on the Dardanelles to strike at the Ottoman capital of Constantinople; he proposed it again in November – but was rebuffed on both occasions. What added new impetus to this idea was an urgent Russian appeal on

> **"WHATEVER MAY BE THOUGHT OF HIS INTELLIGENCE AND SKILL, THE TURKISH SOLDIER IS AT LEAST NO COWARD."**
>
> The War Illustrated,
> *13 March 1915*

2 January 1915 for British help in diverting Ottoman military resources away from the bitter battles it was fighting in the Caucasus. Churchill and Lord Kitchener agreed that a British naval attack on the Dardanelles was the only practical option.

On 13 January, Churchill secured tentative agreement from the War Council for a naval assault on the Straits. Commanded by Vice-Admiral Sir Sackville Carden, it would be carried out by the British ships that had been blockading the eastern Mediterranean since the escape of the *Goeben* and *Breslau*, along with an additional squadron of ships pledged by France. The new super-dreadnought battleship HMS *Queen Elizabeth* was also attached to Carden's fleet: her massive 15-inch guns might as well be test-fired against the Turks as into the sea off Gibraltar.

In early 1915, an attack on the Ottoman Empire appeared to have three sound strategic benefits. First, it offered immediate help to the whole Russian war effort, not only in the Caucasus but also by reopening the Dardanelles for Russia to export grain and import guns. (Were Russia to stop fighting, then the whole might of the German war machine would be free to fall upon the Western Front.) Second, reaching the Ottoman capital could knock the Ottoman Empire out of the war altogether, and it was likely that this act would then draw Greece, Romania and Bulgaria in on the Allied side. Last, there was already a desire emerging to find some way around the stagnation of the Western Front, and to use Britain's new citizen soldiers more profitably than in expending them in the trenches of France and Belgium.

Thus, the assault started on 19 February, when Carden led a mixed British and French fleet into the 4-mile-wide gap between Cape Helles and Kum Kale. For five hours the British and French battleships blasted the outer forts guarding the Dardanelles. But the following day the weather turned rough, and it was not until 25 February that Carden was able to resume the attack. Landing parties went ashore to continue the demolition and confirm that the outer forts were out of action. It came as a surprise when the fleet, returning on 2 and 3 March, was met by accurate fire from the mobile Turkish field artillery batteries that formed the next layer of intermediate defences further along the Straits.

The Ottomans had laid a series of mines across the Dardanelles, and these would need clearing before Carden's warships could advance towards the crucial Narrows. But the only available minesweepers were civilian trawlers still manned by their untrained fishermen. The vessels struggled against strong currents, and their crews suffered under the fire of the Turkish guns, slowing the whole operation. The Admiralty started to apply pressure on Carden to speed up and to storm the Narrows, telling him not to worry about losses – at which point he collapsed from nervous exhaustion to be replaced by his second in command, Vice-Admiral John de Robeck.

On 18 March, De Robeck led a full-blooded assault intended to silence the guns. Disaster struck. In an area believed to be clear of mines, the French battleship *Bouvet* hit one and instantly capsized along with most of her crew. Minutes later the battlecruiser HMS *Inflexible* also struck a mine and had to limp out of the battle. Soon after, the battleships HMS *Irresistible* and HMS *Ocean* were also mined, and both sank. De Robeck withdrew in disarray, intending to return once he had worked out what had happened and organized reliable minesweepers.

It was now clear that military support was required to capture the shoreline and allow the warships and minesweepers to operate free from Turkish gunfire. After much prevarication, Kitchener released the 29th Division from Britain along with the ANZACs, who had been training since December in Egypt. Together with a French division and the Royal Naval Division (RND) – naval reservists and the Naval Wartime Volunteers serving as soldiers – these troops formed the Mediterranean Expeditionary Force. Their task was to capture the Gallipoli Peninsula and thus enable the naval attack to resume. Overall command went to General Sir Ian Hamilton, who was rushed out from London. As he left Charing Cross, Hamilton turned to one of his newly assembled staff and confessed: "This is going to be an unlucky show. I have just kissed my wife through her veil."

He faced a near impossible task. First he had to reorganize his force in Egypt so that it could land in the right order. As a result, security for the expedition evaporated. British agents openly bought up flat-bottomed lighters and war stores in Egypt, and correspondence was addressed to "the Constantinople Expeditionary Force". From mid-April British shipping began to build up in the natural harbours of the Aegean islands, mostly on Lemnos, which became the forward base for the campaign. Faced with limited resources, Hamilton decided to split his forces and launch a pincer attack on the rear of the high ground that guarded the Dardanelles. The main landing would be undertaken by the British 29th Division at the

ANZAC and British soldiers huddle aboard a picket boat, or motorized lighter, as they prepare to return to the Gallipoli frontlines in 1915 after a spell of rest on the Aegean island of Lemnos. There are, unsurprisingly, not too many cheerful faces.

Gallipoli Peninsula's southern tip around Cape Helles. Simultaneously, the ANZACs would go ashore halfway up the west coast near Gaba Tepe. The French would temporarily land opposite Helles on the Asiatic coast and the RND would make a pretend landing at Bulair. It was complicated and ambitious. Ironically, the Ottoman defences were simultaneously reorganized and tightened to great effect by the German General Liman von Sanders.

In the event, and for different reasons, the landings were a shambles. Through a combination of errors, as dawn broke the ANZACs landed further north than they were expecting. They struggled ashore and began to scramble up the steep slopes to the high ground overlooking the beaches. A handful of Australians did reach the peak of the third ridge, from where they could see the waters of the Dardanelles. But behind them the beach, and the confused jumble of hills that surrounded it, was a scene of confusion. Many units charged ahead without orders, officers failed to grasp where men had gone and artillery could not get up the steep hills. Far more damaging was the impact of a near-suicidal counterattack by part of the Ottoman 19th Division, led by its inspirational commander Mustafa Kemal (the future Atatürk), who three times during the campaign was to change the course of the battle and ensure Ottoman victory. On 25 April, it was Kemal who stopped the Australians and New Zealanders on the crucial northern hills. By nightfall the position at what became known as Anzac Cove was deadlocked. Hamilton ordered the ANZACs to consolidate and dig in: they would stay there for another eight wretched months.

Further south, two hours after dawn the 29th Division stormed ashore on five separate beaches surrounding Cape Helles. Because of the strong current flowing out of the Dardanelles, many of the boats were late and the naval bombardment, intended to compensate for landing in full daylight, lifted before they reached the shore. At "W" Beach, immediately north of Helles, the Lancashire Fusiliers met withering fire from the Turkish trenches. But, despite appalling losses, they made it ashore and began to assault the cliffs, an achievement that led to the celebrated award of "six VCs before breakfast".

South of Helles, at "V" Beach, men were to be landed from an old collier called the *River Clyde*, converted with gangplanks and doors cut in the side to put men directly on the beach. But heavy Turkish rifle and machine gun fire mowed down the first two companies as they surged onto the gangplanks. One company commander recorded in his diary: "We got it like anything. Man after man behind me was shot down but they never wavered. I think no finer episode could be found of the men's bravery and discipline than this ... to go to what was practically certain death." It was not until the next day that the men were finally able to fight their way off the beach and join hands with the men from W Beach.

The landings were now locked in rough beachheads, a long way from the high ground inland, and faced increasingly effective Turkish defences. Hamilton tried to break out, both at Anzac and at Helles, but little was achieved and as spring turned to summer the beachheads degenerated into the troglodyte trench conditions already so familiar on the Western Front. In the first five weeks of the campaign the Imperial troops suffered nearly 40,000 casualties, the French a further 20,000.

Gallipoli had become a bloody failure. On 15 May 1915, the First Sea Lord, Admiral Lord ("Jackie") Fisher, resigned over Churchill's handling of the naval side of the campaign; but even at the time Fisher's own petulant and arbitrary behaviour attracted much criticism. Combined with the uproar surrounding the British shortage of shells on the Western Front (*see* Chapters 30 and 40) the political fallout forced Asquith to form a Coalition government with the Conservatives. Their price was Churchill's sacking. Meanwhile, at Gallipoli the campaign stagnated as the summer heat built up. Flies, disease and lack of water and sanitation became the real enemy in the blistering heat of a Mediterranean summer.

In August, the promise of new troops encouraged Hamilton to launch a renewed attack from Anzac Cove. An ANZAC force would break out, sweep north and assault the ridge of hills that dominated the whole area. It would link up with two new British divisions simultaneously coming ashore at Suvla Bay. In the hope of drawing off Turkish reserves, diversionary attacks would also be made from existing positions at Helles opposite Krithia and Anzac Cove at Lone Pine. They all failed. By the end of August it was clear that nothing had been gained except a longer line winding through the same three beleaguered beachheads – Helles, Anzac Cove and now also Suvla Bay. Hamilton refused to contemplate withdrawal, and in October was summarily replaced by General Sir Charles Monro, fresh from the Western Front. Within days Monro had recommended evacuation. As Churchill quipped, "He came, he saw, he capitulated."

But Monro had a point: there was nothing further to be gained at Gallipoli. Whitehall dithered, and Lord Kitchener himself came out to see what conditions were like. He instantly realized that the campaign had to be shut down. A dreadful run of weather at the end of November confirmed his conclusion. First a gale struck,

An Australian soldier carries a wounded comrade to a medical aid post for treatment, on the ANZAC beachhead. Turkish machine guns were deadly enough; but dysentery and other diseases in the fly-infested summer heat, compounded by inadequate water supplies, made even greater demands on the medical facilities.

then there was torrential rain. "Lightning and thunder absolutely incessant for two hours and rain indescribable since the Flood. It simply dropped in lumps, whole chunks of it," wrote one officer at Suvla. Both sides were forced to evacuate their flooded trenches and take shelter, and they huddled on the open ground in an undeclared silent truce of mutual misery. There followed a bitter frost, and immediately afterwards a blizzard, both causing widespread frostbite. At least 30 British sentries froze to death. And then the sun came out.

Evacuation was finally ordered on 8 December, but only for Anzac Cove and Suvla Bay. Between 10 and 20 December the troops extricated themselves from under the very noses of the Turks with great skill, without the loss of a single soldier. In a bow to the inevitable, the evacuation of Helles was also ordered on 24 December. Just before dawn on 13 January 1916, the last Allied soldier left the Gallipoli Peninsula, in a withdrawal as smooth as the earlier one. Indeed, the evacuation was easily the most successful element of the entire campaign – though it did not feel like a success. Leaving Helles in one of the final boats, Joe Murray, who had served there with the RND continuously since May, remembered: "We were so packed we couldn't move at all. We left there like a lot of cattle, being dumped into a lighter and just pushed out to sea, and nobody gave a tinker's cuss whether we lived or died."

As Churchill later observed of Dunkirk, "wars are not won by evacuations". Gallipoli had proved, in Hamilton's phrase, "an unlucky show" indeed.

25

AN ITALIAN TRENCH HELMET
ITALY IN THE FIRST WORLD WAR

1915 TO 1918

In 1914, Italy had existed as a unified state for barely longer than Germany. Her individual duchies, principalities, republics and kingdoms had often fallen under the sway of stronger powers such as France and Austria, and until 1866 Austria still ruled the Veneto region, while the pope exerted temporal rule over a swathe of central Italy until 1870. But the new country needed allies and by 1882 the unified Kingdom of Italy became a fully-fledged member of the Triple Alliance with Germany and Austria-Hungary, and there was a natural expectation when war came in 1914 that Italy would cast her lot with the Central Powers.

However, the legacy of Italy's subjugation in the past and her national interests now created other pressures. Although Italy had long-standing disputes with France over North Africa, they had been settled during secret negotiations in 1902. But keenly felt territorial disputes continued over the northeastern border with Austria-Hungary, behind which ethnic Italian populations continued to live under Habsburg rule, principally along the north coast of the Adriatic – especially around Trieste and Fiume – and inland in the Tyrol. When war came for Italy, it was to be in the mountains, valleys and plateaux of this northeastern region.

The front that opened on the borders of Italy and Austria-Hungary was in some ways totally different from the Western Front. The campaigns were fought high up, in a distinctive mountainous landscape. Battle lines were hacked out of rock as men fought above the clouds and in drifting snow. Yet the stalemate of the fighting still generated barbed wire, no-man's land and trenches, and in the autumn of 1915 the Italians introduced this unique trench helmet. It was made in Milan by the firm of Elmo Farina from three steel plates, riveted together and worn over a cloth pad for comfort. A brow plate protected the forehead and a broad skirt the top of the neck, while a steel cap swept over the skull. The helmet weighed well over 6 pounds and was principally issued to specialist wire-cutting troops, whose job was to move ahead of any attack, clearing the barbed wire before the infantry followed. On occasions it was combined with additional body armour, thick gloves and knee protectors, all worn by the so-called *Compagnie della morte* (the Company of Death). It was claimed that, at 125 metres distance, the helmet was effective against rifle bullets, though few wanted to test out this hypothesis.

Italy therefore found herself in an invidious position in August 1914. Prime Minister Antonio Salandra claimed that the mutual defensive obligations of the

"TO SACRIFICE ONE LIFE WANTONLY IS A CRIME. TO USE A HUNDRED THOUSAND IF NECESSARY IS A DUTY."

General Luigi Cadorna, New York Times, *12 September 1917*

Triple Alliance Treaty did not apply, because neither Austria-Hungary nor Germany had been attacked – rather, they had gone on the offensive. Many Italians could see little advantage in joining their "allies" in war, and there was fear that Italy, as a peninsular nation, was much more exposed to attack by Britain's powerful Royal Navy.

A loose opposition coalition advocated strict neutrality. However, many Italian nationalists saw the war as a chance to seize the "Italian" territories from Austria-Hungary. Faced with these conflicting voices, the government remained neutral, to the ire of the Central Powers. Italy sat on the fence to see which way the war was going, while being wooed by both sides and maintaining secret links with both sides.

As New Year 1915 dawned it was the Allies who tipped the balance. France saw Italian participation as a way of forcing Germany to divert forces away from the Western Front. The Allies dangled promises of Italy taking over Austro-Hungarian territory. The Central Powers could not match such territorial bribes, as Austria was unlikely to surrender voluntarily her own territory in return for Italian support. A Bank of England £50 million loan to finance any Italian war finally clinched the deal, and in the secret Treaty of London (26 April 1915) Italy agreed to enter the war as one of the Allies.

It was a controversial move: an outraged Italian Chamber of Deputies brought a vote of no confidence in Salandra and forced him to resign. It reckoned without the palace, for King Victor Emmanuel III exerted considerable political influence. He refused to accept Salandra's resignation and personally made the decision to declare war on Italy's erstwhile Triple Alliance partner Austria-Hungary on 23 May 1915, invoking Italy's "*Sacro Egoismo*" (sacred self-interest).

Italy was, however, ill-prepared for major European war. In 1914, she was a poor country, the weakest of the warring partners, and her centuries of internal divisions were still palpable. A more advanced, industrializing north contrasted with a south that was primarily agrarian, the latter chiefly populated by peasants whose lives were often little better than feudal serfdom. Southerners were, however, the primary pool of manpower for massive conscription. One-third of them were illiterate. Deficiencies in human resources were matched technically: the Italian army could only muster 120 heavy or medium artillery pieces and about 700 machine guns.

Nonetheless, the fighting started surprisingly quickly. The Italian Chief of the General Staff, General Luigi Cadorna, assembled 25 infantry and 4 cavalry divisions on the Austrian border, and on 23 June launched a major offensive northeast across the River Isonzo towards what is nowadays Slovenia. The river was prone to heavy flooding and was overlooked by steep mountains to the north. Cadorna's strategic objective was the city of Trieste, 150 miles to the southeast: it was vital to the mostly landlocked Austro-Hungarians, because it was their major commercial port.

For their part the Austrians were well prepared in the region and had built a system of trench defences rivalling anything seen on the Western Front. Although the Italians outnumbered the defenders by two to one, their offensive quickly ran out of steam because they were launching frontal attacks uphill against well-dug-in troops and uncut barbed wire. In the two weeks of the First Battle of the Isonzo, the Italians suffered 60,000 casualties. On 7 July 1915, Cadorna called off the attack.

This was only a respite. On 18 July, the assault was renewed using the same tactics but with a heavier bombardment. Although in places the fighting was savage, and even hand-to-hand, the Italians were repulsed with heavy casualties. The battle ended on 3 August when both sides appear to have run out of artillery ammunition. On 18 October, Cadorna tried again, launching a major offensive with over 1,300 guns massed against the whole line of Austrian positions overlooking the river; it was as unsuccessful as its predecessors, and by 3 November had run out of steam. Astonishingly, a week later Cadorna continued the offensive in the Fourth Battle of the Isonzo, hurling another 370 battalions mainly against the fortress town of Gorizia, although the fighting was spread all along the 60-mile river front. Yet again the attack collapsed. An unofficial "live and let live" truce was agreed between the weary combatants as the first serious snows of winter reduced both sides to trying to survive, and operations were halted through lack of supplies.

By the end of 1915 the Italians had lost 300,000 men, mainly through artillery fire, which was even more devastating in mountainous terrain than on the Western Front: it could send deadly razor-sharp splinters of rock flying into its victims. Yet the gain was less than 10 miles of Austrian territory. Cadorna's brutal head-butting offensives appeared to have achieved little. However, they had at least succeeded in alarming the Austro-Hungarian High Command, whose forces had also suffered seriously. Worried by the persistent Italian attacks, Vienna formally requested assistance and reinforcements from Berlin. But Italy and Germany were not yet at war with one another, and for now the Germans resisted the requests.

Specialist Italian mountain troops clamber up Monte Nero, on the limestone Karst Plateau, during the Second Battle of the Isonzo (July 1915). It was a radically different sort of terrain compared to that which the BEF confronted in Flanders or on the Somme, though often as deadly.

Cadorna launched seven more costly offensives on the Isonzo over the next two years. In May 1916, a concerted Austro-Hungarian push in the Trentino was contained by an Italian counterattack, and in the subsequent Sixth Battle of the Isonzo (6–17 August 1916) Cadorna's men finally did succeed in capturing Gorizia. But it was only a relative Italian success. By September 1917, and despite some territorial advances in the Eleventh Battle of the Isonzo, the shattered Italian army was suffering mutiny and disaffection.

The Austro-Hungarians were equally worn down. But things were about to change. In August 1916, Italy had declared war on Germany, and now – with the failure of the last Russian offensive on the Eastern Front – Germany was able to transfer troops to the Italian theatre. Thus the Twelfth Battle of the Isonzo – better known as Caporetto – saw one of the great *German* victories of the war. A new Fourteenth Army under General Otto von Below, with seven German and five Austrian divisions, secretly massed 1,000 guns each with 1,000 rounds in the mountains to the north. On 24 October 1917, a surprise bombardment of mixed gas and High Explosive eliminated the Italian batteries and headquarters as stormtroopers infiltrated the frontlines. Mountain troops seized the mountain defences and the main assault fell down on the Italians in the plain below, routing them and causing havoc as they fell back more than 60 miles in disarray. Italian gas masks didn't work and Cadorna's men fled in panic as the Germans surged forward, capturing whole units miles behind the lines. Many bewildered soldiers just ran away; key generals went into hiding. The offensive only stopped when the attackers ran out of supplies two weeks later.

The Battle of Caporetto ranks as one of the most comprehensive victories of the war: it resulted in the capture of half the Italian army's artillery and inflicted 600,000 casualties on the hapless Italians – the vast majority surrendering or deserting.

There was one silver lining. Despite the threats of revolution in a weakened Italy, the new frontline, on the River Piave, was now on Italian territory and the war had become a defensive one, a war for survival, which concentrated minds. Moreover, the new line was now only half as long and could be held – just. The Italians begged for help and the British and French rushed forces to stabilize the situation – but only on condition that Cadorna was sacked. His tactical stubbornness had been matched by a ruthlessness meted out on his own troops. As Hew Strachan has noted, almost 6 per cent of Italian soldiers faced a disciplinary charge, and "about 750 of them were executed, the highest number of any army in the war". Cadorna had even brought back "decimation" – the Roman practice of executing every tenth man in units deemed to be underperforming – *pour encourager les autres*.

The uneasy stabilization of the line in the winter of 1917–18 gave both the demoralized Italians and their overstretched attackers a breathing space. But in the spring the Germans withdrew most of their troops to support the offensives of March to June on the Western Front. In its turn, the Austro-Hungarian High Command decided to attack along the whole line, with the aim of knocking out what it saw as an enfeebled Italy once and for all.

However, the Italians had learned from their mistakes and their new Chief of the General Staff, General Armando Diaz, had reorganized his battered army. Behind new defences in depth, and with an operational reserve of 13 lorry-borne divisions ready to be rushed to any critical point, the Italians were this time prepared. Good intelligence had alerted Diaz that the attack would start at 03.00 on 15 June 1918, and so he ordered a massed bombardment of the packed Austrian forming-up trenches at 02.30, catching the attackers by surprise and causing serious casualties. The offensive did eventually break in for 5 miles over a 15-mile front along the River Piave, but then stalled as the swollen river tore bridges away and cut off many advanced Austrian units. By 19 June the Italians were counterattacking and up to 20,000 Austro-Hungarians are thought to have drowned as they tried to flee. By 26 June it was all over. The Italians had recaptured all the Austrian gains and had inflicted over 175,000 casualties in the process.

The Battle of the Piave was Italy's first real victory and had decisive repercussions. At the same time Germany's great offensive in the West was running out of steam, and Piave contributed to Ludendorff's growing sense of crisis. It finally dashed any hopes in Vienna that military victory was possible. It also served to accelerate the disintegration of the Austro-Hungarian army, whose destruction was completed by the Italians at the Battle of Vittorio Veneto – but not immediately. Ignoring Allied pleas urging him to press a counterattack, Diaz stopped to regroup and resupply between July and October 1918. Then, on 24 October, the anniversary of Caporetto, Diaz launched his main offensive, pitting his now reinforced and re-equipped 60 divisions against the same number of weak and demoralized Austro-Hungarians. The flooded river plain slowed progress in the centre, but near the river's mouth into the Adriatic at Papadopoli Island on 27 October, Allied troops broke through and crossed the river. Ominously, the enemy units ordered to counterattack by Field Marshal Svetozar von Bojna refused to move and mutinied. In Ludendorff's later opinion: "In Vittorio Veneto, Austria did not lose a battle, but lose the war and itself, dragging Germany in its fall. Without the destructive battle of Vittorio Veneto, we would have been able, in a military union with the Austro-Hungarian monarchy, to continue the desperate resistance through the whole winter, in order to obtain a less harsh peace, because the Allies were very fatigued."

From then on, the Austrian Front collapsed as soldiers voted with their feet, surrendering in droves to the advancing Italian forces who were now threatening to cut off any retreat to the Trieste plain. The retreat turned into a rout as the Austrian divisions fled east. The political consequences of the disaster rippled outwards: on 28 October, the Czechs withdrew from Vienna's stricken empire, to be followed by Hungary herself in November. The Austro-Hungarian Empire fell apart.

By this time, an Austrian Armistice Commission was already in discussions with the Italians, and on 3 November the Armistice of Villa Giusti was agreed. It came into effect the following day. Italy had won her war, and to the victor the spoils of the Trentino/Alto-Adige and South Tyrol, Istria (including Trieste) and portions of the north Dalmatian coast and islands, all as agreed secretly with the Allies in 1915. Many Italians considered this the final act of Italy's long drawn out Risorgimento and reunification.

Yet Italy's victory had cost her over 650,000 dead and a million wounded, and other Italian ambitions (including for colonies) were rebuffed during the subsequent Versailles peace negotiations. An impression grew among many Italians of a "mutilated victory", helping to drive growing political instability after the war – and ultimately the rise of Mussolini and the *Fascisti*.

26

THE HIGHLANDERS' BULGARIAN MAXIM
SALONIKA & THE BALKAN FRONT

1915 TO 1918

Salonika is very much the forgotten theatre of the war. This is a serious oversight as it saw over 600,000 Allied soldiers of half a dozen nationalities deployed to "the Balkan Front" and was – eventually – one of the Allied victories that brought the Central Powers crashing down.

The First World War's opening shots were Austria-Hungary's bombardment of the Serbian capital, Belgrade. Yet Serbia had managed to hold off the Austro-Hungarian armies until the spring of 1915. German involvement and Bulgaria's entry into the war in October 1915 changed all that. With powerful German and Austrian armies to the north and now a major Bulgarian threat from the east, Serbia faced annihilation.

In 1915, British and French plans for a Balkan campaign were driven by three main factors: first, to persuade other Balkan countries – particularly Greece – to join the Allies; second, as part of the reassessment of grand strategy, since the Western Front seemed a stalemate; and lastly as a way of propping up the hard-pressed Serbian army. In the event, the Greek port of Salonika would pay host to a large encampment of Allied soldiers for almost three years. The British became the junior partners in a French-led theatre, where they occasionally battled the enemy, but mostly battled boredom and disease.

Summer was always the worst time at Salonika. In the river valleys life was unsupportable amid malarial mosquitos, forcing the British to fall back to the nearby foothills. In 1917, when the weather cooled in September, the British prepared to re-establish their forward line along the Struma valley – but to cover this move they needed temporarily to recapture the village of Homondos. So, on the night of 13/14 October, a tricky attack attempted to take the village from behind. As D Company, 2nd Battalion, the Cameron Highlanders, moved forward, the Bulgarian defenders rallied around a strongpoint, at the heart of which stood a machine gun. Lieutenant Robert MacIntyre gathered a group of men and charged the gun, killing or capturing all the Bulgars in an action that won him the Military Cross. "Homondos II", as it was called, secured the village and the British line could be rebuilt along the Struma's left bank. MacIntyre's gun, one of three captured by his battalion, was this MG09 Maxim made in Berlin in 1916 for the Bulgarian army. General Headquarters at Salonika took hold of the gun and immediately sent it back to London. Before the end of the year, it was lodged in the (Imperial) War Museum as exhibit number 742. Battle-scarred and still highly prized, it remains on display proudly bearing the defiant message: "CAPTURED BY 2D CAMERON HDRS HOMONDOS 14TH OCT 1917."

"IT WOULD BE VALUABLE IF YOU WOULD KINDLY EXPLAIN TO THE PRIME MINISTER ... WHAT THE NATURE OF THE BALKAN COUNTRY IS ... HE SEEMS TO THINK THAT THERE IS A SINGLE RANGE OF HILLS ... WHEREAS THE WHOLE COUNTRY IS A MASS OF MOUNTAINS ... IN WHICH A SMALL ARMY WOULD BE MURDERED AND A LARGE ARMY WILL STARVE."

Chief of the Imperial General Staff, Field Marshal Sir William Robertson, to Lord President of the Council, Lord Curzon, July 1917

Greece was neutral when Prime Minster Eleftherios Venizelos called for intervention in September 1915 – which the Allies were happy to regard as a legal invitation. Venizelos was soon sacked by King Constantine, who was anxious to preserve Greek neutrality; but there was little the king could do to prevent the landings of French and British troops, which began on 5 October.

The following day, combined German and Austro-Hungarian forces under Field Marshal von Mackensen promptly invaded Serbia. Bulgaria declared war on 14 October and within 24 hours attacked Serbia from the east, before successfully turning back the Allied forces advancing north into Serbia from Salonika. The Serbs now faced two choices: surrender or retreat. By an extraordinary feat of endurance, of the 140,000 men of the Serbian army and refugees who escaped westwards over the snow-covered mountains to Montenegro and neutral Albania, 125,000 survived to take ship and escape to Corfu. The hardy Serbs would themselves arrive in Salonika in May 1916.

The Central Powers' total victory over Serbia opened up the railway from Berlin to Constantinople and ensured that German supplies could reinforce their Ottoman allies. For Bulgaria there was the prize of Serbian Macedonia, a major war aim. British politicians and generals now faced the difficult question of what to do next. The recent débâcle in Gallipoli (see Chapter 24) made most of them sceptical of new fronts. But French internal politics demanded a continuation of a Balkan Front, to be run by the general favoured in left-wing quarters, Maurice Sarrail; there was strong support, too, from Italy, Russia – and of course the Serbs themselves. Thus, the four divisions (three French, one British) that were pushed out of Serbia in December 1915 now fell back to Salonika, there to be reinforced. In vain did King Constantine protest he "would not be treated like some native chieftain" at this ignoring of Greece's neutrality.

The Allies dug themselves into a vast military encampment packed with men and huge stockpiles of war equipment. The whole was surrounded by dense thickets of barbed wire and was known irreverently as "the Birdcage". Eventually, a multinational force under French command held a line that ran from the Adriatic through Macedonia to the Aegean. French, Serbs and others manned the western portions of the line and two British corps held the east. The mystified Bulgarians looked on in amazement, and after a couple of tentative probes left the Allies alone. The force posed no threat to the Ottoman Empire, Austria-Hungary or Germany and was tying up hundreds of thousands of Allied troops to no end. A German journalist sardonically called the Salonika Front "the greatest internment camp in the world": it was.

It was also very unhealthy. Disease was rife, mosquitoes were plentiful and malaria was endemic. Along with boredom, poor food and little action, the conditions sapped the strength and morale of an already badly supplied army, now effectively beached in northern Greece.

The stalemate was interrupted, though, in August 1916, when Romania finally threw in her lot with the Allies, a move helped by extravagant promises of Austrian territory. A Franco-British sortie into Macedonia, to distract the Bulgarians and thereby help Romania, achieved surprise and made progress until November snows halted it. The gain of some territory and the "liberation" of the Serbian town of Monastir provided a morale boost for the Allied effort. Romania was less fortunate. German, Austro-Hungarian, Ottoman and Bulgarian armies swiftly moved to crush Bucharest for its temerity. By December 1916, and after losing 310,000 men, Romania was effectively out of the war, reduced to an isolated rump of an army huddling in the wintry protection of the Russian lines in far-off Moldova.

British military dugouts and bivouacs monopolize a terraced hillside near Salonika (1916). The defensive line around Salonika created the massive encampment dubbed "the Birdcage"; contemporary newspapers criticized its apparent inactivity and failure to take the fight to the enemy.

The forces at Salonika went back to holding the line and waiting. Greece, meanwhile, had fractured into two competing governments when the Allies supported a regional coup by Venizelos; now some Greek forces loyal to his cause joined the Allied force. In April 1917, action resumed, as three British divisions launched an attack in the hills around Doiran as a diversion from a larger Franco-Serb attack west of the River Vardar. Both attacks failed with heavy losses, the offensive was called off and the stalemate returned. But Greece now made up her mind. In June 1917, King Constantine abdicated in favour of his son Alexander, who, under pressure from Venizelos, finally issued the nation's declaration of war.

By early 1918, the force around Salonika – now including Italians, Russians and the Greek army, too– was preparing a major offensive intended to end the war in the Balkans. On 15 September, the new French commander, General Louis Franchet d'Espèrey ("Desperate Frankie" as the British called him), unleashed the main Franco-Serb thrust, and three days later the British once again attacked the well-fortified hills of the Lake Doiran area – only to be repulsed, as before with major losses. However, in the west the French and Serbs finally broke through at Gradsko, then took Skopje, forcing the Bulgarian army into a general retreat as it was harried by the pursuing Allies on the ground and by the Royal Air Force from above. Bulgarian discipline collapsed, and the retreat became a rout. This time no help was forthcoming from the exhausted Germans, already under severe pressure on the Western Front. Faced with faithless allies, a disintegrating army and unrest at home, Bulgaria was finished and signed an armistice on 29 September 1918.

The political effects of this surrender went far beyond the Balkans. The supply route from Germany to Constantinople was finally severed, and the whole Central Powers' southeastern front was now vulnerable. D'Espèrey, forgetting the logistical problems, wrote excitedly on 2 October: "I can with 200,000 men cross Hungary and Austria ... and march immediately on Dresden."

He didn't, and elsewhere the war still had time to run. But there was no doubt that he had struck the Central Powers a decisive blow, albeit at heavy cost. For the British, the battle casualties of less than 20,000 were dwarfed by the 480,000 cases of disease, principally malaria; accusations that the whole thing was a drain on resources lingered long after. Yet, after three years of monotony, sickness and misery, the Salonika Front had delivered a decisive Allied victory and kicked away one of Germany's props, and to that end had finally vindicated itself and helped to end the war.

27

A *LUSITANIA* SURVIVOR'S CAMISOLE
UNRESTRICTED SUBMARINE WARFARE

1915 TO 1916

By spring 1915, although Germany's High Seas Fleet was bottled up at its Wilhelmshaven base, her U-boats were beginning to flex their muscles in increasing numbers. The Royal Navy's senior leadership was acutely aware of how vulnerable even their largest warships were to underwater attack. But it was gradually becoming apparent that the *really* exposed targets were the vessels of the British Merchant Navy, and by attacking these ships German submarines had the potential to threaten a counter-blockade of Britain. In May 1915, all these issues exploded into an international incident with the sinking by torpedo of the Cunard passenger liner RMS *Lusitania*.

On board the *Lusitania* in May 1915, a young British couple, the Reverend Herbert and Mrs Margaret Gwyer, were returning from Canada, where they had recently married. When the ship was struck, they made it into a lifeboat and seemed to be escaping – but their boat lacked oars and remained perilously close to the sinking ship. As the wreck of the *Lusitania* rose in the water before plunging to the bottom, it looked as if it would crush the Gwyers' boat. Margaret never remembered why, but, unnoticed by her husband, she leapt into the water and fainted, coming to in the darkness of one of the liner's funnels. All she could see was a distant light. Suddenly there was a massive explosion as the boilers burst, shooting her clear of the ship as it went down. Margaret, though blackened by oil and smoke, was picked up and deposited safely in Ireland, to be reunited with her frantic husband some hours later. The Gwyers were taken to London, where Margaret tried to get the black stains off her face by washing it "twice with Vim", before she faced the daunting prospect of meeting her husband's parents for the first time. For the rest of her life she carefully preserved the stained camisole she had been wearing on 7 May – a reminder of her miraculous escape.

In 1914, the reappointed First Sea Lord, Lord Fisher, had warned of the threat to merchant shipping; however, the prime minister had pointed to the pre-war international agreements (to which Germany was a signatory), which laid down the accepted rules governing "cruiser warfare": passenger ships were off-limits and enemy merchant ships could only be sunk without warning if they resisted or failed to stop. If neither of these was the case, the ships could only be sunk after the crew had been evacuated. As Germany's scattered cruisers were hunted down worldwide, the German navy pressed the Kaiser to use the growing number of U-boats to attack merchant shipping – including that of neutral countries trading with Britain. German

> **"IT IS STARVATION, NOT INVASION WE HAVE TO FEAR."**
>
> *First Sea Lord, Admiral Lord Fisher*

politicians and diplomats warned of the political dangers. Nevertheless, on 4 February 1915 Berlin declared that from 18 February the waters around Britain would be treated as a "war zone", that all British merchant vessels would be considered fair game, and in a deliberate ploy to scare off Britain's trading partners warned them that "their becoming victims of attack against enemy ships cannot always be avoided".

Neutral powers inevitably reacted angrily, but they continued trading, for there appeared little *tangible* risk to their ships from a few submarines. In 1915, unlike today's nuclear deep-sea boats, submarines were primarily surface ships that submerged only when necessary. Their *modus operandi*, in line with the agreed rules, would be to overhaul a merchant ship, order her to stop and then determine her identity. British-flagged ships were legitimate targets, and the crew would be ordered to the lifeboats and the vessel sunk either by a boarding party or more usually by gunfire rather than wasting one of the submarine's few and expensive torpedoes (of which a U-boat in 1915 carried a maximum of six).

The problem for a U-boat was that while on the surface she was at risk. Even merchant ships could ram a submarine – and some did (*see* Chapter 33). For self-preservation, it made more sense to attack without warning. In January 1915, Captain Otto Dröscher of *U-20* torpedoed and sank three merchant ships without warning, in the English Channel, before going on to damage the fully illuminated hospital ship *Asturias* off Le Havre. During March, *U-28* sank five British merchant ships without warning, including the 5,000-ton *Falaba* and even the passenger liner *Aguila*. By mid-April 1915 the U-boats had made 57 torpedo attacks on merchant ships, of which 38 had been successful. Another 90 ships had been attacked by gunfire.

During May the U-boats also turned their attention to the North Sea, where Scandinavian neutrals suffered most. However, in the waters to the west of Ireland and in the Irish Sea, where shipping had to concentrate to make landfall, U-boats found a target-rich environment. It was here, on 7 May 1915, that the new captain of *U-20*, Walther Schwieger, confronted the 45,000-ton *Lusitania*.

The *Lusitania* had sailed from New York on 1 May 1915, under command of the experienced Captain Bill Turner, with 2,000 passengers and crew on board and a small cargo of ammunition – rifle cartridges, empty shell-casings, non-explosive fuses, but no explosives. All aboard were aware of a warning posted by the German Embassy that passengers travelling on British-flagged ships "did so at their own risk".

During the first week of May, *U-20* had already been busy off the coast of County Cork, attacking six ships and prompting the Admiralty on 6 May to warn shipping of U-boat activity off southern Ireland. On the morning of 7 May, the liner entered what was known as the "Danger Zone", increased her speed to 18 knots, closed all watertight doors, posted double lookouts and swung out all lifeboats "just in case".

At 14.10 Schwieger ordered one torpedo fired at a range of 700 metres. It struck *Lusitania*'s starboard side just below the bridge and was followed by a second explosion – probably the rupturing of high-pressure steam boilers, accompanied by clouds of coal dust from the ship's bunkers. The stricken vessel continued for another 2 miles, settling with a 15-degree list to starboard as water flooded in. Electric power failed and bulkhead doors could not be reopened. Captain Turner gave the order to abandon ship. It took ten minutes for *Lusitania* to slow down and start lowering her boats in the water. But on the starboard side the listing meant they were swinging out too far for people to step aboard, while on the port side several boats crashed down the sloping hull, spilling their occupants into the cold water below. A mere handful out of the almost 50 boats eventually proved usable.

Eighteen minutes after the torpedo struck, *Lusitania* sank, just over 11 miles offshore. By the time help arrived, many of those in the water had died of hypothermia. The final death toll for the disaster shocked the world: of the 1,959 passengers and crew, 1,195 had been lost. The bodies of 885 victims were never recovered.

Most of the reaction swiftly and unequivocally condemned Germany and Captain Schwieger. President Woodrow Wilson had already made plain his view that "no warning that an unlawful and inhumane act will be committed" would be accepted

A German U-boat of the UC-1 type surfaces, and her crew appreciate some fresh air. This particular class of submarine was used mainly for mine-laying, carrying up to 12 mines at a time. Together with their cousins, the attack submarines, U-boats alarmed Allied politicians, the public and traditional naval men alike.

as a legitimate excuse for that act. Of the 139 US citizens aboard *Lusitania*, 128 had been killed. *The Nation* newspaper called the sinking "a deed for which a Hun would blush, a Turk be ashamed, and a Barbary pirate apologise". There was even loose talk of an American declaration of war on Germany.

The furore had an impact in Berlin. Realizing that many Americans were now calling for war, the German High Command bowed to political pressure and imposed strict limitations on U-boat activity. The British continued to lose about 150 merchant vessels a month to the U-boats over the summer, but high-profile attacks on passenger liners were banned. Despite this, on 19 August 1915 the debate exploded once again when *U-24* mistook the liner *Arabic* for a troop transport and sent her to the bottom with a single torpedo. The liner sank in ten minutes with 44 dead, including 3 Americans, and Washington began to make another round of strong protests with a serious undertone of threats. The sinking of an unarmed French-registered passenger ferry, the *Sussex*, in March 1916 again prompted an American threat to sever diplomatic relations with Germany.

In May, the German offensive was called off, in what was known as the "*Sussex* pledge"; it was not worth the risk of US intervention on the Allied side. For the moment, the U-boat war would be confined to the North Sea and to the Mediterranean, where there was an abundance of targets – and few Americans to complain. But submarine warfare was here to stay.

28

A ZEPPELIN'S AMMUNITION BOX
THE AERIAL BOMBING OF BRITAIN

1915 TO 1918

Aerial bombing was not unprecedented at the outbreak of war. But it was outside the experience of most fighting men, and certainly of civilians. That novelty wore off, as most belligerents indulged in aerial bombing to some extent. Mostly it was against military infrastructure behind the lines – railheads, depots, even factories – and sometimes troop concentrations. What was distinctive about the German air campaign against Britain was its scale, the targeting of population centres – and the eerie proliferation of airships.

This aluminium ammunition box belonged to the airship designated *L.31*, commanded by probably the best-known and most effective German airship raider, *Kapitänleutnant* Heinrich Mathy. He and his machine met their end in the early hours of 1 October 1916, northwest of London, when caught by 2nd Lieutenant Wulstan Tempest of 39 Squadron, Royal Flying Corps. Boldly flying through anti-aircraft fire, Tempest made three sweeps along *L.31*, pumping in incendiary ammunition. "As I was firing," he remembered, "I noticed her begin to go red inside like an enormous Chinese lantern." *L.31* and her crew plummeted to earth from almost 15,000 feet, the impact on hitting the ground visible in the way the ammunition box's bullets perforated its soft skin. It was the fourth airship brought down in as many weeks; after months of attack, Londoners were no longer defenceless. As the burning airships lit up the night sky, thousands cheered. But at least one observer, Sybil Morrison, was more reflective. "I was appalled to see the kind, good-hearted British people dancing round in the streets at the sight of 60 people being burnt alive, clapping, singing and cheering. It was like a flash to me that this is what war did. It created this utter inhumanity in perfectly decent people."

The first bombing by aeroplane was in 1911, during the Italian–Turkish War in Libya, when Lieutenant Giulio Gravotta dropped two small bombs. But to deliver a serious payload something bigger was needed, and the German military saw the potential of the airship after Count Ferdinand von Zeppelin's *Z1* prototype took to the air in 1900. With aluminium frames and filled with lighter-than-air hydrogen, these huge silver airships were an awesome sight. Both the German navy and army ordered machines, although the army preferred the wooden-framed Schütte-Lanz model to the Zeppelin. By 1914 Germany had 11 serviceable airships and, when war began, deployed them to forward bases and then to occupied Belgium. On 16 August 1914, the first Zeppelin bomb of the war fell on Liège, in Belgium.

"THE NOISE OF THE GUNS & SHELLS
BURSTING & THE BOMBS BURSTING WAS
TERRIFIC & MOST AWESOME. WOMEN
SIMPLY WENT OFF THEIR HEADS & WERE
DIFFICULT TO CONTROL. I LOCKED MY
LOT, WIFE & ALL, IN THE KITCHEN."

Mr W.A. Phillips, September 1915

A Zeppelin is caught in the searchlights during a bombing run. The aerial equivalent of the U-boats' unrestricted warfare, the attacks by these monsters seemed to betoken a new kind of war that did not distinguish between combatant and non-combatant.

In 1914, German warships had bombarded east-coast British towns, causing civilian deaths and enraging British public opinion. Now the aerial bombing of major cities began with the permission of the Kaiser. Although hail, rain and ice made airships sluggish and unmanoeuvrable, and strong headwinds caused many attacks to fail, on 19 January 1915 two airships got through to carry out the first air raid, dropping nine small bombs on Great Yarmouth and King's Lynn, killing four people.

The first Zeppelin raid on London was by *LZ.38*, on the last night of May 1915, after earlier probing raids that month. It cut a swathe of destruction from Stoke Newington to Stepney, dropping nearly 3,000 pounds of bombs, killing 7 and wounding 35, as well as causing thousands of pounds worth of damage. An angry public turned on the government, which promptly slapped reporting restrictions on air raids and desperately looked for a solution. An air defence organization with searchlights, guns and aircraft was hastily cobbled together to reassure an anxious and indignant public.

Two days later the British had some recompense. As one Zeppelin was preparing to land at its hangar in Belgium, aircraft of the Royal Navy Air Service (RNAS) arrived to bomb the base. Sub-Lieutenant Reginald Warneford dropped his bombs on top of the airship, which burst into flames and crashed. (He earned a Victoria Cross – but was killed ten days later in a crash.)

The short summer nights and moonlight reduced the number of airship raids, but August and September saw a resurgence. One airship, *L.13*, led by the experienced *Kapitänleutnant* Heinrich Mathy, caused over £500,000 worth of damage on 8 September. The sight of the seemingly invulnerable monsters droning slowly through the sky, dealing out indiscriminate death and destruction, infuriated the public. D.H. Lawrence described seeing a Zeppelin "high up, like a bright golden finger, quite small ... It was like Milton – 'then there was war in heaven'." New defensive measures included specialist anti-aircraft guns procured from France and new airfields brought into service to protect London. Nevertheless, on 13–14 October two Zeppelins bombed London's West End, killing 71 and wounding 128 people.

Bad weather put a temporary stop to the raids and Whitehall reorganized yet again, with the RNAS taking responsibility for battling enemy airships at sea and the Royal Flying Corps (RFC) for tackling them over land. From February 1916, ten home-defence squadrons were organized to protect the capital. But before these measures took effect the Zeppelins were back, in January 1916 striking Liverpool, though without doing much damage. At last the guns managed to bring a raider down in March 1916, off the Kent coast.

The RFC fighter pilots were gradually getting the measure of intercepting Zeppelins in the dark – and they had a new weapon: explosive bullets. On 2 September 1916, 12 German airships set out on the biggest raid so far. Dozens of fighters were scrambled to intercept, and three closed in on *SL.11*, coned by searchlights over London. Lieutenant William Leefe Robinson, flying a BE2c, raked the craft from bow to stern with the new incendiary bullets. After his third sweep, the airship caught fire. The hydrogen gas burned the wooden frame, and all over London and Essex thousands cheered as *SL.11* plummeted to her flaming doom. The next day people danced in the street, church bells rang and thousands travelled to see the smouldering wreckage. Robinson received the Victoria Cross. Three weeks later *L.33* was hit by anti-aircraft fire and forced to crash-land in rural Essex. The crew tried to march to the coast but were all arrested by the police. They were lucky. That same night their sister ship *L.32* was caught by another BE2, which brought it down in flames. There were no survivors. A week later Mathy himself was killed with all his crew: he jumped to his death rather than be burned alive. And three further airships were lost in November 1916.

Airship vulnerabilities were spurring German technical developments, and for 1917 Germany unveiled higher-flying airships and Gotha heavy bomber aircraft. The Gotha was a long-range bomber, capable of carrying a ton of bombs for 500 miles at 80 miles per hour. On their first raid, on 25 May 1917 on Folkestone, Gothas killed 96 and wounded 195 people. The advent of successful aeroplane raids led to the Kaiser ordering airship raids on London to be suspended, although he later allowed them to continue under "favourable circumstances". On 19 October, no less than 13 airships tried to attack targets across the British Midlands, but gale force winds brought disaster and four of them were lost. Sporadic airship raids continued into 1918, with the last not until 5 August, but it was clear that Gothas were now in the ascendancy.

It was Gothas that, on 13 June 1917, inflicted the single most *deadly* air raid of the war on Britain, killing 162 people – including 18 young children at a Poplar primary school – and injuring a further 432. All the aircraft returned safely to base. And it was Gothas that, in May 1918, mounted the *largest* raid against London – but this time six were shot down and another crashed on landing, proving that the Gothas, too, were not invincible: indeed, over 60 were lost during their 22 raids on Britain. But now there were other German priorities, and the Gothas were diverted to attacking depots and railheads behind the Western Front, and even Paris, in the struggles of 1918.

The German bombing campaign against Britain killed 1,413 civilians, wounded another 3,408 and caused millions of pounds worth of damage. It diverted aeroplanes, men and guns from the Western Front. However, its greatest impact was psychological. The civilian population, particularly in parts of Southeast England, was undoubtedly traumatized: fearful Londoners were sleeping in Underground stations and hatred of the German "baby killers" reached new heights.

The British learnt from the Germans, too. In 1918, it was bombers of the new Royal Air Force that were roaming from Cologne to Stuttgart, and only the Armistice on 11 November 1918 stopped its first raids with the heavy four-engined Handley Page V/1500 aircraft carrying a 3,000-pound payload. The age of the bomber had truly arrived.

29

A TICKET COLLECTOR'S HAT
WOMEN'S WORK IN WARTIME BRITAIN

1914 TO 1918

Looking back from a hundred years on, it seems inevitable that the huge demands on manpower exerted by the war would be most sharply reflected in the changing role of women. Women's position in British society had already been the subject of heated debate before 1914. But the outbreak of war split the campaign for the vote: Mrs Emmeline Pankhurst and many militant Suffragette followers called a "ceasefire" out of patriotism, as did most other less strident groups, although some radicals continued to agitate. But the demands of a "total war" economy pushed women's roles and rights higher up the political agenda, and transformed the working options for women.

> From leading figures like the pioneering doctor Elsie Inglis – who overcame male hostility to establish hospitals that treated thousands of wounded – to ordinary mothers, sisters and daughters across the country, women stepped out of the shadows during the war to challenge convention in the range and accomplishment of their contribution. Wartime transport was one key area. From 1915 increasing numbers of women began to work on trams, buses and the railways, so that by 1918 there were 117,000 women transport workers – a 650 per cent increase from the start of the war and the highest proportional rise in any sector. This straw hat was part of the summer uniform of a ticket collector on the Lancashire and Yorkshire Railway (LYR), which carried passengers and freight across the Pennines. By November 1918 the LYR employed 4,459 women, three-quarters of whom undertook jobs previously carried out by men. Their uniforms, badges, photographs and statistics were just part of what, as early as April 1917, a specialist War Museum sub-committee of visionary women was starting to gather, to make sure that the full range of women's work in 1914–18 was remembered.

In 1911, the census recorded about one-third of women doing some paid work, but autumn 1914 saw a shake-up. Textile employment fell 43 per cent in the first five months of the war, and many women were laid off. However, as hundreds of thousands of men enlisted in the armed forces a general shortage of employees began to emerge. At first, working women began moving from one major traditional employment – domestic service – into the more obviously "respectable" new jobs such as typing and clerical posts. Other women, mainly from the more leisured classes, rushed to do voluntary work, such as helping with Belgian refugees or setting up, or nursing in, private hospitals.

"WORK GIRLS WORK / MAKE THE SHOT AND SHELL / WORK GIRLS WORK / BLOW THE HUNS TO HELL"

Slogan on wartime ephemera

However, during 1915 women began to move across the workforce in larger numbers and in different ways, stimulating a year-long debate about what jobs were suitable for women. One Suffragette wrote: "There are some jobs for which women are 'naturally suited' such as clerks or teachers", and the burgeoning Civil Service attracted large numbers of women, helping to release men for the Front. Many of these jobs attracted younger, unmarried women, because dismissal or retirement on marriage was still considered normal. In the view of one journalist, "The extremist feminist in her wildest moments would not advocate dock-labouring, mining or road-digging as suitable employment for women." But women's work continued to diversify – over 60,000 were in the banking sector in the later stages of the war, and nearly twice that number in transport, whose numbers were in turn dwarfed by those in local government.

The biggest change, though, in women's work came in factories manufacturing material for the war effort. A government poster showing a woman donning overalls, "doing her bit" as the slogan ran, emphasized that working in a factory was *real* war service. After the advent of the Ministry of Munitions in May 1915 (*see* Chapter 30), women found plenty of jobs as "munitionettes" in the new factories and created the most enduring image of the wartime woman worker. Explosives work generally went to married women, who were considered to be more sensible and "steady"; but single women were often preferred for working with certain explosives, such as TNT, because of their suspected gynaecological hazards. The work could be long, arduous and dangerous. Over a hundred women died from TNT poisoning, and several factories witnessed deadly explosions.

For the trade unions the arrival of women in large numbers was greeted with suspicion and obstruction. Their main concern was "dilution", the threat to wage levels from the replacement of highly paid skilled men with semi-skilled or unskilled workers – which usually meant women. Most new female employees in wartime industry were eventually regarded by the unions as "substitutes", despite the fact that in many cases they were actually extra workers. Women's representatives were not consulted in the discussions over pay, because theoretically the agreements were for the men they had "replaced". Nevertheless, by 1918 women's membership of trade unions had grown threefold, to over 1.2 million.

Some women were concerned that they were producing objects to kill and maim. One wrote in a factory magazine: "The fact that I am using my life's energy to destroy human souls gets on my nerves. Yet on the other hand, I'm doing what I can to bring this horrible affair to an end. But once the war is over, never in creation will I do the same thing again." For many women, work on the factory floor was a liberating – if exhausting – experience. The welfare on offer mattered, and canteens were popular, of which hundreds were established. For particularly older women from the poorer districts, it was the first full meal they could sit down to and eat regularly. On almost 40 munitions sites, government housing was provided, too. It was common later to recall war work as a happy time because of the camaraderie, better wages and jokes with friends, as well as factory-run social activities such as plays, concerts, football matches, and even hair competitions. Many factories had crèches, too, as a way of attracting and keeping workers.

Number Seven Filling Factory at Hayes in Middlesex may be considered typical. It employed 10,000 women, aged 18 upwards, on relatively good wages. Safety and discipline were tight; to set foot in a hazardous area without protective clothing was

Women workers somewhat self-consciously pose for the camera as they fill trays with bullets at Cartridge Factory 5, part of the huge Royal Arsenal complex at Woolwich. The great expansion in munitions production represented the most overtly war-related work that women undertook, though the range of occupations that opened up to women was diverse.

an offence punishable by a fine or dismissal. Production workers worked shifts of a 9½-hour day and a 10-hour night. Workers' facilities included cycle sheds, changing rooms, bathing facilities with plentiful supplies of hot water and canteens capable of feeding several hundred at a time. There was also a medical centre with a resident doctor and dispenser. The morale and spirit of the workforce were high; in the crisis that followed the German attacks of March 1918 workers volunteered to work over the Easter Holiday, many without pay.

Inequalities in wages remained, of course, and it was normal for women to earn less than men, including for doing the same job. Although women formed the majority of the workforce in manufacturing fuses and cartridges, they were still forced to rely on male skilled-engineer tool-setters, to whom they had to pass on some of their wages. Earnings averaged 30 shillings (£1.50) a week – much better than the pre-war average of 11 shillings and sixpence, but still only half the men's wages.

July 1916 saw the largest number of additional women entering the workplace, and during the 12 months from July 1916 to June 1917 women comprised a full half of the workforce. The female contribution to the economy grew still further in March 1917, when the Women's Land Army was set up; perhaps as many as 250,000 women were working the land in 1918. Beyond the Home Front, it should also be remembered that women joined the armed forces in non-combatant roles. By the end of the war, 80,000 women were performing auxiliary roles such as nursing, driving and cooking in new services like the Women's Army Auxiliary Corps.

The trend started to reverse even before the Armistice. There is little doubt that many working women would have welcomed a chance to continue their occupations, and they had demonstrated prowess in hitherto untried tasks from tram driving to forging heavy metal. But the roles began disappearing, or were taken up again by the returning men. Some women went back to domestic service, but far fewer returned to live or work in the great households.

Britain's women had made a significant contribution to the war effort, one that could not now be ignored by politicians. With the passing of the Representation of the People Act in 1918, women aged over 30 finally won the vote. As for the wartime experience itself, many women were very conscious of their efforts and spoke proudly of their contribution. For many individual women, just as for the men, the First World War was a unique defining experience and a radical force for social change.

30

THE MUNITIONETTES' FIRST HEAVY SHELL
THE STRUGGLE TO PRODUCE MUNITIONS

1915 TO 1918

If, in modern warfare, fuel is the blood of victory, then munitions – in all their varied forms– are the muscles and sinews. This raw truth was first understood as the First World War deteriorated into a crude slogging match dominated by guns, shells, machines and the power of industrial output to support soldiers on the battlefield. The Germans even had a name for it, the *Materialschlacht* – the battle of production.

Britain was ill-prepared. With the exception of the recent naval arms race, the Treasury's thinking had always been to deliver the minimal equipment at the cheapest price, and soldiers in 1914–15 paid the price. Part of the problem also lay with the War Office, whose pre-war policy had been to procure light battlefield artillery at the expense of heavy guns. So Britain not only had a shortage of heavy artillery for the siege warfare that evolved in the trenches, but also had no stockpile of ammunition. Worse, there was no manufacturing base to produce shells quickly. It took a crisis, a new Ministry of Munitions (headed by David Lloyd George) and the imposition of state control to turn things around.

> This 8-inch High Explosive shell was the first ever made by women in Britain during the war. As such, it was not sent to be hurled at the enemy but instead preserved for the collections of the Women's Work Committee at the nascent War Museum. It was manufactured in Liverpool, which, on 4 June 1915, David Lloyd George visited to initiate a regional munitions campaign. Within weeks, shells were being made at two Liverpool Corporation-owned sites. The Cunard Steam Shipping Company, owners of the recently torpedoed *Lusitania*, also offered a warehouse in Bootle and the building was quickly adapted. Soon, the Cunard National Shell Factory was making 4.5-inch and 6-inch High Explosive shells, and from September the heavier 8-inch shells, too. Over three-quarters of the 1,000 employees at the factory were women, "mostly drawn from middle class homes, and the majority had not previously been engaged in Factory work", as noted in the factory's History. They worked all the lathes, and the Cunard factory became the first to make 6-inch and 8-inch shells entirely by female labour. This shell was initially displayed at a temporary exhibition at Burlington House in January 1918 and has remained on show ever since, a testament to the immense national effort made by over 900,000 British women in the munitions industries to keep the guns firing.

In 1914, the War Office's Army Ordnance Department – which in peacetime had supplied small numbers of weapons under the watchful eye of the Treasury – was now

expected to mobilize industry as quickly as possible, regardless of expense. In the panic of war hasty contracts were issued to the existing domestic arms manufacturers and to American companies. Unfortunately, most of the early ammunition contracts were for shrapnel shells, which had given good service in the open veldt of South Africa but which proved useless for cutting barbed wire or for blowing up enemy dugouts on the Western Front. The War Office ordered millions of them.

Three key factors now hampered a rapid expansion of the British armaments industry: a shortage of key raw materials, including chemicals; a paucity of the specialist armaments factories, which were already at full capacity; and a fragmented railway distribution network of over a hundred competing companies (which had at least been placed under overall government direction by September 1914).

The result was that the British Expeditionary Force was seriously short of shells in spring 1915. The BEF's Sir John French was bitter. After the disappointment of Neuve Chapelle on 10 March and especially the failure at Aubers Ridge on 9 May (*see* Chapter 40), French briefed Lieutenant Colonel Charles Repington, military correspondent of the *Times*, in detail. He even showed him confidential military documents. The *Times* described the BEF's shortage of shells in graphic detail: "We had not sufficient high explosives to lower the enemy's parapets to the ground ... The want of an unlimited supply of high explosives was a fatal bar to our success." Ironically, the brief "hurricane" bombardment necessitated by the shell shortage had contributed to the preliminary success of Neuve Chapelle. But it was one thing to make a positive tactical choice, and quite another to be in a position of having no alternative.

Thus, a "shell scandal" broke out as an angry public demanded action. This crisis, compounded by the failure of the Gallipoli landing (*see* Chapter 24), effectively brought down Asquith's Liberal government. David Lloyd George – a vociferous critic of alleged War Office profligacy in peacetime – now berated the Ordnance Department for its "dilatoriness and sloth". Under pressure, Asquith formed a new Coalition government, and the War Office lost responsibility for munitions as Lloyd George was appointed to head the new Ministry of Munitions in May 1915. He soon found out the truth. British industry lacked the high-quality modern machine tools and the specialist semi-automatic forging machines needed for shell manufacture, had no chemical industry big enough for the mass manufacture of explosives, and possessed few companies able to manufacture precision fuses. He addressed these with his characteristic energy, helped by the passage of the Munitions of War Act in July 1915, which brought munitions production under state control.

Lloyd George recognized that Britain's whole economy needed to be geared for war. The state now took over direction, with munitions the key industrial priority. An Imperial Munitions Board was set up to ensure that supplies and factories in Britain and Canada were organized to provide adequate shells and other war material for the duration. A huge munitions plant, officially named "His Majesty's Factory", was built near Gretna, on the English–Scottish border outside Carlisle, and by mid-1916 was in production. A large bureaucracy developed to administer the vast state effort. For months to come the shells supplied still reflected orders placed by the old War Office, but during the latter part of 1916 the speed and volume of manufacture was transformed by these changes.

The Ministry of Munitions was staffed by experienced businessmen able to coordinate the needs of big business with those of the state and reach a compromise on price and profit. Government agents bought essential supplies from abroad and then controlled their distribution in order to prevent speculative price rises and profiteering. The government controlled all dealings in metals as well as coal. All over the country factories were converted to munitions production, and machines and skills were adapted to military use. In Birmingham's jewellery quarter skilled craftsmen turned to making hand grenades; pen manufacturers found themselves producing cartridge clips.

The efficient production of munitions required a consistent, ample and stable workforce. "Treasury agreements" had been reached with 35 unions, which, among other things, sought to prohibit strikes and lockouts, created means for arbitrating disputes and allowed for the so-called "dilution" of labour – the replacement of "skilled" men who had enlisted with "semi-skilled" or "unskilled" men and (even!) with women. These measures were then incorporated into the Munitions of War Act, along with restrictions on the movement of labour, which made it hard for workers in vital industries to change jobs.

The government's centralization of control was thus paralleled in the enhanced status of trades unions and their leaderships, who now carried a raft of responsibilities as partners in the war economy. They were initially opposed to the introduction of women workers, whose wages never reached parity with men's, but the facts spoke for themselves. By mid-1917, women dominated fuse production, overcoming a backlog of 25 million fuses. But the general shortage of labour also gave unions considerable muscle, as the law of supply and demand drove wages up to unprecedented levels. Skilled machine operators could command £3 and 10 shillings a week at a time when a private soldier's basic pay was 7 shillings a week. Unsurprisingly, trades union membership doubled during the war, reaching 4.5 million in 1918.

Rising food prices, rising rents and other factors provided reasons for disgruntlement and fuel for militancy, and (the laws notwithstanding) Britain lost 27 million days in strikes – more than four times the number in Germany. By the end of the war, though, it was clear that the overriding need for munitions had been met. At war's end, the Ministry of Munitions had a staff nationwide of 65,000, employing some 3 million workers in over 20,000 factories, including 250 government-controlled ones (143 of them state-owned).

In 1914, British factories produced 300 machine guns; in 1918, they made over 120,000. In 1917, the 76 million shells produced that year was over 150 times the quantity made in 1914. And by the end, many thousands of the new war machines – tanks and aircraft – had rolled off the production lines. As the Germans ruefully acknowledged, they had lost the *Materialschlacht*.

Shells stretch as far as the eye can see at the National Filling Factory at Chilwell, Nottinghamshire. The plant was responsible for packing explosives into many of the shells eventually fired by British forces, but disaster struck on 1 July 1918, when more than 130 workers were killed and a large part of the factory destroyed by an accidental explosion.

31

KAISER BILL TOILET ROLL
PROPAGANDA IN THE WAR

1914 TO 1918

The First World War was the first conflict to witness the full exploitation of the mass media (including film) for propaganda purposes. From the start, the populations of the belligerent nations were flooded with exhortations and emotional appeals, along with demonizations of the enemy and uplifting political assurances such as "This is the war to end war." Governments targeted their own populations to maintain the war effort and motivate the will to fight. But they also wanted to influence neutral, international opinion and, where possible, undermine the enemy – though in an era before broadcast radio, there was relatively little that they could do to *directly* influence the enemy's citizens, beyond dropping leaflets behind the lines.

In Britain, as early as August 1914 the War Propaganda Bureau was established under Charles Masterman to coordinate propaganda at home and abroad, which it did until 1917. It was better known as Wellington House, after its London HQ. Masterman discreetly recruited famous writers such as Arthur Conan Doyle, John Masefield, G.K. Chesterton, Rudyard Kipling, John Buchan and H.G. Wells to draft articles, pamphlets and books supporting the government's line.

The phrase "a scrap of paper" became notorious after German Chancellor Theobald von Bethmann Hollweg used it, on 4 August 1914, to convey his dismissive astonishment that Britain might declare war merely on account of a 75-year-old treaty regarding Belgian neutrality. What he saw as Britain's inflated sense of honour and obligation was, by contrast, regarded in Whitehall as an absolute moral guarantee. Over the coming months, British propaganda seized on Bethmann Hollweg's words to vindicate the very values that he had dismissed, as the words "scrap of paper" appeared on posters and handbills and quickly entered popular culture. Fragmented and tatty, this roll of 1914 toilet paper reflected the essence of Britain's total defiance of Germany's perceived conceit and arrogance. Each sheet showed a picture of Kaiser Wilhelm and offered the opportunity to any British man, woman or child to express his or her contempt in an unambiguous way. Wilhelm's moral bankruptcy was headlined by Bethmann Hollweg's famous phrase. Topping the lot, there was the bold claim: "SCENTED". In a classic piece of bawdy British humour, the toilet roll sardonically suggested that in a crisis any scrap of paper would do.

The official efforts were greatly helped by the impact of the principal mass medium of the day, the daily newspaper. It was less than 20 years since the *Daily Mail* had first appeared, the first truly mass-market daily. To a highly literate public,

> "PROPAGANDA … DRAWS NOURISHMENT FROM THE SINS OF THE ENEMY. IF THERE ARE NO SINS, INVENT THEM! THE AIM IS TO MAKE THE ENEMY SO GREAT A MONSTER THAT HE FORFEITS THE RIGHTS OF A HUMAN BEING."
>
> *General Sir Ian Hamilton*

newspapers were an important tool for war information, aided by posters, magazines, pamphlets and other ephemera. The press – at first not allowed anywhere near the Western Front – tended to fall into line through self-censorship, and anyway had to rely on a government Press Bureau for information about the actual fighting. Indeed, the government–press closeness became explicit later in the war, when Lord Beaverbrook, owner of the *Daily Express*, headed up a new Ministry of Information and Lord Northcliffe, owner of both the *Daily Mail* and the *Times*, was put in charge of an Enemy Propaganda Department.

Allied propagandists were helped early on in the task of demonizing the enemy by the allegations of German brutalities against Belgian civilians (*see* Chapter 13), which came to acquire a life of their own. Starved of real news from the Front, editors relied on uncorroborated tales to sell newspapers. In an enduring visual and verbal vocabulary, German soldiers were depicted as sadistic, bestial violaters and murderers of defenceless women and children and, after the sack of Louvain and the bombardment of Rheims cathedral, as vandals and destroyers of civilization and culture. While German forces may indeed have killed women and children in their reprisals, there is no evidence that they went about cutting off hands, bayoneting women and babies, and crucifying captured soldiers, as some of the propaganda claimed. Despite this, a wave of anti-German propaganda swept Britain, justifying intervention to save "gallant little Belgium". The Kaiser was especially singled out as a fanatical, bloodthirsty tyrant bent on world domination. In 1915, documentary credence was lent to the whole picture when the Bryce Committee Report on atrocities in Belgium appeared. It was mostly rooted in facts as they were understood and based on 1,200 sworn witness depositions. Translated into 30 languages, it had a significant impact, making front-page headlines in major newspapers in Allied and neutral countries, and it was actively promoted by Wellington House.

French propagandists had an even easier task. It was *les sales Boches* who had invaded the sacred soil of France and so obviously had to be driven back, and especially after Verdun a theme of "they shall not pass" emerged (*see* Chapter 50). But they, too, were quick to mine the rich seam of atrocity stories. Even the Americans, recruiting for the war three years later, could fruitfully exploit images of *Pickelhaube*-wearing apes and burning cathedrals to whip up anti-German feeling.

As the war progressed, individual incidents were seized on for propaganda value, especially if they bolstered the "atrocity" theme. The execution of British nurse Edith Cavell in October 1915 (*see* Chapter 32) provided a focus for countless articles, pamphlets, images and books publicizing her shocking end. The torpedoing of RMS *Lusitania* in May 1915 presented, amid its tragedy, another sort of propaganda opportunity, this time with a high international value on account of the 128 American victims (*see* Chapter 27). And the continuing German air campaign over England maintained British outrage (*see* Chapter 28).

Germany's own propaganda apparatus combined a War Press Office and Supreme Censorship Office. But the overall effort lacked focus, and often failed to comprehend how German actions and policies came across abroad – as the ruthlessness in Belgium testified. With her forces on foreign soil, Germany could not very plausibly claim defence against aggression. German propaganda appears to have favoured relatively simple slogans, such as "*Gott strafe England*" ("God smite England"), which was widely distributed on memorabilia. Also popular was the poem *Hassgesang gegen England* ("Hate Song Against England", better known as the "Hymn of Hate"), written by Ernst Lissauer. It was hugely popular, and Crown Prince Rupprecht of Bavaria ordered copies distributed to his soldiers.

For much of the war, German domestic propaganda concentrated on boosting the image of Hindenburg, initially following his victory over the Russians at Tannenberg, and later as the *de facto* leader of Germany's war effort, alongside Ludendorff. But the subordination of political leadership to military men produced its own problems of a relatively inflexible message that risked looking increasingly threadbare, as the population was urged to greater sacrifices with phrases such as "The times are hard, but victory is assured."

As the war ground on, the need to supply it with men, money and machines created the dominant propaganda across the home fronts. In Britain, having first appealed to individuals' patriotism – and before conscription decided the issue – recruitment posters increasingly exploited shame and guilt, asking "Daddy, what did <u>YOU</u> do in the Great War?" or shouting "Women of Britain say 'GO!'". Appeals to people on the Home Front urged them to "Save Wheat and Help the Fleet", to "crush the Germans" by lending the government money, and women were summoned to "enrol at once" for munitions work.

After America entered the war in 1917, as well as being presented with the "brutal Hun", Americans were told that they were fighting for abstract concepts like liberty, democracy and a new postwar world. A long-running campaign to sell "Liberty Bonds" (war bonds), using the powerful symbol of the Statue of Liberty, raised around $17 billion for the war effort, or about $170 per citizen – a huge sum at the time.

Even in 1917 the "atrocity" theme was potent propaganda, as this US Army recruitment poster shows. Adapting a British design, it combines the familiar indicators of German bestiality, brutality and cruelty. In the background is the much-used landscape of a shattered Louvain or Rheims; in the foreground, the Pickelhaube-wearing monster threatens "America" herself.

Perhaps the most audacious piece of Allied negative propaganda was the German "Corpse Factory", which has been described as the "master hoax" of the war. It originated in some disinformation planted by Wellington House in a Chinese newspaper, to take advantage of presumed Chinese horror at the desecration of the dead and so tilt Chinese opinion towards the Allies. But it was supported by the *Times*, which lifted a German newspaper description of a "corpse exploitation establishment" but omitted one important fact: that the corpses being processed for oils and animal feed were of *animals*, not dead German soldiers. The story mushroomed, was taken up all over the world and was helpfully reinforced by later accounts of a misrouted freight wagon full of dead Germans and "confirmations" of the story by interrogated Germans. The outright lie was not officially repudiated by Britain until 1925.

Propaganda, spread through mass media, seemed to work. But as war gave way to peace, a reaction set in. Frank admissions of wholesale lying on the part of trusted governments, especially in Britain and America, were not soon forgotten – and they fundamentally shaped how propaganda would be conducted in the next war.

32

NURSE CAVELL'S SECRET DIARY
THE CREATION OF AN ICON

1915

The story of British nurse Edith Cavell evokes the values of an earlier era. Here was a woman steeped in religion, duty, care for others, with an unflinching sense of right and wrong, and imbued with a sincere patriotism; qualities that, allied to her unbending character, led to her execution at the hands of a German firing squad.

Cavell was born in 1865, the daughter of a rural Norfolk vicar. Reared to share what she had with the poor of the parish, and to respect rules, it was perhaps inevitable that she was drawn to the disciplined and caring world of nursing. Her skill, leadership and strength of character led to her becoming matron at a new nursing school in Brussels, and by 1911 she was training Belgian nurses for hospitals, schools and kindergartens.

Cavell was on holiday in Norfolk when war broke out, and she promptly returned to Brussels. The expected flood of wounded failed to materialize – the war had moved on – but in the harsh winter of 1914–15 Cavell and her nurses began to harbour Allied soldiers caught in occupied Belgium and secretly trying to get to neutral Holland. She became part of a network, in which escapees, equipped with identity documents, were sheltered in Cavell's clinic before being led to the Dutch frontier.

But Cavell was betrayed. On 5 August 1915, she and Sister Elizabeth Wilkins were arrested. Wilkins denied all the charges, but Cavell, characteristically, refused to lie and admitted everything. After two months in a solitary cell she was charged with "conducting soldiers to the enemy" and treason – a capital offence. Despite pleas for clemency from the US and Spanish representatives, on 12 October 1915, Cavell, dressed in her matron's uniform, was shot.

The repercussions were immediate. Newspapers worldwide proclaimed Cavell's death as further proof of German barbarism, with comparisons to the burning of Louvain and the sinking of *Lusitania*. Her steadfast character, womanly status and her caring profession combined to create a lasting propaganda figure for the Allies.

> In solitary confinement in St Gilles Prison, Brussels, Cavell wrote these fragments, recording her feelings and many acts of assistance to escaping soldiers. But they only revealed their secrets decades later. Following Cavell's death, and the return of her personal belongings, her sister Edith received a cushion, which was hard and lumpy. She passed it on to another woman, whose husband later opened it up – to reveal a tightly bound roll of paper. It was only in the late 1960s that the handwriting was identified as Cavell's and the words deciphered. They revealed a secret prison diary and cast new light on one of the war's most remarkable, yet elusive, women.

"PATRIOTISM IS NOT ENOUGH. I MUST HAVE NO HATRED OR BITTERNESS TOWARDS ANYONE"

Cavell's reputed last words, inscribed on the Cavell Monument (1920), London

33

CAPTAIN FRYATT'S WATCH
DEFYING THE U-BOATS

1915 TO 1916

A year after the execution of Edith Cavell, Germany earned British and international opprobrium again with the execution of another civilian. This time it was a captain in the Merchant Navy.

In 1914, Charles Fryatt captained a regular ferry on the Rotterdam–Harwich route, and he continued operating across the North Sea once war broke out, in spite of the hazards of unlit coasts, mines, enemy submarines, aircraft and warships. Unfortunately, ferries became particular targets once Germany, in February 1915, commenced unrestricted submarine warfare (see Chapter 27). At least three attacks were made on railway company ferries, and Captain Fryatt was in command on two occasions.

On 2 March 1915, the SS *Wrexham*, sailing to Rotterdam in neutral Holland, was intercepted and challenged by a U-boat. Fryatt ignored the signal to stop and turned away at high speed, steaming for the Dutch coast. The submarine gave chase but the *Wrexham* gradually drew away, travelling at 16 knots, her funnels on fire. After 40 miles the U-boat gave up. Fryatt was hailed as a hero. Within the month, on 28 March, he had another narrow escape, as submarine *U-33* ordered the SS *Brussels* to stop. Instead, Fryatt commanded "full steam ahead" and proceeded to try to ram the U-boat, which was forced to dive to avoid being hit.

A year later Fryatt paid the price, when the Germans deliberately hunted him down. Five destroyers intercepted the *Brussels* and she was taken into Zeebrugge, in occupied Belgium. On 27 July 1916, Fryatt was charged with attempting to ram *U-33* illegally because he was "not a member of a combatant force", and he was court-martialled at Bruges. Predictably, he was found guilty of "acting like a *franc-tireur*" and condemned to death, a sentence officially described by Germany as a "merited expiation" for his "nefarious" behaviour. His execution, by firing squad, came within 48 hours.

On both occasions when Captain Fryatt outwitted his U-boat attackers, he was rewarded with gold watches. After the first incident, his employers, the Great Eastern Railway Company, gave him this elegant piece, a half-hunter with a small glass cover, to mark "their appreciation of his courage and skilful seamanship". It was only three weeks later that Fryatt turned the SS *Brussels* on *U-33*. To the Germans, his actions were seen as an illegal act of war. By, contrast, the British Admiralty lauded the skipper's feistiness and gave him another gold watch "in recognition of the example" that he had set. For Britons, Fryatt's actions were seen as a fine act of British pluck.

International outcry followed. Neutral Holland and the United States were particularly outraged, describing U-boat attacks as "piracy" and pointing out that a merchant ship's captain had every legal right to defend his passengers and crew. Yet again, German actions translated into a brutal overreaction that alienated world opinion.

34

WILLIAM HARRISON'S NO-CONSCRIPTION FELLOWSHIP CARD
ENLISTMENT TO CONSCRIPTION

1915 TO 1918

Conscription was a vexed topic long before 1914. The distinguished former Commander-in-Chief Field Marshal Lord Roberts VC had eyed the mass enlisted armies of the continental powers and – backed by some of the press, the Conservative Party and the National Service League – argued powerfully for conscription. He was opposed by Asquith's Liberal government and the wider Labour movement, who felt that the compulsion of freeborn Britons was an infringement of their liberty, and by many ordinary professional soldiers.

When war did come, Lord Kitchener's call for voluntary enlistment (*see* Chapter 8) was resolutely answered and took the pressure off any moves to compel men to serve. But the supply slowly dried up during 1915. In the following year, two new concepts in British life became realities: conscription and conscientious objection.

William Harrison was a man of deep-seated principle: a lifelong vegetarian, teetotaller and pacifist. He immediately joined the No-Conscription Fellowship when it was established in 1914, as testified by this membership card. When claiming exemption from the army on the grounds of conscience, he explained to his local Military Service Tribunal in July 1916: "War inevitably means that the nations involved degenerate and become like brutes. This contention is supported by the facts of the present day. Love, mercy, pity, tenderness and forgiveness, things which our Master Jesus bids us practise, are all gone. I love my country too dearly to assist it in coming to such a deplorable state." Despite letters testifying to the sincerity and longevity of his views, Harrison's appeal was rejected. In May 1917 he was arrested, court-martialled and began a sentence of hard labour in Wormwood Scrubs Prison. Released a week after the Armistice, Harrison was arrested again and, still refusing to take any part in the military system, went back to prison, this time in Newcastle. He was not finally freed until April 1919. Throughout his experience, he was sustained by a deep religious faith, which enabled him to emerge from prison free of bitterness and to even see the lighter side. At his first trial, it was reported that the magistrate deducted £2 from his pay as a soldier. Fifty years later, Harrison wondered where that money went: "I never had any pay and have always wondered what happened about the £2!"

The first recognition that something more than voluntary enlistment might be needed came in August 1915, when a mandatory National Register of able-bodied

"CONSCRIPTION ... INVOLVES THE SUBORDINATION OF CIVIL LIBERTIES TO MILITARY DICTATION; IT IMPERILS THE FREEDOM OF INDIVIDUAL CONSCIENCE AND ... DIVIDES THE PEOPLES OF ALL NATIONS."

The No-Conscription Fellowship, response to the Military Service Act, 1916

NO-CONSCRIPTION FELLOWSHIP

A Fellowship for common counsel and action composed of men of enlistment age who are not prepared to take up arms in case of Conscription, whatever the penalties for refusing.

MEMBERSHIP CARD

Mr. _W. Harrison,_   _58, Bonn Road_

Address ~~67, Hyde Grove,~~   _Heaton_

~~Plymouth Grove, Manchester~~ _Bradford_

is hereby certified a Member of the above.

Bradford   Group

Office : 8 MERTON HOUSE
SALISBURY COURT, E.C.   Local Sec.

men was announced. It was primarily aimed at the labour market, and was a natural consequence of the new Ministry of Munitions' need to ensure labour was being used efficiently. But it laid the groundwork for later conscription by identifying those who might be eligible for military service.

It became clear towards the end of 1915 that volunteers would no longer be able to sustain any long-term military effort. The Secretary of State for War, Lord Kitchener, approached Lord Derby, now Director General of Recruiting, asking him to devise a scheme by which all men of fighting age on the Register would be invited to formally "attest" their willingness to serve, but would not have to honour this promise until absolutely necessary. The "Derby Scheme" promised that married men would not be called up until *all* single men had been enlisted. But only just over half the eligible single men signed up, leaving thousands of married men liable to be called forward before those non-signing men. Lord Derby anxiously observed: "It will not be possible to hold married men to their attestation unless and until the services of single men have been obtained by other means." Seen in hindsight, the Derby Scheme was a rather clever piece of political coercion: either sufficient numbers attested, or the case for conscription would become hard to resist.

The Coalition government was split. Liberal sentiment was still strongly opposed to compulsion, but in early January 1916 Asquith proposed the Military Service Bill, whereby single men aged 18–41 would be deemed eligible for military call-up. One Liberal minister resigned over "compulsion", the Labour Party was against it and the Trades Union Congress overwhelmingly condemned it – for one thing, they were fearful of conscription spreading to industry. But behind the scenes the Labour leadership accepted the inevitable, and the Bill became the Military Service Act, coming into force in March.

That was not the end of it. On 25 April a *universal* conscription bill was howled down in the Commons after a bitter debate; but the demands of the trenches, and the army, could no longer be ignored. In May, the Second Military Service Act was enacted, extending conscription to married men.

There were practical obstacles. Politicians, soldiers and industrialists were well aware that a modern war could not be fought if thousands of skilled men were removed from the workplace. The Reserved Occupations Committee, set up under the Derby Scheme, grew into a Manpower Board in late 1916, with the power to identify and direct that certain functions were "reserved occupations".

There were other objections, too. With the new legislation, the former Derby Scheme tribunals were recast as Military Service Tribunals, which heard appeals for exemption – usually on grounds of infirmity, an existing occupation or training (such as religious ministry), or vital domestic or economic responsibilities. More contentious were the appeals on the grounds of morality and principle. The No-Conscription Fellowship (NCF) had been formed by determined pacifists in December 1914, and it had evolved into an active pressure group. Via sympathetic MPs it persuaded the government to extend the tribunals to take into account "conscientious objection to the undertaking of combatant service". The idea of the "conscientious objector" was born.

Pacifism was, for society then and later, a difficult concept, cherished by some, derided by others. A rejection of *all* violence could, arguably, mean either having to live with highly disagreeable consequences or a reliance on non-pacifists to defend those conscientious freedoms. For many pacifists, the principles remained clear.

But the 16,000 recognized conscientious objectors in the war reacted in different ways. About 7,000 did serve in the army, in ways that did not require them to carry weapons: mostly as stretcher bearers and in the Non-Combatant Corps, in which roles they were much respected by their arms-bearing colleagues. Another 3,000 were allowed to do work considered of national importance, such as on farms, or were Quakers who had volunteered for the independent Friends Ambulance Units in France. That left a hard core of 6,000 men who chose to go to prison rather than submit to the state's demands. Of these many later accepted places in work camps under a Home Office scheme, leaving a rump of about 1,500 "absolutists" who remained in the conventional prison system.

The treatment of those arrested reflected the tenor of the times; at least 41 were illegally sent to France and placed under military discipline, court-martialled and sentenced to "Field Punishment Number One" – tying a man to a wagon wheel for two hours a day – and even to death. Asquith's government intervened hastily and remitted them to civilian custody in Britain.

In 1917, Dartmoor Prison was emptied of its regular convicts and renamed "Princetown Work Centre". It was used to house conscientious objectors on the Home Office scheme, eventually numbering 1,100, ranging from anarchists to Bible Students (Jehovah's Witnesses). There they were treated by the prison staff – many of whom had lost relatives in France – with all the prejudice and rigour of the day. Most work was outdoors, and many were subjected to hard physical labour, such as quarrying, and suffered accordingly. Campaigning by women members of the NCF did improve conditions, and even stoked accusations that "conchies" were living soft lives.

The NCF's chairman, Clifford Allen, was one of the "absolutists": he was arrested and imprisoned three times and became seriously ill before the Home Office eventually released him. But some 70 conscientious objectors *did* die in prison or work centres. And even war's conclusion did not end the punishment. Conscientious objectors were banned from voting for a period of five years.

The crisis in manpower that conscription addressed in 1916 was real. And conscription delivered almost 400,000 men to the armed forces that year, dwarfing 1916's crop of volunteers. But it was a watershed in British history, a break with centuries of tradition in response to the exigencies of war, which divided old Whig-Liberal notions of liberty and the small state from the modern fact of an all-powerful state bureaucracy. Conscription drew men away from their workplaces, requiring women to take over millions of jobs. The war compelled almost a third of the male population into uniform and then to undergo the horrors of modern war. Both those who had volunteered and those who were called up never forgot the experience. In a very real sense, conscription changed British society.

Members of the "London and Home Counties Workers' and Soldiers' Council" are ejected from a pacifist meeting at London's Brotherhood Chapel. As revolutionary fervour rippled outwards from Russia's turmoil in 1917, Britain was not immune; but anti-war politics did not necessarily sit easily with the conscientious objection of those spurred by religious principle or moral scruple.

35

THE "MOTHER" OF GUNS
ARTILLERY IN THE FIRST WORLD WAR

1914 TO 1918

The greatest inducer of fear in the First World War was artillery. Shellfire terrified everybody. From the steel flail of a barrage to just the sheer chance of the odd shell – and whether from a long-barrelled cannon or a snub-nosed howitzer with its steeper, plunging fire – "the guns" reduced strong men to nervous wrecks. One who experienced them, Guy Chapman, "could never stand shell fire. I got into a thoroughly neurotic state". He was not alone. Another wrote of "cowering in abject terror, praying that it would stop". Even the Australians, supposedly the toughest of soldiers, were recorded "shaking like leaves and weeping" on receiving their baptism of fire on the Western Front at Pozières.

Such were its technological advances that a weapon which accounted for only 2.5 per cent of casualties in the 1877–8 Russo-Turkish War became one that killed almost 60 per cent of the BEF's dead in 1914–18, and perhaps as many as 80 per cent of German dead in 1917–18. Not for nothing did Stalin, in a later conflict, call artillery "the God of War".

> While the war was mobile, heavy guns played only a limited role. But once positions became fixed, these bigger, heavier weapons came into their own. By 1913 the Coventry Ordnance Works had developed this mighty 9.2-inch howitzer – so big it had to be dismantled into three loads for transport, weighing over 41 tons. Its missing ballast box needed 14 tons of earth to be shovelled in before it could be brought into action. The 9.2 was tested by the Royal Garrison Artillery at its range in South Wales in July 1914 and quickly approved, so that by the end of the year more than 30 were in production. As the trench network spread across France and Belgium, the 9.2-inch howitzer became one of the main British weapons for destroying Germany artillery, and around 450 were eventually used, firing more than 3 million shells. This, that very first one, became known as "Mother", parent to a new generation of heavy artillery. It was sent into action with the 8th Siege Battery, RGA, on 31 October 1914, and the following year, now with the 10th Siege Battery, it fought at Neuve Chapelle and Festubert, before being returned to Britain where the barrel was eventually relined. It saw action in France again in 1918.

The transformation in artillery's deadly capabilities came through developments in four key areas during the late 19th century.

First, new nitro-cellulose propellants were three times as powerful as gunpowder or "black powder", weight for weight, and left little residue to foul the gun's barrel. They also produced little of the smoke that had obscured the battlefields of earlier eras and which had given away the position of the guns to the enemy.

"MOTHER"

PLEASE DO NOT
TOUCH OR CLIMB
ON THIS EXHIBIT

A dramatic example of pinpoint targeting – or a lucky strike – by counter-battery artillery. An American shell blows to pieces a German field gun, as its gunnery team and their horses gallop frantically away.

The second critical development was the introduction of single-case shells, in which the actual shell was married to a brass case as a single piece of fixed ammunition, as in a bullet. Allied with the third development – the invention of a reliable sealed-breech mechanism (more technically, the interrupted-screw, self-sealing breech mechanism) – this meant that a gun's rate of fire could be increased dramatically. The only limitation now was how quickly shells could be loaded into the breech, although some big guns, including for example the 9.2-inch howitzer, continued to use separate charges.

But the fourth, and single greatest, development was the "recoil-less" cannon. In fact, a recuperating mechanism allowed the gun's barrel to recoil but, by absorbing that recoil, enabled the cannon to remain stationary, still aimed at its target. All previous guns had jumped back as they recoiled, forcing the gun crew to drag the gun back into position and re-aim after every shot.

The French 75mm field gun (*see* Chapter 50) – the celebrated *Soixante-Quinze* – was the first mass-produced artillery piece that overcame the gun barrel's recoil by using a recuperating buffer containing hydraulic oil and compressed air. With its independent sighting mechanism and a protective shield for the gun crew, the new gun was triumphantly displayed during the 1899 Bastille Day parade. It was the world's first modern artillery piece, raising artillery to a new level of battlefield importance, and able to shoot further and more lethally than ever before.

In 1914, the guns of the warring nations reflected these changes. The Germans had a 77mm gun, the British their 18-pounder field gun, both of them variants on the "75". The British Royal Horse Artillery and Royal Field Artillery (the most numerous arm of the artillery) went to war with light, mobile, horse-drawn guns designed to be at the forefront of the battle. In 1915, every division was equipped with fifty-four 18-pounders organized into three 18-gun units called "brigades", backed by a brigade of 4.5-inch howitzers and a battery of four heavier 60-pounders. (British cannon were described by shell weight, and howitzers by their ammunition's size/calibre.)

The practice of placing artillery directly on the frontline was rapidly abandoned after events at Le Cateau on 26 August 1914: although the BEF's II Corps stopped the Germans in their tracks, it lost in the process 38 guns, abandoned in the open, and horses and men cut down by German artillery and machine gun fire. For the rest of the war artillery mostly concentrated on "indirect fire", against targets it could not see from the gun position. As the fighting progressed ever heavier guns were deployed, like the massive 9.2-inch howitzer and even a 12-inch railway gun with a range of 8 miles, the longest of any British gun. But most British artillery support relied on the ubiquitous 18-pounder, close behind the lines and able to react swiftly to any infantry call for assistance.

Fire was directed either by an airborne observer, especially later in the war, or more usually by a Forward Observation Officer (FOO) in the trenches. He was connected by field telephone to the gun lines and could nominate targets and correct fire. The guns themselves each had a simple theodolite or "dial sight" that enabled them to be laid accurately on an invisible target several miles away. As the war progressed, anti-personnel shrapnel shells were increasingly replaced by High Explosive (HE), which was much more destructive. With the addition of improved fuses, by 1917 shells could burst on contact, blow in dugouts and tear holes in barbed wire. And they literally blew men to pieces. Guy Chapman recalled "a booted foot and some bloodied earth" as the only record of one victim of a direct hit.

The British heavier artillery was the responsibility of the Royal Garrison Artillery (RGA), which evolved from the fortress-based artillery on British coasts. Although (unlike the Germans) the BEF had very few heavy guns in 1914, by 1917 the RGA had grown into an important combat-support arm, with its heavy, large-calibre guns and howitzers positioned well back but still able to reach out deep into the enemy's rear area, where their immense destructive power also pounded the German artillery. By the end of the war the RGA deployed almost four-fifths the number of heavy batteries (440) as the RFA had field batteries (568).

Life for British gunners was always hazardous. German shellfire frequently targeted gun lines and Royal Artillery casualties reflect the dangers of frontline gunnery – 49,000 of their number were killed during the war. Another challenge – and rarely acknowledged by scornful infantrymen – was the sheer hard work and lack of sleep artillerymen endured. A distress rocket or an urgent call from the trenches meant that a battery's gunners would be turned out at any time, day or night, often to spend hours manning their guns. One infantry officer on the Somme vividly described them in action: "gunners stripped and sweating, each crew working like a machine, the swing and smack of the breech blocks as clean and sweet as a kiss, and a six foot stream of flame from the muzzle, a thunderclap of sound, and away tore the shell over the hills to the Bosche trenches 5,000 yards away".

By 1917–18 the BEF's artillery and heavy trench mortar detachments had become the most important fighting arm; the Royal Artillery comprised 25 per cent of the army. The techniques, science and terrifying destructive power of British gunnery were feared and confirmed by the Germans. Not for nothing did the experienced German infantryman Ernst Jünger call his memoirs *The Storm of Steel*. It was not one-sided, of course, as witnessed by the terrible bombardment of 21 March 1918, as nearly a million shells rained down on British lines in just four hours at the start of the German spring offensives.

Guns were the masters of the First World War battlefield – the cause of trench warfare and the greatest takers of life. If any single weapon defined the Western Front, it was artillery.

"THE DRUM FIRE NEVER CEASED … MEN BECAME HYSTERICAL … EVEN THE RATS PANICKED AND SOUGHT REFUGE FROM THE BRITISH ARTILLERY."

Stefan Westmann, German officer

36

THE VICKERS MACHINE GUN
MACHINE GUNS ON THE WESTERN FRONT

1914 TO 1918

Artillery may have wrought the most destruction in the First World War, but there seemed something very contemporary and uniquely malevolent about the machine gun, which scythed down men in no-man's land.

The Maxim-Vickers (and its international variants) is the device that caused so much of the slaughter. Its earliest forerunner was the American Gatling gun, designed in 1862, ironically to "show how futile war is". But, like the French Mitrailleuse, as used in the Franco-Prussian War, it still relied on a handle being cranked to rotate the barrels. The Maxim, by contrast, was the first true automatic-firing machine gun. Its inventor, the American Hiram Maxim, claimed he was told: "Hell, if you want to make a pile of money, invent something that will help the Europeans to cut each other's throats more efficiently." The Maxim used the recoil power of the fired bullet to reload a new bullet into the breech: as long as the trigger was pressed, the gun kept firing. He demonstrated his patented mechanism in 1884, and from then on the Maxim – and later its British version, the Vickers – was used by the British Army. The patent was eventually exported to many other European countries, including Germany for its efficient MG08, which killed so many Allied soldiers.

The machine gun emerged as the most infamous weapon of the war. Machine guns were directly aimed by men who consciously pulled the triggers, whereas artillery seemed more remote and its casualties more random. The Vickers .303-inch (7.7mm) Machine Gun became the British Army's standard automatic weapon in November 1912. It was a direct adaptation of the Maxim. Vickers literally turned Maxim's design upside down, making it more compact, efficient and lighter. One of its most distinctive changes was the replacement of Maxim's original brass jacket with the lighter corrugated steel jacket, seen here. This contained water to keep the barrel cool during firing. As the water gradually heated, it was siphoned off as steam and condensed into a reservoir to be reused. The standard .303-inch cartridges were fed into the gun on cloth belts of 250. Technically, the Vickers could fire between 450 and 600 rounds per minute, but gunners rarely fired continuously in that way; more commonly they worked in shorter bursts. As the war progressed, machine gun fire became increasingly sophisticated, with guns working in batteries for increased firepower, and unseen, distant targets attacked by firing against specific map references. Such was the success of the Vickers gun that it remained in use by the British Army little changed until 1968, when its retirement from active service was marked by a feature on the front page of the *Times*.

"THE BLUE CROWD OF FRENCH
SOLDIERS SLID ABOVE THE GRASS ...
'TO THE SLAUGHTERHOUSE!' CRIED
LA POULE. RIGHT ON THE HORIZON,
AT THE POINT WHERE THE SKY MERGES
INTO THE LAND, MACHINE GUNS
BEGAN TO SIZZLE AND SPIT, LIKE OIL
IN A FRYING PAN."

Jean Giono, 100th Regiment of Infantry

Before the war, however, the British were reluctant to invest heavily in the new weapon for two reasons: the usual Treasury parsimony; plus the fact that for an infantry battalion that depended on what it could carry on foot, ammunition supply for a weapon that could fire 600 rounds a minute was always going to be a problem. (In the event, the Maxims required carts to carry the weapons and ammunition.) The German army was equally reluctant to press heavy weapons upon its heavily laden infantrymen. The result was that by 1914 British infantry battalions, in common with the other armies, were equipped with a machine gun section of just two guns. In February 1915 this was increased to four, based on the experiences of the previous autumn, but the problem was one of supply. Vickers struggled to manufacture 200 Maxims per week. As a result, in July 1915 the BEF was still over 200 guns short of the full complement.

After the Battle of Loos in September 1915 (*see* Chapter 40), no-one on the Western Front had any doubt about the importance of the machine gun. Assault troops dreaded it; defenders relied on it. Private Harry Fellowes summed it up in his description of what happened to the 12th Battalion, Northumberland Fusiliers, as it attacked across open ground: "All the time we were running across the Germans never fired a shot and then it seemed as if somebody had given an order and they all opened out with machine guns. Men were just mown down. It was slaughter, just suicide, all hell let loose."

The supply situation eased by the autumn of 1915 as the new Lewis gun became available. This was also the invention of an American, Colonel Isaac Lewis, but, having failed to sell it to his own army in 1911, he retired and took it to Belgium, where he intended it to be manufactured under licence. The German forces who came up against it dubbed it "the Belgian rattlesnake". It was a much lighter (12kg) gun than the heavy, water-cooled Vickers. It was also a genuinely man-portable weapon with a 47-round pan magazine. With its adjustable sights and bipod support, the air-cooled Lewis was accurate to 600 yards.

In Britain, BSA bought a licence for it and began volume production after the outbreak of war, and it was formally adopted as the standard-issue British Army light machine gun at the end of 1915. At first it was regarded with deep suspicion by the infantry and the General Staff, who were reluctant to give up the greater firepower of the Vickers. However, by the end of 1915 every British battalion on the Western Front had four Lewis guns.

With the increase in manufacture, by 1917 every infantry section had its own Lewis gun team and each battalion was equipped with 36 Lewis guns. The tactical impact was immense. The Lewis gave every infantry platoon the ability to fight using fire and movement. It was considered the best and most reliable light machine gun of its day, also seeing service with the Royal Flying Corps as an observer's weapon and for forward firing over (or through) aircraft propeller blades, as well as in tanks and armoured cars.

The arrival of the Lewis gun allowed the War Office to withdraw the heavy tripod-mounted Vickers guns from individual infantry battalions and concentrate them instead in a new specialist support unit: the Machine Gun Corps. It provided every infantry brigade with a Vickers machine gun company, and by 1918 these had been combined into Divisional Machine Gun Battalions. (As well as doling out death the Corps suffered, too: of the 170,500 officers and men who served in it, more than 62,000 were killed, wounded or missing.)

After the bludgeon of artillery bombardments, the machine gun was the most feared weapon. Once attacking troops had "hopped the bags" and advanced over the top, they often presented little more than targets for enemy machine guns, and the greater the distance to the enemy's trenches the more vulnerable they were. Where the defenders could man their parapets in time, the attackers were slaughtered. In the rare places where the attackers won their race across no-man's land, the roles were reversed. But usually the machine gunner had already won. Just a single well-placed gun could cut down an attacking infantry unit with ease. Nowhere was this demonstrated with more devastating effect than on the Somme on 1 July 1916. Ernie Deighton of the 8th Battalion, King's Own Yorkshire Light Infantry, was just one of those who suffered their effects:

> As soon as (our lads) started across the machine guns opened up ... The bullets were flying across all over the place. I were in the first row and the first one I saw was my chum Clem. I don't think we'd gone twenty yards when he got hit straight through the breast. Machine gun bullet. He went down. I went down. We got it in the same burst.

However, the machine gun proved increasingly important in attack as well as defence, as armies acquired greater tactical sophistication. By 1917 the British Machine Gun Corps was using its Vickers as artillery. For example, at the Battle of Messines in June 1917, machine gunners were employing massed creeping barrages, with fire falling ahead of the artillery barrage to catch enemy troops moving to the rear and to prevent reinforcements coming forward.

In 1918, the newly arrived American Expeditionary Force equipped itself with an array of home-produced .30-inch Vickers (made under licence, by Colt) and European weapons. It ran into problems with a mis-manufactured batch of the very widely used French Chauchat automatic rifles, but by the autumn it had the excellently designed Browning's automatic rifle, whose propellant gases recocked and fired the gun. In 1918, the Germans and Italians also produced the world's first sub-machine guns, with the Germans employing theirs, the MP18, in some of the final defensive fighting.

The war demonstrated the machine gun's grim potency. In 1939–45, no belligerent would go to war without heavy, medium, light and sub-machine guns in its armoury.

A Lewis light machine gun in action, in a British trench near Ovillers, on the Somme. The Lewis was operable by one man, and portable enough to be carried into the attack. Once British forces had sufficient numbers of them, in 1917, they contributed to the opening up of the battlefield. No longer was the machine gun just identified with fixed, defensive positions.

37

A MESSAGE STREAMER
THE EARLY AIR WAR

1914 TO 1915

Use of the skies was nothing new to battlefield warfare in 1914. The French had occasionally employed air observation balloons during the Napoleonic era, and both the Union and Confederate armies used balloons during the American Civil War. Some nations before 1914 even attempted to drop bombs from balloons: it was banned by the 1899 Hague Convention, but military reality was already outstripping diplomatic ideals. In 1914–18, the air became integral to the conduct of war as never before.

While the public's imagination, then and now, came to be captured by the stories and images of gladiatorial fighter aces and their dogfights, it was the more mundane but crucial work of reconnaissance and observation that provided the real *raison d'être* for the first air war. It began with fragile constructions of canvas, wood and wire, such as the Maurice Farman Longhorn, which accompanied the BEF in August 1914. With its underpowered, unreliable engine and large wings it could wobble through the sky at just over 50 miles per hour on a calm day carrying a pilot-observer. But this apparently flimsy aircraft and its companions would revolutionize warfare.

Throughout the war, aircraft provided armies with their eyes in the sky. In the opening days, pilots collected and sent back vital intelligence as troops moved across Belgium and northern France. They included Euan Rabagliati, a newly qualified pilot with the Royal Flying Corps. Observing beyond Mons just before hostilities began, he was astonished by what was revealed below him: "Instead of seeing a few odd German troops I saw the whole area covered with hordes of field grey uniforms – advancing infantry, cavalry, transport and guns. In fact it looked as though the place was alive with the Germans." But to pass on this information, Rabagliati had to land. He was then driven direct to GHQ and reported to Sir John French in person. For the first few months of the war, RFC aircraft were not fitted with wireless radio sets. Even when they were, communications remained unreliable, so the only alternative while still in the air was to drop messages, either in weighted bags or on coloured streamers. This blue, yellow and red cloth streamer landed near 3rd Division headquarters during the Battle of the Marne in 1914. It was retrieved by the division's senior staff officer, Lieutenant Colonel (later Major General Sir) Frederick Maurice, who donated it to the Imperial War Museum in 1933, of which he was then a Trustee.

After the Wright brothers' first successful manned flight in 1903, aircraft development was fast, and some soon saw its military potential. In September 1910, a young captain called Bertram Dickson took off in a private Bristol Boxkite to locate the "Blue Force" during the annual British Army manoeuvres on Salisbury Plain. Once he had found them, he landed and reported back to "Red Force" HQ by telephone. The next day another aviator, actor Robert Loraine, successfully transmitted a Morse Code signal through a primitive on-board wireless. In 1911, Dickson submitted a paper to Britain's Committee of Imperial Defence, in which he predicted:

> In case of a European war, between two countries, both sides would be equipped with large corps of aeroplanes, each trying to obtain information on the other ... the efforts which each would exert in order to hinder or prevent the enemy from obtaining information ... would lead to the inevitable result of a war in the air, for the supremacy of the air, by armed aeroplanes against each other. This fight for the supremacy of the air in future wars will be of the greatest importance ... .

His prescient submission informed the Committee's recommendation to form a Royal Flying Corps for the army in 1912, while the Royal Navy set up its own Air Service. By 1914 Britain had nearly 100 military aeroplanes and, on 13 August, despatched 4 squadrons to France, when 60 machines flew from Dover to Boulogne.

So it came as no surprise when the armies finally clashed in August 1914 that the aeroplane was the obvious reconnaissance tool to supplement the cavalry's traditional role. The *Official History of the War in the Air* is unequivocal: "The single use in war for which the machines of the Military Wing of the RFC were designed and the men trained ... was reconnaissance." It was near Mons on 22 August 1914 that Captain Charlton and Lieutenant Wadham observed the Germans outflanking and outnumbering the BEF as it advanced into Belgium. Doubtful at first, over the following days GHQ became convinced, and aerial reconnaissance played an important part in allowing the BEF to retreat from Mons in line with the French, and enabling it to fight another day.

And it was French aerial reconnaissance that identified the move that finally derailed the Germans' Schlieffen plan. Aircraft designer Louis Breguet observed General von Kluck's First Army swinging down towards the east of Paris. Joseph Gallieni, the military governor of Paris – and a great pre-war advocate of aviation – seized his chance, ordering the newly formed French Sixth Army to advance due east and drive into the Germans' exposed flank. With the BEF and the French advancing from the south, the resulting rebuff of the Germans that was the "Miracle of the Marne" owed a great deal to the "eyes in the sky".

The Eastern Front was no different. There, in late August 1914, it was German aerial reconnaissance that confirmed intelligence reports of the two invading Russian armies failing to coordinate, and of a huge gap opening between them. The intelligence enabled the Germans to surround and annihilate the Russians at the battles of Tannenberg and later at the Masurian Lakes (*see* Chapter 18).

Once the war had settled into static lines of defensive trenches, aerial reconnaissance became an essential tool for seeing what was happening on what the Duke of Wellington had described as "the other side of the hill". Unarmed aeroplanes flew over enemy lines, reporting the location of gun batteries, supply dumps, the movement of troops and the subsequent location of enemy soldiers.

The efficacy of aerial reconnaissance depended on the ability not only to see, but also to report what was observed in an accurate and timely fashion. But one of the greatest difficulties – as in all areas of command and control in the First World War – was communications. In the very early days, air-to-ground communication had to be a matter of dropping notes (e.g. with bags or streamers), which was not always reliable. Waiting until a flight landed so the pilot could report in person wasted valuable time. By December 1914 developments in Morse wireless transmitters enabled the first reliable sets to be installed in British aeroplanes, finally allowing them to communicate directly to artillery batteries so they could adjust their fire.

Soon, aircraft roles expanded. Cameras were routinely installed to photograph enemy lines (*see* Chapter 74). And aerial reconnaissance spawned the attempt, by both sides, to put out the other's "eyes in the sky". Airmen who, early on, had been exchanging cheery waves with the other side's flyers were now quick to fire at enemy aeroplanes with rifles and pistols. In December 1914, French aviation pioneer Roland Garros noted development work on metal deflector wedges attached to propeller

"THE VICTOR IN THAT AERIAL STRUGGLE WILL TOWER WITH PITILESS WATCHFUL EYES OVER HIS ADVERSARY, WILL CONCENTRATE HIS GUNS AND ALL HIS STRENGTH UNOBSERVED ... EVERYWHERE THE VICTOR WILL SOAR."

H.G. Wells, Anticipations of the Reaction of Mechanical and Scientific Progress upon Human Life and Thought, *1901*

blades, and asked for them to be attached to his Morane-Saulnier aircraft. With this crude installation, on 1 April 1915, he achieved the first ever shooting-down of an aircraft by a machine gun that fired directly through the propeller. On 15 and 18 April 1915, he shot down two more German aircraft. However, on his last sortie he crash-landed and was captured by the Germans who examined the wreck of his plane with some interest.

They promptly devised their own much more efficient system, using an interrupter mechanism that only allowed the machine gun to fire when no propeller blade was in front of it. The Dutch aircraft designer Anthony Fokker quickly fitted this to his new E1 monoplane. With its 7-cylinder, 99-horsepower rotary engine, its single MG14 machine gun and top speed of 80 miles per hour, the Fokker Eindecker went on to become the world's first fighter plane. It was fast, light and well armed, and in the hands of a trained pilot a deadly threat to the slow, awkward two-seaters, already weighed down with their heavy wireless equipment. By the autumn of 1915 the Eindecker had shot down hundreds of Allied aircraft and become the scourge of the skies.

The battle for control of the air had begun, and life for the airmen was becoming highly hazardous.

An almost unimaginably fragile-looking Maurice Farman Longhorn S.7, a two-seater reconnaissance plane, which was also used for training. It was with aircraft like these that the BEF first attempted to monitor the battlefield from the air. Such aircraft were rapidly superseded by more sophisticated machines in the fast-paced innovations of 1914–18.

38

A TRENCH SHOVEL
WAR IN THE TRENCHES

1914 TO 1918

In some ways, trenches should have come as no surprise to the men of 1914. "Digging in" to avoid enemy fire has always been a natural reaction in warfare. For centuries, those besieging fixed positions have sought to push themselves towards enemy strongholds under cover, while building up for a final assault. The somewhat different *battlefield* use of trenches emerged during the American Civil War. In 1863, General Ulysses Grant wrote to a friend in words that could almost come from 1915: "We have our trenches pulled up so close to the enemy that we can throw hand grenades over into their forts. The enemy do not dare show their heads above the parapet at any time, so close and so watchful are our sharpshooters." At Sebastopol during the Crimean War, facing Paris in the Franco-Prussian War and confronting entrenched Boers across the South African veldt – trench warfare taught sharp lessons to all involved.

The Russo-Japanese War (1904–05) witnessed scenes that would, a decade later, become tragically familiar. Over several months, dug-in Russians armed with rapid rifle and machine gun fire repelled massed Japanese bayonet charges. Combined with modern firepower, trenches underlined the growing dominance of defensive capability over attack. The First World War cemented that reality in a way that was unparalleled in duration, and in scale, as trenches sprouted across France and Belgium, the Austro-Italian border, Gallipoli and beyond.

In the dying minutes of 25 April 1915, the commanders of the ANZAC landing at Gallipoli sent a note to General Sir Ian Hamilton asking if they should re-embark their troops after the setbacks of the day. Hamilton knew this was impossible and immediately signalled his response, concluding: "You have got through the difficult business, now you have only to dig, dig, dig until you are safe." It was testament to the fact that throughout the war, in so many theatres, the spade was the soldier's salvation, wherever men went to ground to seek protection from bullets and shellfire. British soldiers carried a small entrenching tool, but this was only for digging shallow scrapes and shelters. For more extensive work – including trenches, dugouts and gun emplacements – a more suitable tool was required. The professional "sappers" of the Royal Engineers, who were trained to dig, used the large, broad-bladed "Shovel, R.E". For wider use there was the "Shovel, G.S." (i.e. General Service), lighter in weight and with a smaller blade. Anyone could use it. This one was found more than 80 years after the war in an excavated Flanders dugout. The thumbs of successive diggers have buffed it smooth, each man no doubt hoping that if he dug, dug, dug he would be safe.

> "ENTRENCHMENTS ARE ONLY TO BE USED WHEN, OWING TO FURTHER ADVANCE BEING IMPOSSIBLE, THE EFFORTS OF THE ATTACKING FORCES MUST BE LIMITED TEMPORARILY TO HOLDING GROUND ALREADY WON."

Infantry Training 1914, *a British War Office manual*

Despite the existence of precedents, the BEF's first commander-in-chief, Sir John French, claimed (surprisingly) in 1919 that "No previous campaign, no conclusion I had been able to draw from the campaigns in which I had taken part, or from a close study of the new conditions in which the war of today is waged, had led me to anticipate a war of positions." But that reality began to unfold as early as 13 September 1914 when trench systems were built flanking Rheims, and within days had also begun to sprout along the Aisne. By mid-November the line was complete. From Switzerland to the North Sea a continuous 400-mile line of trenches effectively created the biggest siege in history. Even the optimistic Foch grumbled that "they have sent me here to manoeuvre, but things are not going too brightly. This eternal stretching out in a line is beginning to get on my nerves."

At first little more than a line of linked defensive ditches, the trench systems that became the Western Front grew in scale and complexity into sophisticated networks as the static war wore on. Communication trenches joined the front and support lines, and a third reserve line of trenches further back acted as a stop line. Trenches were becoming homes to the troops, with deep, secure, well-furnished dugouts, revetting to hold the trench walls back and duckboards to walk on.

The British and French, determined to evict the invaders, tended to build more temporary trench systems than the Germans, who, having invariably chosen to occupy better-sited positions, wanted to consolidate their territorial gains – as springboards for further advances, or as "facts on the ground" to trade in any future peace negotiations. For the Allies, the idea that their own trenches might be permanent was unacceptable – the whole point was to use them to launch attacks and evict the Boche. Consequently, Allied trenches were rarely the deep, concrete-reinforced, relatively comfortable affairs that came to characterize the German lines. Nonetheless, over three years many BEF trenches did take on a permanent air. Thick belts of barbed wire kept any attackers outside grenade-throwing range, and fields of fire were laid out around fortified strongpoints. A daily rhythm of trench life soon became established. Men slept or acted as sentry by day; by night working parties repaired damaged trenches, laid new wire, brought up stores and rations, and twice a day at dawn and dusk "stood to" to repel any attack.

It could also be a confusing, mole-like world below the level of the earth, as Lieutenant Tom Allen, of the Irish Guards, explained in 1915: "For one thing it is not straight for more than four yards (it is 'traversed' to prevent enfilade and shell fire having much effect.) Then there are all sorts of odd turnoffs ... In these mazes ... it is very easy to get lost." Such a maze could be bewildering at night, and getting lost in it was indeed a common experience. So every trench was given a name, which often recalled the highways and byways of a lost civilian life: "Hyde Park Corner", "Northumberland Avenue", "Red Dragon Alley" or "Sauchiehall Street".

Few but the bravest, or most foolish, looked directly out over the parapet at no-man's land. This was more safely done by means of a specialist trench periscope. It revealed what many found baffling: a weirdly empty battlefield, with only shell holes, shattered tree stumps and rusty barbed wire to be seen, and occasional dirty bundles of rags lying on the ground to mark the bodies of men killed in the last attack or fighting patrol. The nature of the terrain varied, of course, down the lines, as the often soggy clay of Flanders gave way to the chalky ground of the Somme. The enemy's lines appeared like a horizontal scar, in wide open country sometimes hundreds of yards away, but in more intense and closer parts of the line within shouting distance.

Trenches varied. In the flooded fields around the River Yser on the Belgian coast they were formed by banks (*levees*) of sandbags piled high. In the rocky Vosges, far to the south, they were sometimes stone and timber fortified positions ("sangars") carved halfway up a mountainside; but usually they were all to a standard pattern: a 7-foot-deep ditch, with a ledge forming a "fire step" cut into the side that faced the enemy, known as the parapet. The rear wall (or "*parados*") was topped with a lip of sandbags also, to protect troops against explosions behind the trench. Into the parapet side, safe from direct enemy fire, would be the dugouts (and the more improvised "funk holes" or scrapes for temporary rest, or sheltering from rain), weapon racks, ammunition pits and latrines.

Whatever their similarities or differences, trenches – with all their hazards and routines, privations and camaraderie, boredoms and lethal excitements – became the way of life for millions of men, across France and Belgium, Italy and Austria, in Germany and Russia, and in Greece and across the Ottoman Empire. In 1897, an obscure Polish banker, Ivan Bloch, had written a statistical analysis entitled *Modern Weapons and Modern War*, in which he said that "everybody will be entrenched in the next war. It will be a great war of entrenchment," which would lead to "increased slaughter on so terrible a scale as to render it impossible to get troops to push the battle to a decisive issue". In such a war, he opined, the spade would be as important as the rifle.

He was right.

39

A PETRIFIED GLOVE
GAS WARFARE & THE SECOND BATTLE OF YPRES

APRIL TO MAY 1915

In the First World War the feared artillery and devastating machine guns may have caused more casualties, but for many soldiers the most detested weapon was – gas. Anthony R. Hossack, of the Queen Victoria's Rifles, gave a graphic description of the first use of poison gas on the Western Front, northeast of Ypres on the late afternoon of 22 April 1915: "More curious than anything was a low cloud of yellow grey smoke or vapour ... What was it? ... For in the northerly breeze there came a pungent nauseating smell that tickled the throat and made the eyes smart ... while over the fields streamed mobs of infantry ... away went their rifles, equipment even their tunics that they might run the faster. One man came stumbling through our lines ... The Zouave was frothing at the mouth, his eyes started from their sockets and he fell writhing at the officer's feet."

The Germans had unleashed 168 tons of highly poisonous chlorine gas on a favourable wind against the northern part of the Ypres Salient. The French troops here – the 45th Algerian Division and 87th Territorial Division from Brittany – broke and fled back towards Ypres, leaving a 3-mile gap in the line, with at least 6,000 casualties.

The reputation of gas as one of the most insidious and malevolent weapons of the First World War endures to this day. It is deeply embedded in the war's cultural legacy through works like John Singer Sargent's painting *Gassed* and Wilfred Owen's poem "Dulce et Decorum Est". At first, gas was released from cylinders and hard to control, because it depended on wind direction. But once it could be placed on specific targets by firing special artillery shells, it became much more dangerous. With the introduction of mustard gas in July 1917, gas warfare seemed to plumb new depths of inhumanity. Mustard gas was a liquid that vapourized on contact with air, but in wet and cold conditions it could remain viscous. Its effects were often delayed, too. In his diary, Sydney Fuller of the Suffolk Regiment noted: "This new gas was invisible and smelt like mustard, rotten oranges etc. The only effect, at first, was to cause much sneezing, but 5 to 10 hours afterwards the victim's eyelids swelled, the eyes became very inflamed, blindness followed and great pain for about 10 days." The damage to human bodies was reflected in what happened to this British officer's glove. In 1948, it was sent to the Imperial War Museum with the explanation that, although once full-sized, it had "shrunk to the size of a child's hand" and become "quite solid to the touch" through exposure to gas during the war. Petrified and wizened, the glove chillingly shows how gas corrupted and deformed everything it touched.

"IF YOU COULD HEAR, AT EVERY JOLT, THE BLOOD
COME GARGLING FROM THE FROTH-CORRUPTED LUNGS,
OBSCENE AS CANCER, BITTER AS THE CUD
OF VILE, INCURABLE SORES ON INNOCENT TONGUES ..."

Wilfred Owen, from "Dulce et Decorum Est", 1917–18

In 1899, the Hague Convention's Gas Declaration contained an agreement "to abstain from the use of projectiles the sole object of which is the diffusion of asphyxiating or deleterious gases". Twenty-seven states signed up. However, the language of this declaration was so limited that it had little, if any, effect during the First World War. The French fired tear gas grenades, of the type used by their police, as early as August 1914, arguing (correctly) that tear gas was not "asphyxiating or deleterious". The Germans used the same argument at Neuve Chapelle in October 1914, when firing a chemical irritant that caused sneezing attacks inside specially adapted shrapnel shells.

Neither case represented a true gas attack. However, German chemists were studying something more potent. By the end of March they had produced cylinders for frontline use that projected chlorine across no-man's land. French and British intelligence picked up clear indicators that – quite literally – something was in the wind: captured Germans were carrying anti-gas masks, prisoner reports talked openly about "cylinders of poison gas" and the Germans muddied the water with a communiqué on 17 April accusing the British of "using asphyxiating gas". Despite this, General Smith-Dorrien, commanding the British Second Army in the Ypres sector, remained unconvinced. Although he issued a warning, he thought that the stories were just scaremongering and propaganda. Once the attack had materialized, however, the British sprang into action with swift remedial measures. By 15 May all soldiers were issued with pads of cotton waste soaked in sodium hyposulphate and carbonate of soda, and by 6 July the first gas masks ("smoke helmets") were issued.

The chlorine released on 22 April 1915 became, though, just the first phase of a much longer offensive, because the Germans failed to take full advantage of their initial success. For 33 days, this Second Battle of Ypres witnessed five determined attacks in a belated attempt to drive the Allied line back behind the city. By the battle's close, over 59,000 British, 10,000 French and 35,000 Germans were casualties. By any rational military appreciation of the situation, the tiny salient east of Ypres was indefensible. However, for political and military reasons, the Allies were determined to hold what they could of it.

The Germans were as surprised as the Allies at the success of the gas that day; the German infantry, not wishing to get gassed themselves, were understandably wary of following up in the dusk and failed to exploit the yawning hole in the Allied lines. By 23 April their advance was stopped, thanks mainly to the Canadian Division, who, with high casualties, took ground to their left to fill the gap, including ferocious fighting in the oak plantation dubbed "Kitchener's Wood".

But on 24 April the Canadians surrounding the village of St Julien were themselves attacked with gas. They improvised gas masks by urinating on or wetting socks and handkerchiefs, to help dissolve the acidic chlorides of the gas. Attempted counterattacks on 26 and 27 April by the newly arrived Indian Army's Lahore Division to retake ground lost four days earlier were routed as the Germans released more gas and machine gunned the advancing lines of men. French efforts to the north and west of the German bulge were uncoordinated and sparse. The Germans then switched their attack to the Canadians' opposite flank and, behind a crushing barrage, bit off another chunk of the salient as far as Gravenstafel. In four days of fighting the Canadians lost 200 officers and 5,000 men.

And all the time the superior German artillery, with seemingly endless supplies of shells, could fire into packed and exposed trenches in the salient from the north,

Men of the 2nd Battalion, Argyll and Sutherland Highlanders, at Bois-Grenier, just south of the Ypres Salient (May 1915). They wear improvised gas protection: goggles and cotton-waste "respirators" soaked in a solution, perhaps sodium hyposulphate. Soldiers carried bottles of the solution to resoak the cotton as necessary.

the east and the south. On the extreme flanks it was even possible to be shelled from behind. Casualties mounted and the British commanders began to consider ways of reducing the tactical trap in which their soldiers now found themselves. The obvious way was to withdraw west in order to straighten and shorten the confused British line. On 27 April, Smith-Dorrien wrote a long letter to GHQ proposing a 2.5-mile withdrawal to a position closer to Ypres. The proposal incensed Sir John French, already no admirer of Smith-Dorrien; French got his chief of staff to sack him. Having rid himself of his most successful general, French then promptly implemented all Smith-Dorrien's proposals by 4 May. Heavy fighting continued around Ypres, with repeated use of gas attacks throughout May, and finally fizzled out on 25 May with the BEF now firmly established along the new "GHQ line" just a mile to the east of Ypres.

The practice of gas warfare, though, did not fizzle out. It was just beginning. The British unsuccessfully tried it, attempting to break through with chlorine gas at Loos on 25 September 1915 (*see* Chapter 40). Germany replied with Phosgene (carbonyl dichloride) in December 1915: it killed by damaging the lungs and preventing oxygen being absorbed. By 1916 both sides were regularly employing gas-filled shells, which were not dependent on wind direction, to make the soldiers' – and horses' – lives more miserable. The arrival of mustard gas (dichlorethyl sulphide) in July 1917 made things worse still. It attacked moist tissue, blistered exposed skin and contaminated the ground. Although it was fatal to proportionally few men (1.2 per cent) it made life extremely difficult for troops.

Gas made a major contribution to the Germans' final great offensive and breakthrough on 21 March 1918, where the BEF's rear areas, HQs and gun lines were drenched with a mixture of gas and High Explosive shells, disrupting communications, preventing reinforcements moving up and forcing even staff officers miles back to work in gas masks. And therein lies the real contribution of gas to the First World War. It killed relatively few, and its wounds usually healed; even mustard gas blindness, familiar from the photographs of lines of soldiers with bandages over their eyes, proved temporary (and the wet bandages frequently seen in images were actually to reduce the pain). But gas –disruptive, debilitating, agonizing, exhausting – sapped the resolve of even the most battle-hardened soldier.

40

CONWAY JACKSON'S PRAYER BOOK
THE BATTLE OF LOOS

25 SEPTEMBER TO 14 OCTOBER 1915

The Battle of Loos, fought in autumn 1915, was the first large-scale offensive in which the British attempted to overcome the problems of trench warfare. But it was fought on the wrong ground, to a weak operational plan, and was marked on the British side by some suicidal tactics, bad staff work, poor communications, weak artillery support and uncoordinated control. It degenerated into a hopeless muddle, at the cost of 61,700 casualties, of whom at least 8,000 died.

There was, though, no reason in the autumn of 1915 to suppose that a great breakthrough was *impossible*. Britain's first independent operation at Neuve Chapelle on 10 March had made – at first – a clear breach in the German lines. Following a hurricane bombardment of only 35 minutes (because of the shortage of shells), British and Indian troops had swept the surprised first-line German defenders away. The British then lost the initiative and were unable to exploit their brief success as German reserves rushed to seal the breach. But, despite 12,000 casualties, Neuve Chapelle proved that at least making a breach was *possible*. It was exploiting it that was the issue. Unfortunately, two problems then arose: the French under Joffre insisted on a major attack from the BEF, which was now a mixture of half-trained volunteers and the survivors of the old Regular army, and an unsuitable battlefield, the slag heaps of Loos.

> Two days before the Battle of Loos, Conway Jackson of the 6th Battalion, King's Own Scottish Borderers, wrote to his mother. It was to be his last letter. "How many things I have to thank you and Daddy for. I know I have always been an anxiety to you both, as I am afraid I am very headstrong." He had been reading the *Daily Light* prayer book his mother gave him and drew strength from the text for 26 September: "If we be dead with Christ, we believe that we shall also live with him." On 25 September 1915, Jackson attacked northwest of the Hohenzollern Redoubt, but his battalion suffered over 350 casualties. Later, the eyes of a German officer moving among the dead "were attracted by the peaceful face of a young officer, the features of which seemed to be transfigured in death. My servant handed me a little book, which lied beside of [*sic*] his body. I took it in my possession, intending to send it to his mother after the war." In June 1919, Captain E. Wynne Jones was billeted in Cologne with the Army of Occupation. He received a request, from a relative of his landlord, to help with returning a prayer book found by her brother on the body of a young British officer in 1915. Through the War Office, Captain Jones sent Conway's *Daily Light* back to Mrs Jackson, adding: "I feel sure you will derive comfort in days to come from this positive proof that your loving son died as you had taught him to live."

"MY NEW FRONT AT LOOS IS AS FLAT AS THE PALM OF MY HAND ... IT WILL COST US DEARLY AND WE SHALL NOT GET VERY FAR"

General Sir Henry Rawlinson, commanding IV Corps, to Joffre

In May 1915, the Allies launched coordinated attacks in Artois, north of Arras. While the British threw themselves at Aubers Ridge, the French attacked – and took (despite heavy casualties) – the dominating positions of Notre Dame de Lorette and nearby Vimy Ridge. However, the French could not communicate with their victorious infantry and their reserves were too far away. Unable to benefit from up-to-date reports, a pre-planned French artillery barrage hit the surviving *poilus* on the summit with murderous accuracy. Isolated, and facing determined German counterattacks, the survivors began to drift back. But they had again shown that an assault could break the enemy lines.

Joffre therefore planned a great offensive for the autumn. As early as 4 June he asked the British to take over another 20 miles of front south of the La Bassée canal, stretching towards Lens and Loos, and to join him in a renewed attack in Artois. General Haig, whose First Army would carry out the operation, objected, pointing out that the ground was totally unsuitable for a large attack. However, Lord Kitchener insisted the BEF join in, pointing out that the British had to pull their weight.

Thus, at dawn on 25 September, the largest Allied offensive of the war so far opened, with 6 British divisions attacking on a 20-mile front among the coal mines, pit villages and slag heaps around Loos (under cover of gas to compensate for the shell shortage). Simultaneously, 16 French divisions assaulted the Vimy-Arras sector while far to their south 27 French divisions launched a second, major attack in the Champagne, also using gas. In every case the Germans were waiting. At Loos the gas turned out be a two-edged weapon. The wind was fluky and much of the chlorine blew back onto some of the assaulting troops, causing chaos and casualties. Bombardier J.W. Palmer noted afterwards: "The field of battle presented a shambles. There appeared to be bodies everywhere ... By the afternoon the faces of our lads who lay in the open changed colour and presented a gruesome spectacle. Their faces and hands gradually assumed a blue and green colour and the buttons and metal fittings of their uniforms were all discoloured ... ."

Nevertheless, some attacking divisions broke through, albeit with heavy casualties, and took several strongpoints. By mid-morning one Scottish division (the 15th) had captured Loos, while another (the 9th) was in the Hohenzollern Redoubt. The German defenders fled back to their second line. For a brief moment success seemed possible.

Unfortunately, there were no British reserves on hand to keep up the momentum. The 21st and 24th divisions had been kept back, with the intention they follow up hard and exploit any breach. However, these two new, inexperienced divisions were firmly under the thumb of Commander-in-Chief Sir John French and GHQ, and based nearly 20 miles back. Remembering the lessons of Neuve Chapelle, Haig had protested. In a decision that eventually cost French his job, they were only released from GHQ control late in the morning of 25 September. It was too late. With roads jammed, the divisions' soldiers struggled forward in pouring rain. Staff officers were unfamiliar with the ground, many orders were contradictory, units got lost and communication trenches were flooded and packed with men. By the time the reserves arrived tired, wet, cold and hungry, and in the dark, there was no possibility of any attack before dawn the next day. Their supposed exploitation of a moment of success thus came more than 20 hours late. On the 26th, they ended up making a massed daylight charge across the open grassy terrain and presented easy targets for the waiting German machine gunners.

The battle now swung the other way. When the final reserve, the Guards Division, joined the attack it ran into fierce German counterattacks and was forced to dig in. By the 27 September it was the British who were now desperately defending, falling back and clinging onto their minimal, costly, gains. The battle degenerated into a struggle to hold on to the thinly held forward British positions across the battlefield. The survivors of the units that had attacked on the 25th were exhausted and the reserves broken up to shore up the defence. The strongpoints previously won – Fosse 8, the Quarries, Hill 70 and the Hohenzollern Redoubt – were all lost.

Sir John French ordered a fresh assault for 13 October. It would be led by the 46th Division, only just arrived from Ypres on the morning of the attack. The 46th had no intelligence about the ground or the enemy, no coordinated artillery support and faced uncut wire and waiting German machine guns. The divisional commander was stopped from carrying out his own plan for the attack and ordered to charge the German lines. For no gains, the division lost more than 3,750 officers and men in less than ten minutes.

Among the casualties, the British lost 2,000 officers at Loos, a further drain of experienced men, including surviving remnants of the old Regular army and Reservists and Territorials who had been out since the spring. On 31 October, the French offensive in Champagne ended, having traded almost 150,000 casualties for barely any gains. The Allied offensives had all failed. As the year's campaigning season drew to its close, the awful sense began to grip commanders and troops alike on the Western Front that there was no war-winning formula. By the end of 1915 spirits remained surprisingly high – but operational bafflement was pervasive. Grinding down the enemy seemed the only option.

Ironically, the experiences at Neuve Chapelle and Vimy had demonstrated very clearly a tactical solution: surprise, short bombardments and infiltration. But, as the Somme and Verdun would prove next year, no-one was yet heeding those lessons. Battles of attrition would supplant any idea of surprise and manoeuvre.

41

THE FULLERPHONE
COMMUNICATIONS IN THE WAR

1914 TO 1918

Good communications have always been vital in war. As the Second World War US General Omar Bradley put it, so succinctly, "Congress makes a man a general, but communications make him a commander." But in the trench warfare of 1914–18, generals invariably lost control of their units once battle was joined, because military communication reflected the technology of the time – and that technology was both primitive and vulnerable, its deficiencies highlighted by contrast with the deadly effectiveness of the latest artillery and machine guns.

Over centuries of warfare, flags and semaphore had replaced horns and trumpets. Two developments revolutionized communications, including military, in the late 19th century: the electric telegraph and the telephone. The former spurred the first ever professional Signals Corps, founded by the US Congress in 1863, during the Civil War. By 1908 the British Army had formed the Royal Engineers Signal Service, which provided communications such as field telephones, despatch riders on motorbikes and crude wireless sets. Field and trench telephones were common in 1914, but their use was limited, and their lines liable to be disrupted by enemy action.

One of the greatest challenges facing British Army communications during the early years of the war was in making them secure. Most field telephones and "buzzer" telegraphs used only a single wire, with the return circuit being achieved by connecting the device to the earth. As a result, British conversations with the frontline could be intercepted by specially designed German "tapping" devices, often installed in dugouts or tunnels. Many perplexed British units wondered how the Germans knew who they were, and exactly what they were planning. The answer was simple: they were using the earth in order to listen. In 1915, this problem was solved by a technically advanced, but relatively simple, invention. It became known as the "Fullerphone" after its designer, the Royal Engineer signals officer Captain A.C. Fuller. He devised a portable Morse telegraph that sent a Direct Current signal through a single wire, but incorporated what was in effect a primitive scrambler. Electrical chopping mechanisms and filters produced a sound in the headphones that was only audible if the devices and circuits at each end were synchronized. Although the signal still passed through the earth, it could no longer be intercepted and understood by the enemy, and it was therefore fully secure. At first, the device was used only for Morse signals, but in time voice communication also became possible. (The model shown here, made in 1917, includes both facilities.) By the end of the war the Fullerphone was the standard way to send secure messages up and down the line.

> **"WITH A BASKETFUL OF MOBILE GSM TELEPHONES YOU COULD HAVE BROKEN THROUGH ON THE WESTERN FRONT IN A WEEK!"**
>
> *Military historian Richard Holmes, CBE*

Wireless communication, meanwhile, was in its relative infancy. In 1896, Guglielmo Marconi had demonstrated his long-range wireless transmitter, and since then radio transmission had been widely used at sea – for instance, to report the *Titanic* disaster in 1912. Yet these primitive devices were large and needed electricity from a generator. Their lack of portability meant that in the war there were no battlefield radios, so the men on the ground depended on other means. But telephone wires could be cut to ribbons by bursting shells, and troops often reverted to older, sometimes ancient, methods: runners, semaphore lamps, flags, mirrors, signal flares and pigeons; even dogs were trained as couriers (*see* Chapter 45). The canine option was not always effective, as soldiers sometimes adopted the dogs as pets, and men would often volunteer to go as runners in their place!

The result of the serious flaws in communications was that once the assaulting troops were in the mayhem and chaos of an attack, they could be cut off from their HQs, from battalion upwards. Brigade, divisional and corps commanders were often totally in the dark about events on the frontline, as demonstrated on the first day of the Somme campaign in 1916, when in the evening General Haig still had no idea of the disaster that had befallen Rawlinson's Fourth Army. Until the last months of the war, generals were effectively trapped in their headquarters, many miles from the front.

Poor communications significantly helped to bring most of the offensives that failed to grief. At Neuve Chapelle in March 1915, having broken through the German first lines, the British waited hours for orders to come, during which time the defenders managed to seal the breach. At a tactical level, without adequate real-time communications with the all-important artillery, infantry could not call in fire support or redirect fire plans – as demonstrated by the French experience at Notre Dame de Lorette and Vimy Ridge in spring 1915. Here, the French infantry (who had stormed and seized the positions) were driven off by accurate *French* artillery fire, unwittingly launched at them because of a rigid prearranged fire plan: there was no means of telling the artillery to change targets.

Naval communications mirrored the problems on land. While an exuberant Churchill could grandstand and deploy individual ships on the far side of the world thanks to the Admiralty's new wireless technology, tactical communication at sea still relied mainly on flag hoists. In the days of Nelson, an admiral could order his fleet in good time; but by 1914, with 20,000-ton steel monsters powering along at 20 knots, filling the horizon and belching thick black coal smoke, flag hoists could be hard to see. Yet admirals remained strangely reluctant to entrust their orders to wireless transmission. They were wary of its novelty and potentially flawed security – "transmission is treason" summing up the view of many old sea dogs. But there was a more practical reason, too. Despite the drawbacks, when ships were close enough and conditions clear enough then flag-hoisting could still be much quicker in practice, and more readily understood, than the process of drafting a signal, tapping it out in Morse Code and decoding it for the captain on the receiving ship.

Lamp signals made life easier, though. Aldis lamps had been used by the Royal Navy since 1867 and were a practical form of ship-to-ship communication, being fairly secure unless the enemy was positioned between the two users. Their range exceeded that of flags, with the larger lights being effective even in daylight, and rates of communication were around 14 words per minute.

In the air, as befitted the new technology of aircraft, communications were surprisingly advanced. At first, reconnaissance pilots and observers in 1914–15 had

Telephonists of the Royal Garrison Artillery coordinate fire from a dugout close to the frontline at Langemarck, during the Third Battle of Ypres (August 1917). They are passing messages from Forward Observation Officers to the batteries. Keeping up with events was a challenge for all those involved in command and control.

to physically drop messages to impart their information between headquarters and forward positions (*see* Chapter 37). But since 1910 innovators had been experimenting with air-to-ground wireless transmissions. During 1914, the British Royal Flying Corps BE2c aircraft were equipped with a crude spark transmitter and this allowed them to communicate what they could see direct to the gun batteries. The difference between communications on the battlefield and in the air was that, as with a ship, an aeroplane had a built-in power supply – though of course it was much more limited as to the weight it could carry. By 1915 the British had airborne radio sets in production for artillery support and reconnaissance, and by 1918 "trailing" aerials extended under the aircraft to make air-to-ground communications a routine possibility.

Strategic-level wireless communications became ever more important as the war progressed. By 1918, radio – still a matter of Morse Code rather than voice transmissions – was routinely used to pass on orders and communications between capitals and higher headquarters. Indeed, when the Germans suspected that the British had tapped their telegraph cables, laid by submarine, they were forced to resort to radio for their diplomatic messages. It is significant that President Woodrow Wilson's conditions for the final Armistice were passed on to Berlin in 1918 not by diplomatic telegram, as would have happened in 1914, but by radio transmission.

By the time of the next war, radio communications between tanks on the ground and aircraft in the skies lay at the very heart of the German *Blitzkrieg* tactics that overwhelmed Europe. In 1914–18, this age of electrical wireless communications was just emerging. Perhaps, therefore, the last word should go to one of its much older cousins, the carrier pigeon, of which tens of thousands were used successfully in the war to carry messages. The British Carrier Pigeon Service was called upon especially when the telegraphs and telephones failed, its birds evading gas and shell bursts to get the message through. In October 1918, one pigeon in US service, Cher Ami, carried the coordinates of a group of stranded and endangered servicemen more than 20 miles back to HQ, enabling them to be rescued. Cher Ami was awarded the Croix de Guerre.

42

A DECEPTIVE TREE
CAMOUFLAGE IN THE WAR

1914 TO 1918

By tradition, military forces marched conspicuously into battle, behind brightly coloured flags, flaunting their presence. Armed forces only slowly came to learn the importance of camouflage when the range and accuracy of weapons improved.

Irregular troops tended to provide lessons. In revolutionary America, riflemen adopted the hunting colours of green and brown, in striking contrast to the bright scarlet of the British Army. In the late 19th century, regular armies also began to blend in with the environment, beginning when army units in British India began to dye their uniforms pale brown, or *khaki*, the Hindi for "earth-coloured".

Other nations followed. The United States adopted khaki by 1902 and in Germany the traditional Prussian blue uniforms were replaced with *Feldgrau* ("field grey") in 1910. And so in 1914 the BEF went off to war in khaki; the French, however, fought the devastating Battle of the Frontiers clad in their traditional blue coats and red trousers – and paid the price accordingly (*see* Chapter 12). By early 1915 they, too, had conformed and were in lighter, horizon blue.

Aerial reconnaissance, and static trench lines, meant that anything rendering units less detectable mattered. First attempts were usually painted tarpaulins hastily thrown over the top of artillery batteries. In 1915, though, a full-time French *Service de Camouflage* was set up, employing artists, designers and architects, whose talents ranged from repainting buildings, hangars and guns to contriving false landscapes and pop-up figures of soldiers to draw sniper fire. "Camouflage" was also coming to mean "deception". The BEF set up its own camouflage section, too, a specialist group of Royal Engineers. By 1918 camouflage had become an integral part of war, from earth-coloured aircraft to painted steel helmets, to the "Dazzle" painting on ships (*see* Chapter 83) that made it harder for U-boats to see them.

The intimacy and claustrophobia of trench warfare made it difficult to hide. Using new wartime skills in the art of camouflage, artificial positions were created, where possible, to overlook the frontlines. In March 1918, the Imperial War Museum acquired this camouflaged observation post that had stood in no-man's land between the lines. Made from thin metal to resemble the battle-worn trunk of a pollarded willow, it is hollow, with irregular-shaped holes cut into the sides for observation. To render them, and the observer, invisible, the holes were covered with painted metal gauze. The trunk contains a thick steel lining to protect the occupant, the necessity of such protection being underlined by the shrapnel and bullet marks peppering the outer shell. Amid the desolate landscape of the battlefield, the tree – and its secret occupant – would probably have passed unnoticed.

"... 'FEAR NOT, TILL BIRNAM WOOD / DO COME TO DUNSINANE!' AND NOW A WOOD / COMES TOWARD DUNSINANE."

Shakespeare's Macbeth, *as the witches' prophecy appears to be coming true – in reality, his enemies were using camouflage as deception*

43

THE GEOPHONE
MILITARY MINING IN THE WAR

1914 TO 1918

Accounts of military mining, as a method of attack on walled cities and fortresses, go back to Classical times: in the 2nd century BC, the historian Polybius was describing how the Romans had tunnelled towards the city of Ambracia – only to meet enemy tunnellers heading the other way. Where the usual above-ground tactics of siege warfare yielded few results, or where the available siege artillery and machines proved ineffective, literally undermining the enemy offered an alternative route.

With the establishment of trench warfare in late 1914, the combatants on the Western Front found themselves in situations comparable to mutual sieges, and they began to consider the potential of mining. In December 1914, the Indian Corps attempted, unsuccessfully, to blow up a German trench using a 45-pound charge of guncotton placed at the end of a shallow tunnel. The German riposte was more successful: on 20 December 1914, the Germans attacked the Indian Corps at Festubert with ten small mines placed under their forward trenches. The shaken survivors fled back to their reserve lines; and at Cuinchy, on 25 January 1915, the Germans repeated their local success. In the years to follow, miners across the Western Front conducted a subterranean battle to outwit their enemy counterparts.

Recent research has resulted in a new awareness of the crucial importance of First World War tunnelling. Military miners fought a private war deep beneath the battlefield, their primary role being to protect the trenches above from underground attack. Most tunnels were dug either in the stiff blue clay of Flanders, employing the north-country "clay-kicking" technique, or in the chalk of Picardy with traditional pick and shovel. In both geologies, while some dug, others listened – probing for sounds of enemy activity. The lives of those working below ground, as well as the infantrymen in the trenches, depended on "listeners", who had to remain fully alert to what was happening around them. They used a number of listening devices, the most popular being the small but highly effective geophone, like the set shown here. A French invention, it resembled a stethoscope linked to a brass or hardwood sensor. The casing enclosed a "sandwich" composed of a pair of vulcanite rubber rings surrounding two mica diaphragms, which held a bed of mercury. The mercury acted upon the diaphragms to amplify underground noises, enabling them to be heard at remarkable distances. To detect direction, the operator moved the two sensors until the sounds were balanced in both ears, and then took a compass bearing. Training and experience gave the listener the distance, allowing the enemy's direction and work rate to be plotted. The sophisticated geophone could mean the difference between life and death.

> "GENTLEMEN, WE MAY NOT MAKE HISTORY TOMORROW; BUT WE WILL CERTAINLY CHANGE THE GEOGRAPHY!"
>
> *General Sir Herbert Plumer, 6 June 1917, prior to exploding mines under Messines Ridge*

The British responded quickly. Major John Norton-Griffiths, who in peacetime was the head of an international engineering company, had already written to the War Office proposing the formation of special mining units, drawing on personnel from a sewer contract beneath Manchester. These men employed a technique known as "clay kicking" for digging tunnels in heavy clay geology. In February 1915, the first of eight "Tunnelling Companies" were formed within the Royal Engineers: the first 18 clay kickers were enlisted on 17 February and, in what is probably the fastest ever passage of a unit from formation to deployment, were shipped to France to start work on shallow mines at Givenchy, near Béthune, on 21 February. By late 1916/early 1917, when the British mining effort neared its peak, there were 33 Tunnelling Companies, including Australian, Canadian and New Zealand ones, controlled from each army HQ. Between 30,000 and 40,000 men were engaged on mining (and construction of subways and forward dugouts) behind and beneath the British lines.

There were two types of mines. While some effort went into offensive work, where quantities of explosive were lodged in chambers to blow up enemy trenches, the tunnellers' primary labour was defensive: thwarting the other side's offensive ambitions, first by detection and then by a carefully controlled "Camouflet" charge, designed to blow in the enemy tunnel and obliterate, gas or entomb its occupants.

The work in the tunnels was hot, arduous and unusually stressful. Knowing at any moment that an enemy countermine could explode and bury you alive made mining particularly nerve-wracking. Frequently, work would stop and everyone held their breath as the "listening men" with their stethoscopes and geophones sought telltale signs of the enemy digging. Sometimes tunnel encountered tunnel, and men fought to the death in the dark with revolvers, daggers, clubs and even picks and shovels. The infantry were of the general opinion that the tunnellers earned their pay.

In the attack on the Somme on 1 July 1916, the British Tunnelling Companies proved their worth beyond doubt. Several mines were detonated that morning in the chalky ground: they included one at Hawthorn Ridge ten minutes before the attack, and others just two minutes before the assault, like the huge explosion at La Boisselle.

The latter, produced by 24 tons of ammonal, resulted in the massive Lochnagar crater that is still today a place of pilgrimage for those remembering the war. Cecil Lewis, a pilot in the Royal Flying Corps, was flying over La Boisselle at the time: "The whole earth heaved and flashed, a tremendous and magnificent column rose up in the sky. There was an ear-splitting roar drowning all the guns ... The earth column rose higher and higher to almost 4,000 feet. There it hung, or seemed to hang, for a moment in the air, like the silhouette of some great cypress tree, then fell away in a widening cone of dust and debris." The Hawthorn Ridge explosion was filmed as it went off, and both the film footage and photographs remain prominent, enduring images of 1 July.

Further north, at Vimy, when the British took over that sector from the French in February 1916, they discovered that the Germans had been active in undermining the French positions. The British Tunnelling Companies then fought an intense underground war with the German tunnellers until the autumn when it settled around a new line. But when the Canadian Corps assaulted Vimy Ridge the following year, on Easter Sunday (9 April), 17 mines and a dozen other charges were used to support the successful attack.

However, the greatest mining attack in history took place in Flanders in June 1917, when General Sir Herbert Plumer's Second Army, in a classic example of "bite and hold" tactics, "earthquaked" the Messines Ridge, just south of Ypres. The assault had been a year in preparation and had all the hallmarks of Plumer's careful generalship. At least nine Tunnelling Companies worked secretly, some for over a year. By Z (Zero) day there were 25 huge mines sitting below the Germans' "impregnable" defended line of trenches, dugouts, concrete bunkers and barbed wire, 20 yards deep.

By the spring of 1917 Plumer had drilled and practised his assaulting divisions again and again on battlefield mock-ups behind the lines. When the British sappers, at 03.10 hours on 7 June 1917, finally fired 19 of the deep mines – 937,450 pounds of explosive, within 30 seconds of each other, along a 6-mile front – the attacking divisions knew exactly what to do and where to go. The detonations were clearly heard in London, and reportedly in Dublin, too. It was a shattering prelude to the most successful British set-piece of the war, in which one of the strongest fortified positions was taken within an hour or so with few casualties borne by the attackers.

The longest, and probably deadliest, mining campaign on the Western Front was, though, not a British affair at all. It was conducted by the French and Germans around the hilltop hamlet of Butte de Vauquois in the Argonne, 20 miles west of Verdun. From April 1915, surface fighting to dislodge the German defenders gave way to subterranean warfare. The French began by tunnelling under German positions on the ridge and detonating the first mine. The Germans retaliated, and in April 1916 exploded the largest mine of the battle (60 tons, over 130,000 pounds), killing over 100 *poilus*. By the time the Germans gave up the underground battle in early 1918, the Vauquois "war of the mines" had witnessed 519 explosions, three-fifths of them French. It had evolved into such a routine that enemy miners were even fraternizing below ground and the two sides were agreeing hours for detonations. The French abandoned a plan to blow the hilltop off the map with a single gigantic explosion. But the village had ceased to exist anyway – as had perhaps as many as 8,000 French and Germans – leaving a deeply pitted landscape to this day.

44

CAPTAIN SHAW'S ESCAPE AIDS PRISONERS OF WAR

1914 TO 1918

Prisoners of War (PoWs) are an unmitigated nuisance to all armies. They divert troops from the frontline to guard them and they have to be caged, fed and watered. Armies in Ancient times tended to feel freer about simply doing away with the problem, and despatching the prisoners they did not want to retain as trophies. But at The Hague in 1899 and 1907 the Western nations agreed a series of international conventions, which included formal rules for dealing with PoWs, declaring them "in the power of the hostile Government, but not of the individuals or corps who capture them. They must be humanely treated. All their personal belongings, except arms, horses, and military papers, remain their property."

In 1914–18, once a soldier had successfully surrendered – in the heat of battle, always a chancy affair – and got over the initial shock of capture, a curious mixture of relief, resignation and apprehension was likely to set in. Some PoWs were used as working parties behind the lines. Most were marched off to railheads, and only there would they be given food and water before being sent to far-off camps. And most would remain as captives, though an intrepid few attempted to forge their own fates. While much has been made of the stories of prisoners of war in the Second World War, the prisoners of 1914–18 had just as many dramatic and harrowing tales to tell.

A week after the Armistice, Captain Jack Shaw received a letter at his prison camp in Holzminden, Germany. Ostensibly a cheery letter from home, it was actually a coded message from a British Intelligence Officer alerting him to the despatch of secret escape equipment. Reading the second character of every fourth word, it told him to "LOOK OUT FOR ARMOUR TONGUE TINS". Shaw's mother had regularly sent him parcels of food, but it was the last one – returned to her because of the suspension of the war – that contained this unusual tin of Armour Tongue. Inside the tin were wire cutters, compasses and thin, rolled maps showing the country between Holzminden and Holland, together with a lead weight to make the unopened tin of "tongue" weigh the same as a real one. A fighter pilot, Shaw had been shot down during the fighting at Messines in 1917. He made his first attempt to escape from Freiburg, and was then sent to the troublemakers' camp at Holzminden. While incarcerated, he developed his secret code to contact London. A leading figure in Holzminden's tunnel, through which 29 officers escaped in July 1918, Shaw was waiting to go through when it collapsed. The experiences he and his fellow prisoners had, and the development of covert links with military intelligence in Britain, paved the way for a new generation of even more famous "great escapers" 20 years later.

The first prisoners on the Eastern Front in 1914 overwhelmed German resources. Around 95,000 Russians alone fell into German hands after Tannenberg at the end of August 1914, and it took until mid-1915 to house and feed them properly. Most were put in hastily built camps. By the end of the war there were 300 PoW camps in Germany, housing almost 2.5 million inmates. On all sides, during the war about 8 million men were held in PoW camps, 2.9 million of them in Russia and about 720,000 by Britain and France.

Conditions in the camps varied. German prisoners housed in Britain had arguably the best, although French camps were generally humanely run. By late 1918 a blockaded and starving Germany meant that PoWs there inevitably went hungry – as did their captors. The Hague Conventions appeared to assume that PoWs would be treated at least as well as the soldiers of the capturing power. But the Ottoman treatment of British and Indian prisoners taken at Kut in 1916 proved the dangers of such thinking (*see* Chapter 23), where over a third of them died on forced marches to camps, or of subsequent malnutrition and lack of medical care.

Regular food parcels from charitable bodies, such as the British Central Prisoners of War Committee, the French *Vêtement du Prisonnier* and the Swiss Red Cross, helped to eke out meagre rations and worn-out clothing. For most men working out how to get by, bad and/or insufficient food and ample boredom were the greatest problems. Food was always poor in Germany, the staples being cabbage soup, *sauerkraut* and bread with the occasional sausage. Prisoners in France and Britain generally enjoyed a healthier diet. Towards the end, food became an obsession. Rifleman Victor Denham remembered: "If a German was in charge of the food store we were sure of obtaining our fair ration, but a fellow prisoner in charge would soon grow fat at our expense." Hunger broke the bonds of discipline and comradeship, and men stole their comrades' food or sold their meagre possessions to the guards. Indeed, some prisoners were so ashamed of what had happened in the camps in the dark days of 1918 that they rarely spoke of it. As the war went on many prisoners held in Germany grew weaker, and disease – mainly typhus – raged in some camps.

Boredom was ameliorated in several ways, not all of them voluntary. Non-commissioned PoWs were obliged to work under the Hague Conventions. They soon became a valuable asset to the workforce, especially in agriculture and mining. Inevitably, some prisoners formed attachments to their employers, particularly on the farm. These more relaxed exchanges with their captors could stretch from honest exchanges of views to romantic liaisons with the opposite sex. The French prisoner Robert d'Harcourt wrote of his German civilian captors: "the inhabitants seemed rather indifferent to the war. The neighbourhood barber's wife ... told me one day: 'What the hell do we care about Alsace-Lorraine? Let them give it to the French and let the slaughter cease.'" It was not unknown for civilians of the captor nation to help prisoners during escape attempts.

For all PoWs, receiving news from the outside world was important, and newspapers were highly valued. Sport provided a form of release. Some PoWs – usually the officers, who were not required to work – formed self-improvement classes or made up amateur dramatic groups or even orchestras, which helped to fill many a long day and night. Camp repertory companies were usually hard at work with a variety of shows ranging from plays to reviews.

The main concern for a minority of adventurous individuals – again mainly officers, given their more leisured existences – was planning escape. For fit young

"PRISONERS? WELL LET ME TELL YOU, IT'S CHEAPER TO FEED THEM THAN FIGHT THEM"

Confederate General "Stonewall" Jackson, 1862

Battling a compatriot at chess might have made a welcome change from battling the enemy on the frontlines for these two German PoWs at Querrieu, on the Somme (1916). Though for much of the time, prisoners other than officers would be put to work, as allowed for by the Hague Conventions.

men it was considered their duty to contemplate it, and the prospect of getting home gave them a goal. Of the 29 British officers who escaped from Holzminden camp on 23 July 1918, through a tunnel they had been digging for months, 19 were recaptured; but 10 succeeded in making their way to neutral Holland and eventually back to Britain. By contrast, four British would-be escapers were executed on 24 June 1918 for the murder of a guard during their attempted flight.

One particularly audacious exploit on the British side was the escape of Major M.C.C. Cartwright and Captain H.A. Harrison from the Burg camp in northern Germany, which they later wrote up in their book *Within Four Walls*. They walked out through the front gate disguised as German officers, gambling on "no German soldier daring to address an officer who failed to show a pass, no matter how strict the rules might be". It worked. By altering clothing and army caps, with two wooden "swords" (highly polished with boot blacking) tucked underneath their capes, the two strolled out of the gates, smoking cigars and acknowledging the puzzled sentry's feeble challenge with an imperious flick of a salute, and casually walked to freedom. Hiding in barns by day and walking at night they made their way 125 miles north to Rostock. They were only recaptured at the last minute trying to board a neutral Danish freighter.

The German pilot Günther Plüschow was more successful. He and a companion named Treffitz escaped from Donington Hall in Leicestershire in 1915 by climbing over several wire fences in the dark. They made their way separately by train to London. Treffitz was recaptured, but Plüschow made his way to Tilbury, boarded a Dutch freighter where he hid in a lifeboat and made a successful "home run" via Holland. He was unique – the only German prisoner to escape from Britain during either world war.

With the Armistice in 1918 the victors demanded "the immediate repatriation without reciprocity", and soon most PoWs had found their way back home. But not all – in one thread of the war that took some time to unravel, over 180,000 Russian prisoners were still on German soil in October 1919, and some of them remained there as late as 1922.

45

"WAR DOG 180"
ANIMALS ON THE FRONTLINE

1914 TO 1918

The exploitation of animals in human conflict – as food sources, beasts of burden, messengers or even weapons – is, of course, very long-standing. The Hittites' chariots are perhaps the earliest recorded example of actual battle uses, though already packhorses were bearing military loads. The breeding of bigger horses led to cavalry, in which the horse became – in a charge – a powerful weapon itself, while the Romans used huge attack dogs, created by cross-breeding the great British mastiff with Greek Molossian hounds to produce very large and aggressive beasts. In 1914–18, a range of animals were involved in the conflict, most famously horses, but also including donkeys, mules, oxen and messenger pigeons.

The mechanization of everything, from transport to killing, that characterized the First World War challenged traditional uses of animals, but it also witnessed ingenious new uses. For example, in the confined spaces of trenches and relatively small distances separating trench lines dogs took on a new role, not as attack beasts but as messengers.

By 1917 the French and British armies had almost 20,000 serving dogs, and the Germans had half as many again. Dogs proved adept among the trenches. They moved quickly, much faster than men; they were hard to spot, being low to the ground and with colouring that blended with the environment; and they were loyal and determined. In Britain, the potential of dogs for war service had first been explored by Major Edwin Richardson over 20 years earlier. But his initial offer to train dogs for the army following the outbreak of war was turned down, and it was not until 1916 that Richardson was invited to establish a dog training school, at Shoeburyness in Essex. He had strong views on dogs, explaining to a visiting journalist that no particular breed of dog stood out as the best, but that he avoided any dog "with a gay tail which curled over its back or sideways" as this seemed "to indicate a certain levity of character, quite at variance with the serious duties required". A Messenger Dog Service was established in France, with its headquarters at Étaples, and dogs became a full part of the army establishment. They carried messages back and forth to the frontline in metal canisters strapped to their collars. This particular collar was worn by War Dog 180, a crossbreed Collie called "Wolf". In August 1918, Wolf was taken to serve with the 14th Battalion, Welch Regiment, on the Somme. He did a good job.

In 1914, despite the development of the internal combustion engine, the prime means of mobility on the frontlines themselves remained the horse – the relationship still expressed in an engine's output being described in terms of "horse power". Road

> "KILLING, WOUNDING OR MOLESTING HOMING PIGEONS IS PUNISHABLE UNDER THE DEFENCE OF THE REALM REGULATIONS BY SIX MONTHS IMPRISONMENT OR £100 FINE."

Notice in Leeds during the war, referring to Defence of the Realm Regulation 21A

It was as beasts of burden, rather than glamorous cavalry chargers, that horses played a fundamental role on the frontlines in France and Flanders. Here, a horse belonging to the 1st ANZAC Corps is loaded up with a Vickers machine gun and ammunition, for an official photograph (August 1917).

and rail took everything, and everyone, most of the way; but horses were vital thereafter. It was inevitable, therefore, that as the armies marched off to war they took with them horses, *millions* of them. Every artillery gun, save for the very heaviest, was pulled by teams of horses, and it is estimated that over 20 million horses took part in the First World War – and that as many as 8 million of them died during it. The British Expeditionary Force alone had upwards of 368,000 horses in 1917. Maintaining the stock, and treating ill and wounded horses, therefore became a mammoth exercise. It is estimated that around 2.5 million horses passed through British veterinary hospitals, of which four-fifths were returned to duty. The horse was so important, so necessary, that it was ubiquitous. Although, as the BEF quickly discovered, more mechanized transport was needed to ferry troops around (*see* Chapter 15), the horse remained vital, along with mules, for most armies in the war. Feeding and watering these millions was, inevitably, a huge logistical effort – though a different sort of challenge than the upkeep of a large fleet of lorries.

Horses were initially the prime means of reconnaissance, at least until the trenches sank into their seemingly immovable shapes on the Western Front. Cavalry warfare was soon highly problematic. The BEF cavalry was undoubtedly the best-trained and equipped at the Front, and the experience of the Anglo-Boer War a decade earlier had taught the British how to use cavalry as mobile infantry. Yet, after a few frustrating charges in the opening weeks of the war, the cavalry was sent to the rear to await the great breakthrough. Apart from a few incidents late in the war at Cambrai and during the open warfare of the last "Hundred Days" (*see* Chapter 88), cavalry remained impotent against the machine gun and barbed wire.

On the Eastern Front things were different, though. The wide spaces there allowed cavalry to roam in the gaps, and at the Battle of Tannenberg in August 1914 and a host of other engagements cavalry proved their usefulness – but only as mobile troops, not through traditional cavalry charges using their weight and power. Mounted troops of the British, Antipodean and Indian contingents also came into their own in Palestine and Sinai, seeing many deployments and culminating in a classic example of cavalry exploitation in the breakthrough at Megiddo in September 1918.

Soldiers of all armies became very attached to their horses. It is perhaps summed up in the words of one Royal Artillery officer, who wrote of one horse: "He (Sailor) would work for 24 hours a day. He was quiet as a lamb and as clever as a thoroughbred, but he looked like nothing on earth, so we lost him. The whole artillery battery kissed him goodbye and the drivers and gunners who fed him nearly cried."

As a beast of burden, the horse was supplemented by the mule, that curious half-horse, half-donkey, highly valued since Ancient Greece. Considered less obstinate, faster and more intelligent than donkeys, mules also offered the advantage of being able to cope with difficult terrain because of their harder hooves. They were also considered easier to train than a horse, and could cover 50 miles in a day with only a few hours of sleep. All sides looked to the mule when the going got tough, and by the end of the war the British Army owned over 230,000 of them. But mules knew when they had had enough. Henry Williamson worked with them as a member of the Machine Gun Corps and noted how: "When a mule lowered both ears, it had given up. It stood awhile in dejection, nosebag and net of hay unwanted. In the black night it sank down, its eyes in the morning were glazed." In situations like that, the mule would normally be put out of its misery.

The different theatres of war demanded different animals. The British formed an Imperial Camel Corps (ICC) in 1916 in Egypt to fight mostly in Sinai and Palestine, making use of the "ship of the desert's" unrivalled ability to endure long distances in the blazing heat. The unit fought dismounted as a multinational infantry brigade and included its own light artillery. Its Australian component had a particularly tough reputation, because unit commanders had used it as a repository for some of their more difficult characters. By 1918 the British Army had 47,000 camels.

In their contribution on the Western Front, dogs played a small but useful role as messengers, and also sometimes in locating wounded men. They presented less of a target to a sniper and could travel over any terrain. One dog is recorded as running nearly 3 miles in less than 60 minutes with an important message to a brigade's headquarters. Perhaps inevitably, soldiers (including a young Adolf Hitler) also adopted dogs as pets, which sometimes prevented the dogs being sent on dangerous missions.

A usually more reliable messenger was the homing pigeon, which saw service on all the battle fronts. They played a vital part in the war, especially when more modern means of communication broke down, as they frequently did. Signallers carried them forward into action to report progress – or lack of it – in special baskets strapped to their backs, and pigeons were also used to send messages from ships at sea. When the French advanced at the Marne in 1914, they took 72 mobile lofts with them, to which, incredibly, all the pigeons returned despite the changes of location. Over 100,000 British pigeons were recorded as flying in action, with an astonishing success rate of 95 per cent in getting the message back. Several birds were even decorated for their exploits (*see* Chapter 41).

All animals had their vulnerabilities in war, as the poignant images of horses sinking into the treacherous Flanders mud in 1917 testify. Occasionally, too, the bond between human and animal broke down. One Australian divisional commander was recorded waiting impatiently for news of an attack when a pigeon from the frontline fluttered back to its loft. The orderly recovered the message and handed it to the general. It read: "I am absolutely fed up with carrying this bloody bird around France!"

46

MAIRI CHISHOLM'S DECORATIONS
MILITARY MEDALS

1914 TO 1918

Napoleon was a great believer in the power of medals. He clearly, and cannily, recognized their importance as motivators and (inexpensive) public rewards. But military history since Ancient times has been littered by visible symbols of achievement, worn by their recipients. The First World War continued this tradition, but also saw new decorations brought in, not only for soldiers but also for women and civilians, too, reflecting service in campaigns and individual meritorious and gallant acts.

This distinctive group of medals was awarded to one of the few women to experience frontline service in 1914–18. Mairi Chisholm and her comrade Elsie Knocker were celebrated as "*les deux madonnes de Pervyse*". In September 1914, 18-year-old Mairi was spotted intrepidly racing her motorbike through London by Dr Hector Munro and invited to join his privately funded ambulance unit. Within weeks she and Elsie, who was a trained nurse, were in the thick of the action providing medical support to the Belgian army. As trench warfare spread, Elsie proposed a forward dressing station to provide faster treatment, and the two women established themselves in the ruined houses of Pervyse not far from Dixmude, north of Ypres. From November 1914 until they were badly gassed in March 1918, they worked in their vulnerable "*poste*" saving lives and bringing comfort to all who passed through. They regularly ventured into no-man's land to bring in the wounded, especially shot-down pilots. It was for this, in particular, that in October 1917 they were two of the few women awarded the British Military Medal (shown second from left, followed *left-to-right* by other British awards: the 1914 Star, British War Medal and Victory Medal).

Most British and Imperial servicemen (along with many women and civilians) were awarded two or three basic campaign medals. Those who served in an active capacity overseas received the British War Medal, and those on a Fighting Front also earned the Victory Medal. (The other Allies had Victory Medals, too, with similar designs and ribbons.) Members of the British services who saw war service during the first 18 months of the war additionally received the 1914 Star or the 1914–15 Star. The former, known widely as the "Mons Star", was the rarest of Britain's campaign medals, with only around 370,000 recipients, whereas over 2 million received the 1914–15 Star. The combination of Star, War and Victory medals was later referred to as a "First World War trio", or, more affectionately, as "Pip, Squeak and Wilfred" after three well-known postwar cartoon characters from the *Daily Mirror*.

Many individuals also received awards for distinguished or meritorious service. The Distinguished Conduct Medal (DCM) was highly prized and regarded as being immediately below a Victoria Cross. It recognized outstanding bravery in the field by private soldiers and NCOs. It was the equivalent of the officers-only Distinguished Service Order but, unlike the DSO – which was often presented to staff officers and senior commanders for first-rate service well behind the frontline – the DCM could only be gained by bravery in *action*. It also had the attraction of conferring a small pension on the recipient.

The new Military Cross (MC), instituted in December 1914, was for "gallantry during active operations in the presence of the enemy". It was aimed at officers of the rank of captain and below and warrant officers (such as regimental and company sergeant majors). It was joined after March 1916 by the Military Medal for non-commissioned ranks, given for "gallantry and devotion to duty when under fire in battle on land": eligibility was backdated to 1914. The army could award it to anyone serving in the frontline, including rare instances of women who performed gallant service in forward positions, such as nurses, members of the Women's Army Auxiliary Corps – and indeed the two "Madonnas of Pervyse". These army awards were paralleled by the Royal Navy's Distinguished Service Cross (DSC) and the Distinguished Service Medal (DSM), and, after 1918, by the Royal Air Force's Distinguished Flying Cross (DFC) and Distinguished Flying Medal (DFM).

Many meritorious acts were publicly acknowledged in a list attached to the official commander-in-chief's despatch or account of a battle. While not a medal, to be "Mentioned in Dispatches" allowed the individual to sew a small bronze oak leaf on the ribbon of their Victory Medal (as Mairi Chisholm did). As well as servicemen, many male and female civilians, and members of the Red Cross, YMCA and YWCA were recognized in this way during the war.

The medal tradition was embraced by all belligerents. Germany had absorbed many of Prussia's longstanding honours and awards. The Iron Cross, instituted during the Napoleonic Wars, was awarded in three classes: the Grand Cross for senior commanders only, then either First Class or Second Class. However, so many of this last category were awarded in 1914–18 (estimated at over 5 million) that it tended to debase the currency. Perhaps the next most famous German medal was the *Pour le Mérite*, originating in 1667 and given its name by Frederick the Great in 1740, when French was still the court language. Germany brought it to popular attention by broadcasting news of its presentation, in early 1916, to young, successful fighter pilots. Famous recipients of the "Blue Max" included the "Red Baron" von Richthofen, Hermann Goering and the young army *Oberleutnant* Erwin Rommel.

The French system of awards continued to reflect Napoleon's policy of recognizing egalitarian merit rather than distinction based on class or nobility. Primarily, Paris relied on the *Légion d'honneur* to recognize outstanding wartime achievements, both civil and military. Like Britain's new Order of the British Empire, the *Légion d'honneur* was organized into five classes, from the lowest Knight to the highest Grand Cross, and shrewdly accompanied by a handsome cash pension. Hardly surprisingly, it was much sought after. However, in 1915 the French brought in the *Croix de Guerre*, awarded for a mention in dispatches by a regimental commander, rising to an army level commendation. Over 2 million were awarded, 20,000 of them to foreigners – and even including whole units. The French also issued an unofficial medal, showing Clemenceau on one side and an attacking *poilu* on the other.

Undoubtedly, the most famous and prestigious British and Imperial medal is the Victoria Cross, the highest possible award for bravery under enemy fire. A number of features make it unique and add to its prestige. It is a wholly egalitarian award, open to any member of the armed forces demonstrating "a signal act of bravery"; it was conceived as a very difficult accolade to achieve, and its rarity preserves its distinction – only 1,360 (to date) since its 1856 inception; and it hinges on service to the British monarch, remaining the only one of the old "Imperial" gallantry medals still awarded across the Commonwealth. The inscription, suggested by Queen Victoria herself, sums up the essence of it: "For Valour". Posthumous awards of VCs commenced only after the Anglo-Boer War, and for those who died in the act of earning it the medal was engraved onto their gravestones.

Six-hundred-and-twenty-eight VCs were awarded during the First World War, all for outstanding and selfless acts. But only one man earned it *twice* in 1914–18, and he didn't even carry a gun. Captain Noël Chavasse was a regimental medical officer with the 1/10th Battalion, King's (Liverpool Regiment), known as the Liverpool Scottish. The words of his citations tell their own story of exceptional, extraordinary heroism:

VC, August 1916 (at Guillemont, Somme): "During an attack he tended the wounded in the open all day, under heavy fire, frequently in view of the enemy. During the ensuing night he searched for wounded on the ground in front of the enemy's lines ... Next day he took one stretcher-bearer to the advanced trenches, and under heavy shell fire carried an urgent case for 500 yards into safety, being wounded in the side by a shell splinter during the journey ... Altogether he saved the lives of some twenty badly wounded men, besides the ordinary cases which passed through his hands. His courage and self-sacrifice, were beyond praise."

Bar to the VC, July/August 1917 (outside Ypres): "Though severely wounded early in the action whilst carrying a wounded soldier to the Dressing Station, Capt. Chavasse refused to leave his post, and for two days not only continued to perform his duties, but in addition went out repeatedly under heavy fire to search for and attend to the wounded who were lying out ... During these searches, although practically without food during this period, worn with fatigue and faint with his wound, he assisted to carry in a number of badly wounded men, over heavy and difficult ground ... this devoted and gallant officer subsequently died of his wounds."

Bravery recognized, at the investiture of Charles William Train. King George V awards him the Victoria Cross at Second Army Headquarters, Blendecques, west of Hazebrouck (6 August 1918). His award was in recognition of his fearless initiative against Ottoman machine gunners outside Jerusalem on 8 December 1917.

4

MUD & BLOOD

47

PRIVATE BÉRENGER'S *ADRIAN* HELMET
HELMETS FOR THE TROOPS

FROM 1915

In the days when warfare was invariably a close-quarters affair, of metal on metal, no self-respecting knight would go into battle without adequate armour, often including a helmet that completely covered the head save for narrow eye and nose slits. In the 19th century, cavalry still wore metal helmets to protect their heads from sabre blows; but in the age of firepower and standing armies, other values such as camouflage and lightness for mobility (and lower cost) came to be considered more important and many armies turned to soft headgear. Nevertheless, at the Battle of Mons in 1914, Walter Bloem, of the 12th Brandenburg Grenadiers, was astonished at the garb of his British enemy: "Could this be a soldier? A man in a grey-brown golfing suit with a flat topped cloth cap?"

In 1914, the Germans still sported a helmet of sorts: the iconic *Pickelhaube*, which, with its distinctive spike, was intended to look martial and aggressive (*see* Chapter 3). But the war revealed two big drawbacks. Its hardened leather offered little protection, while its spike, often visible above the parapets of trenches, provided the enemy with a target. In reality, none of the combatants had anything in the way of personal head protection, and the casualties from modern quick-firing artillery soared, half of them from head wounds. Lethal bursts of shrapnel overhead brought hundreds of thousands of head wounds into the dressing stations. Even men deep in trenches were vulnerable. Within a year, the First World War witnessed the revival of the military helmet, which protected men and helped forge the visually distinctive identities of the nations' armies. Winston Churchill, now out of office, was just one who approved of the new development.

On 5 December 1915, Winston Churchill visited the French Tenth Army at Arras. Having resigned from the Cabinet in November, he had just completed a fortnight's acclimatization in trench warfare with the Grenadier Guards and was fully aware of the dangers at the Front. He was, therefore, impressed when one of the French generals there, General Émile Fayolle, presented him with one of the new "Adrian pattern" steel helmets, observing to his wife: "it looks so nice and will perhaps protect my valuable cranium". By then, it was already doing that for thousands of French troops. Never intended to stop bullets at close range, the popular "M1915" nevertheless performed vital service as a means to protect from shrapnel and shell bursts. This particular M1915 – battle-damaged and lacking its badge at the front – belonged to Private Bérenger of the French 39th Division. At the Somme on 1 July 1916, he went over the top as the northernmost French soldier, the last *poilu* in the line.

> "HEAD-WOUNDS HAVE BEEN MORE THAN USUALLY NUMEROUS DURING THE WAR, OWING TO THE TRENCH-FIGHTING, AND MORE THAN USUALLY SEVERE, OWING TO THE EXTENSIVE USE OF SHRAPNEL. BUT THE DANGER, ALTHOUGH IT CANNOT BE AVOIDED, CAN BE MINIMISED."
>
> Illustrated War News, *17 November 1915*

The French were the first to react. In early 1915, the man responsible to the Ministry of War for army supplies, *Intendant General* August-Louis Adrian, asked a soldier how he had survived his head wounds: he answered that he had worn his metal cooking bowl under his cap. Impressed, Adrian began exploring possibilities for protective headgear. He first tried a design of a simple steel cap before, in April 1915, proposing a helmet based on the existing *casque du pompier* – the helmet used by Parisian firefighters. Introduced from July 1915, the "Adrian pattern" was made from light, mild steel, with a brim and a raised crest to cover the ventilation slot in the top. A stylish Republican crest was embossed onto the front. With its leather liner for comfort, the M1915 helmet was an instant success with the troops, even if its steel thickness of only 0.7mm meant it was less effective than the later British Brodie-pattern helmet (*see below*). On the other hand it was light, comfortable and still gave a level of much-needed protection against shrapnel and flying fragments.

By the end of 1915 more than 3 million *Adrians* had been distributed to the French army. In the words of the army's Controller of *Matériel*, "the rapid delivery of these helmets has saved the lives of many men at the Front". Other Allied armies saw the advantages and were quick to adopt the new helmet, too, and the *Adrian* was worn by Belgians, Russians, Serbs, Romanians and Italians.

Imitation is the sincerest form of flattery, and both the British and the Germans moved to devise new helmets for their men. Britain began to study the question of a "trench helmet" in June 1915 and acquired *Adrians* as a trial for frontline sentries. In September 1915, the War Office confirmed the need for steel helmets; however, the British felt that the French helmet was both too flimsy and too expensive to manufacture and looked instead for something stronger and cheaper. The eventual design adopted was by inventor John Leopold Brodie, based on the medieval "iron hat", or *chapel de fer*, worn by infantry. Brodie's design for "an improved helmet or head shield" (as his patent described it) gave the soldier protection from air burst shrapnel and shell fragments, and was easy to manufacture.

The first helmet, designated "Brodie's Steel Helmet, War Office Pattern", was a shallow, inverted dishbowl with a wide (but rather sharp-edged) brim and a primitive lining made of oilcloth. The lining was attached to a strap riveted to the crown of the helmet, with a chinstrap of two leather straps. Brodie's helmet was tougher than the French helmet, being made from thicker (and later harder, manganese) steel. Most important was its ease of manufacture: it could be easily stamped out using existing machine tools.

The helmets began to arrive in France after September 1915, where they were not issued as personal equipment but stored in the trenches for whichever frontline battalion was there. The Top Brass was not necessarily keen. A rumour circulated that some generals thought they looked "unsoldierly" and that they would make the men go "soft". Nonetheless, by March 1916 the Brodie helmet (known to the troops as a "battle bowler", "tin hat" or – when issued to the US Expeditionary Force in 1918 – as the "Tommy helmet") was widely in service with frontline troops and was an immediate success with them. Weighing 2 pounds, it was heavy and uncomfortable, but soldiers made no protests at such a potentially life-saving addition to their uniform. By the time of the Battle of the Somme in July 1916 every British soldier sported a "tin hat", now in the Mark I version, and was only too happy for its protection. The sharp metal edge was now a folded rim, the shell more khaki and the lining more comfortable, and, while it would continue to evolve, essentially this is the helmet that would identify the Tommy in both world wars.

The Germans came to accept that the *Pickelhaube* was obsolete, and by August 1915 the High Command had approved of the idea of a new helmet. The designs were drawn up in September 1915 by Friedrich Schwerd and August Bier, and by December the German Model 1916 *Stahlhelm* was being trialled by a *Sturm* (Assault) battalion. It, too, drew inspiration from earlier centuries to generate a design that, unlike the shallow Brodie, covered the neck, temples and ears to a depth of over 2 inches. Mass production began in January 1916, and by the beginning of the Somme most German soldiers on the Western Front had them. Units at Verdun were the first to receive them, and, as with all the armies, the incidence of serious head injuries fell dramatically. The *Stahlhelm* was the heaviest of them all – nearly 3 pounds – but effective, as Lieutenant Walter Schulze realized when shrapnel flew his way in July 1916: "If I had, as had been usual up until a few days previously, been wearing a cap, then the Regiment would have had one more man killed."

Like the Brodie, the iconic *Stahlhelm* served on in the Second World War. It proved to be an outstandingly successful design, giving protection to the skull and, with its flaring neck-guard, to the shoulders. Today, the modern American Kevlar helmet follows the original German design of 1916 closely and is aptly known as "the Fritz".

Statistics comparing deaths from head wounds before and after the introduction of the steel helmet clearly show its impact. However shocking the numbers of dead and seriously wounded were during the war, there can be little doubt that they would have been more horrific still without the contributions of Adrian, Brodie and Schwerd & Bier.

Proof of the Brodie helmet's efficacy. In this official War Office photograph, the unsurprisingly relieved British soldier shows where the shrapnel entered. He suffered his injury while in action near Hamel, on the Somme, in December 1916.

48

WILLIAM SHORT'S BRODIE HELMET
THE ROAD TO THE SOMME

AUTUMN 1915 TO FEBRUARY 1916

At the midpoint of the middle year of the First World War, an offensive began that came to embed itself in British folklore and memory – as a futile and bloody débâcle. However, although the Battle of the Somme was undoubtedly a bloodthirsty affair, it was certainly not futile and it was far from a defeat. In fact, as German observers ruefully admitted after the battle, "the Somme was the muddy grave of the old German field army". The truth is that over a campaign lasting 142 days, the British and French attackers fought the German defenders to exhaustion, as what started out as a grand design by the Allies to break through the German lines became instead a drawn-out battle of attrition, with heavy casualties on both sides, and many individual acts of extraordinary sacrifice and heroism.

Foremost in the first consignment of artefacts sent back to London's new War Museum in 1917 were several "Brodie-pattern" steel helmets worn during the Battle of the Somme. The characteristic, broad-brimmed helmet, introduced from late 1915, was already seen as a lasting symbol of the BEF's experience of the trenches. This one, battle-scarred and worn, belonged to Private William Short, from Eston in Yorkshire. He joined up within the first month of the war, and by 1916 he was taking part in the great offensive on the Somme with the 8th Battalion, Yorkshire Regiment (Green Howards). On 6 August, as the Australians desperately struggled to consolidate their hold on the village of Pozières, on their flank the 8th Yorkshires were ordered to attack a strong German position known as Munster Alley. Short was one of the battalion's expert bombers. Quickly wounded in the foot, he still carried on bombing intensely. A German shell exploded and destroyed most of one leg below the knee, but he continued to fuse new grenades and pass them forward to the men who could still stand, right up to the moment of his death. A month later Short was posthumously awarded the Victoria Cross. Plain and simple, this ordinary helmet still reflects the gritty bravery of an extraordinary Yorkshireman.

The road to the Somme started in the late autumn of 1915. The year was ending as a round of major disappointments for the Allies. Whereas in spring 1915, General Joffre had been confident of expelling the Germans from their salient of conquered French territory – the so-called "Noyons Bulge" – by the autumn, it was clear the attempts had failed. At Neuve Chapelle, Aubers Ridge, Vimy, Loos, Notre Dame de Lorette and in the Champagne, even where there had been initial success it had dissipated into expensive failure (*see* Chapters 39 and 40). Beyond the Western

"THERE ARE THEREFORE NO REASONS FOR CONSIDERING THAT THE PROSPECTS FOR A SUCCESSFUL OFFENSIVE NEXT SPRING ARE ANYTHING BUT GOOD"

General Sir William Robertson, Chief of the General Staff to the BEF, to Prime Minister Herbert Asquith, 6 November 1915

Front, from Mesopotamia to Gallipoli to Greece, the French and British Imperial forces were faring no better.

Senior figures began to pay the price. In Britain, crisis over Gallipoli and the shortage of shells had already produced a new Coalition government (and seen the exit of Churchill as First Lord of the Admiralty). In France's Third Republic, René Viviani, premier since the outbreak of war, resigned in October 1915 and was succeeded by Aristide Briand, who also took on the portfolio of foreign affairs. He was joined as Minister of War by the former colonial soldier Joseph Gallieni, who was widely credited – to the French Commander-in-Chief Joffre's chagrin – with setting in train the "Miracle of the Marne" in 1914 through his robust military direction when governing Paris. Even Joffre's reputation was beginning to tarnish, while the commander-in-chief of the British Expeditionary Force, Sir John French, was on borrowed time for his perceived mistakes at Loos.

New faces did not mean, though, instant or novel solutions to a war that resembled a long siege. The elusive goal remained to find a way to shatter the enemy's line and exploit a breakthrough. And at this stage, both British and French General Staff officers could not see much alternative to bigger attacks and more shells, fired for longer. Surely a larger pounding must kill more of the enemy, destroy more defences, induce greater demoralization? On 6 November 1915, when still the BEF's Chief of the General Staff, Sir William Robertson sounded a genuine note of optimism to the prime minister: "Given adequate artillery support there is no difficulty in overwhelming the enemy's ... lines ... There are therefore no reasons for considering that the prospects for a successful offensive next spring are anything but good." If anything was going to win the war in 1916, it would have to be something on a scale hitherto untried.

On 5 December, Prime Minister Herbert Asquith, accompanied by his Secretary of State for War, Lord Kitchener, and others, met a French delegation including Briand and Joffre in Calais to begin thrashing out the next moves. Kitchener argued forcefully the British case for ending the French-led Salonika campaign (*see* Chapter 26), which seemed a pointless drain of men and resources. Briand agreed, but immediately the socialists in his government threatened to resign, and he – with other Allies – pressed Britain not to abandon Salonika. Not wanting to cause friction for Briand's fragile government, the British agreed.

That, and much else, was worked through at French army headquarters at Chantilly, northeast of Paris, on 6–8 December, where the Allies gathered to plan a common strategy for 1916. It was chaired by Joffre, with representatives from Britain, France, Italy, Serbia and Russia. For Sir John French, it was his swansong. Finding himself isolated by his subordinates, notably generals Haig and Rawlinson, *and* his superiors – notably Kitchener, but even the king – he had accepted the inevitable and written his resignation. His compensation was a peerage and command of the British Home Forces, in the unlikely event of a German invasion, while Haig's intrigues finally won him command of the BEF on 18 December. Robertson was promoted, too, as Chief of the Imperial General Staff in London and the Cabinet's sole military advisor.

At the conference, Joffre pointed out that the Allies' forces were spread around the periphery of the Triple Alliance, so Germany always had the advantage of being able to swing her forces from front to front quickly via excellent interior railway lines. Only coordinated and simultaneous offensives could prevent German reserves from being sent to reinforce a single threatened Front. He was strongly supported by the Russian delegation, represented by General Yakov Zhilinski.

The French then circulated a "Plan of Action Proposed by France to the Coalition", proposing simultaneous large-scale offensives for 1916. It also called for the evacuation of Gallipoli, the strengthening of defences in Egypt and Salonika, the occupation by Italy of Albania and all efforts to keep Romania free of German control. An agreement on joint Allied strategy was finally reached whereby:

In the Principal Theatres
1. Great Britain, France, Italy and Russia will deliver simultaneous attacks with their maximum forces on their respective fronts as soon as they are ready to do so and circumstances seem favourable. This is our essential aim, the principal means by which we expect to force a decision.
2. Until this can be done, the Austro-German forces will be worn down by vigorous action, to be carried out principally by those powers which still have reserves of manpower. (Great Britain, Italy and Russia).
3. Each of the Powers will unceasingly continue to accumulate material and equipment. Russia and Serbia will be helped by their Allies to reorganize their armies in this respect.

B. In the Secondary Theatres
The Allies will allot to the secondary theatres only the minimum forces required – in principle, those which are already in the East – and will use them to bar the way to German expansion ... One commander-in-chief for all the Allied forces in the East will be charged with its execution: the other Allied nations would launch offensives of their own whenever any other Allied nation came under clear threat.

Here at last was a clear statement of Allied grand strategy for 1916. The generals' various political masters agreed. As more details were worked out, there was a notable twist. Although Haig wanted the BEF to mount its planned attack in Flanders, on 20 February 1916 he agreed to accept a joint offensive in the summer along the line of the river in Picardy where the French and British armies met – the Somme.

There was also a significant fly in the Allied planners' ointment. One party naturally not invited to Chantilly was the Germans. And the absentees had plans of their own. Just one week after Haig agreed the joint offensive, the first German shell crashed into the bishop's palace at Verdun.

The emergence of a coordinated strategy. Allied generals from the Western, Italian and Eastern fronts gather at the French army's HQ at Chantilly in December 1915 to consider the large question: how to beat the enemy? In the middle of the group Joffre plays host (in profile); left of him Sir John French listens, in the knowledge that his days as the BEF's commander-in-chief are numbered.

49

HAROLD STARTIN'S TRENCH CLUB
TRENCHES – A DAY IN THE LIFE

1914 TO 1918

There is a popular impression that soldiers on the Western Front invariably spent their time immersed in mud and water as shells rained down around them. While true for some, at certain times and in certain sectors, for most the *daily* trench life was different. German soldiers might well spend months in forward trenches, living (by 1916) in relatively warm and dry, concrete-reinforced, deep dugouts; but then for much of the time their priority was defending territory gained. For the British, by contrast, trenches were always supposed to be temporary, the jumping-off point for driving out the Germans.

This was reflected in the way British units were rotated. The average unit was only "in the line" – the fire trench facing the enemy – for perhaps one week each month, and rotated back to do a week in support, then a week in reserve, followed by a rest away from the trenches. Charles Carrington recorded that his battalion spent only 65 days in the frontline in 1916. During great offensives or crises, that changed of course; but such intensity was the exception, not the rule. And rightly so, for the forward trenches were governed by an exhausting regime, where the stresses of daily life could be compounded by being sent out on patrol, or even a raid, into no-man's land – where meeting the enemy could be a brutal affair indeed.

Harold Startin was one of the original BEF, an "Old Contemptible". He arrived in France with the 1st Battalion, Leicestershire Regiment, on 9 September 1914. As the war descended into trench warfare, he became a specialist "bomber", fighting with hand grenades in the close quarters of no-man's land. In spring 1915, the Leicestershire's bombers were ordered to leave their rifles behind when going out between the lines. But this left them feeling vulnerable – no-man's land was a ruthless place where men fought to the death, eye to eye – so they decided to arm themselves with improvised weapons. They placed entrenching-tool handles in clay moulds and poured in molten lead. As Startin later explained, this made "what we called cudgels", also known as "trench clubs" – rudimentary and plain looking, but brutally effective. He began using this cudgel at Hooge, outside Ypres, its first victim being "a Sergeant of the Württemberg Regiment in July 1915". The following October, Startin went home on four days leave and took the cudgel with him to show his father. When he returned to the Front, he left it at home. Half a century later, in August 1964, Startin presented it to the Imperial War Museum. In the simple words of the man who knew, the cudgel had been "a most effective weapon, especially when used on listening patrols between the trenches when silence was really golden".

"AFTER SIX DAYS OUT AT REST WE CAME BACK INTO BRIGADE RESERVE FOR SIX MORE AND THEN UP INTO THE LINE AGAIN. IT GETS JUST LIKE GOING TO AN ORDINARY DAY'S WORK."

Sergeant F.W. Bilman, 9th Battalion, East Surrey Regiment, June 1916

Every day started with the dawn "stand-to", when all ranks would be at their battle stations fully armed ready to repel any attack in the dim half-light between night and day. Half an hour after dawn, the men would be stood down. That, for many, was the best moment of the day; everyone got a mouthful of the army's rum ration, usually from jars labelled "SRD" ("Supply Reserve Depot" – although the wits called it "Seldom Reaches Destination"), and breakfast would be cooked – usually bacon sandwiches and strong tea. A glance through a sentry's trench periscope might well reveal the smoke from the cooking fires of the Germans across no-man's land, and in most sectors, for much of the war, both sides coexisted in an unwritten "live and let live" around breakfast.

Next, rifles were cleaned and inspected, and men washed and shaved when possible; water was usually in short supply in the forward trenches. They might then play cards or sit yarning round a fire, while trying to exterminate the lice (known as "chats") in their clothes – giving rise to our phrase "chatting". After this time, the serious business of the day would begin. Platoon sergeants would detail off men for the long list of potential chores: sentry duty, sandbag filling, excavating better dugouts, fusing Mills grenades, filling ammunition belts, repairing blown-in trench walls, and so on.

Platoon officers would inspect their sectors, and the company commander and company sergeant major would make their daily rounds of the line, gauging discreetly the health and temper of the men. Whenever possible, between tasks, soldiers would try and sleep by day. They were watched over by vigilant, if weary, sentries. Lunch would normally be bully beef, cheese and biscuits, and more hot, strong tea.

Officers would be called away to battalion HQ for orders, and to struggle with the endless reports and returns required by the army's bureaucracy. A battalion might have to account for some missing trench stores, for rations that had mysteriously disappeared, or even – exceptionally – for a soldier who had failed to come back from leave and had to be posted as a deserter. As the day wore on, the shape for the coming night would emerge. A quiet one normally meant just a lot of hard work; and a dangerous one could involve a patrol or raid into no-man's land.

The "quiet" nights were often anything but. After the ritual of the dusk stand-to, replicating that of dawn, working parties would beaver away in the darkness. Hot food and water might be carried up from the rear; trench stores such as barbed wire, ammunition and corrugated iron would be dumped at the head of a communication trench; nervous wiring parties could set out into no-man's land to lay more barbed wire or repair breaches. They would have to do an awkward job in the dark as quietly as possible, praying that the Germans wouldn't hear them, and freezing motionless if a flare went up. If a machine gun opened up, everyone went to ground, cursing and praying for the light to go out. Back in the trenches the sentries would be doubled, the officers and sergeants would patrol regularly, and very few men would be able to sleep. Trench warfare was primarily a nocturnal activity.

If a raid was being mounted, then the night became a dangerous one for all concerned – on both sides. The usual justification for patrols or raids was "to dominate no-man's land" or snatch a prisoner for intelligence purposes. The truth was that for the British High Command, the urge for activity of any sort was too strong. Half the raids failed, and the result was a serious drain of casualties. Between December 1915 and June 1916 nearly 6,000 men were killed and 120,000 wounded in these "minor operations". In a typical raid, a group – usually of volunteers – would steal across no-man's land armed with clubs and knives until the raid kicked off. If all went well they would return, perhaps clutching a frightened German, often wounded and invariably battered.

But a lot could go wrong. If the wire was not cut, if the raiders were spotted by an alert sentry, if the supporting artillery got the timing wrong, then the raid was compromised. A storm of rifle and machine gun fire accompanied by a counter-barrage of artillery would fall upon the would-be raiders. One officer recorded a major battalion raid – almost a night attack – where of the 650 men who set out, only 194 returned unscathed. By 1917 trench raids were very often the source of some very un-soldierly "negotiating" between commanding officers and higher headquarters, involving promises of extra home leave, and decorations to order for the leaders.

For all the men in the line the biggest day-to-day challenge was the elements. There are numerous tales, especially in the winter of 1914–15, of trenches flooding in really bad weather, when both sides clambered out and walked around on top. The war went on hold. Worst of all was really cold weather. In sub-zero winter temperatures in northeastern France, men, equipment, food and water froze. And with a thaw came cold, glutinous mud. Hours spent standing in the damp, cold and dirt could bring the sores and swellings of "trench foot", which if untreated would turn gangrenous. With the vermin, the ever-present rats, a poor diet and erratic sleep, the surprise is not that the men went sick or cracked, but that so many soldiered on, grumbling but sticking to their time in the frontline. With these hardships to contend with, very often the enemy was often seen as a mere distraction, and the collapse of a trench from an artillery barrage or a trench mortar seen as just another chore.

It was no wonder that the principle of rotation was so important. At least a British soldier could usually say to himself, "Only another two days to relief."

The semi-permanence of trench life made for ever more ingenious ways to adapt holes in the ground to make life more bearable. This chicken house would have been a considerable boon for its British unit, bringing the welcome prospect of fresh eggs for breakfast.

50

THE *SOIXANTE-QUINZE* FIELD GUN
ASSAULT ON VERDUN

FEBRUARY TO DECEMBER 1916

It was barely more than two months after the Allies agreed, in December 1915, to coordinate future offensives (*see* Chapter 48) that the Germans delivered a shock of their own – a massive attack on the fortress complex of Verdun. It would signal the start of the biggest, bloodiest and longest battle on the Western Front.

Verdun was supposedly chosen as the target because it was the place that France would *have* to defend to the end, thereby expending valuable French lives and resources. After the war, Chief of the German General Staff Erich von Falkenhayn claimed that he wrote a memorandum to this effect for the Kaiser over Christmas 1915, outlining his attritional plan to "bleed France white", saying: "the French will be compelled to throw in every man they have. If they do so the forces of France will bleed to death."

Whether he really did intend such a bloody, grinding battle, Falkenhayn's decision set in train a titanic Franco-German struggle that has become synonymous with mass slaughter and which resonates to this day. By the time the field guns, including the French "75s" and their heavier equivalents, had finished pounding one another, around three-quarters of a million French and Germans had been killed, wounded or were missing.

The French M1897 75mm Field Gun revolutionized the way wars were fought. It used a combination of liquids and gas in a recuperator to absorb the energy of each shell. While the barrel shot back nearly 4 feet on the carriage, nothing else moved. The wheels remained in place and, once the barrel had returned to its starting position, the gun could be fired again and again at the same target. It was its speed and accuracy that made the "75" so effective. The Germans tried to copy the gun's technology for their own M1896 77mm Field Gun, as did the British for their 18-pounder. But the French kept the 75's details secret and it arguably remained the supreme field gun for much of the war. Fully aware of this, in September 1919 the Imperial War Museum asked the French for a 75 with a good war history. This particular gun fought throughout the war with the 2nd Battery, 61st Field Artillery Regiment – playing key roles on the Marne and north of Ypres (1914), in the Argonne and in Champagne (1915), at Verdun (including the battles for Fleury Ravine and the hill of *Le Mort Homme*) and the Somme (1916), on the Aisne (1917), and again on the Somme and the Argonne (1918). Since it was first displayed in 1920, it has provided an enduring reminder of both the heroic efforts of the French army and the close bond that existed between Britain and France during the war.

"DEAFENED BY THE NOISE, DIZZY WITH SMOKE, SUFFOCATING WITH GAS, THEY ARE THROWN AGAINST THE GROUND OR HURLED AGAINST EACH OTHER IN THE BLASTS. PIECES OF SHRAPNEL WHISTLE PAST THEIR EARS. THE SOIL, THE STONES, THE RIFLES, THE BEAMS OF THE SHELTERS AND THE EQUIPMENT ALL SPRING OUT AND THEN FALL DOWN AROUND THEM."

Sub-Lieutenant Jacques Péricard, reservist and journalist, author of Ceux des Verdun *(1917) and other works on the battle*

Today, Falkenhayn's motives in attacking Verdun are questioned. His "memo" has never been found, no record existing except in his memoirs. And French aerial reconnaissance detected new German railway lines and supply routes being laid towards Verdun as early as November 1915, suggesting longer planning. It seems more likely that Falkenhayn's claim was made after the event to explain away what the battle actually became when at the time he really sought a breakthrough. However, one *undoubted* reason for choosing Verdun was that the German artillery could be supplied with ammunition by direct railway line from nearby factories in Diedenhofen. Some of the shells arrived at the gun lines "still warm from the manufacturers".

Verdun's defences had been deliberately run down during 1915 by General Joffre. The shock of the Germans' super-heavy artillery, which had shattered the Belgian forts at Liège and Namur in 1914, had convinced many in the French military that static forts were now just helpless targets. So Verdun's heavy guns had been removed to support Joffre's great offensives of autumn 1915. However, the local French governor, General Frédéric-Georges Herr, and Lieutenant Colonel E.A.C. Driant, who was commanding two battalions of Chasseurs at the Front, both warned that they would be unlikely to withstand any determined German offensive.

As Driant was also a Deputy in the French Parliament, it was difficult to ignore his publicized concerns, and a commission went to Verdun to investigate, but an angry Joffre dismissed its findings. In some parts of the frontline at Bois des Caures, Driant's sector on the north of Verdun, there were neither trenches nor continuous barbed wire. Among the thick woods the French defence consisted of bunkers and foxholes, not all linked; and telephone cables had not been buried to protect vulnerable communications from shellfire. Worse, Germany had secretly massed nearly as many shells for *each* of her 50 gun batteries as the French had for all their 75mm guns in the Verdun sector.

The German plan was based on breaking across a narrow front of 7.5 miles along the eastern bank of the River Meuse, which flowed north from Verdun. Falkenhayn had planned a concentrated, intense but short bombardment followed by a swift advance. Strict secrecy was maintained, and overhead German fighter pilots maintained a ruthless air supremacy over the outclassed French reconnaissance planes. French intelligence slowly became aware of the German build-up during January 1916 as they detected massive new concrete troop shelters (*Stollen*) being built in the woods, and artillery moving into position, while deserters warned of a major offensive. However, the French General Staff discounted the warnings. The local chief of operations told concerned intelligence officers: "When you show me trenches 150 metres from our lines than I will believe you." The problem was they had only identified 34 enemy battalions on the east bank of the Meuse, most of them nearly half a mile back from the French frontlines, and an estimated 260 guns. In fact, there were 72 assault battalions being massed and over 1,200 guns.

The attack was scheduled for dawn on 12 February. However, at first light, both sides looked out on a raging blizzard. For over a week the weather delivered high winds, freezing snow and thick fog. Crown Prince Wilhelm, commanding the German Fifth Army, fretted, noting in his diary: "we passed an agonizing time. Every hour lost diminished our prospects of speedy success."

When the weather finally cleared on 21 February, the attack began. Across a 19-mile front the artillery pieces roared into action. For 12 hours the bombardment raged, much of it concentrating on the northeasterly Bois des Caures, turning it into

"HE WHO HAS NOT FOUGHT AT VERDUN, CANNOT COMPREHEND MISERY"

Jacques Péricard

a wreck of splintered trees, shattered bodies and smoking shell holes. Finally, at 16.00, in the gathering winter dusk, German assault troops probed forward, led by flamethrowers and grenadiers. Astonishingly, they ran into serious resistance. Although only about 20 per cent of Driant's Chasseurs had survived the bombardment, those that could fought on. Infiltrating through the wrecked wood, little groups of attackers surrounded the French posts and pressed on into the gloom. At first light the woods on either side of the Bois de Caures endured more bombardment, to be followed by a more serious onslaught. The woods were overrun.

Eventually recognizing he was outflanked and the position was hopeless, Driant ordered his surviving men to pull back. As he stopped to help a wounded soldier, he was shot in the head and killed. His soldiers' stand had successfully delayed the Germans for a vital 48 hours but still the Germans pressed on, and late on 24 February they finally took the last French reserve line, even moving up to the first of Verdun's protective forts at Douaumont. The sector commander, General Fernand de Langle de Cary, now planned to pull back and evacuate the whole east bank of the Meuse. Joffre despatched his chief of staff, General de Castelnau, to report on what looked like a major defeat. De Castelnau restored order and Joffre promptly ordered the replacement of de Cary with the infantryman Philippe Pétain, with strict instructions to hold on at all costs.

It seemed a logical choice. Pétain, commanding the Second Army to the south of Verdun, had always believed that modern weaponry gave pre-eminence to the defence. He had a saying: "*le feu tue*" ("firepower kills"). The immediate problem was that he could not be found. His *aide de camp* eventually ran him to earth at a hotel in Paris, ensconced with his mistress. He confirmed that he would leave for Joffre's Chantilly HQ at daybreak, and afterwards travel to Verdun, adding imperturbably: "meanwhile, the night has other duties".

Life and death, cheek by jowl. A German soldier near Fort Vaux crouches in a depression and aims his rifle, ignoring the torso-less legs of a French defender to his left. The fighting at Verdun became a byword for the worst of the Western Front's attrition and greed for human life.

Pétain set up his headquarters in the south at Souilly, arriving on 25 February just in time to learn of the devastating loss of Fort Douaumont that day. As the French infantry retreated, a small garrison had remained there, but it took to the lower levels to escape the shelling. Eventually, it took just one enterprising German, Pioneer-Sergeant Kunze of the 24th Brandenburgers, to put the fort out of action: he broke in through a shell hole and single-handedly captured the small gun crew. He was followed by two captains of his regiment with their sections, Hans-Joachim Haupt and Cordt von Brandeis, who rounded up the rest of the garrison without a shot. German children were given a day's school holiday to mark the occasion and both officers were awarded Germany's highest military decoration, the *Pour le Mérite*. Sergeant Kunze was ignored.

For the French, Douaumont's fall was a public disaster. It commanded the whole northeastern approach to Verdun itself and had huge symbolic value. As the French consolidated on the last line of hills only 3.5 miles north of the city, the situation was looking desperate for the French – and now for Pétain himself. The 60-year-old had contracted pneumonia in the freezing winter weather. Yet, wrapped in blankets, he proceeded to fight the battle by telephone from his bed and his desk. His early decisions and orders were unequivocal: "hold on", "re-man the forts" and, most famously, "They shall not pass!" ("*Ils ne passeront pas!*"). The French artillery now began to disrupt fresh German attacks, and the Germans found it difficult to drag their heavy guns forward across the shell-cratered battlefield. Their advance slowed.

Another Pétain decision was to set up a permanent supply line to the beleaguered town through a narrow road corridor from Bar le Duc in the southwest. This became known after the war as *"La Voie Sacrée"*. Nearly 80 per cent of men and materials involved in the defence came along this route, with the residue arriving on a narrow-gauge railway line. Over 220 French divisions rotated along the 45 miles of the *Voie* during the ten months of the battle, and 23 million shells passed along it. The road was maintained by a small army of 10,000 troops, and patrolled from the air. One calculation is that a truck passed along it every 15 seconds, night and day.

The battle itself, fed by enormous resources on both sides, developed into a vast artillery mincing machine. The successful German advances on the eastern side of the Meuse had, though, exposed their right flank to bombardment from the French positions on the west bank. The Germans had not counted on such a withering barrage from these superb, massed French "75s". More and more batteries of these quick-firing guns blasted the German attacks as they sought to struggle forwards, forcing Falkenhayn to tackle the problem head-on and widen his front. On 6 March, the Germans attacked the west bank of the Meuse to push the French back. Instead, they became embroiled for months in a battle of attrition for two west-bank hills, *Côte 304* and, nearer the river, the ominously named *Le Mort Homme*.

As spring arrived, on both sides of the Meuse the battle deteriorated into the familiar pattern of trench warfare, with endlessly mounting casualties. This was a different scenario to the desperate defence in February, and by May Joffre promoted the defensive-minded Pétain away to be commander of the Army Group Centre and put the more aggressively-minded General Robert Nivelle in charge at Verdun. Meanwhile, on the east bank, the Germans slowly pushed further south. On 7 June, after bitter fighting deep underground, the Germans captured Fort Vaux and pressed closer to the city itself.

Everything changed on 1 July, when the British and French launched their Somme offensive to the north. Along with recent Russian resurgence in the shape of Brusilov's offensive on the Eastern Front (*see* Chapter 51), Falkenhayn was so alarmed, by 12 July, that he ordered the attacks around Verdun to be stopped in order to move vital reserves to counter these new threats. The Germans had lost the initiative and were now on the defensive. But the mutual shelling continued all summer long. Gradually, things were turning to the French advantage. Air superiority over the battlefield was regained and finally, in October, Nivelle began a slow and bloody counteroffensive to retake the forts, culminating in the recapture of Fort Douaumont on 24 October. Fort Vaux was retaken, too, on 2 November.

By December 1916 the battle was finally over as the Germans found themselves back on the attack lines from which they had set out on 21 February. At Verdun, France and Germany had fought themselves to a standstill. It had been one of the longest, most indecisive, greediest battles (in terms of human life) in history. There has been dispute about casualties, but however viewed they are horrific: French official numbers are 377,231, including 162,308 dead, while German estimates are 337,000, including at least 100,000 dead.

The landscape bears the scars of battle a century later. Whole villages are represented only by a sign and a rolling series of grassed-over silent shell holes in the woods. The battle appeared to teach lessons. For one French sergeant called André Maginot, who was wounded near Verdun in 1914, the stubborn durability of the fort complex suggested it was still the way to protect France. In the 1920s, when Minister of War, his proposed "Maginot Line" was supposed to stop German aggression once and for all. Fifty years later, in the very different atmosphere of 1984, Verdun was the place where German Chancellor Helmut Kohl and French President François Mitterrand held each other's hands for a public act of joint remembrance, beneath the shadow of the towering monument and the massive Douaumont cemetery (*see* Chapter 99).

51

POSTCARD FROM THE EASTERN FRONT
THE BRUSILOV OFFENSIVE

JUNE TO OCTOBER 1916

The disastrous defeats and retreats of 1915 (*see* Chapter 18) had left the Russian army's High Command, *Stavka*, dispirited and pessimistic. Despite its huge size, the army still did not have enough artillery, machine guns or even rifles – indeed, it had lost thousands of guns to the Germans. Russia's inefficient industry was incapable of delivering enough new arms, while the Allies' failure at Gallipoli prevented the possibility of imports via the Black Sea. A scanty Russian rail network and inefficient logistics compounded the problem. At the Chantilly conference in December 1915 (*see* Chapter 48), the Allies had committed themselves to simultaneous attacks in the summer of 1916. But it was not clear how the Russians could contribute.

Logistically, the vast spaces of the Eastern Front, like the Western Desert a quarter of a century later, were a nightmare. Yet, perhaps surprisingly, many soldiers felt an affinity with the outdoors way of life on the Eastern Front. The landscape of lake, steppe and forest was arguably more bearable, even in trench lines – and despite the sometimes ferocious weather – than the concentrated proximities in which the armies in the West fought.

For Germans and Austrians, centuries-old traditions linked men to the vast forests of Central Europe and, unlike British trenches with their corrugated iron or sheets of expanded metal, German and Austrian trenches were lined with something much more natural and familiar – wood. In February 1916, one Austrian reservist by the name of Wündsam sent this small slice of wood back to his boss in Vienna. It was a piece of dried birch bark, cleaned, pressed and turned into a postcard. Wündsam was serving in *Landsturm Infanterie Regiment Nr.1* somewhere in *"Russland"*. All Austrian men were liable for military service between the ages of 19 and 42, and their last ten years were spent as members of the Landsturm, a reserve unit which remained ready to be called up in the event of war. Curiously, Wündsam's boss in his day job, and the addressee of the postcard, was British. In 1914, F.G. Stickings was living in Vienna as the head of Kodak in Austria. When war began his family returned to Britain but he had to remain behind. He was not interned, as he would have been in Germany, but allowed to continue working "on parole". This unusual postcard, from a serving infantryman to an "enemy alien", evokes a trusting relationship that transcended the politics of war.

This landscape was, though, an operational general's paradise – given the right general. And in 1916 Russia found him. During March, Alexei Brusilov was appointed

"IF THERE REMAIN ANY GERMANS STILL HOPEFUL FOR THEIR CAUSE, LET THEM REALIZE THAT TODAY, WHEN THE CENTRAL POWERS HAVE LOST THE INITIATIVE AND ARE FINDING A DIFFICULTY IN REFILLING THEIR RANKS, RUSSIA HAS NOT YET REACHED THE ZENITH OF HER POWER"

General Alexei Brusilov

commander-in-chief of the armies of the Russian Southwestern Front. This Georgian was an energetic and offensive-minded cavalry general, whose commands had done well in 1915, pulling back only to conform with the defeated Russian armies on his flanks. At his first meeting with the Tsar Nicholas, Brusilov took a brisk no-nonsense approach and insisted on Russia taking the offensive.

By contrast, the Imperial Council of War that met at Mogilev on 14 April 1916 reflected the Tsar's prevailing pessimism and indecision. The offensive around Lake Naroch, near Minsk, the previous month had been seen off by the Germans with

100,000 Russian casualties. The other two Eastern Front commanders, generals Alexei Kuropatkin and Alexei Evert, argued for a policy of "defend and wait", pleading shortages of guns and ammunition. Brusilov disagreed vehemently, advising an attack on *all* fronts. Supported by the Inspector General of Artillery, he insisted that he could mount an offensive with the armies and equipment he already had. There was a somewhat shamefaced agreement that Russia had to do something to honour her promises to her allies, so reluctantly the Tsar and other generals agreed: Brusilov's armies in the south would mount the first phase of a broader attack, to be continued by Evert further north.

Brusilov threw himself into the task with his customary energy. His 55 divisions were opposed by 49 Austro-Hungarian ones in three solidly fortified defensive lines. Brusilov's concept of operations was, for 1916, revolutionary – it anticipated future innovations on the Western Front. He planned to attack along the whole of his Army Group's 280-mile front. His orders emphasized surprise, deception and new infantry infiltration tactics designed to bypass strongpoints. The attack would be preceded by a short, intense bombardment concentrating on targets behind the frontlines to degrade command and control. His four armies each had an "active" sector, too, to confuse Austrian intelligence as to where the real blow might fall: units were deployed forward in an obvious manner, artillery fire intensified and there was blatant aerial reconnaissance.

Brusilov meticulously prepared his subordinates. Aerial photographs revealed details of the enemy defences; attacking units were briefed using terrain models of their objectives and rehearsed in their roles. Reserves moved quietly at night right up to the frontline where they dug huge bunkers in which they could hide from enemy observation. To take the first enemy line quickly the Russians secretly dug saps forward to within 100 yards of the Austrian lines. (Some opposing trenches on the Eastern Front were up to a mile apart.) By late May everything was ready, despite Evert's foot-dragging over his supporting attack to the north.

Surprise was complete when Brusilov's guns began their four-hour hurricane bombardment on 4 June. His northernmost army rapidly broke through around Lutsk, pushing the broken and demoralized Austrian Fourth Army back 10 miles on the first day, with thousands surrendering. By 8 June the Russians had captured the communications centre at Lutsk. As the Austrian command tried to work out where to deploy its reserves, Brusilov's southernmost army attacked into Galicia towards the Carpathians and commenced a rapid advance to the River Pruth. By the end of July Brusilov's men had progressed 60 miles across the Front and taken 350,000 prisoners. Conrad, the Austrian commander-in-chief, begged for German help.

Things now began to go wrong for the Russians. The offensive by Evert's Army Group, positioned around Minsk, was postponed, and when it did go in it was weak and badly prepared. On 24 July, German divisions counterattacked north of Lutsk. The Russians were stopped and Evert characteristically used the lack of success as an excuse for doing nothing further. Now *Stavka* did the very thing that Brusilov had begged it not to: it transferred troops by rail from Evert's sector to Brusilov's Southwestern Front, claiming that the new divisions would exploit the success of his initial attack. All they did was clutter and clog an already groaning resupply network.

The move also gave Hindenburg and Ludendorff, in effective overall command of German forces on the Eastern Front, the very clue they had been seeking. They promptly ordered the German reserves – including some hastily transferred

It is a tight squeeze for these German and Austro-Hungarian supply wagons as they negotiate the narrow Transylvanian mountain pass at Kirlibaba in 1917, near Romania's northeastern border with Russia. The Central Powers were under pressure in the region after General Brusilov turned his attention to supporting the Romanians.

divisions from the Western Front – to the far south where, because of their superior rail network, they arrived first. Brusilov had resumed his own offensive on 28 July, pushing hard towards the Carpathian Mountains, which his advance units reached on 20 September. But by then events were overtaking the Russian general: his supply lines were over-extended; ammunition was low; his men were exhausted; German counterattacks were slowing the advance; and Russian units now had to be transferred to help Romania, which – partly inspired by Brusilov's success – had unwisely thrown in her lot with the Allies on 27 August, and was soon overrun as a result. With Russian casualties numbering at least half a million, the offensive ground to a halt in early October.

Nevertheless, Brusilov's offensive had far-reaching effects. The German Chief of the General Staff, Falkenhayn, was sacked in August 1916: the Brusilov "shock" plus failure at Verdun, German losses on the Somme, and Romania were all too much. Austria-Hungary had lost some 16,000 square miles of territory and a staggering 1.5 million men (including 400,000 prisoners), and her hopes of victory in the East were ended. More than that, her subordination to Germany was complete. Germany was eventually forced to transfer no less than 35 divisions from the Western Front to bolster her ally. Austro-Hungarian attacks in Italy were stopped on German orders and her divisions recalled. The German General Staff now realized that with the Austro-Hungarian defeat it had arrived at its two-front nightmare and was now "shackled to a corpse".

But Brusilov's success would ironically help to accelerate Tsarist Russia's downfall, too. His victories had prompted initial rejoicing, but disillusionment set in when the offensive petered out. Dissatisfaction with a regime that could send men into battle without the basic necessities and could not feed its people led to widespread discontent. Behind the frontlines national morale slumped in the winter of 1916–17, as shortages caused by the diversion of resources to the war effort caused rioting and hunger took hold in the cities. Brusilov's failure would indirectly contribute to the Tsar's abdication just five months later.

52

BILLIE NEVILL'S FOOTBALL
THE FIRST DAY OF THE SOMME

1 JULY 1916

The first day of July 1916 – the beginning of the Battle of the Somme – retains a uniquely grim reputation. Quite simply, it was the day on which the British Army suffered its greatest number of casualties ever. The tally of killed, wounded or missing was 59,470, the recorded dead alone counting for 19,240. Moreover, because the British regimental system was based on region and locality, the painful news back home was concentrated on individual towns, villages and even streets. Well might the day be remembered a century on as a national tragedy. It was. Yet it was also the occasion for extraordinary bravery, where Britain's new "citizen army" of volunteers began to learn its rough and brutal trade, albeit the hard way. Inexperienced they may have been, but they faced the day with optimism, courage and some acts of inspiring leadership.

Wilfred "Billie" Nevill was always cheerful. In July 1915, he told his mother: "I feel as happy as I ever have in my life." The previous year he had been at the University of Cambridge, where he planned to become a schoolmaster. Instead, on the outbreak of war he became an officer in the 8th Battalion, East Surrey Regiment. He proved to be a capable, natural soldier and, quickly achieving promotion, he decided to make the army his career. In August 1915, the 8th East Surreys reached the Somme, where the British had recently extended their line, and for the next ten months it moved in and out of the trenches, with an increasing sense of battle looming. In May 1916, when home on leave, Billie bought two footballs to take to the Front, with the idea that his men could kick them forward and follow them when the attack materialized. He believed this would give them something familiar to think about as they crossed no-man's land under fire. On 1 July, Billie's company duly kicked off in the direction of Montauban – a moment that was later featured in the international press, though in Germany it was portrayed as a clear act of English madness. The attack succeeded as the battalion took its objective, but it did so without Captain Nevill and his second in command, who were both killed within their first few yards. The footballs fared better. They were retrieved from the German barbed wire, and this one was given to the regiment, which has held it securely ever since – a symbol of inspirational, unorthodox leadership.

For a week before the battle, a bombardment rained more than 1.5 million shells onto the German lines. It was more than all the British shells yet fired in the war. As zero hour approached – the attack had been put back a day because of bad weather

> **"I HAVE NOT GOT AN ARMY IN FRANCE REALLY, BUT A COLLECTION OF DIVISIONS UNTRAINED FOR THE FIELD. THE ACTUAL FIGHTING ARMY WILL BE EVOLVED FROM THEM."**
>
> *General Sir Douglas Haig,*
> *29 March 1916*

– the British detonated ten mines under the German defenders. The most memorable, on Hawthorn Ridge, was captured on film at 07.20, as 40,000 pounds of high explosive blew a German company to pieces. It was timed early, so as not to shower the British attackers with debris. Surely, there could be few German survivors along the line? The 8th Battalion, King's Own Yorkshire Light Infantry, was even told: "When you go over the top, you can slope arms, light up your pipes and cigarettes, and march all the way to Pozières before meeting any live Germans." At 07.30, along a 12-mile front, 150,000 British infantrymen climbed out of their trenches and began their advance. Battle was begun.

The background to it all lay in the Allies' Chantilly conference of 1915 (*see* Chapter 48). But what was intended as a massive French-dominated attack astride the Somme and Ancre rivers, in Picardy, had been compromised by the German onslaught on Verdun, from February 1916 (*see* Chapter 50). Faced with an increasingly embattled French ally, General Haig was forced to bring forward his plans and accept the fact that his 13 British divisions would now provide the bulk of the attackers. A second drawback was the weakness of the operational plan. Expanding the British Army from 6 to 56 divisions in 18 months was a colossal achievement, but it could not generate experienced, well-trained officers – and particularly staff officers. That deficiency compounded differences at the top. Haig believed in the possibility of breakthrough and exploitation, with a short but deep bombardment, whereas his general charged with planning the attack, Sir Henry Rawlinson, had more cautious ambitions. The plans for the "Big Push" thus veered between the over-simplistic and the overcomplicated, and from dreams of breakthrough to acceptance of attrition.

Rawlinson, commanding the Fourth Army, which would undertake the attack, was an experienced infantry officer but had to wrestle with three factors: first, the artillery needed to crush the German defences, but a week's bombardment sacrificed any chance of surprise; second, as most of his assaulting divisions were only half-trained, they would have to attack in waves, most at walking pace, making them more vulnerable; and third, to keep the reserves available for immediate use, they would have to follow close behind the assault forces and so were ordered forward on a pre-set timetable. All three factors contributed to the failures of the day.

The bombardment by 1,400 guns started on 24 June. It looked formidable on paper but was patchy in execution: most of the guns were field guns firing shrapnel, but the lead balls did not cut barbed wire. Heavier guns firing high explosive were diverted to help the wire-cutting, with the result that only 283 heavy guns targeted the well dug-in German trenches. Many German strongpoints and supporting artillery remained undamaged, and the barbed wire was only cut in places.

The assault went wrong from the start, especially on the left/northern flank. At Serre, the waves of "Pals battalions" (*see* Chapter 9) that formed the 31st Division were cut down by machine guns; a little further south, at Beaumont-Hamel, soldiers were slaughtered as they struggled through gaps in the barbed wire; and at Ovillers most of the leading waves were felled as they advanced across several hundred yards of open ground. Although the Ulstermen of the 36th Division successfully stormed the strongpoint of the Schwaben Redoubt, near Thiepval, in a running advance, their initial triumph ended in failure. They pushed further on, but as the formations on their flanks failed to advance and the German counterattacks increased, the survivors, short of ammunition and bombs, reluctantly fell back after dark.

An expression that says it all, as a soldier carries a wounded member of the 29th Division on 1 July 1916. The caption accompanying this long sequence from the contemporary documentary film The Battle of the Somme *records that the man being carried "died 30 minutes after reaching the trenches".*

Worse was to come after the initial assaults. As the first waves fell or took cover, others followed as the reserve lines advanced steadily, to be cut down in their turn. At La Boisselle, the Tyneside Irish were shot even before they reached the *British* forward trenches. The attack stalled. Along the line the British survivors, many badly wounded, cowered in shell holes in the blazing sun.

But it was not the same picture further south, around Montauban, where the well-drilled 18th Division (including Nevill's East Surreys), led by the able Major General Ivor Maxse, achieved all its aims. In fact, aided by well-cut wire, a new "creeping" barrage, mines, flamethrowers and catching the German defenders in the middle of their relief in the line, XIII Corps (including also the "Pals" of the 30th Division) seized all its first-day objectives, albeit at the cost of 6,000 casualties. Further west, the 7th Division of BEF Regulars gained the village of Mametz, forcing the Germans to abandon their nearby garrison at Fricourt.

These were, though, limited and expensively bought successes compared with the achievements of the French, albeit along a narrower front. General Marie Émile Fayolle's Sixth Army, straddling the Somme, took all its objectives comfortably. French heavy guns had pulverized the German trenches, counter-battery work had neutralized German artillery and the experienced *poilus* had infiltrated their way forward using fire and movement.

By midnight the scale of the day's disaster for the British slowly became apparent. Brigades and divisions reported unheard of numbers of casualties. The medical facilities were overwhelmed. Exhausted doctors worked late into the night and into the next day. Shocked chaplains wept over dying and broken bodies. The PoW cages remained largely empty. Numbed officers counted the shattered remnants of their once proud battalions, now reduced to company strength. The Newfoundland Regiment reported 700 dead or wounded from its 900 attackers. The 10th West Yorkshires' losses were worse. French casualties, by contrast, totalled just 7,000.

Further back, realities took longer to sink in. Haig actually wrote in his diary that some troops had not left their trenches, not realizing that dead men cannot advance. But as the next day dawned, and the cries of the wounded in no-man's land slowly faded and then fell silent, it became apparent to most that the first day of the Somme had been a bitter, bloody setback.

53

HAROLD COPE'S JACKET
CONTINUATION OF THE SOMME CAMPAIGN

JULY TO SEPTEMBER 1916

The thought of giving up after the first day on the Somme never occurred to General Haig or the British High Command. Even if they had wanted to stop, the French, the Russians and the British Cabinet were determined that the offensive should continue, to back up their mutual pledges to press the Germans on all fronts and to draw enemy reserves away from the hard-pressed French at Verdun. Just to make sure, General Joffre visited Haig on 3 July. The two men disagreed sharply on what to do next. Joffre wanted Haig to regroup and make a big push to gain Thiepval Ridge, while Haig insisted on carefully continuing local actions in those sectors that had seen success. Rawlinson, instinctively wishing to push on with greater urgency, acquiesced to Haig's caution; a month later he bitterly regretted what he felt was a lost opportunity in these early days of July to make a bigger impact: "it makes me sick to think of the 'might have beens'". Over the following weeks, making good this error would bring fighting as fierce as anything the Western Front had to offer.

By August 1916 Delville Wood on the Somme was one of the worst places on the Western Front. Death, decay and corruption permeated every inch. "Devil's Wood", some soldiers called it. Partially captured on 14 July, it was bitterly contested. For three weeks the South Africans fought through the broken trees, barbed wire and shell holes. Then their positions were taken over by men from northern England, including the 7th Battalion, Border Regiment, which moved into the fiercely fought-over eastern half of the wood and was immediately ordered to push the Germans from their remaining positions. Among its junior officers was Harold Cope, who had joined the battalion in May. At 4.30 p.m. on 7 August – Bank Holiday Monday – Cope rose up and led his men forward, only to be instantly cut down. He fell into a shell hole, severely wounded, his right arm hanging helplessly by his side and bleeding profusely. He was picked up, sent back to a dressing station and there, to tend his wound, the sleeve of his jacket was cut off. In March 1966, conscious of the forthcoming 50th anniversary of the Somme campaign, Cope offered his jacket to the Imperial War Museum. The remains of its right sleeve still hung limply off the shoulder, and streams of dried, brown blood covered the pockets. Another 50 years on, Harold Cope's bloody jacket remains a chilling testament to the brutal reality of life and death on the Somme battlefield in 1916.

What followed over the next two months was effectively a drawn-out slogging match as the British tried to push on with a series of hastily organized local attacks,

"BY THE END OF JULY ... THE GERMAN INFANTRY HAD MADE NOT LESS THAN SIXTY-SEVEN COUNTER-ATTACKS ... THIS WAS THE TEXTURE OF THE BATTLE: ATTACK, COUNTER-ATTACK; ATTACK AGAIN, COUNTER-ATTACK AGAIN."

Historian John Terraine,
The Smoke and the Fire, 1980

which the Germans resisted by equally hasty piecemeal counterattacks, over 300 of them in the summer. The German High Command soon became seriously alarmed at the ferocity of the fighting: the flow of reserves to Verdun was stopped, and by 10 July, 14 reserve divisions had been diverted to the Somme to reinforce General von Below's Second Army defenders. The British offensive was achieving at least one of its goals in the wider strategic context, as Joffre acknowledged.

On 14 July, Rawlinson got his chance for something larger. Ignoring Haig's worries about the inexperience of his Fourth Army volunteers, Rawlinson launched a skilful dawn attack after a night approach march towards the woods around Bazentin, supported by a short, highly concentrated bombardment. They took the Germans completely by surprise, overrunning the defences, seizing a 3.5-mile length of German second-line trenches and securing Longueval and Bazentin-le-Petit. But once again the chance to exploit was lost through poor communications; cavalry that could have captured the unoccupied High Wood to the northwest of Bazentin were not released until late afternoon – by which time the battered defenders had filtered back into the wood. The Battle of Bazentin Ridge was therefore an unfinished victory. But it showed that the British "New Armies" were learning.

To keep the pressure on, Haig gave Lieutenant General Sir Hubert Gough's Reserve Army responsibility for the battle above the Albert–Bapaume Road, which bisected the battlefield southwest to northeast, leaving Rawlinson to concentrate on the areas south of the road, including the local woods and the villages of Ginchy and Guillemont. The fighting rumbled on as the Fourth Army mounted over 90 separate attacks throughout late July and into early September, many of them small-scale, single-battalion affairs. In places like Delville Wood, where the South African brigade distinguished itself (with great losses), and High Wood, now reduced to splintered, leafless stumps, the German defenders clung on as the British tried to flush them out at close quarters.

On the night of 22/23 July, in Gough's sector, the Australian divisions of I ANZAC Corps entered the fray. Their objective was to capture Pozières, which had defied four British assaults since the battle's start, and its commanding position on the ridge astride the Albert–Bapaume Road. The 1st Australian Division tore into the village, but six days later the 2nd Australian Division failed to finish the job. At the same time,

Another still from the film The Battle of the Somme, *from the sequence "The Attack", in which a British Army unit and officer clamber into no-man's land. The scene might have been specially staged, away from the fighting, but nonetheless it conveys the vulnerability of infantry going "over the top" from a very shallow trench.*

Rawlinson's army was attacking between Pozières and Guillemont, and taking large casualties. It took two weeks of savage fighting before Pozières and the area around it finally fell on 7 August. Raising their heads from their hard-won victory, the Australians looked over at their next target, the well-fortified strongpoint of Mouquet Farm just short of Thiepval. It would take another month of hard fighting and 6,300 further casualties before the German defenders were finally driven out on 5 September.

Across the English Channel, British civilians were beginning to get a sense of the battle. Between late June and 8 July, two *ciné* photographers, Geoffrey Malins and John McDowell, filmed the build-up and the early fighting. Malins was "embedded" in the 29th Division around Beaumont-Hamel: it was he who famously filmed the Hawthorn Ridge mine going up. Shortly afterwards he had a near miss as a German shell blew his tripod over. McDowell was working further south and filmed captured German trenches near Fricourt and Mametz. The pair returned to London and put together an hour-long documentary, in which footage of actuality was intercut with specially staged continuity scenes such as shell bursts and soldiers going over the top. The film was later criticized for such creativity, though given the technology of the day and the need to convey narrative and the atmospheric, if not literal, truth this approach was perhaps inevitable.

After a private showing to the royal family, *The Battle of the Somme* was released in 34 London picture houses and distributed widely abroad. It was a sell-out. The *Times* opined that "it was wise that the people at home should have this glimpse of what our soldiers are doing and daring and suffering in Picardy". However, many spectators were shocked by the scenes of dead and wounded men, shutting their eyes to blot them out. "Oh God! They're all dead," gasped one woman. The film was generally recognized as a successful attempt to support the war effort and raise morale, while also conveying, for the first time, a sense of what the frontlines were like.

The Battle of the Somme was even shown to new drafts, if only to help them prepare for the horrors to come. Because, as the summer faded and the weather broke, the momentum of the real Battle of the Somme continued unabated, now under the grim and calculating heading of "attrition". In early August, Haig had ordered his commanders to press on with an unending series of smaller attacks. The casualties continued to mount – on both sides.

The impact of the entire Allied effort was undoubtedly taking its toll on the Central Powers. The French were now counterattacking at Verdun, Brusilov had driven the Austrians back in the east, and by the end the Somme was to suck in 42 extra German divisions to shore up its defence. On 29 August, Falkenhayn was dismissed, and Hindenburg and Ludendorff were brought from the Eastern Front to take over. They swiftly ordered a change of tactics. Instead of counterattacking as soon as possible, the defenders were urged to "let the attacker wear himself out, bleeding himself white" and reminded that "the fundamental consideration is the saving of personnel". It was the beginning of a new defence-in-depth approach, which in due course would see the German defenders retire to a new line of concrete defences.

But before that could happen, Haig was planning another big push for 15 September. And this time he intended to break through, using a new British secret weapon – the tank.

54

A FILM PROGRAMME
TANKS & THE END OF THE SOMME

SEPTEMBER TO NOVEMBER 1916

By September 1916 the British high hopes of June for breakthrough on the Somme had turned into a grim determination to keep up the wear and tear on a tenacious enemy. One prospect, though, of transforming the nature of the battle lay in the novel and highly secret weapon that the British had been developing: the tank. General Haig now planned to unleash it in a new offensive timed for 15 September, where the British would fight on a 1.5-mile front between Courcelette and Flers supported by the French to the south.

Of the film *The Battle of the Somme* (*see* Chapter 53), civilian Frederick Robinson had noted in his diary: "Londoners cannot go to the front to see the war, but the war has been brought to London for Londoners to see." He was one of the estimated 20 million Britons who saw that film, Britain's biggest-ever box-office hit. It recorded the battle's opening phase and, in the way that would come to typify the film industry, its success prompted a sequel. Thus *The Battle of the Ancre and The Advance of the Tanks* filmed the closing stages of the Somme campaign and highlighted the extraordinary phenomenon of the tank. The film was released in London on 15 January 1917, and this programme accompanied one of the first West End showings. The public were again captivated by the sight of genuine soldiers, the men they knew, fighting a real war. But this time there was the added excitement of seeing the new secret weapon. The films were, Robinson felt, totally absorbing: "You see in an hour more than you could see at the front itself in a month and all this is compressed into sixty strenuously exciting minutes. No wonder after the ordeal you come away both mentally and physically exhausted."

Notions of an armoured vehicle had existed before 1914. But it was the harsh realities of artillery, machine gun and trench warfare that supplied the impetus for action. As early as 24 August 1914, the French Colonel Jean Baptiste Estienne expressed the view that "Victory in this war will belong to the belligerent who is the first to put a cannon on a vehicle capable of moving on all kinds of terrain."

In November 1914, Major Ernest Swinton, later commissioned in the British Royal Engineers, suggested the idea of an armoured tracked vehicle to the War Office. The project was taken up, perhaps surprisingly, by the Admiralty in early 1915. Winston Churchill, as First Lord of the Admiralty, formed a "Landships Committee" charged with the design and construction. The first "landships" were built in conditions of great secrecy and called "tanks" to disguise the true purpose of the large

"I HEAR THAT OUR NEW FORM OF ARMOURED CAR WAS MENTIONED IN THE COMMUNIQUÉ YESTERDAY. THEY ARE A WONDERFUL CONTRIVANCE AND ARE EXACTLY LIKE A CREATION OF H.G. WELLS, OR JULES VERNE. THEY ARE ON THE CATERPILLAR PRINCIPLE, AND CAN GO OVER AND THROUGH ANYTHING."

Captain Arthur Gibbs, Prince of Wales Company, Welsh Guards, in a letter to his mother, 18 September 1916

THE BATTLE OF THE ANCRE AND THE ADVANCE OF THE TANKS.

PART III.

At 6.20 a.m. the attack is launched. The men climb "over the bags" and stream across the rugged waste of "No Man's Land." The Scottish troops stand to arms, eager for the signal. A "Tank," impressive in its power, surges forward over wire, hillocks, and craters. Another "Tank" is far away, well on to the enemy's lines.

As the attack progresses, waves of men are seen pouring into the German positions. The first prisoners arrive from "No Man's Land," their faces expressing great relief. As our reserves watch the progress of the battle the brave stretcher-bearers can be seen at work under a heavy shrapnel fire.

OF THIS PHASE SIR DOUGLAS HAIG REMARKS IN HIS DESPATCH:—

"Our assault . . . . met with success altogether remarkable for rapidity of execution and lightness of cost. . . . At 9 a.m. the number of prisoners was actually greater than the attacking force."

PART IV.

The wounded are carried in as the action continues, a Padre assisting a disabled Tommy with the devotion that has been so characteristic of "the cloth" in every battle. Scenes in the dressing station show how friend and foe receive the same attention. A large column of prisoners is assembled for removal to the compounds. Hot tea and sandwiches are given to the wounded, the lesser injured being sent to hospital in motor char-a-bancs.

Batteries of the R.H.A. move off to follow the advance.

Among the prisoners one observes a Hun colonel and his staff, captured in Beaumont Hamel. Our anti-aircraft guns are actively at work preventing the German scouts from reporting on the fight. At the close of the battle the mail arrives and the weary lads are gladdened by the latest news from home.

The Royal Naval Division assembles after seizing Beaucourt. The troops march back to rest laden with mud and glory. German helmets of two varieties—both the traditional Pickelhaube and its later relative the shrapnel headguard—appear to have been taken in profusion.

PART V.

At the close of the battle, the weary lads await the char-a-bancs that carry them back to billets. The West Yorks and the Worcesters are seen returning.

The shattered trail of war is seen in the condition of Beaumont Hamel and Martinpuich as they appeared on the British entry. Scottish troops are seen resting in the former. Australian gunners discourage their musician as they rest around a campfire. A view of the Ancre from the elevated bank, shows the inundated valley and the wire entanglements half hidden in the flood. Our men stormed through these obstacles and drove the Germans out.

The "Tanks" return triumphant, with an escort of cheering Tommies. The victors enjoy a meal in the captured German lines.

The return of the Cameron men. Irish heroes enjoy a well earned rest. The boys clean arms in readiness for the next attack, while a stern bombardment is maintained throughout the night.

And all that night, in a long drawn twilight, the shadowy forms of men and transport move forward to continue the Fight for Freedom.

GOD SAVE THE KING.

Programme

OF THE

Official Pictures of the British Army in France

Presented by

The War Office Cinematograph Committee.

The Battle of the Ancre

AND

The Advance of the Tanks

PRESENTED AT . . .

CINEMA HOUSE,
225, Oxford Street, W.

MONDAY, January 15th, 1917
And Throughout the Week.

metal objects being transported by rail. Ostensibly, they were water tanks for Mesopotamia and for the Russians.

In December 1915, the first real prototype, "Little Willie", proved that the concept was feasible and demonstrated its basic features: an armoured box to protect the crew, sitting upon caterpillar tracks to get across muddy fields. Two questions remained: how to cross trenches, and what type of armament should it could carry.

In January 1916, a new design was trialled, called "Mother", with a distinctive rhomboid-shaped frame over which the tracks extended. It could easily cross gaps of 9 feet, and its guns – normally two Hotchkiss 6-pounders (in a "male" tank) or four Vickers machine guns (in a female) – were mounted in two "sponsons" protruding from the sides, intended to sweep enemy trenches. The War Office ordered its first 100 machines into production, with a new Heavy Section of the Machine Gun Corps designated to operate them.

During August 1916 over 50 of the new Mark 1 tanks were shipped to France, and Haig agreed that they should be trialled during his upcoming offensive. On 4 September, the French Tenth Army began attacking the wider southern flank, below the Somme. Then, on 15 September, the British went into action, and Captain H.W. Mortimore achieved a historic first as he took his tank, *D-1*, into Delville Wood. But of the 49 tanks committed that day, only 32 made it to the start line, and only 21 of those actually advanced. They proved too easily prone to breakdown and mechanical failure, and too easily trapped in the pulverized, rain-swelled mud.

One tank, *D-17*, commanded by Lieutenant Stuart Hastie, was more successful than most on 15 September, smashing through the barbed wire protecting Flers. The sudden appearance of this mechanical monster shocked the Germans as it crunched through their trenches before driving through the village, blasting the defenders in the houses on either side. One overexcited reporter wrote of a tank "walking up the High Street of Flers with the British Army cheering behind". Overall, though, there weren't enough tanks and they didn't work very well. So their first attack – and many of the tanks themselves – petered out, leaving the infantry still to take the strain.

At Morval, later in September, General Rawlinson's Fourth Army did just that, demonstrating how well his men were learning their trade. Under cover of a tightly controlled creeping barrage, attackers of the 55th Division literally walked into German frontline trenches before the terrified defenders could emerge from their dugouts. And finally Thiepval fell on 28 September, with the 18th Division of Gough's Reserve Army showing once again that good training, limited objectives and tightly controlled artillery were the keys to success in trench warfare.

Throughout October Haig kept the pressure on, but only in the face of growing opposition from his own officers. The men were exhausted and conditions in the field were terrible. A series of attacks in the autumnal rain and chalky mud yielded few gains. Quite why Haig persisted remains a puzzle, but it can probably be attributed to French pressure. The fact that a major Allied strategy conference was scheduled for 15–16 November would also have made him aware of the need to try and secure a success to bring to the conference table.

It was against these realities that Haig ordered a final push on the northern flank of the line, against Serre and Beaumont-Hamel – both uncaptured strongpoints from 1 July – and up the River Ancre towards Beaucourt. The assault went in on 13 November and, in spite of yet another failure against Serre, was largely successful. The 51st (Highland) Division seized Beaumont-Hamel, taking thousands of

"AND WE SAW THESE TANKS COMING OVER FOR THE FIRST TIME; THEY'D NEVER BEEN USED BEFORE. IT WAS A FUNNY SENSATION TO SEE A DOZEN TANKS COMING OVER SHELL HOLES, NO STOPPING. DIDN'T MATTER WHAT THEY CAME OVER, THEY GOT OVER IT ALRIGHT, AND IT WAS HORRIFYING."

Gunner Sidney Taylor, 250th Brigade, Royal Field Artillery, recalling the sight of tanks near Flers, 15 September 1916

Tank C-19, Clan Leslie – a "male" type – rumbles along the curiously named Chimpanzee Valley on the Somme in September 1916. Visible are its grenade screens and rear steering wheels. It was commanded by Captain Archie Holford-Walker and intended for the debut of tank warfare on 15 September. Unfortunately, damaged axles en route to the starting line prevented its committal to battle – which was not a unique story.

prisoners. On its right, the 63rd (Royal Naval) Division, a curious hybrid of Marines, naval reservists and wartime volunteers organized as infantry, surprised the German defenders of Beaucourt, where the high morale of the "Navy's soldiers", inspiring leadership, and a fierce but brief artillery barrage swiftly smashed through the Germans' frontline. This Battle of Ancre was also another outing for the tanks of the (now renamed) Heavy Branch MGC. Once more, the deficiencies of these early machines limited their tactical usefulness; however, their sheer presence induced enough fear to make some Germans simply give up and surrender.

By 19 November, as thin snow covered the corpses and litter of the battlefield, the main fighting on the Somme was over. The British and French had gained a maximum depth of territory of around 7 miles. Was it worth it? In the six months between build-up and November at least 128,000 British and Imperial troops were killed, an average of nearly 900 men a day. Frustration at the campaign fed a political crisis (*see* Chapter 65) that brought in Lloyd George as prime minister. Despite all this, the national mood remained remarkably resilient. But it was different. From the press, from the films and from troops on leave, the British public was becoming only too well aware of the sacrifices being made. Lloyd George may have been shocked at the casualty figures, but he could come up with no alternative solution. A grim determination to see it through now became the prevailing British mood.

On the German side, though, the outcome of the Somme was greeted with something akin to horror. Ludendorff admitted that "the Army has been fought to a standstill and was utterly worn out". Over 100,000 irreplaceable regular NCOs, the backbone of the German military structure, had fallen. Moreover, the probability of worse to come in 1917 weighed heavily on German strategic planners, and would underpin the decision that year to fall back to the formidable defences of their new Hindenburg Line, now being constructed.

For the British Army, the Somme was merciless. But the BEF was now much better trained to fight a modern war. Operational and battle staffs acquired hard-won experience, new weapons and tactics had been forged, and it is no exaggeration to say that the battle-hardened BEF that went into battle from 1917 was a very different force to the hopeful amateurs that attacked on 1 July 1916.

55

ARMY RATIONS
FOOD IN THE TRENCHES

1914 TO 1918

In normal trench life, by far the greatest comfort – after sleep – was food. The rhythm of life was often set by meals, from rum, bacon, bread and tea for breakfast, to "bully" (corned) beef, cheese and army biscuits in the middle of the day, and – with luck – a Dixie can full of hot, all-in stew carried up after dark. Food punctuated what Lord Moran –then an infantry doctor and later Churchill's physician – was to call "the awful sameness of those years of trench warfare".

It was quite different in periods of action, or under heavy bombardment, as survival came first. But whenever there was an opportunity, creature comforts reasserted themselves. With a barrage over, men would immediately brew up tea. The staple, bully beef, was always ready to be eaten warmed up or cold. Old Regulars who had served in India might even chuck in a handful of curry powder. To improve this basic diet the army provided tins of pork and beans, Maconochie's Army Ration (meat and vegetables in gravy), plum and apple jam, and condensed milk to be shared among a mess group of four. Maconochie rations were generally deemed quite palatable hot; cold, it was a different matter, as R. Derby Holmes recorded: "The first man who ate an oyster had courage, but the last man who ate Maconochie's unheated had more."

> In the trenches, food was often tinned: corned, or bully, beef, Maconochie rations, and pork and beans. In September 1917, Ernie Rhodes was in a shell hole near Ypres when another soldier dropped in beside him. As Rhodes remembered, his visitor said, "Ooh, I'm hungry", to which he replied: "Well, listen, I've got a tin of pork and beans in my haversack. You can have it. He had a little 'Tommy Cooker', which was a little tin with fat in it. You could light it and hot things up. So, in this shell hole we got this going and when I smelt these beans warming up – I'd told him I didn't like beans – but I said, 'Well, I'll have some of that.' And that was the finest meal I've ever had in my life. I was really hungry and it was absolutely wonderful. I'll never forget it." In adversity, even the plainest of army rations could bring solace.

Variety was limited, especially as the war ground on, and parcels from home were eagerly awaited. They could contain all sorts of items to supplement the army basics, such as chocolate, biscuits, sweets and cakes, but the favourites were Oxo Cubes, Bovril and, above all, tobacco. After the capture of High Wood in 1916, during the Somme campaign, the Public Schools' Battalion even donated parcels sent for its now-dead gentlemanly comrades to another regiment: one of the grateful recipients remembered that as a result they "lived on luxuries for the next few days".

"THIS IS A RED LETTER DAY. MY PARCEL CAME THIS MORNING WITH A TIN OF PEACHES, LOAF AND BUTTER, FISH PASTE, TOBACCO, SLEEPING HELMET, CHOCOLATE, A PAIR OF SOCKS AND A TOWEL. HAD PEACHES FOR SWEET AT DINNER AND FISH PASTE FOR TEA. GRAND."

Private Frank Bass, 9th Battalion, Norfolk Regiment

Officers dined on the same food as the men, although prepared by their orderlies. Their own supplements might be rather grander – perhaps a hamper from Fortnum & Mason, or local produce such as chickens and eggs. Whisky figures large in officers' diaries: it was drunk at all hours, laced with water from old petrol tins.

Out of the line, food was readily available to all ranks. *"Estaminets"*, or cafés, sprang up everywhere to accommodate the British soldiers' hunger for egg and chips, washed down with plentiful draughts of "plonk" – *vin blanc* – or French beer (*see also* Chapter 56). Some soldiers' memoirs record happy nights out of the line in the company of good food, strong drink and complaisant young women ... a world away from Maconochie rations.

56

A DUMMY CALLED "DOUGLAS"
RELAXATION AT THE FRONT

1914 TO 1918

War is a social activity, even if an unusual kind. But the men at the Front could also look forward to rather more conventional, more pleasurable social situations, where they could relax. When rotated out of the line, they first looked to get clean, have an undisturbed night's sleep and eat hot food, but then they looked for entertainment and diversion. Games and gambling were always much in demand, as were sport and increasingly theatricals, together with the perennial attractions of wine, women and song. There was a place for anything that could take the men's minds off the grimmer business of their frontline lives.

Arthur Harden always reckoned that Douglas saved his life. Harden had enlisted in November 1915, apparently under the Derby Scheme, and, as a married man of 26, was mobilized in March 1916. He joined the newly formed 59th Divisional Ammunition Column where his commanding officer, Colonel K.C. Brazier-Creagh, discovered he had a special talent. Harden was a ventriloquist who had with him his *papier-mâché* dummy "Douglas" (possibly named after General Haig), and they no doubt made a fine pair. Since soldiers were always glad of any distraction, Colonel Brazier-Creagh quickly realized the pair's value for keeping up his men's morale. To keep Harden safe, he was appointed to the orderly room and eventually promoted to sergeant. As he often remarked: "The Colonel enjoyed Douglas so much that he prevented my posting elsewhere and mildly discouraged me from taking a commission." Harden and the 59th DAC arrived in France in March 1917. They pursued the Germans to the defensive Hindenburg Line, fought at Ypres and took the full force of the German attack of March 1918. Douglas, too, came under fire: his suitcase was torn by shrapnel. Yet the double act survived the war, with Harden living to the age of 93. On Harden's death in 1983, Douglas was passed to the Imperial War Museum. By then, like many older gentlemen, his hair was thinning; in later performances he had been forced to wear a yellow woolly hat. But, despite these challenges, Douglas continues to entertain visitors today, testament to an enduring life well lived.

One of the first things soldiers did was to write home. If urgent, as after a big battle, they often used a British Army Field Service Postcard, containing pre-printed statements such as "I am quite well" or "I have been admitted into hospital sick/wounded", which men could strike out or underline. A soldier was also entitled to two free letters home a week. These were censored by sometimes embarrassed company officers, many of whom discovered hidden depths among their soldiers.

"THE GAMBLING WAS ON A SMALL SCALE, NECESSARILY, THE BRITISH SOLDIER NOT BEING AT ANY TIME A BLOATED PLUTOCRAT. AT THE SAME TIME THE GAMES WERE CONTINUOUS"

R. Derby Holmes, who volunteered with the BEF, from A Yankee in the Trenches, *1918*

A female impersonator from the Canadian Concert Party "The Maple Leaves" makes up and prepares to don his wig, which is being combed by the kneeling officer. Theatrical productions were always popular behind the lines, and most concert parties could boast at least one drag artist.

The future prime minister, Harold Macmillan, wrote of the job as being his most valuable experience of the war as it "gave him knowledge of the poorer classes".

After having reassured the folks back home that he was still fine ("in the pink" was a favourite phrase), many a Tommy looked for diversion. This often took the form of cards or gambling games. A popular game was the North Country miners' "Pitch and Toss", where pennies were thrown at a line and the nearest scooped the pool – after the table had taken its cut, naturally. Others were "Over and Under" and "House" or Bingo. Authority tolerated these but not the most popular of all, "Crown and Anchor", in which men threw special dice – marked with the four playing-card suits, a crown and an anchor – in an effort to match their stake on a board of the same symbols. The "board" was usually a blanket, for quick concealment. The game was invariably run by a well-practised syndicate of three: a patter merchant; a money man; and a lookout, watching for any sign of approaching authority. One Tommy, Frank Richards, wrote ruefully of losing all his backpay during a long evening's gambling on the day the Armistice was signed.

A more active diversion, and antidote to cramped trench life, was football – played everywhere, at any opportunity, and by almost everybody. Officers marvelled at their soldiers' energy and willingness to play "footy" every moment they could. "However tired the rascals may be for parades, they always have enough energy for football!" observed one general. When troops were on rest, inter-platoon, inter-company and inter-battalion soccer matches were commonplace.

Organized sports extended far beyond football. Officers at rest or stationed behind the lines carried on their field sports as if back home in the country. The Northamptonshire Yeomanry kept a pack of hounds and when possible hunted fox and hare. Some officers kept dogs – the Earl of Feversham and his deerhound were killed and buried together on the Somme. Shooting game was common, mainly of the fat, over-fed partridges that would whirr out of cover at dusk heading for the loose grain and oats where the horses lined up. The chalk streams of the Somme were a dream for the dedicated angler. One reported taking 70 trout while at Blangy, saying "it was the best moment in my war service". His bait was, it seems, processed cheese.

Once the sun had gone down, off-duty soldiers would head for the canteen, "wet" or "dry". In those days, before the NAAFI was set up to organize such things, canteens were often run by charitable organizations such as the Salvation Army or the YMCA, where men could get a cup of tea and a bun. Many preferred the wet canteen with its beer, and even more soldiers would head out of camp looking for local hospitality at an *estaminet* (small café) with its invariable omelette and chips, *vin blanc* (often mixed with grenadine, as many soldiers craved sweetness) and the company of other men – and women. Indeed, every base camp attracted the attentions of local entrepreneurs. Cafés, bars and brothels quickly sprang up to service the off-duty soldier's needs and to relieve him of his money. In towns, business boomed for the *restaurateurs*. At Montreuil, well behind the lines and home of GHQ, the establishments in town were strictly segregated: "for Senior Officers", "Officers Only" and even "NCOs Only".

The three liveliest towns – magnets for soldiers on a very brief holiday from the horrors of the trenches – were Poperinghe (just 8 miles behind the Ypres Salient), Armentières near the Belgian border, and Amiens on the Somme. Here, an off-duty soldier could find almost anything he wanted, provided he paid. For the officers at Poperinghe, champagne was available at a popular club presided over by Madame Beutin and nicknamed "Skindles" after a similar hotel in Maidenhead, Buckinghamshire.

Sex was much in demand, and many soldiers lost their virginity in France. Young unmarried officers, often straight from public school, found much to excite their curiosity, and many soldiers had serious relationships with French and Belgian women – some going on to marry them. But for most men, the overriding aim was more transitory – to sleep with a woman before death or injury knocked on the door. Decorum could slip away – one soldier on the way up to Ypres remembered seeing a Highlander, kilt up, quite openly making love to a local girl. Later in the war, the stream of British nurses and WAAC drivers meant there were more women intermingling with the men, on duty and off, a proximity that contributed to an unwarranted reputation for "availability".

Other kinds of off-duty entertainment were organized by officialdom. Out of the line, Christmas dinner or regimental days were usually, as in peacetime, a sumptuous regimental feast served by officers to the men, washed down with lashings of drink. Perhaps the most amusing memories for many BEF men were the various semi-official concert parties playing to packed houses behind the lines. The 4th Division's "Follies" were in existence as early as December 1914, and by 1918 a whole series of well-organized official concert parties shadowed the popular music hall back home, putting on reviews and making fun of the Army, the General Staff, officers, NCOs and stingy quartermasters in a mix of ribald humour and sentimental songs and sketches, many performed by young men in drag.

On the last day before having to go back into the line, many companies and battalions organized "smokers" for the men: a day of more contemplative relaxation – drinking beer, perhaps listening to a talented member of the regiment singing or an officer playing a borrowed piano, while swapping cigarettes and talking with chums, all the while knowing that the next day the war would reassert its rigours and regime of fear. After a round of singing together, often ending with sentimental favourites like "There's a long, long trail a'winding, into the land of my dreams" or "Keep the home fires burning", all ranks would disperse to their billets, wondering just what tomorrow might bring – and just how many of them would be at the next smoker ... .

"IN SPITE OF – INDEED PERHAPS *BECAUSE* OF – THE IMMINENCE OF DANGER, CONCERTS AND FILM SHOWS (WHICH WERE EQUALLY POPULAR) WERE OFTEN HILARIOUS AFFAIRS ... EVERYBODY IS READY TO LAUGH AT EVERYTHING & MIRTH IS THE PREDOMINANT FEATURE OF THE WHOLE PERFORMANCE."

2nd Lieutenant E.W. Jacot,
14th Battalion, Royal
Warwickshire Regiment

57

A FRENCH PHRASE BOOK
THE BRITISH SOLDIER ABROAD

1914 TO 1918

In 1914, many regular soldiers of the British Army had already had experience of service abroad, or had heard stories from those who had served somewhere in Britain's Empire. But for the hundreds of thousands of volunteers and conscripts that followed in their wake, the shock of modern warfare was accompanied by the strangeness of living amid foreign places, people and cultures.

For most British soldiers in the First World War, little was familiar, from the brutal, dehumanizing nature of fighting to the alien environments in which they found themselves living. In Palestine, men who had grown up in houses with a family bible now found themselves walking through the ancient Holy Land where ploughs were still pulled by an ox and an ass. Battles were fought within sight of the Plains of Troy or close to Agincourt. Yet for the ordinary Tommy perhaps the most troublesome feature of life was language. All the natives spoke funny. Places had strange, unpronounceable names and it is no wonder that Ypres became "Wipers" and Auchonvillers "Ocean Villas". To help with this, handbooks were published like this one, the *Familiar French* pocket guide to French conversation and slang, or a *Soldier's Language Manual*, giving useful tips on how to be understood. With goodwill and a cocky smile, a little bit of "Franglais" went a long way to bridging the cultural divide.

On the Western Front, locals and their uninvited guests came to terms with their coexistence, and a relationship flourished that was based on supply and demand. Small towns, many packed with refugees, were swamped by foreign troops with money in their pockets and – never knowing if the next shell was for them – eager to spend it on the better things of life.

In the trenches, soldiers lived in sealed worlds, cut-off from the wider environment. But they became different creatures once out of the line and at rest. In towns and villages they were billeted on locals (who were well paid for the disturbance to their lives) or, more likely, were dropped off on a large farm with barns and a farmhouse, and left to their own devices for three or four days to rest and recuperate.

Relations with the locals continued, for the most part, according to a mutual suspicion balanced by a desire for mutually satisfactory commerce. Interaction, so far as it went given language barriers, was often about trading, whether it was buying wine at an improvised *estaminet* or, higher class, a restaurant, or even purchasing some female company at one of the officers' brothels in Poperinghe (*see* Chapter 56). Relations could be strained if the balance was put in jeopardy by some

"MY MAN BOBETT NEARLY MAKES ME DIE WITH LAUGHING SOMETIMES AS HE GESTICULATES TO THE PEASANTS FOR EGGS: SQUATTING DOWN, FLAPPING HIS ARMS AND SQUAWKING. HE THEN GRUNTS AND MAKES AS IF HE WERE SLICING BACON. FOR MILK HE SAYS 'MOO, MOO', BUT YOU SHOULD SEE HIM TRYING TO GET BOOT POLISH."

2nd Lieutenant Cyril Rawlins,
1st Battalion, Welch Regiment,
June 1915

of the heartier soldiers' behaviour (stealing wood, milk, chickens and fruit; getting roaring drunk; seducing farmers' daughters), and none of the French locals were anxious to share the soldiers' lice. For their part, the soldiery was not impressed by entrepreneurial locals attempting to overcharge their captive market.

But commerce wasn't everything. Some soldiers came away as married men. And for many soldiers, the locals offered the possibility of domesticity. When they were hosted by kind, hospitable civilians, with children or pets, sentimental soldiers often broke down, such was the contrast with the frontline. Such relationships reminded them of the things the soldier dreamed of above all others: freedom from fear; comfort; love; and hearth and home.

58

TUBBY CLAYTON'S CHALICE
CONSOLATION & HUMAN CONTACT

1914 TO 1918

People have always looked for some outside controlling influence to explain events and their lives. Believers call it religion, non-believers call it superstition. For the soldiers of the British Expeditionary Force, facing death in all its forms in the forward trenches for at least a week in every month, it meant (as for all other armies) that *some* mechanism of coping was obviously necessary, if a man was to stay sane.

Many did not. A sizeable minority of men were driven insane through their experience and the constant stress and fear: some temporarily; some forever. The problem was compounded by the fact that in 1914–18 the selection of would-be warriors had no psychological screening. A volunteer was a volunteer. The result was, as many observed at the time, that men were often accepted as physically "A1" for the army when their psychological profile left them extremely vulnerable. It is perhaps no wonder that men sought consolation wherever they could find it, from camaraderie to communion, from the spirits in a bottle to the spirituality of contemplation.

One of the hardest things for soldiers to find was spiritual peace. There was rarely any true respite from the war. Even out of the firing line and away from danger, routines continued and the pressures of military life remained. Faith gave hope to many, yet even the strongest beliefs could be tested at the Front. That was what made Talbot House so special. Usually called "Toc H", after its initials in the First World War's phonetic alphabet, it was founded by two chaplains at the end of 1915 as a new soldier's club in the quieter backwaters of Poperinghe, behind Ypres. The Reverends Neville Talbot and Philip Clayton were determined to create a place where men could go to recharge and rebuild; a place that was mentally distant from the war. As the sign outside said, it was "Every Man's Club". Inside, there were no ranks. Officers and ordinary soldiers met on equal terms. There were many places they could go to find release: a library to borrow books, a kitchen to make simple food and a beautiful garden, just like the ones remembered back home. But above all, discreetly placed in the Upper Room of the loft, was the chapel. For three years Clayton, whose short, round physique inevitably meant he was known to all as "Tubby", used this elegant but solid chalice and paten to dispense the holy sacrament. Through his services at Toc H, Tubby Clayton's quiet, practical Christianity provided salvation for thousands of lost souls.

The most vulnerable men could take very little extra stress. The writer Robert Graves, who was badly wounded on the Somme, reckoned that it took a man three

"NOT MANY OF US ARE RELIGIOUS IN THE TRUE SENSE OF THE WORD THOUGH A LOT OF US TURN TO GOD FOR HELP AND COMFORT WHEN WE ARE AFRAID: THAT DOES NOT MAKE US RELIGIOUS"

Private Archie Surfleet, 13th Battalion, East Yorkshire Regiment

months to learn how to survive in the frontline and then three months to start to break down as he saw his friends wounded and killed. Then many men cracked. One observer records a man wandering off after a bout of shelling "with his clothes off, believing he was going to bed". The authorities struggled with the concept of "shell shock" as being much more than insufficient backbone; even in 1922, a War Office committee stated that "No soldier should be allowed to think that loss of nervous or mental control provides an honourable avenue of escape from the battlefield." No less than 65,000 ex-soldiers were still receiving medical attention in 1929.

Others managed better, and a remarkable stoicism and endurance was often witnessed. Frank Richards, of the Royal Welsh Fusiliers, recorded numerous incidents when the survivors of a bloody attack or a ferocious bombardment would settle down to drink and gamble, shrugging off the horrors of the day. "San Fairy Anne" (*Ça ne faire rien*) seems to have been the old soldiers' universal sentiment – "it doesn't matter". Such fatalism was perhaps the only way of coping with the arbitrary nature of enemy shells or the chance of getting killed by a bullet.

The main support came from a man's friends. Soldiers didn't fight and endure for King and Country; they stuck it as part of a mutual support system with their chums in the trenches. Shared talk, shared hardship and shared fears helped many a man to cope with the horrors.

Officers and NCOs seem to have coped better because of the burdens of responsibility. When an officer led his men down a communication trench under fire, pretending to be as cool as a cucumber, or "hopped the bags", going over the top, he was keenly aware that his men were watching him closely for a lead and example. For an officer to run away screaming in terror was deemed unthinkable. (The struggle to stay in control later featured in R.C. Sherriff's play *Journey's End*.) Regimental pride and loyalty became extraordinarily powerful if intangible influences.

In an age when religion mattered, there were many who found comfort in their faith (*see* Chapter 40). The role of the chaplain or padre changed dramatically in war and the various incumbents reacted to it in different ways. Church parades were impossible in the trenches and only seem to have been held in reserve or rest billets. Increasingly, padres found themselves talking to the wounded at dressing stations, or even going round the line distributing chocolate or – as in the case of the Reverend Geoffrey Studdert Kennedy, nicknamed "Woodbine Willie" – giving out cigarettes to frightened soldiers; and, of course, burying the dead. Actual observance varied. To give but two contrasting examples, the Catholic Connaught Rangers held a well-attended Mass before going over the top at the Somme on 1 July 1916, but, despite the strong Welsh Chapel influence, the 2nd Battalion, Royal Welsh Fusiliers, seems to have delighted in substituting obscene words in the hymns at compulsory church parades.

Nevertheless, religion undoubtedly had a close hold on many in the line between 1914 and 1918, and it is no surprise that the Reverend Tubby Clayton's "Toc H" retreat in Poperinghe became a magnet for all ranks, offering an oasis of normality and an opportunity for spiritual contemplation. It went on, after the war, to become the centre of an international Christian movement.

Superstition, too, remained ever present. If someone casually said "touch wood" it was taken deadly seriously. Many men carried lucky mascots, or had bibles or letters from home in their breast pockets (*see* Chapter 40). Others carried their superstition to more practical levels. Major Buckley of the Northumberland Fusiliers recorded a premature explosion of a rifle grenade that scored his steel helmet: "After that I would never part with that helmet, though newer ones were issued later." Another soldier, Charles Edmonds, admitted an obsession with omens and fetishes as a way to grapple with the randomness of shellfire and "the absurdity of dark, overpowering fatalism".

An extraordinary example was Private Dann of the Royal Welsh Fusiliers. At Hulluch in 1915, he was suddenly confronted by "the biggest black rat I have ever seen". Dann decided it was an omen, and told his comrades that "when I go west [die] that

"GOD HEARD THE EMBATTLED NATIONS SING AND SHOUT / 'GOTT STRAFE ENGLAND' AND 'GOD SAVE THE KING!' / GOD THIS, GOD THAT, AND GOD THE OTHER THING – / 'GOOD GOD!' SAID GOD, 'I'VE GOT MY WORK CUT OUT!'"

J.C. Squire, satirical verse in his Epigrams, *1916*

rat will be close by". His mates told him not to be daft. Two months later Dann was sniped through the neck, and as he died he pointed to a huge black rat watching on the parapet. The next moment, an explosion killed the rat, which lay dead at his side.

Alcohol helped. For many, of all ranks, the constant danger and fear of the trenches could be dulled by copious libations of drink, which lent a particular importance to the morning half-gill rum ration, ceremonially dished out in an officer's presence. Indeed, when Authority interfered with sacred matters like the rum ration – as when a teetotal quartermaster thought pea-soup powder would make a more edifying beverage – morale slumped and soldiers became resentful. Alcohol in its many forms became the universal panacea. It relaxed tortured nerves, and encouraged blissful sleep and a few hours forgetfulness of ever-present dangers.

Beyond the community of the men, and such human comforts as the local French inhabitants could provide, there was the bond with home maintained through letters – millions of them – and parcels. By mid-war the BEF's well-oiled postal service ensured that no letter took longer than four days to reach a soldier, even in a frontline trench, and parcels with their creature comforts would be waiting when the battalion went into reserve. Soldiers treasured this link with a different, safe, *normal* world, and would endlessly reread the letters. All ranks agreed that this reminder of the outside world was one of the most powerful and important props to keep a soldier content. And if, at post call, a soldier turned away disappointed, a luckier friend might even say, "Here, d'you want to read mine?" It was a close-knit world.

Like Santa at Christmas, a cheerful artilleryman near Aveluy, on the Somme, bears gifts of parcels and packets for his battery (July 1916). Any small and practical comfort or comestible sent from home was highly prized. The British Army understood the value for morale and put considerable effort into ensuring an efficient postal and distribution service.

59

A BODY DENSITY MAP
CASUALTIES ON THE WESTERN FRONT

1914 TO 1918

The idea of war conjures up a stark duality of life versus death. In real war, though, there is much in between that can turn a soldier – or civilian – into a "casualty". The Latin root, *casualitas*, literally means an "unfortunate accident". Although these undoubtedly occurred in the frontline, from a carelessly dropped hand grenade to – quite common – kicks from a horse or mule, unsurprisingly they were a tiny percentage of the war's overall casualties. Most casualties comprised the wounded and the sick, the captured (*see* Chapter 44) and the missing – as well as the dead.

It is a stark fact that the concept of "the missing" was new in 1914. Industrial-scale warfare, modern artillery fire and churned up ground meant that thousands of soldiers were literally blown to bits. Battle created a landscape of overlapping shell holes, where wounded men could simply disappear without trace, or their graves were obliterated. The huge numbers of "missing" resulted in vast memorials at places like Thiepval on the Somme, the Menin Gate at Ypres and the Tyne Cot in the shadow of Passchendaele. For over 150,000 British and Imperial soldiers, the names inscribed on them are all that remain.

In the autumn of 1914, a British Red Cross officer called Fabian Ware realized that no-one in authority was recording where the British dead were being buried. Voluntarily, he took on the task, which was soon formalized in the Graves Registration Commission and then, in May 1917, the Imperial War Graves Commission. The task of building permanent cemeteries began the following year. Lieutenant Colonel Arthur Messer, Assistant Director of Graves Registration & Enquiries in France, undertook a survey between December 1918 and July 1919 of the locations of all the crosses and known burials across the battlefields that lay outside the recognized cemeteries. To inform the Labour Companies who would have to find, disinter and rebury these outlying bodies, a series of large-scale maps was drawn up, on which the number of crosses or known burials was noted in blue pencil in each map square. These maps, now held in the Imperial War Museum, became known as "Body Density Maps", and the detail given here (from Map 57c) shows the old 1916 Somme battlefield. Each numbered square 1–36 (further sub-divided into four) is 1,000 yards by 1,000 yards. Some of the bloodiest fighting took place from July to September 1916 in the short distance between High Wood and Flers – on the overlap between squares S5 and S11, to the north of Longueval. The density of the losses here is chillingly visualized by four simple blue numbers: in this small area alone there had been over 2,400 burials.

"IN THE BOTTOM OF A SHELL HOLE ... WAS A SOLITARY HEAD. IT STOOD UPRIGHT IN THE CENTRE OF THE CRATER AND THERE WAS NO TRACE OF THE BODY TO WHICH IT BELONGED"

Captain Alfred Pollard VC, in his Fire Eater: The Memoirs of a VC, *1932*

Over half a million British and Imperial soldiers on the Western Front were killed – almost 60 per cent of them the victims of artillery. The possibility of death was always with soldiers in the line, and the dead were much in evidence. After a battle, no-man's land was littered with bodies. Most soldiers were revolted by the sight at first, but slowly became inured to it. On the Somme, Corporal Joe Hoyles of the Rifle Brigade witnessed a staff officer's first sight of death. Staring across at the bodies of the slain, the officer exclaimed: "Good God! I didn't know we were using Colonial troops." He was wrong. A week in the blazing sun had turned the dead men's bodies black.

With the accumulation of bodies came the unenviable task of collecting and burying them. Hoyles describes it well: "There was a terrific smell. It was so awful it nearly poisoned you. The old German front line was covered with bodies – seven or eight deep and they had all gone black. Our job was to put the bodies on [stretchers] and with a man at each end we threw them into that crater. I'll never forget that sight." Because British battle dead were buried close to where they had fallen, the sites – as later documented by the Graves Registration Commission and its successors – in themselves mapped the fighting.

Wounds were the subjects of mixed feelings – mostly feared, but sometimes welcomed. The technology of the day meant that when a shell exploded its fragments could be of any size, and chunks of red hot steel whizzing around could – and frequently did – slice off arms and legs, rip stomachs and chests open and cut off faces. Most men had seen the horrific effects of shellfire on the bodies of their friends. One shell exploded near Lance Corporal William Moon of the Cheshires in 1915, blowing his friend's head off and splattering Moon with his blood and brains – an experience that shook him so much he refused to go into the line, for which he was eventually executed. The bullet wound most dreaded was being shot in the stomach – it was frequently fatal. Despite the ravages of wounds, however inflicted, over 80 per cent of British wounded returned to active service.

The wound most wanted, by contrast, was a coveted "Blighty one" – the wound that didn't cripple or disable, but which took the victim away from the horrors of the frontline with his self-respect intact, perhaps even back across the Channel. The future writer Stuart Cloete was a Coldstream Guards officer in August 1916 when he was shot while tackling the enemy: "As I ran at him he fired. I spun round and sat down. I felt no pain. I felt as if someone had hit me in the shoulder with a great wooden mallet with such force as to knock me over ... Now I had my blighty one".

"Blighty ones" were not always unexpected, though. Frank Richards recalled that soldiers would actively court a nice clean bullet wound. In the winter of 1914–15 he remembered bailing out the flooded trenches, and "a man called Davies had his thumb shot off whilst bailing. Every one of us volunteered to take his place, but one man got the bucket first. He deliberately invited a bullet through his hands by exposing them a little longer than necessary; but the bucket got riddled instead."

When a soldier was hit in no-man's land many heroic acts were performed in getting the him back. Unarmed stretcher bearers risked their lives on countless occasions: it is no coincidence that the most decorated British non-commissioned soldier of the war was a stretcher bearer – Sergeant William Coltman VC DCM and Bar MM and Bar. Once a wounded man was back at the Regimental Aid Post, the wound was cleaned and, if possible, stabilized and then he would be passed back to a Field Ambulance behind the lines or a Casualty Clearing Station (CCS), where major surgery could be carried out. The "walking wounded" would make their own way back. A badly wounded man would then either be moved to a Base or General Hospital, which had all the facilities of a normal civilian hospital, or sent to Étaples, Boulogne or Rouen before transit back to England on hospital ships.

Once in the casualty evacuation system most wounded men felt relief and an immediate loss of any sense of personal responsibility, after they had surrendered their bodies to the great, and increasingly well-organized, medical machine. After crossing the Channel they would be met by trains and dispersed to a network of voluntary and military hospitals across the country. Wounded soldiers were provided with a special blue uniform and were a common sight in provincial towns. Britain's *Official History* of the war states that while 36,879 men died in hospital, 169,842 returned to duty after treatment.

The final – and, perhaps surprisingly, the biggest – source of casualties between 1914 and 1918 was disease. Indeed, it was not until the Second World War that combat deaths came to outstrip deaths from disease. In Africa, Mesopotamia, Palestine, Gallipoli and Salonika soldiers sickened and frequently died from malaria, dysentery, typhoid and typhus. On the Western Front few soldiers died of trench foot or venereal disease, but both incapacitated large numbers of men – as did "trench fever", which was passed on by the ever-present lice. This infection, of which the BEF reported 800,000 cases, was rarely fatal, but it required a hospital stay and was totally incapacitating with its combination of fever, severe headache, pains in the muscles of the trunk and characteristic shin pains. Among the British Imperial forces, over 5,688,000 men were hospitalized from some form of disease during the war. That is nearly twice as many as the official total of battle casualties, 2,937,600.

After four years of war, the number of British and Imperial dead alone – from whatever cause – was well over a million, half of them "missing". And these losses were the least among the original belligerents. Nothing had prepared the warring nations for such numbers.

In a haunting image, a wounded man is wheeled on a stretcher along the road somewhere between Amiens and La Boisselle in July 1916, silhouetted against the setting sun. In its formal composition, the photograph has a stately, funereal air about it.

A BAIRNSFATHER CARTOON
SOLDIERS ON LEAVE

1914 TO 1918

While a spell out of the line in a base rest camp was a welcome break for soldiers on the Western Front, the most sought-after relief was home leave. By 1915 the British Army's bureaucracy had settled on a clear, relatively humane and efficient leave system for soldiers in France and Flanders. In fact, many argue that the promise of regular leave, which did not exist for the French until reforms in 1917, was one of the things that made the British soldier so resilient between 1914 and 1918. But the experience of leave was not always unalloyed joy: it could be a difficult business of acclimatization for soldier and civilian alike.

Seven days away from the war, with family, was something to be cherished, but it also carried an emotional price, as captured in this drawing by officer cartoonist Bruce Bairnsfather. He was best known for his humorous images of the trenches, particularly those featuring the well-known character "Old Bill". Published by the *Bystander* magazine, these "Fragments from France" were collected in a series of anthologies from 1916 onwards. At the end of each one, Bairnsfather included a serious drawing touching on the reality of life for the men in the trenches, and this one captured both the intense joy of leave, but also the lingering sadness that invariably hung over it. Leave had to end. Men had to return to the destroyed and broken world of the frontline, made visible here by Bairnsfather behind the domestic foreground. The distress of this left many wondering if the temporary joy had been worth the pain of renewed separation. London restaurateur Hallie Eustace Miles found herself at Victoria Station in March 1915 as the leave train was arriving. "In one instant the doors all flew open, and strange objects poured out. They seemed to resemble Arctic explorers, or Esqimax, than ordinary soldiers. Most of them had on sheepskin coats, strange fur caps and woollen helmets; and their khaki was black. They all looked *dreadfully* tired. I did so long for someone to start cheering the War-worn heroes: it was so horribly English and silent. I noticed that the men who came back home looked nearly as sad as those who went back."

The system favoured commissioned ranks slightly, reflecting the social standards of the day. Officers were held to be more responsible and therefore more deserving of extra leave; however, in practice the difference was small and no-one got much: officers about three weeks, the other ranks two weeks each year, and that included travelling time, and leave was temporarily suspended during crises, such as enemy offensives. The army tried hard to be fair, carrying out an enormous task that

demanded the movement of 40,000 men every day. But sheer distance meant that a soldier from Ireland or Scotland might get home for just three days out of a week's leave; by contrast, men from London and the Southeast could be home in bed on the day they left France.

The selection of men to be sent on leave varied from unit to unit and sometimes involved urgent compassionate reasons – or some colourful variation of them. Lieutenant Bennett of the Leinster Regiment awarded leave to "the best liar in the section. It was apparent from his story that the entire fate of the British Army depended on his going home to see his father, who is, I believe, confined to bed with a slight chill." When leave was granted, the news usually came at short notice. Then men would rush from their trenches, take extraordinary risks hurrying to the rear and, having collected their passes and warrants, beg a lift to the nearest railhead, where special leave trains would be waiting.

At Boulogne or Le Havre new clothing and "vermin free" certificates would be issued. Then anxious men would finally realize that fear and hardship really were suspended, and pile aboard cross-Channel steamers for the voyage home and the fast train to London. By the time the Tommies walked out of Victoria Station – often to be accosted by the innumerable prostitutes – they became aware of (re-)entering a very different world, one that did not share their values.

The first thing most men did – after a good meal and perhaps trying to explain to a dubious family and neighbours just what life at the Front was really like – was sleep. Some men on leave found soft civilian beds uncomfortable and actually slept long hours on the floor. But others resented every moment asleep and used every waking hour to savour the comforts of home. Some men gorged on rich food; others spent far too much time in the pub.

One universal experience was a growing awareness by the soldier on leave of just how uncomprehending civilians were of what life was like at the Front. This was perhaps the most troubling aspect of leave and was commented upon by many. One King's Royal Rifle Corps soldier wrote: "I became increasingly uncertain of the value of returning to England for periods of leave ... Not being able to discourse about the things at the forefront of one's feelings. Such was England's attitudes I ought to have known". Some men even felt that their modest leave was too long. As bad as life at the Front was, at least one's pals there could *empathize*.

The sense of alienation was increased by many civilians' conversation and behaviour. During the last two years of the war men on leave heard endless complaints about shortages, having to queue, lack of fuel, rising prices and the other hardships that civilians were enduring. One thing that particularly irked the soldier on leave in England's Southeast was to be told by civilians that they were sharing his dangers, especially if an anecdote about a Zeppelin or Gotha air raid could be invoked. It all baffled soldiers, who could find no vocabulary to explain the yawning gulf between the real terrors of the trenches and the worries of civilians back home. Most men chose not to do so. There was no comparison.

Insult could be added to injury by civilians in public. In 1914–15, there were numerous incidents of self-righteous women thrusting a white feather into the hand of a hapless young man on leave in civilian dress, with the stern exhortation that he should join up and do his bit. Yet when in uniform, soldiers on buses and trams could sometimed find themselves shunned.

One area of resentment was the realization that many folks back home were doing very nicely out of the war. A soldier on leave would contrast his pay – which could be as low as a shilling a day – with the £3 and 10 shillings per week paid to some skilled munitions workers. Others noticed that profiteering was rampant. Pre-war interest rates on war-related equity shares such as steel, oil, shipping and motor vehicles had rocketed, and some investors were getting very rich indeed while the average soldier risked his life abroad. Such anomalies troubled thoughtful soldiers.

The putting of so many young men into uniform, who then struggled to square their frontline experiences and home life, could bring social disruption. A sizeable minority of men on leave took their frustrations out on their countrymen by going on the rampage. Drunken soldiers were a common experience, and the military on leave figure strongly in contemporary reports from the magistrates' courts. Indeed, what with drunk and disorderly behaviour, sexual misconduct, petty theft and assaults on other citizens – even on policemen – soldiers on leave seem to have cut a minor swathe through the God-fearing communities of Britain.

Civilians, other than the nearest and dearest, were often glad to see the back of soldiers when they headed to the Front again. And the feeling could be mutual. But while a spell of leave might, for some, fuel a desire to get back to chums in the trenches, many found the moment of return deeply depressing. A not insignificant number of soldiers on leave took the chance to desert – but many were caught and returned, under guard, to France to face court-martial. Drunken soldiers at Victoria Station were commonplace and even hard-headed Military Police found the scenes heartrending as weeping sweethearts and newly married young wives saw their men off, often for the last time. It was thus with very mixed emotions that men waved from the windows as the train pulled out, taking them away from a peaceful, but alien, civilian world back to the well-understood dangers of the trenches.

Members of the BEF on leave, still in their full trench kit and carrying rifles. They queue to change their hard-earned French francs into pounds sterling at London's Victoria Station. Railway stations, and Victoria in particular, were the scenes of high emotion for civilians and soldiers alike. All knew that the return trip to France or Flanders could be the final one.

61

LAST REMAINS OF HMS *INDEFATIGABLE* THE BATTLE OF JUTLAND

31 MAY TO 1 JUNE 1916

By the middle of the war, the German High Seas Fleet had still not found a satisfactory way of confronting Britain's Grand Fleet without exposing itself to unacceptable dangers. At the root of the problem lay the disparity in numbers: by 1916 the Germans' 16 dreadnoughts were outnumbered by the Royal Navy's 28. Thus, German naval policy had resorted to other means: using its U-boats, where possible, and occasional provocations, such as the raids on Britain's northeast coast, to try and coax manageable portions of the Royal Navy onto a superior number of German guns. But following the Battle of Dogger Bank (*see* Chapter 16), the Kaiser had once more opted for caution.

In February 1916, though, the High Seas Fleet acquired a new and more aggressive commander, Admiral Reinhard Scheer. He persuaded Kaiser Wilhelm into a new scheme to trap part of the Grand Fleet in an unequal battle with his reinvigorated fleet, in the hope of inflicting enough losses to destroy the British numerical advantage. His plan was complex, involving Zeppelins as reconnaissance scouts and battlecruisers under Admiral Hipper luring the target ships onto German battleships. It resulted in the largest clash of battleships in history and the only direct confrontation between the Grand Fleet and the High Seas Fleet: the Battle of Jutland.

> The battlecruiser HMS *Indefatigable* formed part of Admiral Sir David Beatty's Battlecruiser Fleet, the object of Scheer's destructive plan. She did not survive. At around 15.50 on the day of battle, *Indefatigable* squared up to the German battlecruiser SMS *Von der Tann* and the pair started to slug it out. The ships were evenly matched, except that German fire control was better. Within ten minutes, *Indefatigable* was rocked by the full weight of a salvo of *Von der Tann*'s shells. Reeling, *Indefatigable* fell out of the British line and was immediately hit by a second salvo. Signaller C. Falmer was up in the crow's nest. Fifty years later he explained: "There was a terrific explosion aboard the ship – the magazines went. I saw the guns go up in the air just like matchsticks – 12-inch guns they were – bodies and everything. Within half a minute the ship turned right over and she was gone." Almost nothing remained of the ship. This battered lifebelt was one of the few fragments picked up from the water on the next day by the British battleship HMS *Bellerophon*; Falmer was one of only two survivors, the remaining 1,017 of his shipmates all dying instantly. The battle killed 6,094 British sailors and 2,551 Germans in just 12 hours. Compared to some of the war's land battles, like Verdun or the Somme, the losses were small, but the speed at which these numbers died was shocking.

"ANY DISASTER TO OUR HEAVY SHIPS LAYS OUR COUNTRY OPEN TO INVASION AND ALSO GIVES THE ENEMY THE OPPORTUNITY OF PASSING COMMERCE DESTROYERS OUT OF THE NORTH SEA"

Admiral Sir John Jellicoe, to Grand Fleet admirals, April 1916

The stakes were high, for both sides. Winston Churchill summed it up in his later description of the Grand Fleet's commander, Admiral Sir John Jellicoe, as "the only man who could have lost the war in an afternoon". For the British, destruction of the Royal Navy's superiority could open the way to Germany once again having a true "high seas" fleet, able to circumvent the British blockade – the ramifications for Britain, her empire and the Allied cause would be enormous. For the Germans, it was a probably unrepeatable gamble that could seal the fate of the High Seas Fleet for good.

Unfortunately for Scheer, the British were, with their access to German codes (*see* Chapter 16), able to read his "secret" signals. On 30 May, the Grand Fleet put to sea, prepared to meet the German sortie. The next day, off the Skagerrak waters between Norway and the Danish Jutland coast, 20 years of Anglo-German naval rivalry reached a head as 151 British warships converged upon 99 German vessels.

Shortly after 15.45, Admiral Beatty's six battlecruisers – the target the Germans were hoping to draw out and isolate – made contact with Hipper's leading Scouting Group of battlecruisers. The Germans promptly turned tail and ran hard to the south, intent on drawing the pursuing British onto the advancing guns of Scheer's battleships. Beatty was happy to do this, for his objective was to locate the main High Seas Fleet and draw it, in turn, back towards the Grand Fleet. But, as battle began, and Beatty pursued the German battlecruisers, disaster befell the British ships. They were struck time and again by accurate German gunnery. HMS *Indefatigable* and HMS *Queen Mary* were both sunk by plunging shellfire followed by massive magazine explosions. The best witness to the destruction was Commander Georg von Hase, the First Gunnery Officer aboard the German battlecruiser *Derfflinger*:

> The enemy was shooting superbly. Twice the *Derfflinger* came under their infernal hail and each time she was hit. But the *Queen Mary* was having a bad time; engaged by the *Seydlitz* as well as the *Derfflinger*, she met her doom at 16.26. A vivid red flame shot up from her forepart; then came an explosion forward, followed by a much heavier explosion amidships. Immediately afterwards, she blew up with a terrific explosion, the masts collapsing inwards and the smoke hiding everything.

Beatty's own, memorable, observation was: "There seems to be something wrong with our bloody ships today!" He was right. The Royal Navy had got into the habit of leaving the metal doors open in its turrets, in order to speed up the supply of shells from the magazines down below, even leaving extra shells and volatile explosive in silk bags in the area beneath the turrets to increase the rate of fire: British pre-war doctrine had been to "smother" enemy ships with shells. The results were disastrous in practice, because when a British turret was hit the explosion started a flash fire that went straight through the open doors to the magazines, blowing the ship apart. It was a danger that the Germans had narrowly avoided at Dogger Bank, and they had adapted accordingly: afterwards, German warships closed all internal doors and kept minimum propellant charges safely out of the way.

Despite the losses, Beatty's ships had done their job. Having closed to within 20,000 yards of the main High Seas Fleet, his remaining battlecruisers now turned and ran back north shortly after 16.30, to lead the Germans onto the guns of the Grand Fleet. But here another British failing was revealed. Beatty was still relying on

Two young seamen aboard HMS Chester *attempt to clear and repair some of the damage inflicted on their ship after the ravages of the Battle of Jutland. Damage from shell bursts is visible behind them. It was a close call for* Chester; *she escaped thanks to the skills of her captain, but it would take more than a broom to get her fully operational.*

hoisted flag signals to communicate his orders. Across 5 miles of sea, thick with funnel smoke, signals often went unread. As a result, when Beatty turned, his supporting squadron of fast battleships – the most modern ships in the world – were slow to realize and fell behind, coming under heavy fire from the guns of Scheer's battleships as they came within range. Now, as the High Seas Fleet chased Beatty north and the Grand Fleet progressed from the other direction, 250 ships of the two fleets were converging.

Admiral Hood's 3rd Battlecruiser Squadron was steaming southeast, ahead of Jellicoe's battleships, to try and locate the Germans, with the light cruiser HMS *Chester* scouting ahead. Suddenly, at 17.40, four German light cruisers emerged from the murk and subjected *Chester* to crippling fire, hitting her 17 times in three minutes. Three of her ten guns were disabled and one-fifth of her crew were either killed or wounded, including the entire crew of the forward 5.5-inch Quick-Firing Gun turret where 16-year-old Jack Cornwell was stationed as sight-setter. The protective gun shields did not reach down to the deck, and a storm of steel splinters swept underneath, slicing legs and cutting down men. Shells bursting behind sprayed red hot metal into the gun crews.

A huge pall of smoke rises from the barely visible HMS Queen Mary, *as two of her magazines are detonated by shells fired by the German battlecruisers* Derfflinger *and* Seydlitz. *Less than 40 minutes after the hostilities of Jutland began,* Queen Mary *sank, with the loss of 1,266 lives.*

But the 16-year-old Cornwell stood firm at his post, although mortally wounded. Posthumously, he earned the best-remembered of the four VCs of the battle. He was found alive, still standing at the gunsight, his chest ripped open by shell splinters, but died the next day. *Chester*'s captain, Robert Lawson, was able to save his badly damaged vessel through some extremely adroit seamanship, managing to manoeuvre out of the line and out of range of the German ships. And as he did so, the two battle fleets collided.

Scheer was still ignorant that he was sailing into a trap. But to the northeast, Jellicoe was facing the biggest decision of his life: he had to decide how to deploy his columns of battleships into the line of battle, either to port or starboard. But where would the German ships emerge, from the haze ahead? Despite repeated requests for more detailed information, Beatty was little help. The dashing leader of the battlecruisers failed in his duty to report the enemy's exact whereabouts at a crucial moment in the war. Jellicoe had to make up his own mind, lacking much of the information he might reasonably have expected.

At 18.15, Jellicoe made a decision. He ordered his columns to turn to port. The battleships swung round one by one into a line heading northeast, their huge guns nosing out to the south. By setting the fleet in a line at right angles to the oncoming German column Jellicoe had successfully "crossed the T" of Scheer's approaching fleet – achieving the position that all admirals dream of reaching at the start of a battle, to maximize firepower against the enemy's line – and was waiting when the leading German battlecruisers suddenly appeared. Hipper began to suspect trouble and signalled Scheer, warning: "Something lurks in that soup."

As the Germans emerged from the smoke and confusion of the running battle with Beatty's battlecruisers off to the west they were suddenly confronted by this solid line of British battleships blasting disciplined salvoes. Scheer now realized:

"It was now obvious that we were confronted by a large portion of the English fleet. The entire arc stretching from north to east was a sea of fire. The flash from the muzzles of the guns was seen distinctly through the mist and smoke on the horizon."

As a hail of shells fell on the leading German vessels, at 18.30 Scheer ordered a simultaneous about-turn by all his ships and retreated to the west, covered by a smokescreen laid by his destroyers. To the puzzled British – who did not know this manoeuvre – it was as if the German ships had disappeared by magic. The Grand Fleet sailed south peering out to the west for the missing Germans.

At 19.00 they found them. The problem for Scheer was that the Grand Fleet was now positioned between him and his home waters. He ordered a second battle turn east, and thus reversed course, which inevitably meant re-engaging the British ships. Clearly silhouetted against the western horizon, the oncoming German battleships were deluged by a rain of shells. After about 20 minutes, Scheer ordered a third turn-about and fled, calling for Hipper's battlecruisers to cover his retreat "and ram", in what became known as the "death ride". Eighteen British battleships fired at the four oncoming German battlecruisers: it is a tribute to their construction that they survived, as they took 37 hits by heavy shells before turning away as German destroyers charged in to cover the retreat. Jellicoe ordered his battleships to turn away from any torpedo attacks, thereby opening the gap for Hipper's fleeing ships. The fleets pulled apart.

As dusk fell both sides took stock. Jellicoe had no wish to become involved in a messy and confused night action. British pre-war night exercises had convinced him that action in the dark was a very chancy affair. He ordered his fleet to stay in line and head south to cut the High Seas Fleet off from its bases, and so recommence battle at first light. Out to the west, Scheer, desperate to use the cover of darkness to escape his predicament, ordered his ships to steer southeast and try and pass behind the main British fleet, which had closed its line for the night. Thus, in the dark the German fleet crossed through the rear of the Grand Fleet. In a series of chaotic, running encounter battles with the British rearguard, the heavily outgunned British destroyers fought hard – and lost five ships. But the Germans also lost two cruisers and an elderly battleship. Jellicoe's battleships saw flashes and heard gunfire astern, but thought that they were night attacks by the German destroyers rather than the High Seas Fleet; unfortunately, nobody in the British rearguard saw fit to alert Jellicoe. By dawn it was all over. Jellicoe and the Grand Fleet looked out on an empty sea, and the battered German fleet limped back to its bases.

The Kaiser promptly declared the battle a triumph. In one sense he was right. His ships had sunk three British battlecruisers, three cruisers and eight destroyers, while the British had only sunk one old battleship, a single battlecruiser and nine smaller ships. And of the 8,645 dead, two-thirds were British. But those statistics hid deeper truths: the badly battered High Seas Fleet was in no condition to fight, and it was four months before it could steam out again. By contrast, the British were ready for action again in 24 hours. Most importantly, Jutland had shaken German – and Scheer's – confidence. Despite what could be publicly represented as a tactical victory, the Kaiser and his admirals were well aware that they had escaped disaster by the skin of their teeth.

Perhaps the most accurate verdict on Jutland came from an American journalist: "the High Seas Fleet has assaulted its jailor; the High Seas Fleet is still in prison." Once again, Germany had no choice but to look to her submarines.

62

A U-BOAT'S WIRELESS RECEIVER
SUBMARINE WARFARE AFTER JUTLAND

1916 TO 1918

The Battle of Jutland (*see* Chapter 61) had confirmed a basic truth by June 1916: that the German High Seas Fleet was only safe in port. It was not quite the end of the story as regards the fleet's forays into the North Sea, but German strategic thoughts were turning back to what seemed the only way of breaking the Royal Navy's deadlock and imposing their own counter-blockade on Britain: the resumption of unrestricted submarine warfare against merchant shipping. It was a potent threat, for there seemed little that could be done to counter the predations of the underwater killers. But during 1917 the British, despite Admiralty conservatism and faulty analysis of the problem, found tactics and technology that, while not eliminating the threat, could at least reduce it to manageable proportions.

In 1914, the Royal Navy had no answer to the U-boat threat, and over the next two years only 46 U-boats were destroyed by British countermeasures, mostly mines. Gradually the Royal Navy's armoury developed, so that by mid-1917 effective depth charges were allowing British warships to hit back hard. The next 18 months saw a ruthless campaign against U-boats in the waters around Britain, and one of its victims was *UB-110*, which entered service in March 1918 and undertook two patrols along Britain's east coast. Her second patrol began on 5 July. For ten days, *UB-110* was depth-charged daily by British warships. She still managed to attack an oil tanker, which did not sink, and a steamer carrying iron ore, which did. On 19 July, *UB-110*'s periscope was sighted as she approached another coastal convoy, and the submarine was saturated with depth charges. With her hydroplane damaged, inhibiting control of diving, she was forced to the surface where she was rammed by the destroyer HMS *Garry*. Badly damaged, *UB-110* sank. The following October, the wreck was raised by the Royal Navy and towed back to Newcastle for evaluation. Several valuable items, including codebooks were found, and some of the salvaged objects were passed to the Imperial War Museum in January 1919, including this high-frequency wireless radio receiver. Plain and technical it may appear, but it provides a tantalizing glimpse into the claustrophobic world of the bitter war fought beneath the waves.

After Jutland, Admiral Scheer initially tried to raise morale among his fleet with another sortie in August 1916. But the signals intelligence analysts at Room 40 warned the Grand Fleet. The British submarine *E23* put a torpedo into the battleship *Westfalen*, and a Zeppelin misreported approaching ships as being the Grand Fleet; Scheer fled back to safety. In October, he tried again, only to lose the cruiser *München*

> **"COMMANDERS OF GERMAN UNDERSEA VESSELS HAVE ATTACKED MERCHANT SHIPS WITH GREATER AND GREATER ACTIVITY... NOT ONLY UPON THE HIGH SEAS SURROUNDING GREAT BRITAIN AND IRELAND, BUT WHEREVER THEY COULD ENCOUNTER THEM, IN A WAY THAT HAS GROWN MORE AND MORE RUTHLESS, MORE AND MORE INDISCRIMINATE"**
>
> *President Woodrow Wilson, Address to US Congress, 19 April 1916*

to another British submarine; again the German ships turned tail, and later nearly lost the battleships *Grosser Kürfurst* and *Kronprinz* to British torpedoes.

Scheer had better luck raiding off Dover with his light forces. On 28 October 1916, his torpedo boats sank a destroyer and six fishing vessels, and a month later he bombarded Margate in broad daylight. But increasingly the weight of German naval action was being borne by the U-boats. Events prompted a post-Jutland shake-up at the Admiralty, with Jellicoe moved to become First Sea Lord in London, leaving Beatty as Commander-in-Chief of the Grand Fleet in Scapa Flow.

There was a taking stock in the German navy, too. Ever since Jutland, German naval staff had been pressing for a resumption of unrestricted submarine warfare, and the numbers of U-boats in service had been rising. Admiral Henning von Holtzendorff now played his trump card. He prepared a statistical analysis that showed that if Germany could sink 600,000 tons of shipping for four months, and thereafter a monthly total of 400,000 tons, it would bring Britain to the brink of starvation within less than six months. The Kaiser accepted that only by wrecking Britain's economic existence could Germany now hope to win the war; an Imperial War Council on 9 January 1917 ordered the resumption of unrestricted submarine warfare from the beginning of February. Chancellor von Bethmann Hollweg opposed the plan, pointing out the dangers of alienating the United States, but was overruled.

With over 100 U-boats operational, sinkings of merchant vessels now rose alarmingly, from 520,000 tons in February to over 860,000 tons in April. If sinkings continued at this rate, by the end of the summer Britain would no longer be able to sustain the war; supplies of coal to French war industries would dry up; and Britain's reserves of food might dip below their current low of just six weeks' supply. The Grand Fleet's exercises even had to be cut back because of shortage of fuel. Despite the looming danger, the Admiralty – and Jellicoe in particular – solemnly advised an anxious War Cabinet that there was absolutely nothing the Royal Navy could do.

A helping hand came from a quite different direction, as predicted by the German chancellor. The United States, after strong protests to Berlin, severed diplomatic relations with Germany. On 26 February, President Wilson asked Congress for authority to arm American merchant ships: no country could permit attacks on her shipping on the high seas, and in addition Wilson had learned of the explosive contents of the "Zimmermann telegram" (*see* Chapter 66). Berlin was taken aback by the peaceable Wilson's reaction, but continued with its attacks, sinking three US-flagged vessels on 15 March. On 2 April, Wilson alerted Congressmen that the German unrestricted submarine campaign was "a war against all nations" and advised them that "the status of a belligerent had been thrust upon us" by Germany. Within days came the US declaration of war.

Once settled in at the Admiralty, a tired and overworked Jellicoe could think of little to beat off the U-boat menace. In spring 1917, there was no real means of detecting a submerged U-boat, and no very effective weapons with which to attack them. There was also no coordinated response to their attacks. Jellicoe's first move was to set up an Anti-Submarine Division of the naval staff under the bright Rear Admiral Alexander Duff. Despite his efforts, the Admiralty continued to insist that all it could do was step up the anti-submarine patrols, and that looking for submarines in the broad oceans was like looking for a needle in a haystack. Sinkings continued to rise. In fact, the solution lay right under the Admiralty's nose but it refused to accept it: convoys (*see* Chapter 83).

Two crew members of a U-boat in the torpedo room of their vessel; the cramped conditions on board are evident. Jutland forced the German navy back towards a naval policy based on U-boats, reigniting British fears of the underwater killers.

Ever since 1914 troop transports had sailed in convoys, with minimum losses, and in February 1917 coalers to France began adopting convoys, too. But until the late spring of 1917 Jellicoe and the navy's commanders at sea rejected the wider implementation of convoying. But when it did become policy, it came with a bonus, because convoys brought the attacking U-boats directly into contact with the escorts, now armed with their better depth charges. U-boat losses, which had only been 14 in the first three months of the campaign, began to climb to 10 a month, a loss ratio that could not be replaced by new builds. The U-boat campaign was effectively over by the end of the year – as was a war-weary Jellicoe, dismissed on 24 December 1917 by Lloyd George to be replaced by the more aggressive Admiral Sir Rosslyn Wemyss. The initiative in the naval war was back with the Allies. Although Scheer's cruisers made two sallies from port in late 1917, destroying two Scandinavian convoys, they fled back to port as soon as British dreadnoughts closed in. It merely confirmed that the fleet war had already run its course.

The naval war finally petered out in the autumn of 1918 when Berlin realized that Germany was doomed while submarine attacks persisted. On 21 October 1918, Germany – already putting out peace feelers – finally abandoned U-boat attacks on passenger ships, at the insistence of the country whose entry into the war had been forced, to a large degree, by unrestricted submarine warfare: the United States.

63

EDWARD THOMAS'S LAST WORDS
A "LOST GENERATION"?

1914 TO 1918

After the war, the expatriate American writer Gertrude Stein was watching a particularly ham-fisted French garage mechanic at work. She asked the owner, sarcastically, where his employee had been trained. He replied that apprentices were easy to train, but men in their mid-twenties to thirties who had gone into the war were *une génération perdue* – "a lost generation". It was a phrase – and an idea – that took hold. Ernest Hemingway took inspiration from it: to him the lost generation were rootless, disorientated postwar survivors. In Britain, however, the phrase has more literally been applied to the idea of a generation swept away between 1914 and 1918.

The war was not fussy. It cut down men regardless. But the loss was perceived to be greater where it seemed disproportionately high. Justifiably could the mothers of Barnsley or Accrington feel that their sons, dying together in the Pals battalions (*see* Chapter 9), were not only their own personal tragedies but also represented a chasm in their communities. In the wider culture, an idea of talent and potential cut short exerted a powerful influence, creating an impression of so many future artists and scientists, poets and painters, thinkers and leaders, prematurely felled by war.

At 07.36 on the morning of 9 April 1917, Edward Thomas's pocket watch stopped dead. The Battle of Arras had been raging for two hours and Thomas was an officer on its southern flank, directing the heavy guns of the 244th Siege Battery, Royal Garrison Artillery. A German shell passed so close to him that the shock wave sucked all the air from his lungs, which collapsed. It froze the hands on his watch and creased the pages of this, his diary, hidden deep inside his greatcoat pocket. But it left no mark on his body. Thomas's death robbed English literature of one of its most lyrical poets. Although a professional writer for over ten years, it was only in November 1914, at the encouragement of his friend the American poet Robert Frost, that Thomas began writing verse. Between then and his departure from Britain in January 1917, he wrote 144 poems, though none of them in France. Mostly his poetry considered the fragile transience of life in contrast to the reassuring permanence of the countryside. Such was his connection to the land that when, as a 37-year-old family man, he enlisted in 1915 and was asked by a friend what he was fighting for, he picked up a handful of soil and said: "Literally for this." People might come and go, but the English hills, trees and fields would always be there. His final poem, "The Sorrow of True Love", is shown here: it was written two days after saying goodbye to his wife and children for the last time.

> **"THERE SEEMED TO BE NOTHING LEFT IN THE WORLD, FOR I FELT THAT ROLAND HAD TAKEN WITH HIM ALL MY FUTURE AND EDWARD ALL MY PAST."**
>
> *Vera Brittain, describing her dead fiancé (Roland) and her brother in her memoir* Testament of Youth, *1933*

The light of the new moon & every star

And no more singing for the bird —
Never understood quite what was meant by God.

The morning chill & clear hurts my skin while
delight my mind

Neuville in early morning as
its steep straight street with
houses (see Drawing [illegible])
the beauty [illegible] silent bright & clear [of]
no inhabitants & hid to those who
don't know why I couldn't once & didn't

The sorrow of true love is a great sorrow 29
And true love parting blackens a bright morrow:
Yet almost they equal joys, since their despair
Is but hope blinded by its tears, & ~~there~~ clear
Above the storm ~~that~~ the heavens wait to be seen.
But greater sorrow from less love has been
That can mistake lack of despair for hope
And knows not tempest & the perfect scope
Of summers, but a frozen drizzle perpetual
Of drops that from remorse & pity fall
And cannot ever shine in the sun or thaw,
Removed eternally from the sun's law.
                                        13.1.17.

Did Europe lose so many young men that it threw society out of kilter? In the words of historian Hew Strachan, "in the crude statistics of the rates of marriage and reproduction there was no 'lost generation'". Of the 6 million men from the British Isles who served in the war, one in eight died. As a proportion of the total population this figure is much smaller than that of France or Germany. It is hard to maintain a literal claim for a lost generation due to the war. But that has never been the point. It has always been about perceptions and concentrations, about loss not statistics.

The memorials at institutions of learning, from schools to universities, bearing the names of the dead, created just such impressions of loss concentrated in groups and communities. For the elite public schools particularly, supplying so many of the officer class, this is the case. Eton College, that bastion of privilege and wealth, records a hefty 1,157 of its sons who lost their lives between 1914 and 1918, and the melancholy tributes at Oxford and Cambridge colleges tell a similar story. Other schools lost as many former pupils as there were attending the school at any one time: a sobering numerical equivalence.

Privileged, wealthier young men tended to volunteer early and proportionately in greater numbers than other groups in society. They often had no job or dependants to maintain, and so were freer to volunteer. More than that, by the standards of their time, as fit, public-school-educated young men over 18, they were automatically deemed officer material. By volunteering, they had sentenced themselves to becoming platoon commanders on the frontline – the most dangerous position in the British Army. Educated by a regime of muscular Christianity that stressed

Proud, pre-war members of Eton College's Officer Training Corps stand to attention as they are inspected by Edward, Prince of Wales (the future Edward VIII), in June 1914. A sizeable proportion of the sons of the top public schools would go on to fight, and die, in the war, contributing to the impression of a generation's fallen elite.

team games and cold baths, and which concentrated on history and the Classics, they were imbued with Sir Henry Newbolt's famous poetic line: "Play up! Play up! And play the game!" and, like Billie Nevill on the Somme (*see* Chapter 52), genuinely believed that it was their duty to set an example to inspire their men.

The conditions of the Western Front meant that proportionately more of this particular social class was killed by the war than any other. The heavy casualties among young army subalterns in the trenches are no myth. Estimates for the *mortality* rates among these officers (below the rank of captain) range from 55 per cent to 81 per cent, depending on the battle. This – even at its lowest estimate – is double the rate for non-commissioned ranks. This statistic is true across all the warring nations. The Germans had higher mortality rates for officers and lost over 50 per cent of the males aged 20–24 in their officer class. The sense of a layer of society being sliced off was encapsulated in historian A.J.P. Taylor's verdict: "The slaughter of the subalterns in World War I destroyed the flower of the English gentry."

Such statistics fuelled the idea that the conflict had deprived society of the brightest and best – a generation of luminaries in their fields. The handsome young poet Rupert Brooke, who died in Greece from blood-poisoning in 1915, is often cited as epitomizing this concept of some lost *jeunesse d'orée*. Hugh Dalton, who was later Chancellor of the Exchequer in the 1945 Labour government, had known Brooke at Cambridge and wrote: "with his passing, a bright light seemed to go out of my life, and a bright hope out of the future". Churchill's own eulogy to Brooke summed up a certain ideal of intellectual and physical prowess joined together: "Joyous, fearless, versatile, deeply instructed, with classic symmetry of mind and body, he was all that one would wish England's noblest sons to be."

Brooke stands alongside Edward Thomas, Isaac Rosenberg and Wilfred Owen as fallen poets, while the war also took away the composer George Butterworth, the brilliant scientist Henry Moseley, and many others. In France, the politician and writer Maurice Barrès calculated that of the 161 students of the elite *École Nationale Supérieure* in 1911–13, half (81) were dead or missing and 64 wounded by 1918 – a 90 per cent casualty rate. We can, of course, never know what outstanding leaders, what great inventions or what great literature and art perished in the trenches – we cannot know what might have been. Writers such as Owen and Rosenberg never got to be just "poets" – their early deaths forever defined them and fixed their reputations as war poets. Arguably, that narrow legacy explains their potency.

That sense of a generation fixed in sepia is not limited to the "brightest and best". The playwright Alan Bennett wrote of his late uncle, Clarence, who died in Flanders: "He was always twenty all through my childhood, because of the photograph on the piano at my grandmother's house in Leeds. He was her only son ... When Uncle Clarence's name comes up it is generally in connection with the undisputed nobility of his character." Bennett wryly identifies the very human wish to make some sense of a young man's death by investing the individual with the finest of humanity's qualities. The belief that a dead comrade or relative was a good person gives comfort to the bereaved and makes it seem less of a waste. And, away from the public figures and the elites, Bennett returns us to the ordinary but much more pervasive sense of loss, affecting households everywhere. However much they came to grip the postwar imagination, the "brightest and the best" and the sons of Eton remain but a small part of the lost generation compared to the widespread loss among ordinary families. For every Brooke, there were thousands of photographs on pianos after 1918.

64

THE EASTER REBELS' SURRENDER
IRELAND'S EASTER RISING

24 TO 29 APRIL 1916

In August 1914, Ireland appeared to be on the verge of civil war (*see* Chapter 2). However, the outbreak of European war had the effect of suspending partisan strife among most groups in the face of a greater common enemy. The British government put implementation of the much-disputed Third Home Rule Bill on hold for the duration, and Ulster Unionists and the Irish National Party, the latter led by John Redmond, agreed to suspend their differences. Irishmen of all political hues volunteered for the armed forces. However, for the more radical Nationalists – such as the revolutionary Irish Republican Brotherhood (IRB) – the struggle with Britain remained paramount. For the IRB, its policy by 1914–15 was that "England's troubles are now Ireland's opportunity". And it seized its moment on Easter Monday 1916.

The Irish insurrection at Easter 1916 remains arguably the most important event in modern Irish history. But at the time it lacked popular support. Many moderate Irish men and women felt the rebels were mad. What eventually swayed public opinion and kick-started a wider movement towards an independent Irish nation was the brutal treatment of the rebels by the British authorities, and the executions of its leaders. Padraig Pearse, James Connolly and Tomas MacDonagh had surrendered, after six days of resistance, by signing this document. Pearse signed first, at 3.45 p.m. on 29 April, with Connolly following suit on the same day. MacDonagh was some distance from Dublin's city centre and did not sign until 3.15 p.m. on 30 April. Pearse and MacDonagh were among the first to be shot on 3 May. Connolly, who had been badly hurt in the fighting, was too sick to stand and was executed in a chair: his treatment, above all, inflamed public opinion, in exactly the way the leaders of the insurrection had hoped. Moderate Irish opinion quickly began to lose faith with constitutional efforts to achieve Home Rule and turned increasingly to the newly formed Sinn Fein to voice political frustration. The roots of the popular republicanism that followed lay not in the act of rebellion, but in the inept response of the British authorities to the rebel leaders' surrender.

If the IRB's idealistic but determined leaders, including Padraig Pearse, were clear on their political aim – "to control Ireland's destiny" – they were never really clear on how this was to be achieved. However, in 1915 the IRB established a military council charged with planning a general uprising. Leaders of the paramilitary Irish Volunteers, who had men scattered throughout the island, were co-opted into it – as was James Connolly's underground Irish Citizen Army, consisting of about

> ## "THE TREE OF LIBERTY MUST BE REFRESHED FROM TIME TO TIME WITH THE BLOOD OF PATRIOTS AND TYRANTS"
>
> *Thomas Jefferson, letter to William Stephens Smith, 13 November 1787*

In order to prevent the further slaughter of Dublin
citizens, and in the hope of saving the lives of our
followers now surrounded and hopelessly outnumbered, the
members of the Provisional Government present at Head-
Quarters have agreed to an unconditional surrender, and the
Commandants of the various districts in the City and Country
will order their commands to lay down arms.

P. H. Pearse
29th April 1916
3.45 p. m.

I agree to these conditions for the men only
under my own Command in the Moore
Street District and for the men in
the Stephen's Green Command.

James Connolly
April 29/16

On consultation with Commandant Ceant
and other officers I have decided to
agree to unconditional surrender also.

Thomas MacDonagh.
30. IV. 16.
3.15 p. m.

250 armed men, and the Socialist Women's group, plus a group of boys to act as messengers. The conspirators were helped with money from the Irish-American organization *Clan na Gael*, which shared their aims and provided the secret communication channel between the rebels and Germany, from whom they hoped to receive military backing.

Intelligence sources in the Royal Irish Constabulary and in Dublin Castle (the British GHQ) were well aware that the IRB was planning an uprising. London was tracking the movements of the pro-Nationalist Sir Roger Casement, who had travelled secretly to Germany specifically to bring arms to Ireland. As Casement landed from a U-boat in County Kerry on Good Friday 1916, he was promptly arrested; the next day the German ship carrying the arms was captured.

This setback split the rebels. Eoin MacNeill, leader of the Volunteers, warned that without the rifles any uprising was off. But Pearse and others were determined to go ahead, even though it was obviously now a hopeless – if not suicidal – venture. Tempers flared and orders, counter-orders and confusion reigned, with personal recriminations flying. British intelligence seems to have been aware of this dispute and of the messenger boys bicycling around Ireland telling Volunteers on Easter Sunday that the rising was off and to "stand down". It may account for GHQ's surprise when, at noon on Easter Monday, 24 April, dumbfounded Bank Holiday crowds in Dublin were suddenly joined by 1,200 armed men. They were marching to seize five important locations – the General Post Office; the Law Courts (where they used heavy law books as sandbags); the South Dublin Union (workhouses); St Stephen's Green; and Boland's Flour Mill – and to proclaim a "Provisional Government of the Irish Republic". An attempt to seize Dublin Castle was chased off.

The battle was on. As the rebels barricaded themselves in and prepared for defence, the British cautiously tried to find out exactly what was going on. Martial Law was declared. A troop of Lancers reconnoitring in the crowded streets was shot down. Most of Tuesday was spent throwing cordons around the rebel strongholds and bringing in reinforcements; some Dubliners, aggrieved at the rebels' actions, got into violent confrontations with them – while others took cover as firing broke out.

Wednesday, 26 April brought serious fighting. The rebels, outnumbered by twenty to one, came under fire as the British brought the *Helga*, a small gunboat, up the River Liffey and bombarded Connolly's regular HQ, Liberty Hall, which the rebels had prudently vacated. Fires were started in the city and, with no food coming in from the countryside, large-scale looting was reported, exacerbated by the removal of the police from the streets. British reinforcements marching in from the coast were ambushed at Boland's Mill by men led by an Irish Volunteer, Eamon de Valera. Despite casualties, the soldiers fought their way through to clear St Stephen's Green. The rebels retreated and set up a new strongpoint in the College of Surgeons.

On Thursday, 27 April, the army closed in on Boland's Mill and the South Dublin Union, and artillery firing over open sights set the General Post Office on fire. Connolly was badly wounded in the foot but kept going on morphine. Much of Dublin was now also alight, and any male in civilian clothes seen in the streets risked being shot by trigger-happy soldiers, as barricades were thrown up and the army prepared for the final assault.

By Friday it was clear that the end was in sight. Connolly ordered the women who had fought in the General Post Office to leave the building, which was now in danger

"IRISHMEN AND IRISHWOMEN: IN THE NAME OF GOD AND OF THE DEAD GENERATIONS FROM WHICH SHE RECEIVES HER OLD TRADITION OF NATIONHOOD, IRELAND, THROUGH US, SUMMONS HER CHILDREN TO HER FLAG AND STRIKES FOR HER FREEDOM"

Padraig Pearse, from the Proclamation of the "Irish Republic", 24 April 1916

of collapse. Later he and Pearse fled as the red-hot bricks crashed down around them. The survivors took cover nearby, but it was now only a matter of time. A last battle was fought for King's Street, where the South Staffords finally stormed the remaining rebel stronghold –and bayoneted any male they found hiding in the cellar. On Saturday morning, Pearse and the survivors surrendered. The rising in Dublin was over – and smaller uprisings in Ashbourne, Wexford and Galway had also been extinguished. But much of the city was battered, and while the dead included 64 rebels and 132 British soldiers, over 250 were civilians.

As the surviving rebels were marched away they were hissed at, pelted with refuse and denounced as "murderers" by angry Dubliners; only their soldier guards saved them from being manhandled by the crowds. Under government orders, and following a wave of arrests, the commander-in-chief, General Sir John Maxwell, swiftly court-martialled around 200 rebels. Fifteen were executed immediately, including all seven signatories to the Proclamation. The wounded Connolly, who was unable to stand, was shot strapped to a chair. De Valera was spared: for one thing, he could claim US nationality.

A wave of revulsion swept Ireland and the United States at such draconian punishment. How could Englishmen denounce the shooting of Edith Cavell and yet justify summary executions of Irishmen? Anti-British sentiment ran high in America and the executions were universally denounced as "tyrannical". The *New York American* wrote: "Thank God for freedom's martyrs in every age and land." Suddenly, thanks to Britain's maladroit response, instead of the foolish and suicidal gesture it was, the Easter Rising became a martyr's cause. It shifted public support away from the moderate stance of Redmond, and radicalized and broadened Nationalist feeling.

Pearse, Connolly and their comrades had not died in vain. Their sacrifice bore fruit. In the short term, it focused attention on the London government's failure to secure universal backing for the war effort throughout the British Isles. Unsurprisingly, conscription was never introduced in Ireland. In the longer term, the roots of the demise of the British Empire can be traced back to London's clumsy response to the Easter Rising. And one of the Easter Rising's surviving participants, de Valera, would go on to become leader of an independent Irish state.

65

MODEL PRIME MINISTERS
A CHANGE OF LEADERSHIP

DECEMBER 1916

With hindsight, it is clear that 1916 was in many ways the pivotal point of the war. The onslaughts and massive losses of Verdun and the Somme, the clash at Jutland, Brusilov's Russian offensive, the British evacuation of Gallipoli and surrender at Kut, the collapse of Romania and Zeppelin raids over England – all these brought home the totality and scale of the war. The warring nations were in too deep, their politics, economies and societies configured to fuel the war effort. By the end of the year any chance of a negotiated peace was off the table and both sides were resigned to a war to the death.

This hardening of attitudes had a major impact on the existing political leadership in both Germany and Great Britain. In the former, Hindenburg and Ludendorff – the "Duo" – took over military leadership of the Western Front, and were soon beginning to exert their commanding political voice in both Germany and her increasingly enfeebled ally, Austro-Hungaria. In Britain, the year ended with political intrigues culminating in what was a form of palace coup, which toppled Asquith and brought in a very different sort of Liberal as prime minister: Lloyd George.

First-World-War Britain saw two very different prime ministers. In 1914, the urbane and intellectual Herbert Asquith had already been in charge for six years. But his style of government proved too indecisive for a nation at war and in December 1916 he was replaced by the dynamic and charismatic David Lloyd George. As Chancellor of the Exchequer, Lloyd George had been one of the most radical members of Asquith's pre-war Cabinet. In May 1915, he became the first Minister of Munitions and demonstrated an energy and ruthlessness lacking in Asquith. Made Secretary of State for War after Kitchener's death in June 1916, Lloyd George went on to engineer Asquith's downfall within months, leaving himself the only credible candidate to take over. These contrasting personalities are clearly reflected in two wooden figures bought by the new War Museum in 1917 from the Lord Roberts Memorial Workshops. The workshops were established after the Anglo-Boer War to provide vocational training and employment for men disabled in the fighting. They expanded rapidly in 1915 with new branches across the country, each specializing in different practical skills. In London, the men made wooden toys including dolls, houses, vehicles and figures like these. In a style developed by the sculptor Edward Carter Preston, Asquith is shown (left) in majestic elegance as "The Last of the Romans". Utterly different, the sharp and modern Lloyd George carries two heavy shells, one under each of his movable arms.

"THE ONE PREDOMINANT TASK BEFORE THE GOVERNMENT IS THE VIGOROUS PROSECUTION OF THE WAR TO A TRIUMPHANT CONCLUSION."

David Lloyd George, written message to the House of Commons after being appointed prime minister, 11 December 1916

Crowds gather outside Parliament, hoping to catch a glimpse of their new prime minister, David Lloyd George (20 December 1916). The "Welsh Wizard's" populist and pragmatic streak meant that he always had a sharp sense of the political impact of decisions. His charismatic appeal was a far cry from the quiet, reserved Asquith.

For much of 1916 it seemed unlikely that there was any alternative to the wartime Coalition government presided over by the dignified and distant figure of Asquith, and it was generally assumed that there could be no general election in the middle of a major war. However, the political crisis of December 1916 changed things.

The roots of the crisis can be traced to the death of national icon Lord Kitchener, Secretary of State for War, on 5 June 1916, when his ship struck a mine on the way to talks with the Russians. He had already become sidelined in the Cabinet; now there was the question of who would succeed him. The choices were limited, and Asquith's consideration of Lord Derby was blocked by Lloyd George and Conservative leader Andrew Bonar Law. One other figure stood out – Lloyd George himself.

Lloyd George was a highly controversial figure. A gifted and natural demagogue in the Welsh Chapel tradition, he was also a successful social reformer and a Machiavellian political intriguer. His string of sexual conquests earned him the well-deserved nickname of "The Goat", and this anti-Establishment former solicitor was trusted by few; but – and it was a huge "but" – he got things done. His restless energy and sharp mind had transformed Munitions and helped marginalize Kitchener.

Asquith's character was entirely different. He was a cautious, consensual politician, without passion, much admired for his calm, steady reliability. By 1916 he had overseen nine years of revolutionary reform in Britain's domestic politics and he was tired. A barrister by background, he had dedicated his life to Parliament and a Liberal Party memorably described in 1935, by historian George Dangerfield, as an "irrational mixture of Whig aristocracy, industrialists, dissenters, trades unionists, quacks and Mr. Lloyd George". Discernible here is Asquith's dilemma. Giving Kitchener's job to the big beast Lloyd George would inevitably make a serious rival even more powerful. Nevertheless, and reluctantly, Asquith did so. His perceptive wife noted in her diary: "We are out: it can only be a question of time now when we will have to leave Downing Street."

In July 1916, with Britain embarked on the Somme offensive, Parliament, the great newspaper magnates and even his own Cabinet noted Asquith's lack of urgency and vim. By contrast, Lloyd George took to his new task with characteristic energy and drive. He initially backed the generals, and in September was confidently predicting "a knock-out blow" before winter. But by November, as the promised gains were not delivered, he was expressing serious doubts about political decisiveness and military strategy. Concerns were reflected in the press: "Unless the Coalition shows more grip than it latterly has," wrote the *Daily Chronicle*, 'it seems to us in serious danger of coming to grief ... Its arch defect is its inability to make up its mind.' This was a shrewd thrust at Asquith. Crushed by the recent death of his son on the Somme and unwilling to give up the hallowed procedures of peacetime, the prime minister was losing his authority.

Unbelievably, Asquith had no real Cabinet secretariat. Its methods were those of another age with no agenda, no order of business and no formal minutes, except for the prime minister's hand-written reports to the king. Lloyd George described Cabinet meetings as a "daily disastrous essay in the dilatory". He was now determined to seize control of the political process by means of a new cabal within government. In this project he found powerful allies – first and foremost Bonar Law, who disliked Lloyd George but recognized the need for change, and Sir Edward Carson, leader of the Ulster Unionists. They were supported outside the Cabinet by both Lord Northcliffe and Max Aitken (soon to become Lord Beaverbrook), controllers of the *Times*, the *Daily Mail* and the *Daily Express*.

Thus, on 25 November, the three politicians presented to Asquith an announcement for the formation of a new body with executive powers, described as a new "Civilian General Staff", to oversee the strategic conduct of the war, and asked for Asquith's signature. Lloyd George would be its chairman, with the prime minister as merely its figurehead. After (the usual) delay, Asquith turned the scheme down flat. A week of political infighting followed. While Bonar Law's Conservative colleagues wanted nothing to do with the "*parvenu* Welsh lawyer", all sides recognized that a Lloyd George resignation could bring down the Coalition government. So did Lloyd George, and on 1 December 1916 he fired an ultimatum at Asquith demanding that he "withdraw from the Presidency of the War Council in favour of another".

The press agreed. Northcliffe considered Lloyd George the lesser of two evils. On 3 December, a worried Asquith promised to negotiate with Lloyd George, after meeting Bonar Law and seeing Unionist support slipping away. He announced that he was advising the king to "consent to a reconstruction of the government".

Conservatives and Liberals alike then rounded on Asquith for giving in to Lloyd George's blackmail. Asquith was trapped. He wrongly concluded that a devastating attack on his premiership in the *Times* was the work of Lloyd George and Northcliffe, and he now informed Lloyd George in frosty terms that, while he did propose to form a new government, Lloyd George should not automatically expect to be part of it.

Lloyd George struck. He reproached Asquith for going back on his word and, on 5 December, resigned as Secretary of State for War. It was too much. Believing that neither Lloyd George nor Bonar Law would be able to form a government, Asquith resigned the same day. But his bluff failed. When Bonar Law was summoned to the Palace, he advised the king that only Lloyd George could unite the people, Parliament and the squabbling politicians.

Two days later, after Lloyd George had secured sufficient support, Britain had a new prime minister and – at last – a war leader.

66

THE STARS & STRIPES
AMERICA ENTERS THE WAR

JANUARY TO APRIL 1917

In 1914, the prospect of Europeans gearing up "to cut each other's throats" (*see* Chapter 36) was an enormous blessing to the economy of the United States. Industrial production, and stocks and shares that had been in the doldrums during the summer, soared in the autumn of 1914 as the British and French placed massive orders for weapons with American companies. The war was distant – confirmed by President Woodrow Wilson's declaration of strict neutrality on 19 August – and profitable.

But the New World found it much harder, in practice, to put the Old World out of mind. As reports of German atrocities in Belgium became worldwide news, attitudes began to harden. Many Americans were genuinely shocked, and there were some open calls for war. But over a quarter of Americans were either German immigrants or of German descent, and there were many vociferously anti-English Irish-Americans, too. Although most Americans did genuinely regard the Kaiser's Germany as an anti-democratic, militaristic power, the US Congress supported a strongly isolationist foreign policy and, with one eye firmly on the melting pot of US voters, saw itself as no more than championing the rights of neutral nations. The prevailing view was that it was not in the US interest to get involved in the "Europeans' War". But in 1917 two German blunders completely alienated American sentiments. And with that radical swing of popular opinion, the scales of war tipped decisively.

It would have been almost impossible for France and Britain to win the war without the United States. During the years of US neutrality, both France and Britain received huge material support from the government and individuals across the United States, spending around $7 billion on American goods. To sustain this level of support, it was vital that France and Britain were well favoured by American public opinion, and both countries fared well in the propaganda war – in contrast to the Germans. But French and British statesmen knew that, in the end, the war would only be resolved when the United States finally committed herself to the Allied cause, even if eventually this was not as a full member of the alliance but only an "Associated Power". The US entry into the war on 6 April 1917 was greeted with relief and muted celebration by the two leading Allied nations. In Paris, they marked the day by hoisting this American "Stars and Stripes" over the Hôtel de Ville, headquarters of the city's civil administration. This was seen as so significant an act of respect and welcome that within only a few weeks the flag was heading the list of acquisitions destined for the new War Museum in London.

"IT IS A FEARFUL THING TO LEAD THIS GREAT PEACEFUL PEOPLE INTO WAR, INTO THE MOST TERRIBLE AND DISASTROUS OF ALL WARS, CIVILIZATION ITSELF SEEMING TO BE IN THE BALANCE. BUT THE RIGHT IS MORE PRECIOUS THAN PEACE."

President Woodrow Wilson, Address to Extraordinary Session of US Congress, 2 April 1917

In the neutral years, the powerful capitalists of Wall Street realized that financially, the United States and the Allies were becoming entwined. The huge sales of war materials to the Allies and the decision to invest in bonds of Allied governments meant that US bankers and industrialists had a major stake in an Allied victory. The billionaire banker J.P. Morgan was, in January 1915, appointed chief UK purchasing and contract agent in America, with thousands of contracts to award, worth several billion dollars. He knew that his client now owed American companies huge sums of money, and that US banks had extended millions of dollars of credit. Were the Allies to lose the war, there would be a danger they could not repay what they owed, an unpaid debt that could deal a severe blow to the American economy. Understandably, Morgan and his friends lobbied for a pro-Allied policy.

Neutrality also had a challenge from an entirely different quarter, in the shape of a spillover from Mexico's turbulent revolutionary strife. The northern Mexican warlord Francisco "Pancho" Villa attacked the US border town of Columbus, New Mexico, in March 1916, causing shock waves throughout the United States. A retaliatory expedition of 12,000 men under General John Pershing promptly invaded Mexico and penetrated about 200 miles to try (unsuccessfully) to hunt him down. The sense of being under threat seemed closer for many Americans, and the "Preparedness Movement", encouraged by Republican politicians such as Theodore (Teddy) Roosevelt, reflected this growing concern. Thousands of Americans marched through the streets carrying national flags and calling for "greater national readiness", and many joined drill clubs and practised marching.

By the summer of 1916 dark rumours of German-inspired industrial sabotage (some justified), supposed poisoning of water supplies, kidnapping of individuals and penetration of American labour unions were circulating. These rumours added to the growing distrust of German intentions and the anger roused by Germany's indiscriminate submarine actions, notably the sinking of *Lusitania* in 1915 (*see* Chapter 27). Public concern ensured that the National Defense Act was passed in June 1916, authorizing the expansion of the US Army from 90,000 to 175,000 men and a quadrupling of the territorial force of the National Guard to 450,000 men.

The November 1916 presidential election campaign spelled out the issues clearly. After a closely fought campaign, the idealistic Princeton jurisprudence professor Woodrow Wilson was re-elected on a ticket promising "peace, progressivism and prosperity". While the majority of Americans still opted for neutrality, nevertheless war seemed to be getting closer. In an effort to stem what many were beginning to see as an inexorable slide, Wilson launched a diplomatic peace mission over the winter of 1916–17 in order to identify the belligerents' real war aims and seek some compromise peace. It merely exposed the warring nations' irreconcilable differences.

Just as Wilson was considering one last initiative came the news of the German resumption of unrestricted submarine warfare (*see* Chapter 62). The sometimes excitable Wilson was furious and broke off diplomatic relations with Germany on 3 February 1917. America's "man of peace" was now having to contemplate war; two weeks later a diplomatic bombshell made it virtually certain.

On 24 February, an astonished Washington learned of the "Zimmermann telegram", and the press got to know a week later. In 1914, when the German undersea cable had been cut, Sweden let Berlin use the Swedish cable to send its diplomatic telegrams to embassies worldwide. But this cable was routed through Britain and the British codebreakers could read the German signals. The so-called "Swedish roundabout" suddenly produced pay-dirt on 17 January 1917, when Admiralty codebreakers intercepted and deciphered a set of instructions from the German Foreign Minister Arthur Zimmermann intended for the German Minister in Mexico City, letting him know that Germany was about to resume unrestricted submarine warfare. More importantly, it also instructed the minister to offer Mexico an alliance with Germany on the promise that they "make war together, make peace together" and Berlin could offer "an understanding ... that Mexico is to reconquer the lost territory in Texas, New Mexico and Arizona".

The British sat on this explosive document for over two weeks, in the hope that events might anyway tip the United States into war. The Germans duly restarted their unrestricted submarine campaign. But the British also managed to obtain a second copy of the actual telegram delivered to the Germans in Mexico City. The problem now was how to tell the world of the Germans' plans without letting them know their top-secret cable traffic was being intercepted and read. London's second, Mexican version of the telegram provided the solution. When the Americans were handed the formal copy of it, they were told that it had been obtained by "an agent in Mexico". To British astonishment, Germany confirmed this deceit, and Zimmermann himself admitted it was no forgery.

And yet, even when confronted with this open evidence of hostile German intention, Wilson still hesitated to call for war. He only briefed his Cabinet on 20 March, nearly a month after he had first seen the "Zimmermann telegram". By then, US public opinion, incited by new U-boat hostilities against US merchant and passenger ships and the incendiary content of Berlin's telegram, had swung decisively against the Kaiser's Germany. On 2 April, Wilson briefed Congress, calling for a declaration of war. In true idealistic style he sold the war as a great moral crusade: "The world", Wilson declared, "must be made safe for democracy." On 6 April 1917, the United States declared war on an unrepentant Germany.

Optimistic Allied hopes of any *immediate* infusion of US armed forces were fantasies. America's army was still tiny, with 128,000 men and 125,000 National Guards. There was no air force – in 1914, the army had only 6 planes and 16 pilots – and the navy was undermanned and relatively unprepared. But with their new partner there was the promise of raising and equipping massive fighting forces and the prospect of almost limitless resources. The most important immediate benefit was therefore the psychological boost to morale.

The Americans were in.

President Wilson addresses an "extraordinary session" of the joint houses of Congress to put his case for war against Germany (2 April 1917), declaring that "The world must be made safe for democracy." He highlighted Germany's unrestricted submarine warfare as "warfare against mankind".

67

A BOLSHEVIK BANNER
RUSSIA IN TURMOIL

1916 TO 1917

By the autumn of 1916 there were many signs that a major crisis was looming for Russia. The ultimate failure of the summer's Brusilov offensive (*see* Chapter 51) had left both the army and the country dispirited, and the prospect of another winter in the trenches lowered morale still further. However, Russia's greatest problems were behind the lines. The combination of mass migration of peasants into the cities, rising costs, inflation and shortages of food led to growing public anger. The massive industrial complex around the capital Petrograd (now renamed from the Germanic-sounding "St Petersburg"), whose population had soared to run the wartime industries, became a natural hotbed of industrial action and demonstrations calling for bread and fuel to withstand the Baltic winter. But the Russian railway system was breaking down under its own inefficiencies and the demands of the army. Before the war, Petrograd received 90 grain wagons a day; by early 1917, it was receiving only 50.

It was these basic shortages of food and fuel that provided the principal catalyst for a political storm. In 1917, Russia witnessed not one, but two, revolutions – or more precisely a revolution and a *coup d'état* – and the rise of the anti-war Bolshevik Party would suddenly fragment the war's Allies.

The Allies knew that any Russian exit from the war would allow the Germans to move large numbers of troops to France and Belgium. They were also worried that weapons and other resources previously sent to Russia might fall into either Bolshevik or German hands. In the months after the October Bolshevik Revolution, pressure grew for Allied intervention, and Britain and France sent troops to the northern Russians ports of Murmansk and Archangel. They included Sergeant Leslie Clarke, who had spent much of the war since 1915 training men to use Lewis and Hotchkiss machine guns, and was now on his first overseas posting. By July 1918 he was in the isolated Russian town of Kemi Karelia, where British troops were forced to break up massed protest meetings, firing into the crowds and even killing locals. Clarke explained: "These Bolshevik agitators had brought with them 3 or 4 Socialistic-Revolutionary Banners which had been used in Petrograd during the first upheaval. The Banners were of red bunting, painted in white Russian lettering, with the translated manifesto: 'Workmen of all nations come together! By fighting you will obtain your rights!'" Somehow Clarke managed to keep one and brought it back when he returned, sick, to Britain the following spring. Coarse and home-made, it still exudes the raw power of revolutionary zeal.

> "IN THE DAYS OF THE GREAT STRUGGLE AGAINST THE FOREIGN ENEMIES ... THE LORD GOD HAS BEEN PLEASED TO SEND DOWN ON RUSSIA A NEW HEAVY TRIAL. INTERNAL POPULAR DISTURBANCES THREATEN TO HAVE A DISASTROUS EFFECT ON THE FUTURE CONDUCT OF THIS PERSISTENT WAR."

Tsar Nicholas II, Abdication Proclamation, 2 March 1917 (Old Style date)

ПРОЛЕТАРІИ ВСЕХ СТРАН СОЕДИНЯЙТЕС"! В БОР'БЕ ОБРЕТЕШ ТЫ ПРАВО СВОЕ!

Once Tsar Nicholas had assumed overall command of the Russian armies in 1915, he became absorbed by military matters at the Russian headquarters in Mogilev. He devolved much domestic government of his autocratic state to his wife, Tsarina Alexandra, but her German lineage and dependence on a coterie of advisors – including, until his assassination in December 1916, the notorious "mystic" Rasputin – made her extremely unpopular with the Russian aristocracy and wider populace. She did little to counteract the growing suspicion that the Germans, capitalist profiteers and "speculators" were bringing the country to her knees. Popular opinion was that treachery started at the top. As early as October 1916, the Tsar's secret police were warning him that Petrograd's people were "on the verge of despair" and "quite ready to involve themselves in the worst excesses of a hunger riot". And in his last audience with the Tsar, in January 1917, British Ambassador Sir George Buchanan undiplomatically warned his host that that the country was heading for "revolution and disaster".

The spark that kindled revolution was a series of demonstrations on 9 January 1917 (in the Old Style Russian calendar, which was 13 days behind the rest of Europe). This was the anniversary of "Bloody Sunday", when the Cossacks had opened fire on rioters in 1905. By 25 February huge crowds were looting shops and fighting with the exhausted police. The Tsar ordered troops in to restore order, but this time the discontent was so deep that the army sided with the rioters. On 27 February, the authorities lost control. The elite Volynsky Regiment mutinied, shot its colonel and, by 28 February, the majority of the Petrograd garrison had joined the rioters. The president of the Duma (Parliament) cabled the Tsar: "Anarchy in the capital, government paralysed. Supplies of fuel and food completely disrupted." By now, street and soldiers' strike committees were formed, calling themselves soviets ("councils"), and factory committees were passing resolutions while conventional authority disintegrated. In a desperate attempt to impose order, the Duma ignored the Tsar's command to disband and stayed in session. A revolution had begun.

On 1 March, the Tsar headed to Petrograd by train, but was not allowed to enter the city. The next day, under intense pressure from his generals, Tsar Nicholas II agreed to abdicate – along with his son and heir – in favour of his brother Grand Duke Mikhail, who promptly refused the throne. Overnight the Romanovs were gone, and the Duma's "Provisional Government", led by Prince Lvov, was now in charge. But it was not the *only* centre of new power in Russia. The hundreds of socialist-inspired soviets had nominated the overarching Petrograd Soviet to represent their collective views. The upshot was that there were now two hubs of political power: the Duma and the Petrograd Soviet's Provisional Executive Committee (*Ispolkom*) of workers and soldiers, dominated by socialist-revolutionary "Mensheviks". In the rest of this vast country there was now no structure of government except for scattered local councils.

The Provisional Government now confronted two great questions: first, should the war continue? Second, what to do about the collapsed economy and runaway inflation? The first was easy. Neither the Socialist intellectuals who dominated *Ispolkom* nor the military High Command wanted to stop fighting. The Socialists thought that if the war stopped, their revolution would be overthrown; the generals and the Duma were driven by what appears to be genuine nationalism and the commitment to the Allies not to pursue a separate peace. The Minister of War, Alexander Kerensky, ordered a new offensive for the summer of 1917, while the Duma desperately sought to restore normal economic life.

Into this maelstrom there returned in early April 1917 a figure who had his own disruptive agenda – the exiled leader of the radical revolutionary Bolshevik Party, Lenin. The Germans calculated that he could be relied on to undermine Russia's stability, and therefore facilitated his return in a sealed train from Switzerland.

Lenin quickly set out his manifesto: an end to the war; the nationalization of all property, land, banks and great commercial concerns; a "people's militia"; and the slogan "all power to the soviets", since he saw the councils as ripe for takeover as the Bolshevik power bases. These radical "April Theses" shocked many, including his own supporters. Lenin was serious, however. When militants of the Petrograd garrison refused to go to the Front in early July, to take part in a renewed Russian offensive ordered by Kerensky, Lenin supported the soldiers, calling for a coup. However, the Provisional Government had enough loyal troops to suppress the uprising and took the opportunity to arrest leading Bolsheviks: once again, Lenin fled into hiding, now in Finland. At the same time, the Provisional Government acquired a harder-headed leader in the shape of Kerensky.

The Petrograd Soviet was, though, now at its most vulnerable. On 25 August, the recently appointed Russian commander-in-chief, Lavr Kornilov, planned to move loyal troops into Petrograd to disarm the militants and close down the Petrograd Soviet. Kerensky and Kornilov had already clashed over the latter's demands, and Kerensky now saw Kornilov's attempt as a military putsch, but seemed powerless to do anything. Instead, a united front by thousands of Bolshevik Red Guard militia, led by Leon Trotsky, combined with disaffected soldiers among Kornilov's forces to stymie the attempt. By September it was all over. The army had fragmented completely, Kornilov was under arrest, Kerensky's credibility was shattered and control of the Petrograd Soviet had passed into Bolshevik hands. In October, Lenin was back, sensing an opportunity and promising "peace, land and bread".

On 24 October, the Bolsheviks, organized by Trotsky, struck, mounting a coup to seize control of key locations around Petrograd. On the night of 25 October, Bolsheviks stormed into the Tsar's former Winter Palace and arrested the astounded members of the Provisional Government still sitting arguing around the table. By the next morning Petrograd awoke to its new government of the "Council of People's Commissars" with Lenin at its head. In Petrograd at least, the quick takeover had been almost bloodless. Even Lenin was surprised at his success, saying to Trotsky: "*Es schwindelt!*" – or more colloquially, "I'm gobsmacked."

One of his first acts was to issue a unilateral Russian Decree of Peace. Russia was out of the war – for the moment.

Bolsheviks and banners. Lenin, surrounded by the paraphernalia of popular protest, addresses packed crowds in Petrograd after his return from Swiss exile. His uncompromising "April Theses" gave way to the more practical matter of getting power: toppling the Provisional Government and gaining control of the Petrograd Soviet.

68

CULLEY'S SOPWITH CAMEL
THE BATTLE FOR THE SKIES

1915 TO 1917

With the importance of aerial reconnaissance established (*see* Chapter 37) – as a way to observe enemy positions, help plan battles and direct and vary artillery fire – aircraft were soon changing the way battles were fought. A junior officer in the air now had the responsibility to select and prioritize targets for a whole corps' artillery. This very success meant it was essential to remove the enemy's eyes in the sky – that aircraft needed to attack and drive off the enemy's aircraft. The war would see a host of new machines, new technologies and new tactics as the constituents of an "air war" – so familiar in the next world war – were born.

Aviation developed with astonishing speed under the urgency of the war. In only three years, the slow, underpowered machines of 1914 had grown into fast, robust modern aircraft. Perhaps the best remembered British aeroplane is the Sopwith Camel, which entered service in the summer of 1917, helping to transform the Royal Flying Corps' fortunes. It was a quirky machine, driven by a rotary engine that turned so powerfully that if not fully controlled it could throw the aircraft to the right so quickly it would spin out of control. But skilful pilots used this unique characteristic to whip around faster than other aircraft and move them into a dominating position behind their opponents, turning the Camel into a superb fighting aircraft. This one, serial number N6812, was part of the newly formed Royal Air Force in 1918, though it was actually in naval service, towed on a floating launch ramp behind a destroyer. On 11 August 1918, it was patrolling the North Sea. Previous patrols had been threatened by Zeppelins flying overhead, and when one was spotted in the distance, Canadian-born Lieutenant Stuart Culley was ordered to take off from his precarious platform and shoot it down. For over an hour, Culley climbed at full throttle towards the distant airship. Once in position, he turned to attack with his two Lewis guns fixed on the upper wing. One jammed, but Culley still poured all the bullets from the other into the airship. As he pulled away, the Zeppelin ignited and plunged 18,000 feet towards the waves – the last ever to be shot down. Culley's famous aircraft has been on display at the Imperial War Museum since 1935.

By August 1915 the innovative forward-firing Fokker Eindecker was taking its toll of Allied reconnaissance planes – and aircraft equipped to drop bombs. The French were already fielding what can be defined as the world's first bomber force, which was raiding railway junctions in the Saar valley, dropping converted 155mm shells with considerable effect. On 25 August 1915, a formation of 62 bombers attacked the steelworks at Dillingen, and another raid the following day against an aircraft factory prompted its relocation further east. However, the French pilots began to encounter serious opposition from the German "attack" machines and began to insist on having an escort of the new "fighters", such as the diminutive but highly effective Nieuport 11, known as the *Bébé*, which appeared in January 1916.

In early 1916, two developments moved the aerial war on further. Under the influence of successful "aces" Oswald Boelcke and Max Immelmann, the Germans began to improve fighter tactics and group their fighters in teams. In their turn, the British began to escort their reconnaissance missions with fighters. These included planes of the "pusher" type (with rear-mounted propellers), such as the new FE2,

DH2 and the Vickers FB5 "Gunbus", a light, manoeuvrable aircraft with a forward-firing machine gun and more than a match for the Fokker Eindecker.

The first great aerial clash of the war was the struggle for air supremacy over Verdun in 1916. The Germans mounted "barrage patrols" to protect their build-up of troops and *matériel* from the prying eyes of French reconnaissance planes. The French were outclassed by the newer German machines like the two-seater Roland C-III, and forced out of the sky. In response, special *escadrilles de chasse* (including the famous volunteer American Lafayette squadron) were hastily formed with orders to "seek out the enemy, fight him, and destroy him". At Verdun, by engaging the German aircraft in this intensive way, the French launched the first independent air campaign in history. They redressed the balance of power in the air, albeit at heavy cost; Georges Guynemer, one of the first aces, was shot down, wounded, as were many others.

Further north, the Royal Flying Corps (RFC) was preparing for the Somme. The first British single-seater fighter squadrons reached France by spring 1916, and from July onwards the pusher fighters and "tractor"-type Sopwith 1½ Strutters (with propeller at the front) ended the so-called "Fokker scourge" as the RFC gained air supremacy over the battlefield. One German soldier wrote: "During the day one hardly dares to be seen in the trench owing to the English aeroplanes." The British had also developed their own effective "interrupter" mechanism, which used the turning of the propeller to fire the machine gun through the rotating blades. And the British were now even able to boast their own *bona fide* fighter ace and national celebrity in the shape of Albert Ball, whose tally of "kills" was 17 by the end of August.

However, by autumn 1916 the air war began to swing back again as the first of the fast, streamlined Albatros D1 fighters appeared in new hunting groups (*Jagdstaffeln*), organized under the influence of Boelcke, who was emerging as Germany's leading air-war tactician and theorist – and its pre-eminent ace, especially after Immelmann was killed in June 1916. In two months Boelcke shot down 20 RFC and French aircraft. The British doggedly tried to maintain air superiority, but were completely outclassed. The single-minded strategy of Major General Hugh Trenchard, the RFC's commander, remained resolutely offensive, so patrols were maintained at all times over German lines; this brought the inevitable result that damaged planes could rarely get home and the prevailing westerly wind meant air battles drifted deep behind German lines, which is exactly what the Germans wanted. Air casualties mounted as the ground offensive petered out. By November 1916 the RFC had lost 782 planes, and – with 499 airmen killed – there had effectively been a 100 per cent casualty rate since 1 July.

British reaction was confused. The government's Royal Aircraft Factory was castigated for turning out slow and inefficient designs. In Parliament, MPs accused the government-designed and obsolete BE2 aircraft of "murdering our pilots". Fortunately, the civil aircraft industry was responding and innovative new designs were slowly coming into production. In France, the new Spads were a match for any German fighter.

For spring 1917 it was, however, too little, too late. The first four months of the year rammed home the hard truth: in the air, numerical advantage was no answer to technical superiority. Obsolete aeroplanes, poor training and slow delivery now brought the RFC into real crisis. In just five days before the Battle of Arras opened at Easter (*see* Chapter 69) the RFC lost 75 aircraft and 105 aircrew. Another 56 aircraft were lost through crashes. During "Bloody April" of that year, some new pilots arrived

"THE BLAST OF WIND FROM THE PROPELLER DISTURBED ME ENORMOUSLY. IT WAS IMPOSSIBLE TO COMMUNICATE ... MY CRASH HELMET KEPT SLIPPING, MY SCARF LOOSENED, MY JACKET WAS NOT BUTTONED SECURELY. IN SHORT, IT WAS MISERABLE"

Future German ace Manfred von Richthofen, remembering his first flight, May 1915

on the squadrons with just ten hours flying experience and thought themselves lucky to survive for three weeks. The German combination of better aircraft, better organization and superior training – plus, of course, an abundance of slow and vulnerable targets – made them formidable and dangerous opponents.

The air war escalated into a series of epic battles. On 23 April 1917, 68 RFC fighters came to the rescue of vulnerable artillery observation aircraft circling over their German targets. At the same time, aircraft of the fighter squadron (*Jagdstaffel 1*) directed by Germany's latest ace, Manfred von Richthofen, tried to shoot them down. The RFC suffered heavy losses after an hour-long dogfight with Richthofen's "Flying Circus" – so called because of the brightly coloured way their aircraft were painted (Richthofen's own plane was red) and the regular movement of their canvas hangers like circus tents. The new two-seater Bristol Fighters, of which much was expected, suffered 60 per cent casualties on their first sortie due to faulty tactics. The overall statistics were devastating: between March and May 1917, 1,270 British aircraft were lost.

Fortunately, by mid-May the worst was over. The arrival of 56 Squadron with its new Royal Aircraft Factory SE5s began to tilt the balance. Within the next two months, new machines capable of outfighting the German fighters would at last begin to pour in from England and, along with them, better-trained pilots. Together with Sopwith's extraordinarily manoeuvrable Camel (credited with shooting down 1,294 enemy aircraft, more than any other Allied fighter of the war), the SE5s and the reorganized Bristol Fighters would wrest aerial superiority from the Germans by the end of 1917.

The Sopwith Camel proved an adept and versatile, if quirky, addition to the Royal Flying Corps' repertoire of aircraft, and helped tilt the air advantage away from the Germans. This particular one had an unfortunate end, although the fact that it is still in one piece suggests it did not fall from too great a height.

69

A TRENCH MORTAR FROM VIMY
THE BATTLE OF ARRAS & NIVELLE'S OFFENSIVE

APRIL TO MAY 1917

The year 1916 left the armies on the Western Front battered and exhausted. Huge amounts of ammunition, weapons and lives had been consumed on the Somme and at Verdun. Both campaigns had degenerated into protracted battles of attrition with no breakthrough, and had left the combatants reeling. The question was: what now? The early months of 1917 would see a strategic retreat of the German armies, but also a renewed Franco-British offensive. Spring 1917 would bring disaster for the French and a rather limited success for the British – yet for the Canadian divisions of the British Army, it produced one of their finest moments of the war.

On 9 April 1917, fighting side by side for the first time, the four Canadian divisions in the BEF captured Vimy Ridge. In 1915, the Germans had defeated repeated French attempts to take the ridge and regarded the position as impregnable. The meticulously planned operation was covered by a massive artillery bombardment. At 05.30, 15,000 Canadian soldiers surged over the ridge. Four hours later, fresh troops crashed through the fortified villages on the far side. By the end of the second day, the entire ridge was in Canadian hands: it had been a complete triumph. In freezing rain and sleet, the 31st Battalion from Alberta had overrun the village of Thélus and, among its shattered ruins, they found this 25cm heavy trench mortar, or *Minenwerfer*, which the Germans had used for bombarding enemy trenches too close to be shelled by field guns. Within weeks it had been passed to the new War Museum in London as a symbol of Canadian victory. The capture of Vimy Ridge showed the world the skill and strength of Canada's soldiers. The French press hailed their success in snatching the positions that had thwarted their own soldiers and portrayed Vimy Ridge as an Easter gift from Canada to the people of France. It is fitting that today, in a reciprocal act of gratitude, Canada's national memorial to its dead of the First World War stands astride Vimy Ridge, on land freely given by France.

First, however, there was a change of personnel. By December 1916, Joffre's star as French Chief of the General Staff was waning, as criticism of his handling of the war arose on every side. Despite his steady leadership and legendary sang-froid he was increasingly seen as a man devoid of ideas. French Premier Briand, under intense pressure from the Chamber of Deputies, faced a choice: either his government fell or Joffre went. Unsurprisingly, the politician ditched the general, appointing him "Military Technical Advisor to the Government", with a small office in Paris.

"BUILDINGS WERE DEMOLISHED, TRENCHES OBLITERATED AND WIRE SMASHED TO ATOMS. THERE WAS HARDLY AN INCH OF GROUND THAT DID NOT BEAR WITNESS TO THE TREMENDOUS EFFECT OF OUR GUNS"

Battle report of the 31st (Alberta) Battalion, regarding the capture of Thélus, 9 April 1917

His replacement was General Robert Nivelle, who had risen remarkably quickly from a mere colonel of artillery in 1914. At the Aisne in 1914, and at Verdun in 1916, he had handled his guns with great skill, and he was responsible for the successful counterattacks that retook the Verdun forts of Vaux and Douaumont. According to the British Liaison Officer at French GHQ, he was "good-looking, smart, plausible and cool"; he had two other advantages: he spoke fluent English, thus commending him to his British allies; and, as a Protestant and a Republican, he was not deemed a threat in the snakepit of French politics.

Nivelle proposed a double offensive for spring 1917. The British would mount an attack around Arras, in Artois; and, once the German reserves had been committed, the French would then attack further south in the Champagne. Unfortunately, Nivelle overplayed his hand, announcing that he had a confident plan to "rupture the enemy's front line in such a manner that the rupture can be immediately exploited". These claims excited war-weary politicians, especially as Nivelle claimed that he now had his "method". This consisted of a two-day bombardment against a selected area, which would turn into a creeping barrage as the infantry closed up to attack. Enemy artillery would be swamped by brisk counter-battery fire once it had revealed its position. Many of his military contemporaries had doubts, arguing that what may have worked on a small scale at Verdun could not be guaranteed on the 23-mile frontage now proposed.

Unfortunately, Nivelle soon fell out with the recently promoted Field Marshal Haig over how much of the Front the British were prepared to take over from the French. Nivelle wanted to hand over another 20 miles south of the Somme. Haig would only accept 8 miles. Nivelle then embarked on an intrigue with Britain's new prime minister, Lloyd George, which damaged relations between the Allies and – worse – left Lloyd George and Haig distrusting each other for the rest of the war. At Calais on 26 February, Lloyd George unveiled a surprise proposal to place Haig under Nivelle's command, without having consulted the Cabinet, Haig or the astonished Chief of the Imperial General Staff. After a furious exchange the idea was whittled down to a temporary subordination for the spring offensives; relations between Haig and the slippery Lloyd George were damaged irreparably.

Events now reared their head. Having suffered heavy losses on the Somme and at Verdun in 1916, the Germans had decided to withdraw to a better defensive position. The result was the building of a shorter, heavily fortified line between Verdun and Loos, incorporating deep and mutually supporting defences: the *Siegfried Stellung*, or "Hindenburg Line" as the British called it. In late February 1917, the Germans began a large-scale strategic withdrawal to this new position, and over two months this retreat, codenamed Operation Alberich, dissolved the "vulnerable" salient that the Germans had been defending at high cost – and took away many of the very positions that Nivelle had proposed attacking. France now had more of her sacred soil back, but it threw Allied planning into disarray.

Political turmoil was also wracking the Allies: there was a revolution in Russia as the Tsar abdicated (*see* Chapter 67); and during March, Briand's government fell in Paris. A number of politicians and senior military figures began to express doubts about the forthcoming attack. But Nivelle insisted and threatened to resign. A special Presidential Council of War was formed and only when Nivelle had received a unanimous – and mendacious – assurance that the new government backed his plans did he agree to continue. As it was, he was forced to postpone his attack for a month.

Canadian troops in the remains of a battered trench at Vimy Ridge (1917). The shell-torn landscape beyond, denuded of any sort of vegetation, is a testament to the ferocity of battle.

When it did get underway, at Easter 1917, it began in the north with the British "diversionary" attack, a week ahead of the main French offensive. The aim was to pin down German forces, draw in reserves and act as the anvil for Nivelle's hammer when he broke through further south. Unfortunately, German withdrawal to the Hindenburg Line meant that the British had been forced to replan their whole attack. Nevertheless, it became clear that the Germans had committed a number of errors in their redeployment. The main German reserves were being held about 30 miles to the rear and the local reserves had been pushed well forward – well within range of any British bombardment.

To the north of Arras the primary objective was the long slope of Vimy Ridge, which climbed gently up to a crest before falling sharply away to give a spectacular view of the Douai plain as far as German-occupied Lille. Drawing away to the southeast was Arras, with both positions undercut by an ancient network of caves and quarries that had been used to provide the stone to build the city, and which now provided well-lit, well-ventilated, but above all safe shelters for up to 30,000 soldiers.

Lieutenant General Sir Edmund Allenby's Third Army was to launch the main thrust of the battle out of Arras itself, flanked by the First and Fifth armies to the north and south. Allenby had a bold plan. Eight infantry divisions would emerge from the ground on the Germans' doorstep, to attack with the support of 70 tanks to crunch through the wire. The assault would be ushered in by a meticulous artillery fire plan using 2,000 guns, of which 700 were heavies. The main thrust was only 7,000 yards wide, but was supported by subsidiary attacks on the flanks, of which General Sir Henry Horne's First Army assault on Vimy Ridge was the most important. Once through, Allenby genuinely believed he would be able to release cavalry onto the Douai plain and exploit his breakthrough.

Bad weather postponed the attack for 24 hours, but on Easter Monday, 9 April 1917, it went in covered by sleet and snow showers. The infantry erupted from their warm tunnels and bunkers and rushed the dazed and frozen German frontlines. But for the

51st (Highland) Division, on the left flank of the Third Army, things went badly wrong. Major General Sir George Harper was an old-fashioned soldier, who had little faith in his machine guns and even less in the tanks. His men rushed in, but they met strong resistance in the shape of uncut German wire and a spirited defence from the elite 1st Bavarian Reserve Division. The fighting became confused. One of the Scottish battalions lost its way in the snowstorm, ended up facing the wrong way, halted and promptly dug in.

Fortunately, the attack in the centre went much better for the British. The 34th and 9th divisions swept all before them as they took their phase-one objectives, causing the 14th Bavarian Division to flee in panic and prompting Ludendorff to observe acidly: "One of our divisions failed." The problem for the defenders was that the British bombardment had drenched the German lines in gas, forcing their gunners to handle their weapons in gas masks, which slowed their rate of fire. Worse, so many horses were gassed that ammunition could not be brought forward. Germans died, fell back in confusion or surrendered. The success in breaking into the German line now allowed the 4th Division to successfully exploit and carry forward the attack, as planned and hoped, pushing on towards the strongpoint at Fampoux, nearly 4 miles behind the German first line. Thousands of prisoners were captured, including one surprised and angry general.

The main British axis was the Arras–Cambrai road. Here, tanks led the attack of the 15th (Scottish) Division against stiff resistance. One tank, *Lusitania*, kept stopping as it overheated. The German defenders unwisely assumed that the attack had stalled, only to be gunned down by the tank as they emerged. *Lusitania* continued to grind forward supporting the Scots, who everywhere were gaining the upper hand, overrunning the German defence lines and capturing 60 guns in the process. The Northamptonshire Yeomanry actually managed to ride through the gap and was busy taking prisoners. Unfortunately, the rest of the cavalry was back in Arras and it was getting dark. The assault troops stopped and dug in for the night, giving the Germans a precious breathing space.

The night of 9/10 April was bitterly cold, and many wounded infantrymen who were caught in the open died of exposure. The resumption of the offensive next day

A French casualty during Nivelle's offensive in the Champagne is carried off for treatment. April and May 1917 represented the nadir of morale in the French army, and for some individuals and whole units this disastrous and costly offensive was the last straw.

was spent sorting out the muddles of the previous day, with teams of 12 or 14 horses (double the usual number) needed to pull the guns forward to their new firing lines. The cavalry arrived in a snowstorm and was ordered to wait as the attack slowly got underway again. Yet again a vital chance was lost as precious hours trickled away and German reserves poured in to stem the advance. By the morning of 11 April the skies had cleared. Three surviving tanks led an attack on the village of Monchy, which finally fell as two regiments of cavalry charged across the battlefield at full gallop. German fire soon put a stop to that presumption, and the dismounted survivors swiftly reverted to the infantry role. The Germans now began a counterattack – and slowly the new front solidified.

However, further north the Canadian Corps won a much clearer-cut victory. General Sir Julian Byng's staff had planned their attack to seize Vimy Ridge in fine detail and with particular care for the artillery programme. There were 383 heavy guns in direct support of the Canadians, plus 720 field guns firing the new "106" instantaneous fuse, optimized for destroying barbed wire. As the attack went in, it would be preceded by a creeping barrage with new "curtain barrages" to seal off the flanks and prevent enemy reserves moving in. Units down to individual infantry platoons were briefed and rehearsed on their objectives.

At 05.30 on Easter Monday the Canadians attacked. By 06.05 the German first line, by now just a crater- and corpse-strewn ditch, had fallen and by 09.30 most of the objectives were taken. One strongpoint on Hill 145, where the majestic Canadian memorial now stands, held out and was stormed the next day after a swift bombardment. Vimy Ridge had been taken in a classic, carefully planned "bite and hold" operation. It cost the Canadian Corps 10,500 casualties, but is rightly remembered, and memorialized, as a magnificent feat of arms, made possible by the preparation, good coordination and sheer courage on the part of the Canadian soldiers. Vimy Ridge endures in Canadian history as the day the nation made its mark on the war, and indeed on the world.

In the wider Battle of Arras, there was to be no breakthrough as the fighting petered out in May into the usual stalemate marked by exchange of artillery fire and digging in. The BEF had suffered 158,000 casualties and the Germans about the same. Ludendorff was so shocked by what he viewed as the defensive failure at Arras that he convened a Court of Enquiry and sacked the local commander.

By May, Nivelle's larger French offensive was also over. It began on 16 April, along 25 miles of the Chemin des Dames and the Champagne. The attack was a disaster. The Germans had captured the complete operation order; worse, the British and French military attachés in neutral Holland had been astonishingly indiscreet about Nivelle's plans. Given the consequent lack of surprise, the unreconnoitred terrain in front of the new German positions and the steep country of the Chemin des Dames, it is surprising that the French made any gains at all. The artillery bombardment was too dispersed, and the new French tanks were too few, unreliable and badly handled. The Germans, waiting in their deep bunkers, inflicted heavy casualties. By the end of the first day the French had lost over 120,000 casualties. Although Nivelle persevered for a week, by 25 April the government ordered the offensive stopped. It had cost France another 187,000 men – for a gain of just 4 miles.

It also cost Nivelle his job. On 15 May, he was sacked. His doomed offensive left a bitter legacy, too. Already rank and file French soldiers were deciding they had had enough of following orders and risking pointless slaughter. They went on strike.

70

A TOY SOLDIER
MUTINIES IN THE FRENCH ARMY

FROM APRIL 1917

Even before the end of 1914, the French army had suffered over half a million men killed, wounded or missing. It was a pattern of loss that continued throughout 1915 and 1916, and it was beginning to tell on the frayed nerves of the rank and file. Nivelle's disasterous offensive (*see* Chapter 69) was the last straw. On its second day, men of the 108th Regiment refused to advance; on 29 April, 200 men of the 20th Regiment left their barracks at Châlons and hid in the woods, rather than go back to the Front. They had had enough.

> Once strikes and mutinies rippled along the French line, it was months before morale was restored – and it was a sign of how stressful the war had become, as the archetypal French soldier had previously been seen as a figure of great resilience and stoicism. Known since Napoleonic times as the *poilu*, or "hairy one", after his big moustache and unkempt appearance, he was the face of France. This superb *poilu* doll was one of five bought in August 1917 from the famous Parisian toyshop *Au Nain Bleu* (the French equivalent of London's Hamleys); others, equally detailed, represented French colonial soldiers, including a Zouave and Chasseur d'Afrique. They formed part of a collection of over 500 toys, models, dolls and games built up in 1917 by London's new War Museum for its Children's Section, where they were seen as a way of ensuring that the underlying strength and fortitude of France would be remembered by generations of adults and children to come. Over 1.35 million French soldiers were killed in the war, a proportionate loss twice that of Britain's: the *poilu* had done his duty.

Desertion rates had been rising since the bloodbath of Verdun. News and rumours also spread that made soldiers restive: that their wives were being molested by "colonials", that well-paid civilian workers were going on strike, that the Germans were organizing a peace movement. By early May 1917 more and more units were effectively downing tools. On 19 May, two regiments of the 18th Division refused to go back into the line; on 27 May, the 36th Division rebelled against an order to leave its billets at Villers-sur-Fèrre. Shots were fired and only the arrival of a force of Gendarmerie stopped the men boarding a train for Paris. Troops coming back from Paris were singing the communist "Internationale" and calling for peace. In all, between 49 and 68 divisions were affected over the next six months. Even Ludendorff, hearing the rumours, was worried about possible contagion among *his* men.

In May, a worried French government stepped in. General Pétain succeeded Nivelle as commander-in-chief, and his reputation as a defensively minded general,

"WE DECIDED NOT TO MAKE ANOTHER ATTACK. WE EXPRESSED OUR EXTREME EXHAUSTION, OUR MISERIES, OUR SUFFERING. THE HIGH COMMAND WILL DOUBTLESS CONCLUDE SOMETHING ELSE."

The words of a poilu, *after the Nivelle offensive, April 1917*

not prone to rash, costly adventures, matched the moment. He moved swiftly to stem the growing unrest and refused to agree to harsh "repression", instead adopting a policy of carrot and stick, well spiced with appeasement. True, there were 3,427 courts martial, at which 23,385 men were convicted of mutinous behaviour. And a total of 554 men were sentenced to death. But only 49 were actually executed.

At the same time he began long overdue improvements to the French soldier's conditions. His top priority was leave, backed by a programme of rest camps, better beds, better rations and a discreet patriotic propaganda campaign. Above all, he forbade any offensives. Realizing that he was facing "despairing peasants, not revolutionaries", he determined to hospitalize his "sick army", understanding that the soldiers were prepared to defend France but were in no mood to risk their lives in futile attacks. His motto now was: "wait for the tanks and the Americans".

Once again Pétain, "*le medécin de l'Armée*", was the nation's hero.

71

A GERMAN OFFICER'S CAP
THE THIRD BATTLE OF YPRES –
"PASSCHENDAELE"

JULY TO NOVEMBER 1917

By the summer and autumn of 1917 the French army, under Pétain, was tending to its own much-needed recuperation (*see* Chapter 70); and the prospect of a flood of American troops was still distant. If there was going to be any Allied offensive on the Western Front, it would have to be borne by the British and Imperial forces – and it was. The successful assault on Messines Ridge in June 1917 was just the prelude to the Third Battle of Ypres. It has come down to us under the grim heading of "Passchendaele", the village around which the wretched fighting of its last weeks took place: a name redolent as a symbol of a futile struggle, with needless slaughter, in appalling conditions of flooded, churned-up fields.

The truth is, however, that Field Marshal Haig's Flanders offensive of 1917 was far from futile. It was fought for sound strategic reasons. Although it failed in its principal stated objectives, at great cost, it succeeded in further weakening the German army on the Western Front by making it suffer unacceptable losses at a time when it could have been doing serious damage to the Allied cause elsewhere.

Passchendaele was remembered by many as the worst the war had to offer. Unseasonably heavy rain turned the battlefield into an unimaginable quagmire. Men struggled as much against Nature as the intensive shelling and meticulous German defences. But for a month, between early September and early October, in dry weather British and Imperial troops made a series of clear leaps forward. Montague Moore was involved in the first, on 20 September, around the Menin Road. He was a young officer in the 15th Battalion, Hampshire Regiment. Despite having already attacked that morning, the Hampshires were ordered over the top again late in the afternoon. Moore and two other officers collected together around 100 men and led them across 500 yards of open ground towards a collection of pillboxes known as Tower Hamlets. Only Moore, one sergeant and four men reached their objective. But Moore burst into the position, throwing bombs and destroying all resistance, and capturing 28 prisoners, one machine gun and an artillery piece. Using men sheltering in no-man's land, Moore consolidated the position and held it against intensive counterattacks for 36 hours. At one point, he later told his sister: "I was standing next to a German officer when, crack, and down he went with a bullet through the head, evidently meant for me." That officer, from the Württemberg Regiment, was wearing this cap – Moore retrieved it, and sent it home as a souvenir of his close shave. Six weeks later, after his medal had been announced, he was able to tell his family: "You were quite right. It's the VC."

> "WHAT A SACRIFICE THIS OPERATION ENTAILED, AND YET SO NECESSARY IN THE GREAT FINAL VICTORY."
>
> *General Sir David Watson, commander of the 4th Canadian Division in the final assault at Passchendaele, 1917*

Haig's belief in 1917, reinforced by GHQ intelligence, was that the Germans were at breaking point, and he welcomed the chance to mount an independent campaign. At the Somme in 1916 and Arras in April 1917, the BEF had been obliged to fight in conformity with French plans. Now Haig had a free hand to strike when his force was at its peak and under the local command of General Plumer, whose Second Army had held the line around Ypres since 1915. The Ypres Salient held great strategic significance for the British, as the forward defensive line of Britain herself and the bulwark that kept the Germans from the Channel. Pushing the Salient east would make this stronger and at the same time greatly damage German logistics and communications if their vital railway hub at Roulers could be rendered inoperable.

The prime minister, Lloyd George, was very wary of incurring more heavy casualties after Arras and preferred to stay on the defensive and wait for the Americans. But the pressure of events forced him to come around to Haig's view. For one thing, German attention needed to be diverted from the stricken French army, lest advantage be taken of France's current weakness. Further pressure came from the Admiralty, despairing at the U-boats that were picking off merchant ships in their hundreds in Germany's new unrestricted submarine campaign (*see* Chapter 62). If the BEF could cross the Flanders ridges, it could attack the U-boats' secure pens at Ostend and Zeebrugge. Haig added this thrust towards the Belgian coast to his growing list of objectives, and there was even talk of an amphibious operation to match. He had every reason to be optimistic: the BEF was up to strength in men and munitions; its artillery was growing more powerful every day; and logistic stockpiles had never been higher.

But first the Messines Ridge to the south of Ypres had to be occupied. Anyone sitting on its slight eminence could see and enfilade the southern and eastern approaches to Ypres, so the Germans would have to be evicted. On 7 June 1917, 19 huge mines were detonated beneath their positions (*see* Chapter 43), and 9 well-rehearsed assaulting divisions seized the ridge from the shocked German survivors with modest casualties, capturing 7,354 prisoners, 48 guns, 218 machine guns and 60 trench mortars. Two days after the battle Ludendorff sacked General Maximilian von Laffert, the local German commander.

But Lloyd George still hesitated before approving any further major offensive. The politician had been shocked by the casualties on the Somme the year before. All his instincts now were to avoid a repetition, and he recoiled from the harsh reality that to win the war the German army in the West had to be confronted and defeated. Moreover, he wanted to bring Haig under political control so that Lloyd George, not the BEF's commander-in-chief, would decide when and where to attack. He didn't trust Haig, believing that he would just squander more lives, and so Haig was summoned back to London on 19 June and interrogated before a new Committee on War Policy that was reconsidering strategy. Haig stood firm: the BEF could lock in the Germans, wear them down and seize the high ground to the east of Ypres, stressing that with the French army effectively now only good for defence it was essential to divert German attention away from Pétain's "convalescent" troops. General Sir Henry Wilson and the Chief of the Imperial General Staff agreed, and they were supported by a gloomy and tired Jellicoe, now First Sea Lord, who reiterated the view that "unless Zeebrugge and Ostend are taken from the Germans by 1917 they would lose the war due to insupportable shipping losses".

Eventually Lloyd George acceded, but Haig's Flanders offensive was conditional on a "bit by bit" approach, minimizing casualties, which could be called off at any stage, giving Lloyd George a degree of control. Lloyd George and the Cabinet – seemingly without realizing it – were calling for an attritional battle, not a breakthrough. But the political wrangling and indecision in Whitehall had now squandered valuable time and momentum since the success at Messines. The Germans had moved reserve divisions into the Ypres sector. They had already had three years to prepare their defences around Ypres, which were based on nine different lines built around concrete pillboxes with interlocking arcs of fire and supported by 1,500 guns. The frontline was thinly held by the forward divisions. Behind them reserve divisions were kept well back to act as counterattack forces.

To the surprise of many, within days of the triumph of Messines Haig chose the BEF's Fifth Army, under General Sir Hubert Gough, not Plumer's Second Army to spearhead the new offensive. On paper that looked reasonable. Gough had

"IT WAS DARK, BUT THEN ILLUMINATED BY A LINE OF BURSTING SHELLS. WE MUST ALL HAVE BEEN QUITE DEAFENED BY THE NOISE. I LOOKED AT HERBERT, I COULD SEE HIS LIPS MOVE – I SHOUTED BUT I COULDN'T HEAR MYSELF AT ALL. I WANTED TO TELL HIM WE WOULD KEEP TOGETHER SO I GRABBED HIS HAND AND WE WENT OVER THE TOP TOGETHER AS WE HAD GONE TO SUNDAY SCHOOL – HAND IN HAND."

Private Alfred Warsop, 1st Battalion, Sherwood Foresters, 31 July 1917

a reputation as a "thruster", whereas Haig felt Plumer was too cautious. Gough arrived at Ypres on 10 June and immediately began to lay down plans. He intended to make good use of his 2,300 guns, many of them heavy; with one gun for every 5 yards of front this was an artillery concentration ten times larger than that on the Somme. He believed his infantry could then advance 5,000 yards in its initial assault, sweeping over places that were to become infamous, such as Langemarck, Polygon Wood, Broodseinde and Passchendaele, and driving up the Menin Road towards Gheluvelt. His vision was wholly unrealistic.

For two weeks before 31 July, the Germans were on the receiving end of over 4 million shells. On the last day of July, Gough's men attacked east and northeast out of the Ypres Salient, supported by 135 tanks. Initial gains were made at the cost of 35,000 casualties. However, that day the beginnings of another sort of battle began – against the rain-sodden terrain. On 31 July, it began to pour heavily, continuing the next day and for virtually every day in August, with no sun to dry anything out. Within 48 hours the clay soil, its drainage ditches already shell-torn, could absorb no more, and the persistent downpour turned the surface into a viscous wet mud. The tanks sank in the boggy ground and were little use. After four days, with an advance of only just over 2 miles, Gough was forced to suspend his attacks for a week.

Later, on 16 August, as soon as the weather allowed, the British struck again. They managed to take Langemarck and St Julien, but once again were frustrated further south towards Gheluvelt, where German counterattacks pushed them back.

The view from a captured German pillbox, near the Wieltje–Gravenstafel Road, during the fighting for Polygon Wood (27 September 1917). It seems to offer a little oasis of calm, amid the mangled trees and broken concrete. In the background, the puff of smoke signals a German shell, targeted at the British lines.

On 24 August, Haig handed responsibility back to Plumer, much to the relief of the subordinate commanders under Gough's command, who disliked and distrusted Fifth Army's slapdash staff methods. Plumer (whose motto was "Trust, Thoroughness and Training") characteristically called a halt to consider how best to resume the attack. The weather too improved, as Second Army planned a series of deliberate "bite and hold" operations along the southern part of the Front, to capture the vital Gheluvelt plateau on the Menin Road. Plumer himself insisted on a break between each phase of the attack to bring the artillery forward, so that his troops would always be covered. This pause was to puzzle the Germans, who thought each time that the offensive was over. On 20 September, Plumer unleashed his first assault on an 8-mile front, astride the Menin Road, with orders to seize objectives only 1,500 yards away, then stop and dig in. These were achieved, for 21,000 casualties, and German counterattacks were cut to ribbons by the defensive fire of Plumer's massed artillery and machine guns.

On 25 September, Second Army pushed on again northeast through Polygon Wood. After another pause, a third operation was ordered for 4 October against Broodseinde Ridge, beyond Zonnebeke, which by sheer chance coincided with a major German counterattack. Australians and Germans collided head-on in no-man's land. However, the British gunners were able to destroy the exposed Germans, who were forced back with heavy losses. In three bounds, Plumer had moved his British and ANZAC forces onto Passchendaele Ridge. Crown Prince Rupprecht, the German regional commander, even ordered his staff to begin to prepare withdrawal plans. The heavens had by now opened again, and within hours the battlefield had returned to a quagmire, with both sides floundering in the mud; yet Plumer, under

A British stretcher-bearing party up to its knees in mud, during the fighting around Boesinghe, on Pilckem Ridge (1 August 1917). It is scenes such as these, of atrociously waterlogged ground trying to suck in men and beasts alike, that contributed to the association of the Third Battle of Ypres with the worst Western Front conditions.

pressure to maintain momentum, attacked at Poelcapelle. With the rain, and the lack of time to prepare, this attack was a dismal failure.

Haig now considered halting the offensive for the winter, but the line would be almost impossible to maintain, and so he ordered a fresh attack on Poelcapelle and the final ridge at Passchendaele for 12 October. The British and ANZACs got nowhere in the sea of mud as the web of machine guns in pillboxes cut the exposed attackers down. It was clearly time for fresh troops, and Haig replaced the two battered ANZAC corps with the Canadian Corps, which had been carefully husbanded for the final assault. The Canadian commander, General Sir Arthur Currie, protested against his orders for an immediate attack and proposed a three-phase assault spread over two weeks to give time for supplies to be brought up.

The terrain of the battlefield by now almost defied description: a blank moonscape of mud with the waterlogged shell holes sometimes linking to form shallow lakes. Artillery pieces sank into the ooze and were lost. The mud was so bad that large numbers of shells sank and did not explode, or just blew large fountains of mud harmlessly into the air. Men and mules struggled forward across narrow paths of duckboards. Despite this, by 1 November Canadian patrols had entered Passchendaele village – or its shattered remnants – and two Canadian divisions had finally assaulted the ridge and dug in by 10 November.

The Third Battle of Ypres was over. There had been no breakthrough. In terms of disrupting the German rail network or threatening the U-boat bases, it had been a strategic failure. Yet the salient was deeper and Ypres felt more secure. The battle had taken its toll all round. But the morale of the now poorly rationed Germans was harder hit than the well-supplied BEF. What no-one denied, then or now, is that the conditions of the battlefield were a byword for suffering and hardship – for both sides. Corporal Randall Heffer MM recalled one poignant example near Wieltje: "Our stretcher bearers found an Englishman and a Fritz with their arms round each other's necks trying to comfort each other. They were lying in a shellhole and were already waist deep in water."

Ever since, argument has raged about the battle's purpose, its alleged futility and the dreadful conditions, and above all about its casualties. The British lost about 275,000 men and the Germans rather fewer, perhaps 200,000. In his self-serving postwar memoirs, Lloyd George devoted two chapters to explaining how he tried to prevent the Passchendaele campaign – even though he failed to intervene at the time. And since the 1950s, British opinion about the campaign has been dominated by the "Butchers and Bunglers" school of thought, picking out "Passchendaele" as the nadir of the war, a complete waste and disaster.

The soldiers' descriptions of the conditions and their experiences are plentiful and undeniably harrowing. Throughout, however, Haig was convinced that the Germans could not afford their heavy losses and were close to cracking, and that view appeared supported by Ludendorff, who credited the BEF with sustained success as 80 German divisions were fed through what he called the "Flanders mincing machine". "Once more," Ludendorff later described, "we were involved in a terrific struggle in the West. October came and with it one of the hardest months of the war."

Perhaps the final word should rest with General Sir David Watson, who commanded the 4th Canadian Division in the final assault: "What a sacrifice this operation entailed, and yet so necessary in the great final victory."

72

GORDON HASSELL'S TANK MASK
THE BATTLE OF CAMBRAI

NOVEMBER TO DECEMBER 1917

Cambrai ranks as one of the most curious battles of the war. It is axiomatic that military operations have a single clear aim; Cambrai initially had at least three: to "destroy the enemy's personnel and guns, to demoralise him and disorganise him, and not to capture ground". This plan originated with Brigadier General Hugh Elles and the staff of his recently named Tank Corps. It was conceived as a gigantic "tank raid" on the open rolling downland south of Cambrai, in Artois. But it quickly grew in scale.

At Cambrai, on 20 November 1917, the British deployed tanks in concentrated force for the first time. They vindicated the faith of those who believed they represented a way forward, including one young participant, Gordon Hassell. After fighting in France in 1916, he had become a Tank officer and took command of tank H7, known as *Harrier*. Frustrated by the mud of Ypres, in mid-November 1917 Hassell was sent south – and "the next three weeks were days of sheer pleasure" he remembered, 55 years later. On 20 November, Hassell led *Harrier* up, over and through the Hindenburg Line, reaching his objective at Premy Chapel cleanly. But, ordered onto the Flesquières Ridge, *Harrier* was hit three times and its tracks were ripped off. Hassell's day ended there, but, undaunted, he still sent his parents an exultant message: "Have come through yesterday's glorious success perfectly well and without hurt. Have had a good time." A week later, Hassell was in the thick of the German counterattack as tanks fought defensively for the first time. When his machine became stuck, it was hit by German fire. "Slivers of red hot steel began to fly in the tank – bullets hitting the armoured plates melted and the splash was dangerous to the eyes. For protection, we used a small face mask." Hassell's mask, shown here, seems to blend the medieval with the modern, King Arthur with *Star Wars*: it is an appropriate emblem of the transition of war's technology from the old to the new.

After the débâcle of tanks floundering in the muddy slough of despond at Ypres, Elles was only too keen to demonstrate just what his machines could do given favourable terrain. This was a curious idea. Demonstrations in war cut two ways, and to offer the enemy a dress rehearsal of what these new weapons could achieve *en masse* seems quixotic. However, General Byng, who had replaced Allenby in command of the Third Army, which faced Cambrai and that section of the Hindenburg Line, thought it a good idea. So did Brigadier General Hugh Tudor, Commander Royal Artillery of the 9th Division. He was keen to undertake his own

> **"I'LL BET THAT GHQ ARE JUST AS MUCH SURPRISED BY OUR SUCCESS AS THE GERMANS AND QUITE UNREADY TO EXPLOIT IT."**
>
> *Colonel Ernest Swinton, Tank Corps, 20 November 1917*

experiment, trying a surprise bombardment using "unregistered" guns and shooting "off the map", entailing flash spotting, sound ranging and other new tactics. By September the limited tank raid had developed into a breakthrough operation, ending with Byng's cavalry divisions passing through the breached Hindenburg Line to cause havoc behind German lines. An additional attraction for Haig, frustrated by Ypres, was the chance to confound his political critics in London with a military success. On 13 October, he approved the attack.

Detailed orders issued by Third Army on 13 November 1917 defined it as a *coup de main*, to "take advantage of the existing favourable local situation" where "surprise and rapidity of action are ... of the utmost importance". It called for a deep attack on a 6-mile front, which would be "widened as soon as possible" to allow the cavalry to pass through and isolate Cambrai and its railway network from the rear. The original brief tactical operation had become one of seizing and holding ground, although not aiming at securing a strategic breakthrough.

The attack commenced at 06.20 on 20 November 1917. Seven British divisions followed the tanks, with a single infantry and three cavalry divisions in reserve. The attack was preceded by Tudor's intensive barrage by around 1,000 guns trained on the Hindenburg Line and key points to the rear, which caught the Germans completely by surprise, followed by a creeping barrage behind which the tanks and infantry advanced. Led by Elles in one of the Mark IV tanks called *Hilda*, 476 machines – of which over 350 were fighting tanks – crunched through the German wire, dragging it apart with grapnel hooks, dropping huge bundles of wood ("fascines") to cross wide trenches and spreading widespread panic among the shocked garrison. Within an hour all the Third Army's first objectives were seized as the defenders surrendered or fled, some of them "off their heads with fright" according to a German officer. The British success was due to four main factors: good intelligence; surprise; the tanks; and especially the new artillery techniques.

There was an exception, however. In the centre, the 51st (Highland) Division, under its old-fashioned leader General Harper, refused to keep close to the assaulting tanks, which he felt put his men at risk because tanks attracted fire. At Flesquières, as the unsupported tanks reached the German gun lines they were knocked out by artillery; the local German commander was one of the few who had specifically trained his gunners to engage tanks. By last light, 39 tanks in the sector were out of action (including Gordon Hassell's), 7 of them to a single brave gunner.

Elsewhere, progress was good. On the right, one cavalry squadron raided 4 miles behind the lines at Cantaing and captured a German HQ; and, apart from a lack of progress by the rest of the cavalry, the attack had succeeded. An excited Captain Stair Gillon of the 29th Division wrote: "The Battle of Cambrai ranks as one of the most thrilling episodes of the whole war. Tanks at last came into their kingdom. The notion that the Hindenburg Line was impregnable was exploded."

"The enemy was himself taken by surprise by the extent of his success," the German High Command recorded. Haig was delighted and, encouraged by the gains of the first day, ordered Byng to press on with the attack. During the night the 51st Division moved into Flesquières, now abandoned by the Germans. The question was: what next? The unwelcome answer came from the Germans, who were slowly regaining the initiative. A major battle developed for control of Bourlon Wood, which dominated the left-flank approaches to Cambrai, and which Byng had ignored Haig's recommendations to strengthen. Byng's lack of reserves also began to tell. Although fresh troops were committed it was apparent to the High Command that while church bells might be ringing in Britain to celebrate a victory, things were going wrong.

One last effort was made on 27 November as 2 divisions, supported by 30 tanks, made a final attempt to take Bourlon and Fontaine in the centre. Casualties were heavy and the attackers driven back. The battle had degenerated into the familiar piecemeal and costly shambles. Now the weather broke and it started to snow. Haig ordered the attack called off and, on 28 November, Byng ordered his men to dig in. It was too late.

Two days later, the British received a massive shock. At 07.30 the Germans struck back in a brilliantly planned and executed counterattack with 20 fresh divisions – the biggest German assault against the British in two years. The plan was to attack from

A Mark IV tank attempts to negotiate a trench, just to the west of Cambrai, during the battle. The shock of these machines moving towards the German defenders had its own effect, notwithstanding the technical deficiencies that plagued the early days of tanks. The tank's bark was sometimes worse than its bite.

the southeast to trap the overextended British divisions around Bourlon. It nearly succeeded. Within an hour, by using short "hurricane" bombardments and new infiltration attacks to bypass centres of resistance, supported by new ground-attack aircraft, the Germans had penetrated almost 3 miles into the right flank of Byng's Third Army, rolling it up as they sliced laterally through the defences. As the Germans' new tactics cut across British divisional boundaries the command structure broke down. The headlong retreat became a rout. Norman Cliff of the Guards Division recorded: "First we had to struggle through the flood of terrified men ... nothing seemed to stem the torrent of frightened men with eyes of hunted deer, without rifles or equipment, among them half-dressed officers presumably surprised in their sleep." Byng's army gave up all its gains of 20 November.

After such promise, the attack at Cambrai ultimately failed. It achieved little at the expense of over 44,000 casualties, 6,000 of them prisoners. Its purpose was unclear from the start. It had grown beyond a tactical raid, but once the cavalry failed to move through *en masse* it could not effect a strategic breakthrough. Its achievements were to show what massed tanks could do, to prove the efficacy of new artillery tactics – and to give the Germans an opportunity to battle-test their new infiltration tactics.

The War Cabinet called for an investigation, which Haig pre-empted by setting up his own Court of Enquiry to examine what had gone wrong. Predictably, it blamed junior officers.

73

A SIMPLEX TRENCH LOCOMOTIVE
LOGISTICS IN THE WAR

1914 TO 1918

"Logistics" – supplying troops with everything they need, from food to ammunition – has always been the lifeblood of war. The First World War was no exception to the iron rule that "armchair generals talk strategy and tactics – professionals talk logistics and intelligence".

More technically, military logistics means "supply, transport and re-supply". Transport had been revolutionized by the coming of the railway, which offered the ability to move vast numbers of men and *matériel* quickly over long distances. Throughout the First World War, railway networks remained the arterial system for most armies, enabling that lifeblood to flow – albeit at different levels of efficiency. As the war developed, temporary rail lines also sprang up, to service the frontlines.

In the First World War, moving anything around in quantity depended, in the first instance, on railways. But standard-gauge trains could not move men and supplies all the way to the trenches. From distant railheads, men and stores had to move forward by road and on foot, and as the fighting became more intense this system became harder to sustain. From late 1916, a network of narrow-gauge railways was laid down to transport men and shells to the frontlines, and eventually it extended to over 600 miles of track along the Western Front. A rugged petrol locomotive was developed to pull trains in the dangerous battle zones. Built by the Motor Rail and Tramcar Company of Bedford, the Simplex 40-horsepower "rail tractor" came in three variants. One was completely armoured; another was "protected" front and back, with a solid roof and sliding doors but open windows; and the simplest kind had protection only at the ends with canvas doors on the sides. The "protected" Simplex was the most common, with over 220 built for use mostly on the Western Front but also in Italy, Salonika and Palestine. After the war, this particular example was used by Newall's Insulation and Chemical Company at its works in Renfrew. It was restored to working order by Newall's apprentices and later displayed, first at Beamish North of England Open Air Museum and, more recently, at the Imperial War Museum's Duxford site. Despite looking a little like an armour-plated garden shed on wheels, this rather strange vehicle was a vital cog in the machinery that kept the Western Front working.

The problem confronted in 1914 was that once the fixed rail lines stopped, the armies were not that much more mobile than in Napoleon's day. They still relied on horses, hundreds of thousands of them (*see* Chapter 45), and increasing numbers of motor vehicles – with the war seeing the use of London buses to ferry many

"AN ARMY MARCHES ON ITS STOMACH"

Napoleon's famous dictum of military success

of the BEF (*see* Chapter 15). And the armies still had to march, carrying whatever they could.

These logistical limitations were starkly revealed in the miscalculations of the Schlieffen plan, the Germans' opening gambit to knock out France (*see* Chapter 11). The sheer distance of the lengthening supply chain as the German armies moved across Belgium, complicated by Belgian resistance, destroyed bridges and wrecked railway lines, contributed significantly to the plan's failure. Most of the fodder to feed the horses was being consumed by the *other* horses further back in the chain, and the further the Germans advanced the worse it got, until the frontline horses were having to survive on green corn from French fields or dying of disease and malnutrition.

Once the war solidified into the trench lines of siege warfare, the supply problem changed. Although the frontlines were now largely static, they consumed unheard of quantities of *matériel*. "Trench stores" needed wood, corrugated iron, sandbags and barbed wire, sometimes even concrete, especially for the Germans who were consolidating territory won. Ammunition expenditure rocketed with the variety of static targets available to shoot at. Casualties had to be moved; food and water had somehow to be got to the frontline – usually by solders in carrying parties. The problems were compounded by the French and British imperative to attack and try to eject the invaders, which required massive logistical build-ups. By mid-1916, for example, the British stockpiled – and fired – a million shells on the Somme, more than they had used in the entire war to date. Such quantities had to be transported, and now everywhere behind the lines, especially on the Western Front, the narrow-gauge trench railways grew up, snaking forward as far as they dared to feed the men, horses and guns in the combat zones.

The biggest supply problem in the first years of the war was ammunition. Before the war the French had planned for 10,000 shells a day: in fact, by the end of 1915 they had to manufacture and move 200,000 per day. The Germans at Verdun (*see* Chapter 50) laid new railway lines direct from the factory to bring up shells. The French only survived the first month of Verdun by their own logistical lifeline, the road dubbed *La Voie Sacrée*, which delivered almost 80 per cent of the 48,000 tons of French ammunition used. When it came to ammunition, the British were initially even worse off, because British industry was unprepared. By 1915 the "great shell scandal"

A column of British lorries and horse-drawn wagons threads its way along the Menin Road, in the Ypres Salient, between emaciated trees (November 1917). In conditions like these, to slip off the road into the water-filled shell holes could spell disaster.

erupted (*see* Chapter 30), forcing the government to issue compulsory contracts to manufacturers and introduce a programme of emergency war industrialization, as well as the new Ministry of Munitions.

Britain also had a unique transport problem: everything from a bullet to a bandage had to be sent by sea. The solution was a huge new military port at Richborough on the North Kent coast. As Southampton was used primarily to recover casualties and Folkestone to ferry drafts across the Channel, Richborough, with its excellent railway lines, sidings and loading docks, supplied the British Army on the Western Front. The port was run by the Royal Engineers (RE) and the Army Service Corps, and even had a "roll-on, roll-off" ferry for complete railway trains. The biggest commodity was fodder: it amounted to 25 per cent of all the stores that passed through the port. The British Army had almost 370,000 horses and 82,000 mules on the Western Front by 1917. The cavalry, now much reduced, accounted for only a tiny percentage, but all the beasts had to be fed.

Another particular logistical problem for the British was the Grand Fleet in its northern base at Scapa. Most of its ships were coal-burning ones and literally millions of tons of coal were produced, which then had to be transported from the coalfields of England and Wales by trains called "Jellicoe Specials". It is no exaggeration to say that the Royal Navy depended on the railways for its wartime operations, as did the army in France. Royal Engineer Railway Companies were used behind the lines, laying miles of track, with spurs to take shells straight to the guns, ambulance and tank-train sidings, and even bridges. The aim was always to take standard-gauge railways as close to the Front as possible, and only then to use narrow-gauge systems, horsed transport and manpower. By 1918 there were no less than 45 RE Train Companies, including in theatres such as Egypt and Salonika. In 1916, the problem of managing this vast logistical and transport network, including canals, was given to a civilian railway manager, Sir Eric Geddes, one of the businessmen brought in by Lloyd George when Minister of Munitions to energize government: he was even made an honorary major general at Haig's HQ.

Beyond the Western Front, the other theatres of war raised their own logistical difficulties. In Sinai and Palestine water was a perennial problem, as it was in Mesopotamia, and it directly influenced the fighting. Indeed, in Sinai the British advance depended on the laying of a waterpipe, along with a railway and a wire-netting "road". In Mesopotamia the absence of road or railway meant the rivers were vitally important: the Tigris and Euphrates became the main supply routes, used with great success. And across the desert environments, the stamina of camels played an important role.

Whatever other criticisms may be thrown at them, British generals and their hard-pressed staffs proved themselves to be thoroughly professional in their administration as they dealt with the British Army's global supply problems. The horses were watered, and the men were fed – no mean feat for the unprecedented demands of the First World War. This logistical competence – plus the combined effort of British industry – truly supplied the "sinews of victory". It is telling that German infantrymen were astonished at the well-stocked BEF food and ammunition dumps they captured in 1918 during their last attempts to snatch victory. It is no wonder they paused, to Ludendorff's ire, in order to sample the bully beef, biscuits, warm clothing, whisky and service rum left by the retreating British. It was a far cry from what they, or their hungry compatriots back home, could get.

"THE DECAUVILLE LIGHT RAILWAY, WHEN IT HAD BEEN LAID UP TO THE BATTERY, WAS A GREAT SAVING TO THE WAGON LINES ... THE TRACK WAS LAID UP OUR SHALLOW VALLEY WHICH WAS SUBJECT TO HEAVY GERMAN FIRE. THE DRIVER OF THE ENGINE DID NOT ALWAYS LIKE THIS, AND UNCOUPLED HIS ENGINE AND WENT BACK."

Major Roderick Macleod, 241st Brigade, Royal Field Artillery, 27 August 1917

74

THE "C TYPE" AERIAL CAMERA
BRITISH INTELLIGENCE DURING THE WAR

1914 TO 1918

In the first decade of the 20th century, a sense of growing threat from Germany gave rise to "spy fever" in Britain. When added to fears of Germany's blatantly anti-British naval programme and German commercial penetration of British markets, the idea that Germany was one day planning to invade the British Isles seemed only too believable. The lead-up to war saw new dedicated intelligence organizations emerge in Britain, and the war itself saw the latest technology and techniques ingeniously harnessed for information gathering and intelligence purposes.

In the troglodytic world of the trenches, possibly the most valuable intelligence either side could possess was knowledge of what was happening beyond the opposing frontline. Direct observation on the ground was almost impossible. Accurate and methodical reconnaissance from the air was needed to fill this gap, and soon cameras were in use in the skies. Basic cameras were first used by the British as early as September 1914, but it was not until the formation of an experimental photographic section in January 1915 that aerial photography began to develop. A hand-held wooden camera, the "A Type", took images on glass plates, but it was complicated to operate. One observer remembered: "You had to take your slide out of the box – with your glove off of course – get it into the camera, take your photograph, close up the plate, take the slide out of the camera, back into your box. By that time your hand was so cold that over and over again I've lost the plate as I took it out of the camera. I've cried with numbness and the pain in my hand." The "C Type", shown here, was introduced in summer 1915. Fixed to the aircraft's fuselage, it produced a more consistent quality of photo. In addition, after each exposure, a semi-automatic mechanism changed the plates within the camera frame. The "C Type" facilitated a widespread expansion of aerial photography, allowing it to keep pace with the Royal Flying Corps' rapid growth. New cameras appeared – lighter, stronger and with better focal lengths. By 1918 no-one could fight a battle without taking pictures from the skies.

In 1909, a worried Committee of Imperial Defence set up a Secret Service Bureau, with a Home Section under Army Captain Vernon Kell, and a Foreign Section under a passed-over naval officer, Commander Mansfield Cumming. These were the forerunners of today's Security Service (better known as MI5) and Secret Intelligence Service (MI6). At the outbreak of war, Kell vindicated his appointment: he ordered police throughout the country to lift 21 of the known 22 German agents he had identified – the 22nd was in Germany on leave – and thus Britain disabled the

> **"THERE WAS MORE IN THOSE EYES THAN ANY COMMON TRIUMPH. THEY HAD BEEN HOODED LIKE A BIRD OF PREY, AND NOW THEY FLAMED WITH A HAWK'S PRIDE … THIS MAN WAS MORE THAN A SPY; IN HIS FOUL WAY HE HAD BEEN A PATRIOT."**
>
> *Richard Hannay's verdict on a captured German spymaster, in John Buchan's 1915 novel of pre-war espionage,* The Thirty-Nine Steps

German spy network in Britain for the rest of the war – with one notable exception (*see below*). Kell's organization was renamed MI5 ("Military Intelligence 5") in 1916.

As war began, the War Office had no troops trained in intelligence matters. It quickly identified a number of army officers, Metropolitan Police officers and qualified civilians and invited them to join the newly formed Intelligence Corps to go to France with the BEF. They were divided into the Intelligence Police, responsible for security, and an Intelligence Branch, working for the General Staff. The new corps was soon in action providing field intelligence on the advancing Germans and interrogating refugees and prisoners of war. Behind the frontlines the former police officers of the Field Security Police ensured that the rear areas and lines of communications remained free from the threat of subversion, espionage and sabotage, and identified enemy agents.

One new area for intelligence lay in interception of cable traffic and wireless signals. Signals intelligence – "Sigint" – soon became invaluable. In the first month of the war the French used the Eiffel Tower to listen in to signals of German units at the Marne. And early on, the British severing of Germany's transatlantic cable forced the Germans to depend on neutral Sweden's cable – conveniently routed through Britain. In fact, Sigint had, unknown to the Allies, already scored its first victory in August 1914: the outcome of the Battle of Tannenberg owed a great deal to radio intercepts informing the Germans exactly where their Russian enemies were and what they were going to do next (*see* Chapter 18).

Much Sigint was simple direction-finding to locate enemy units. British Sigint was helped enormously by the acquisition of three German maritime and diplomatic codebooks. Despite this, in May 1916 Sigint was blamed for a significant intelligence lapse when the Director of Naval Operations, Captain Thomas Jackson, asked the specialists of "Room 40" (*see* Chapter 16) where German Admiral Scheer's call-sign "DK" was. Room 40 replied truthfully: "still in port" at Wilhelmshaven, which Jackson duly passed on; in fact, Scheer and the High Seas Fleet had already set off into the North Sea. The trouble was that Scheer always left his call-sign in port, and used a different one for sorties. Jackson had asked the wrong question. As a result, for a while Jellicoe and the Grand Fleet were wrong-footed in the lead-up to the Battle of Jutland, unaware that the Germans were out.

By contrast, Room 40's greatest success was to change the balance of the war. The interception and decoding of the "Zimmermann telegram" (*see* Chapter 66) by British Sigint revealed that Germany was a genuine threat to the United States and finally brought America into the war.

Telephone lines were vulnerable to interception, too. German monitors quickly developed a system of exploiting the vulnerability of British battlefield telephones (*see* Chapter 41). The Allies only became aware of the German eavesdropping equipment in early 1916 and swiftly ordered new security measures, while copying the technology. By the end of the war the Signals Service of the Royal Engineers could monitor German signals from a buried landline 3,000 yards away.

Aerial photography was also becoming increasingly important. Photographs revealed enemy trenches, defences, artillery locations and railheads, and the Royal Flying Corps' aerial reconnaissance and artillery target-spotting role expanded quickly. By 1916 some cameras were even able to produce stereoscopic imagery. And by 1918 the British had processed over half a million aerial photographs. Beyond the Western Front, aerial photography's mapping role was even more important.

An official Ministry of Information photograph shows a British intelligence officer scrutinizing some captured German correspondence for valuable nuggets of information. By the First World War, intelligence gathering was already acquiring its modern breadth of means and techniques, from good old-fashioned spying to radio intercepts.

Ostensibly trackless wastes in Palestine and Mesopotamia could be plotted and maps issued to everyone who needed one. As generals of all eras have agreed, good intelligence in the first instance is an accurate map.

To coordinate Allied intelligence, in 1917 an Inter-Allied Intelligence Bureau was created at Folkestone, Kent. This brought together reports from German-occupied territory on defensive works, shipping movements, technical details of artillery and aviation developments, as well as economic intelligence on German purchases abroad. Its main contribution, though, was in sifting reports from spies.

As in any war, by far the most difficult area for intelligence was what is nowadays called "human intelligence" or "Humint". Running sources and agents, especially behind enemy lines, was always difficult and chancy. The key Allied task was watching trains in occupied territory to identify the movements of German units: essential information for drawing up an accurate enemy order of battle. In 1918, the French landed a Lieutenant Baschwitz-Meau in Germany. There he set up a train-watching service that was able to observe the movement of German troops across the Continent and provide timely and accurate indications of German intentions on the Western and Eastern fronts.

Perhaps the most famous spy was the Dutch exotic dancer "Mata Hari". As a neutral, Margaretha Zelle (to give her real name) was able to cross national borders freely. In 1916, she was arrested and interrogated at length by Scotland Yard and she admitted to working for French intelligence. However, in February 1917 the French arrested her and tried her as a double agent working for the Germans. Despite flimsy evidence she was found guilty and executed. A more discreet and successful agent was the German Jules Silber, who had served with the British in the Anglo-Boer War and passed for an Englishman; in 1914, he came to London and was able to get a job as a British postal censor. Using his access to "Cleared by the Censor" stamps, he posted intelligence gleaned from reading the mail back to Germany via neutral capitals. Silber survived the war, even receiving a glowing testimonial letter from the Director of Military Intelligence, before returning home to Germany.

By the end of the war intelligence had proved its worth as the ultimate "force multiplier". But in the euphoria of victory and peace, MI5 almost disappeared and the Intelligence Corps was disbanded. In the absence of war, it was time to save money – and Britain's superb intelligence organization was dismantled.

75

PRIVATE HIGHGATE'S CHARGE SHEET
MILITARY DISCIPLINE & DESERTERS

1914 TO 1918

All armies throughout history have had some code of military discipline, because an army without law is just an armed mob. Discipline is the glue that binds an army together. British Army discipline in 1914 was strict and reflected the values of its day. For the British, it was outlined in the 1913 *Manual of Military Law* and its companion, *King's Regulations for the Army* as approved by parliamentary statute. Both are clear on military law as it stood at the time and how it was to be administered. Even in the best-behaved military forces there are exceptions to the law-abiding rule, but military discipline in the BEF of 1914, on active service, was uncompromising.

On 8 September 1914, Private Thomas Highgate of the 1st Battalion, Royal West Kent Regiment, became the first of 266 British soldiers to be shot for desertion during the war. Judged by modern standards it seems a callous punishment, particularly in the speed with which it was carried out. As a regular soldier, Highgate had arrived in France on 15 August and withstood the ferocity of the German assault at Mons. After retreating for two weeks, on 6 September he left his battalion, took off his uniform and put on civilian clothes. He was found in a barn by the British gamekeeper of Baron Edouard de Rothschild. A former soldier, the gamekeeper claimed that Highgate said: "I have lost my army and I mean to get out of it." A Field General Court Martial was immediately convened and, as noted in this formal record, Highgate was found guilty and sentenced to death. The sentence was confirmed first by the commander of II Corps, General Sir Horace Smith-Dorrien, and then the commander-in-chief, Field Marshal Sir John French. At 7.07 a.m. on 8 September, only 36 hours later, Highgate was shot by a firing squad and buried. Ever since, the execution of British soldiers has remained a controversial subject and has been constantly debated. In 2007, this led to the issuing of a blanket pardon by the British government. Yet it is vital to remember the historical context in which these punishments took place. However severe they were, many at the time considered them essential to maintain the fighting spirit of the BEF.

Most petty military offences were dealt with summarily by company commanders, who could award extra parades and "CB" (Confined to Barracks) to rein in petty malefactors for such crimes as drunkenness, being late on parade or having a dirty rifle. More serious charges were dealt with by commanding officers, who could strip junior NCOs of their rank and impose sentences of up to 28 days in the guardroom, with loss of pay. On active service in the field a soldier could instead be sentenced

"I COULD NOT LOOK ON DEATH, WHICH BEING KNOWN, / MEN LED ME TO HIM, BLINDFOLD AND ALONE"

Rudyard Kipling, "The Coward", one of his Epitaphs of the War, *1922*

4

SCHEDULE.

Date 6th September 1914   No.

Name of Alleged Offender (a)	Offence charged	Plea	Finding, and if Convicted, Sentence (b)	How dealt with by Confirming Officer
No 10061 Pte Thomas James Highgate 1st West Kent Regt.	When on Active Service Deserting His Majesty's Service	ABD Not Guilty	Guilty To suffer death by being shot.	Confirmed H S Smith Dorrien General Comdg 2. Corps 6 Sep 14. Confirmed [signature] F. M. C-C.

H S Smith Dorrien General Comdg 2nd Corps —

Sentence executed at 7.7a.m on 8th Sept 1914

[signature] Capt
A.P.M. 5th Div
7.15 a m 8.9.14

(a) If the name of the person charged is unknown, he may be described as unknown, with such addition as will identify him.

(b) Recommendation to mercy to be inserted in this column.

H S Smith Dorrien
General
Convening Officer.
Comma... [signature]

A B Dunsterville Colonel
Comdg II Army Corps Troops
President.

to "Field Punishment Number One", which meant being tied to the wheel of a gun for two hours a day. Not for nothing was it known as "Crucifixion".

Major breaches of military law went to a court martial. The most common on active service was the Field General Court Martial (FGCM), consisting of a president – usually an experienced major or more senior officer – plus two officers who had been commissioned for over a year. Under the Army Act they had the power while on active service to sentence an offender to death for serious military offences, subject to confirmation by the commander-in-chief.

In 1914, capital punishment was the norm in all countries for serious civil offences such as murder. In time of war, death was accepted as the ultimate punishment for a range of military offences, too, such as "sleeping on sentry", an offence which in peacetime is a mere misdemeanour but in war can threaten the lives of hundreds of men. The German, Italian, Russian, French and Belgian armies all executed deserters, murderers and mutineers during the First World War. The French shot over 600 of their men, and the Italians over 700. The true figure for the Tsar's army is unknown. Britain executed 306 men for military offences out of the more than 5 million who went through the army between 1914 and 1919.

Thomas Highgate was the first deserter shot, but the speed and nature of his case was unique. It was far from typical of the rest of the BEF's capital courts martial, which rapidly became much more organized as the war settled down. The records of those courts martial show that every one of those executed received a legal trial as approved by Parliament. They were, in fact, painfully slow because witness statements were written down laboriously in longhand, and the court stopped frequently to thumb through the *Manual of Military Law*. Contemporary records show that these courts followed the letter of the law in the *Manual*, literally line by line.

The verdict always began with the most junior officer voting first, so as to ensure that the opinion of the senior officer present did not sway the final outcome. They were not kangaroo courts but a determined attempt to follow the law as it stood at the time. And, as the BEF settled into a routine, in 1915 two key legal measures were introduced: a plea of "not guilty" became mandatory for any soldier charged with a capital offence; and the "Suspension of Sentences Act" meant that soldiers sentenced could continue to serve in the line, effectively on probation.

Witnesses were cross-examined on oath, and the accused could object to the composition of the court and was encouraged to speak up in his own defence or have a "prisoner's friend" act as his defence advocate. By 1916 the army was appointing experienced court martial officers from the hundreds of lawyers in its ranks, until by 1918 the courts martial were mainly staffed by professional, legally trained officers.

If the accused was found "guilty as charged" the court sent its papers for confirmation at every level of command. At the time, before the advent of the Court of Appeal in English Law, this was felt to be extremely fair. However, this confirmation process was the weakest part of the system. At brigade, division, corps and army headquarters the various commanders would give their own opinion, frequently based on prejudice or the need to set an example. Nevertheless, only 18 British soldiers were executed for cowardice during the war. And while 266 were shot for desertion, the great majority of soldiers sentenced to death had their sentences commuted by the commander-in-chief. Haig refused to confirm 90 per cent of the

"THEY DIDN'T SHOOT ANY AUSTRALIANS. THEY WOULD HAVE RIOTED. THEY WEREN'T LIKE US. WE WERE DOCILE."

Private George Morgan, 18th Battalion, West Yorkshire Regiment (2nd Bradford Pals), reflecting on the execution of two of his comrades just before the Battle of the Somme

death sentences, preferring, in his own words, "to give the man another chance". Most convicted men received suspended sentences and soldiered on.

Part of the problem in reaching a verdict was that lawyers and the doctors could not agree on battle fatigue ("shell shock") as a genuine problem until well into 1916. As a result, a small number of men were sentenced to death who today would have been hospitalized with Post-Traumatic Stress Disorder (PTSD). But in the early years of the war there were no mitigating factors: the law only recognized a stark distinction between "brave soldiers" or "cowards and deserters".

Deserters had little sympathy from their (former) comrades. Frederic Manning's fictionalized but nevertheless highly realistic account of his service on the Western Front, *Her Privates We,* reflected the prevailing view:

> When Miller disappeared just before the Hun attack many of the men were bitter … in their judgement of him … they were to go through with it while he had saved his skin … if one were to ask any man who had been through that spell of fighting what ought to have been done in the case of Miller, there would only have been one answer: Shoot the Bugger!

It is against this background that the British government's decision to issue a "blanket pardon" in 2007, to all the executed, aroused considerable controversy. Their cases could be very different, as the circumstances surrounding the three officers shot during the war illustrate: one was genuinely stricken with battle fatigue that today would have been diagnosed as PTSD; the second abandoned his wounded men to die in freezing shell holes; the third was a long-term deserter living with a French prostitute and who shot the military policeman that came to arrest him. As the military historian Sir Michael Howard pointed out in a 1997 debate: "If the law of the time was obeyed at the time, then we should not interfere. The lesson appears to be that we should not try and judge the past by the standards of the present. We cannot re-invent the past to suit our modern prejudices."

76

SIEGFRIED SASSOON'S REVOLVER
WRITERS AT WAR

1914 TO 1918

The First World War is distinctive in many respects. In at least one, it is unique, certainly within a British context, and it is summed up by the military historian Brian Bond: "Why can't the British approach the First World War through history, not through poetry?"

He had a point. There is a sense in which literature, and its teaching, has tended to dominate the British view of the war – to the detriment of a detached historical perspective. No less than 16 poets of the Great War are commemorated in Westminster Abbey, including Siegfried Sassoon, the arch critic of the trenches. As with many of the others, he knew the Western Front directly and intimately.

> Sharp, clear and easy to understand, for many people Siegfried Sassoon's bitter, accusing poems still offer the most powerful indictment of the horror, futility and pain of this bewildering war. He is also remembered for his stand against the war in 1917, when his "Finished With the War: A Soldier's Declaration" rebelled against military authority. Thanks largely to the intervention of his friend and fellow poet, Robert Graves, instead of being punished for this "act of wilful defiance" he received medical treatment for shell shock. Yet these elements in Sassoon's story often overshadow his military achievements. He joined the 1st Battalion, Royal Welsh Fusiliers, in November 1915 and served with them in France until August 1916. He was awarded the Military Cross for his bravery during a trench raid in July 1916. In 1917, he served again in France with his regiment's 2nd Battalion, and the following year with its 25th Battalion in Palestine and France for the third time. Sassoon bought this standard issue Webley Mark 6 revolver from the government at the end of the war. Most officers obtained their own equipment, and he also had a privately purchased Browning pistol. Both weapons are important reminders that, as well as poet and protestor, Sassoon was also a courageous soldier and his experience in battle makes his condemnation of the war hard to question.

The poets of 1914–18 reflect their times. Universal education, self-improvement and literacy flourished in late-Victorian and Edwardian Britain. And in a world before radio, television, the internet and computers, the principal domestic relaxation available to most people was either music – pianos were common in many homes – or reading. The fortunate conjunction of a universal ability to read and write, combined with a widespread appreciation of classical and English literature, meant that Britain's citizen-soldiers were a very literary lot. Among the officers, an

"MY SUBJECT IS WAR, AND THE PITY OF WAR. THE POETRY IS IN THE PITY"

Wilfred Owen, draft preface for his intended poetry collection

awareness of literature reflected the educational *mores* of the time. The intersection of what Paul Fussell calls the "aristocratic and the democratic" established a unique respect for literature among the men in the trenches that remains to this day.

Not just officers, either; any trawl through the 30,000 soldiers' letters in the Liddle Collection in Leeds, or the diaries and memoirs held by the Imperial War Museum, is a sobering experience. Even the humblest private from the backstreets could write in a clear, cursive hand and seems to have been able to express his feelings clearly. Allusions to literature of all kinds are common. Indeed, many soldiers of all ranks went off to war with a book; significantly, the *Oxford Book of English Verse* seems to have been the most popular, along with an earlier verse anthology, *Palgrave's Golden Treasury*. Poetry, whether read or written, became the distilled essence of the trench experience. Siegfried Sassoon is even recorded charging a German trench and then, instead of signalling for reinforcements, sitting down to read a volume of poems. Most did not take their love of words that far.

Among the poets, principally remembered are Sassoon, Graves and Edmund Blunden, together with those that did not survive, like Rupert Brooke, Wilfred Owen, Edward Thomas and Isaac Rosenberg, whose "Break of Day in the Trenches" is arguably one of the most profound literary pieces of the war. But how to account for the enduring power of the poetry? In part, the answer lies in the traumatic shock to the young authors of the murderous realities of industrial warfare: trenches, gas, indiscriminate slaughter from artillery barrages, maimed and mangled casualties in unbelievable quantities. Wilfred Owen, who wrote the excoriating "Dulce et Decorum Est" (1917–18), evoked the terror of a gas attack in language that was a world away from the pre-war optimism of the so-called Georgian poets:

> If you could hear, at every jolt, the blood
> Come gargling from the froth-corrupted lungs,
> Obscene as cancer, bitter as the cud
> Of vile, incurable sores on innocent tongues

He succeeded in crystallizing both a sense of modern war's horror, and then laying it at the door of the generation that sent the young men out:

> My friend, you would not tell with such high zest
> To children ardent for some desperate glory,
> The old Lie: *Dulce et Decorum est*
> *Pro patria mori.*

Owen was killed in the very last week of the war. His disillusion is surprisingly echoed by Rudyard Kipling, to whom the loss of his only son at Loos was a shattering, guilt-inducing blow. In *Epitaphs* he wrote very much in the bitter vein of an Owen or Sassoon: "If any question why we died, / Tell them, because our fathers lied." (*See also* Chapter 99.)

Owen and Sassoon's work represents the war weariness and loss of hope after 1916 and stands in stark contrast to the fervour embodied in Rupert Brooke, who in his sonnets *1914* could proclaim: "Now, God be thanked Who has matched us with His hour, / And caught our youth, and wakened us from sleeping". Brooke's lines reflect the mood of the early months of the war. The death of this handsome young man *en route* to the Dardanelles transformed him into a national hero, thanks to strong support from influential friends. However, unlike Brooke, few people had heard of Owen until his mentor, Sassoon, edited (with Edith Sitwell) his poems in 1920. With Blunden's fuller, better known edition of 1931, Owen matched the zeitgeist of the "no more war" appeasement movement of the 1930s.

Although poetry is regarded in Britain as the major literary genre, the war provided grist for the prose mill too. Graves wrote his memoir, *Goodbye to All That*; Ernest Hemingway reflected his personal experience driving ambulances on the Italian Front in *A Farewell to Arms*; and the dark horror of J.R.R. Tolkein's Mordor in *The Lord of the Rings* was influenced by his experiences on the Western Front. For many well-known writers too old to fight, propaganda was a natural way of using their talent (*see* Chapter 31). Enduring prose legacies include Frederic Manning's *Her*

"THREE HOURS AGO, HE STUMBLED UP THE TRENCH; / NOW HE WILL NEVER WALK THAT ROAD AGAIN: / HE MUST BE CARRIED BACK, A JOLTING LUMP / BEYOND ALL NEEDS OF TENDERNESS AND CARE."

Siegfried Sassoon, from "A Working Party", published 1918

Privates We (1929), a novel of the Somme, and two memoirs: Captain J.C. Dunn's astonishing *The War the Infantry Knew* (1938), which gives some soldierly insights into Graves and Sassoon, and Frank Richards' down-to-earth *Old Soldiers Never Die* (1933). C.S. Forester's fictional *The General* (1938) remains perhaps the subtlest critique of the BEF's High Command. A less nuanced critic was George Bernard Shaw, whose Fabian views and Irish contempt for the English upper classes led him to openly oppose the war and attack the government in his pamphlet "Commonsense About the War". An infuriated Asquith privately averred that he should be shot.

Other nations produced their own classics – in France, Henri Barbusse's novel *Le Feu* (1916) or Guillaume Apollinaire's poetic evocations of the gas, fear, darkness and blood made a deep impression on the public consciousness of the war. In Germany, the message of Ernst Jünger's postwar memoir of frontline life, *Storm of Steel* (1920), is equally as powerful. Jünger frequently survives the jaws of death, and the work becomes a search for something noble and truly heroic amid the horror. It is very different to Erich Remarque's *All Quiet on the Western Front*. Significantly, this was published later – in 1929 – and was the first of a flood of books critical of the war, with its lines: "I am young, I am twenty years old; yet I know nothing of life but despair, death, fear, and fatuous superficiality cast over an abyss of sorrow. I see how peoples are set against one another, and in silence, unknowingly, foolishly, obediently, innocently slay one another."

But not every young man could afford despair when they somehow had to carry on. For a perhaps representative view, the troops' own newspapers tell a different story to that of the anguished poets. The classic is the *Wipers Times*, first published by the Sherwood Foresters in 1916, which went on to be distributed across the BEF. Never officially sanctioned by Authority, it was nevertheless popular among all ranks with its gallows humour (such as a bogus advertisement for a new film: *Over the Top! – A screaming Farce*) and irreverence about the war and army life. Interestingly, much of the copy submitted was poetry. Some was excellent and some was doggerel – but the quantity was such that the journal had to announce: "An insidious disease is affecting the Division, and the result is a hurricane of poetry".

A British soldier takes the opportunity of a quiet moment and a conveniently unused stretcher to catch up on the news, somewhere amid the blasted landscape of the Somme. A hunger for the written word was ubiquitous among men at the Front.

77

JOHN SINGER SARGENT'S *GASSED*
ARTISTS' RESPONSES TO THE WAR

1914 TO 1918

Although the British art of the First World War did not inform later generations' sense of what the war *was* to quite the same extent as its poetry, it nevertheless left a large and varied body of work, and a core of undoubted masterpieces. At one level there was the popular, graphic art of the day, from cartoons in *Punch* to magazine illustrations and posters, much of it inspired by a propaganda or morale-boosting purpose. Those genres generated the single best-known war-related image: the Kitchener recruiting poster (*see* Chapter 8). In fine art, this new industrial war of mass production and mass killing resulted in experimentation with styles to match the unprecedented scenes and experiences that unfolded. The result was many powerful and moving works of art, undertaken both by artists who experienced the war in the frontline as well as established figures who were too old to fight.

John Singer Sargent was one of the best-known painters of the Edwardian era, famous for his society portraits. In March 1918, he was commissioned by the British War Memorials Committee to paint an epic work that would form the centrepiece of a planned Hall of Remembrance. So in July Sargent journeyed to France to find a suitable subject. Late on 21 August, he and fellow artist, Henry Tonks, drove past a dressing station between Arras and Doullens, which was overrun by men temporarily blinded in a mustard gas attack. Both were stunned by what they saw. Tonks later explained: "Gassed cases kept coming in. They sat or lay down on the grass, there must have been several hundred, evidently suffering a great deal." Sargent captured the scene in possibly the best-known painting of the entire war. Using his gift for subtle composition within a monumental frame, he bathed the agony of the wounded men in languidly beautiful light from the evening sun, while offering hope beyond their present suffering through the sight of healthy men playing football in the distance. In *Gassed*, Sargent delivered the grand subject he had been asked to find and, in a way that is possible only through art, he encapsulated the essence of the war in a work that still deeply affects people a hundred years on.

At the outbreak of war, artistic responses were mainly in the field of ephemeral, graphic art: patriotic drawings and political cartoons in satirical magazines like *Punch* in Britain, *Simplicissimus* in Germany or, from 1915, *Le Canard Enchaîné* in France. One of the earliest exponents was Britain's Bernard Partridge, who trained as an architect before joining *Punch* in 1891 as a cartoonist. His mixture of the realistic

The dashing Captain Bruce Bairnsfather, as depicted on a 1916 postcard. His wryly humorous cartoons, compiled in book form in Fragments from France, *captured the soldiering zeitgeist and turned him into something of a celebrity.*

and the allegorical is seen at its most powerful in drawings such as *Danse Macabre*, where the Kaiser dances with the Angel of Death. His colleague Frederick Henry Townsend's *Bravo Belgium* was one of the best-known drawings in this vein, showing a sausage-laden Teuton armed with a club advancing on a little Belgian boy standing before a gate marked "No Thoroughfare". In their use of stereotype and stark, simple contrasts, they encapsulated the indignant British mood of the time.

Another graphic artist whose work remains popular is Bruce Bairnsfather (*see also* Chapter 60). Relatively unsuccessful before the war (he could only get work in advertising), once in the field in the Royal Warwickshire Regiment, from 1914, he drew scenes of trench life, which were published from 1915 in the *Bystander*. That year, he was wounded and deemed no longer fit for active service; but in 1916 he was appointed an official cartoonist for the Allies. He is chiefly remembered for the humorous cartoon series based on "Old Bill", a grumpy Regular old soldier with a walrus moustache, which achieved huge popularity at home and – as a mark of the way the cartoons captured the essence of things – among the troops.

The first *official* British War Artist was the Scotsman Muirhead Bone, who specialized in black and white drawings. He was recruited in May 1916 by Charles Masterman's War Propaganda Bureau (*see* Chapter 31), and his drawings of the war had the advantage of being easily reproduced in newspapers and magazines. After the Somme campaign, he returned home to record Britons at work on the Home Front, and Glasgow School of Art-trained Francis Dodd was sent to France in his place. Dodd worked in a variety of materials, producing drawings and portraits of commanders and informal glimpses of ordinary sailors at sea

After that, Dodd was followed to the Western Front by a further clutch of officially appointed artists, including the established portrait painters William Orpen and John Singer Sargent, and William Rothenstein. They were joined in this capacity by men who had previously served at the Front, or behind the lines, and whose talents had come to the attention of Masterman's department. This group included Christopher R.W. Nevinson (*see* Chapter 80) and (Percy) Wyndham Lewis of the contemporary "Vorticist" school, and Eric Kennington and Paul Nash.

Orpen in fact had offered his services in 1915, but had ended up doing routine office work until his friend, the Quartermaster General Sir John Cowans (whose portrait he was painting), commissioned him to paint military portraits of generals, privates and politicians, including a surprisingly amiable Sir Douglas Haig. After experiencing the Front at first hand, he produced one of the war's starkest works, the bluntly named *Dead Germans in a Trench* (1918), an eerie form of still-life. He would go on to be appointed the official portrait artist at the Paris Peace Conference in 1919, for a fee of £3,000. He painted *The Signing of the Peace*, a subtly critical work that came to seem a premonition of the days to come. It contrasts the fragmented world as literally shown in Versailles' Hall of Mirrors with the rather diminutive delegates in the foreground, believing they have secured Europe's future (*see* Chapter 93).

Paul Nash has been regarded as a "soldier artist", but he was a Slade School-trained professional artist before joining up with the Artists Rifles – the 28th Battalion, London Regiment – in 1914. (His younger brother, John Nash, followed a very similar trajectory from the Artists Rifles to official War Artist later on.) At the Slade, Paul had shown little talent for life drawing and had sensibly gravitated towards landscapes. He favoured the new dynamic style of Vorticism, an offspring of international Futurism, which rejected Victorian and Edwardian aesthetics in favour of bold lines and bright colours to draw the eye towards the centre of a dynamic world. In the words of Wyndham Lewis, the movement's godfather, Vorticism was "a whirlpool. At the heart of the whirlpool is a great silent place where all the energy is concentrated." It launched itself onto the world a few months before war broke out, via the movement's magazine *Blast*.

Nash served in the Ypres sector, where he sketched, but in 1917 he was invalided home. An exhibition led to his appointment as an official War Artist in 1917 with a roving commission. Now he could flex his talent properly and unite it with his deep experience of trench life to produce his great war paintings such as *The Ypres Salient*

"I AM NO LONGER AN ARTIST INTERESTED AND CURIOUS, I AM A MESSENGER WHO WILL BRING BACK WORD FROM THE MEN WHO ARE FIGHTING TO THOSE WHO WANT THE WAR TO GO ON FOR EVER."

Paul Nash, letter, 1918

at Night, *Howitzer Firing*, *The Mule Track* and *We Are Making a New World*, with their typically jagged lines and strong diagonals, full of movement, full of colour. Yet Nash also came to appreciate art's expressive limitations in the face of the full dimensions of Western Front realities, writing in a letter: "no pen or drawing can convey this country".

Nash's adoption as a War Artist owed something to his Vorticist friend Nevinson, another self-consciously modern artist. Before the war Nevinson subscribed to the notion that war could cleanse society of the old and stagnant, so when it began he was desperate to be part of it. But, physically unfit for frontline service, he had to join a Red Cross ambulance unit. Within days Nevinson was working in France and Belgium, driving ambulances and tending French casualties in squalid, makeshift clearing stations. What he saw quickly disabused him of any idea that the war was a welcome scourge. Having witnessed an early air raid, he later said: "I was one of the first men to see a child who had been killed by it. There the small body lay before me, a symbol of all that was to come." It later inspired his painting *A Taube*, in which a dead child lies among the debris of a broken building: the title evokes both a common German aircraft name in 1914 and its English translation – "Dove".

His experiences inspired other powerful paintings. *La Mitrailleuse* (1915), portraying French machine gunners in a strange, intimate synthesis with their deadly weapon, was even hailed as "the most authoritative and concentrated utterance on the war in the history of painting". But by the end of the war Nevinson's approach had developed considerably, away from Vorticism's angular and boldly coloured abstractions towards a finer-detailed grim realism. This is discernible in the sardonic *Paths of Glory* (1917), whose title and concept was inspired by Thomas Gray's poem *Elegy Written in a Country Church-Yard*. It shows two dead British soldiers slowly decomposing in a field of mud and barbed wire, and is typical of his later style and subject. Nevinson witnessed the scene at first hand, but his painting was too much for the censor. Nevertheless, Nevinson defiantly exhibited it in London, in 1918, with the label "Censored" over it. Along with *The Dead Stretcher Bearer* by Gilbert Rogers, it remains one of the most disturbing images of the real human cost of war.

Wyndham Lewis, another Slade School alumnus, eventually joined the Royal Artillery, where he served as a Forward Observation Officer in the Ypres Salient. This was dangerous frontline work, calling in fire from British batteries. From December 1917, as an official War Artist, he produced some powerful and well-informed works including *A Canadian Gun-Pit*, *A Battery Shelled* and *The Battle of Vimy Ridge*, all highly stylized. His postwar memoir, *Blasting and Bombardiering*, portrays an unusually thoughtful and mature artist, his earlier wildness tempered by the fires of war.

In contrast to much of the Vorticist output was the work of Eric Kennington, another professional artist pre-war, who served as a Territorial soldier in the "Kensingtons" – the 13th Battalion, London Regiment – in 1914. Wounded in 1915, he was invalided out and took the opportunity to paint, unusually on glass, *The Kensingtons at Laventie, Winter 1914*. When exhibited in 1916 it was critically acclaimed for its depiction of exhausted ordinary soldiers (including himself) at the Front, their khaki standing out against the luminous snow. Kennington's *Over the Top, Bringing in the Prisoners, Soldier's Grave* and *Gassed and Wounded* all showcase his versatility with materials and technique, and his often unusual visual perspectives to highlight particular qualities of the subjects. His pastel portrait drawing *Raider*

Getting stuck in. It was doubtless something of a shock for established artists to be exposed to the grime and gruesomeness of the Western Front, but official War Artists came to truly appreciate the soldier's lot. This is Muirhead Bone, the first official War Artist, near Maricourt, on the Somme (September 1916).

with Cosh, showing a member of a raiding party calmly handling his trench club (*see* Chapter 49), oozes quiet menace – and his closely observed portraits of soldiers in the field are as powerfully drawn as any portrait study by a Great Master.

Along with the pre-eminent artists of the war, whose images shone a forensic light on what was happening and those who fought it, there were others who worked in a more popular, commercial vein, and whose milieu tended to be less the artistic movements and exhibitions and more the printed media. Their work has often not stood the test of time, but it fed the contemporary appetite for accessible scenes that evoked the war and its emotions. One example, with an overtly realist and commercial aesthetic, was the Italian Fortunino Matania. His work links the advent of mass photography with a well-trained draughtsmanship. Having studied in Paris and Milan he moved to London and became a war illustrator on the Western Front. His drawings – such as *Field Guns on the Western Front* and *How the Wounded Helped the Wounded* – are marked by an unusual mixture of technical accuracy and dramatic, emotive composition. His drawings were much sought after and became a series of signed prints produced for the *Sphere & Tatler* magazine in 1916, and Matania went on to do much work in magazines and advertising.

Finally, one of the most eloquent artist's insights into the war came from a German artist who served on the frontline but whose reputation stems from his postwar work. Influenced by the new wave of Futurism, as well as by *naïf* forms such as graffiti and children's drawings, the German satirist Georg Grosz achieved popularity when businessmen, mutilated old soldiers, whores and scar-faced Prussian officers became the subjects of his savage pen and ink drawings during the Weimar years. Looking back, he summed up his inspiration: "The war was a mirror; it reflected man's every virtue and every vice, and if you looked closely, like an artist at his drawings, it showed up both with unusual clarity."

78

A HANUKKAH LAMP FROM JERUSALEM
THE PALESTINE CAMPAIGN

1915 TO 1917

On 26 January 1915, an Ottoman force invaded Egypt's Sinai Peninsula in an attempt to capture the strategically vital Suez Canal. The attack on the canal began on 3 February, and was beaten off by the British and Imperial defenders, forcing the Ottoman forces to retreat east of the canal. A new theatre of war had opened. But soon it would be the Ottoman forces who were on the defensive, during a campaign across Ottoman-ruled Palestine that would deliver a prize of major symbolic and psychological significance – the Holy City of Jerusalem.

> The Allied capture of Jerusalem on 9 December 1917 ended 730 years of Islamic control over one of the world's most venerated – and fought over – cities, a place at the heart of Judaism, Christianity and Islam. First seized during the Crusades in 1187 by the renowned Islamic warrior Saladin, it was absorbed almost 350 years later into the Ottoman Empire. But in 1917, Jerusalem surrendered with no real fighting. The moment coincided with the start of the Jewish festival of Hanukkah, which marked the liberation of Jerusalem's Temple 2,000 years earlier, allowing it to be cleansed and rededicated for worship. For the small Jewish population in and around Jerusalem, the departure of the Ottoman rulers therefore invested Hanukkah that year with the quality of a double liberation and a heightened sense of celebration. This Hanukkah lamp was used on that occasion, one of three from Palestine given to the Imperial War Museum in 1918. Its glistening, polished copper still seems to exude a confident glow of release and rebirth.

The Ottoman withdrawal back across the Sinai coincided with the beginning of the Dardanelles campaign (*see* Chapter 24), which then absorbed the energies of both sides. The British and Ottoman positions beyond the canal remained largely quiet. But in spring 1916, following the evacuation from Gallipoli, the troops sent back to Egypt were organized into a new Egyptian Expeditionary Force (EEF), under General Sir Archibald Murray. With enough men and supplies built up, Murray now began to push the British defensive line eastwards. Progress was slow and steady, and, although the Ottomans launched counterattacks in April and August 1916, by the end of the year almost all of the Sinai had been taken. In January 1917, a new phase opened: the British and ANZAC forces took Rafa, on the border, and advanced north into southern Palestine.

Anticipating this continued British thrust, the Ottomans reinforced their defences, from Gaza on the coast inland towards Beersheba, near the base of the

General Sir Edmund Allenby to the commanding officer of 60th Division, December 1917. The biblical verse in question reads: "Our feet shall stand within thy gates, O Jerusalem."

Judean Hills. But Murray's successful advances had caught the attention of Britain's new prime minister, Lloyd George, who encouraged him to push deeper into Palestine. Lloyd George had noted the comparatively low casualties of the desert victories and was looking for a cheap success. Unfortunately, London had no comprehension of the logistical difficulties involved. Murray's army was totally dependent on its single-track railway, a wire-netting "road" and a water pipeline, all of which had been constructed to enable the advance through the Sinai. Supplying a desert army with rations, water and ammunition, let alone the 9.5 pounds of grain a day that each horse required, was a nightmare.

Murray nevertheless agreed to a deeper offensive in southern Palestine. On 26 March 1917, a force under Lieutenant General Sir Charles Dobell attacked positions at Gaza. The assault troops only had food, water and ammunition for 24 hours. Despite the fact that the Ottomans had ample warning of the impending onslaught, the operation was remarkably successful and penetrated into the town. However, three Ottoman divisions were marching to counterattack and a nervous Dobell ordered a withdrawal, snatching defeat from victory. He and Murray were unprepared to risk a retreat by dehydrated men and horses.

As the British pulled back, the local German commander of the Ottoman Eighth Army, General Friedrich Kress von Kressenstein, reinforced the region. He began a 13-mile series of fortified strongpoints along the Gaza–Beersheba defence line. The result was that the second British assault on Gaza three weeks later was an even bigger disappointment. There was naval gun support, along with a few tanks (of the outmoded Mark I variety) and the ineffectual use of 4.5-inch gas shells – the first gas used on the Ottoman Front. But the British infantry divisions' frontal attack was beaten back, with 6,000 casualties. London was not impressed. Murray was sacked shortly afterwards, to be replaced by General Sir Edmund Allenby, fresh from the Western Front. Haig had found Allenby's command at Arras disappointing – but in the desert, Allenby would find his *métier*.

He arrived in June 1917, when the summer heat prevented any fighting, so he used the time to build up his logistic stocks. Work had begun to double-track the Sinai railway, and rail supplies were augmented by coastal shipping from Egypt landing their cargoes over open beaches. The EEF built up a major network of forward supply depots and ammunition dumps behind the frontline.

Now ready logistically, the British made their third attempt on Gaza at the end of October 1917. By now the EEF was up to seven infantry and three mounted divisions, around double the enemy's numbers. Allenby was a career cavalryman and was determined to use the mobility of his mounted troops to unlock the Gaza position. He planned a three-phase offensive to seize vital water supplies and to outflank key defences. The principal, initial thrust would be directed inland against Beersheba, with the aim of capturing its all-important wells, while a simultaneous infantry attack at Gaza would pin the Ottomans in their defence lines. A clever deception plan convinced the Ottoman commanders that the Beersheba attack was just a diversion from the real assault on the coast at Gaza. Instead, Allenby's mobile forces would swing east, deep in the interior, and seize Beersheba's wells, with the Arab rebel irregulars under Emir Feisal and T.E. Lawrence (*see* Chapter 79) covering their exposed right flank. Once the wells were in British hands, the Desert Mounted Corps would move westwards out of the hills and reach the coast behind Gaza, thus cutting off the 46,000 Ottoman troops in the Gaza–Beersheba pocket.

On 31 October 1917, the assault began on the main Beersheba defences, pinning the Ottoman garrison in the town. Meanwhile, ANZAC mounted divisions rode in a wide arc through the Judean foothills east of the town to attack from the rear. As the day wore on, Lieutenant General Sir Henry Chauvel, commander of the Desert Mounted Corps, asked Allenby for permission to pull back and water his horses. Allenby responded by pointing out that if his men captured Beersheba, they would have all the water they needed. Dramatically charging forward on its horses under heavy fire – utterly different to the Western Front – the 4th Australian Light Horse Brigade overran the Ottoman trenches and took the town.

The Gaza phase of the battle had begun earlier, on 27 October, with a massive artillery and naval bombardment. Then, on 1–2 November, two infantry divisions attacked the coastal defences and (to the surprise of attackers and defenders alike) broke through, outflanking the Gaza defences on the beach side and pushing north along the coast. Logistical problems caused by the lack of water delayed the start of the next phase until 6 November. By then Kressenstein knew his forces in Gaza would be cut off, so late on 5 November had begun withdrawing north. Allenby had won a great victory, although the Ottoman divisions had escaped his trap.

Allenby now pursued the Ottomans north for another month, advancing 65 miles in 17 days and capturing the port of Jaffa and much of southern Judea, before moving against his symbolic objective: Jerusalem. The overall direction of the Ottoman campaign in Palestine was in the hands of General Falkenhayn, commanding yet another theatre in his varied career. But both he and Allenby were under strict instructions to avoid fighting in or immediately around Jerusalem. Allenby gave the task of capturing the city to Sir Philip Chetwode, commanding XX Corps, who, on 8 December 1917, attacked on two axes, cutting off the city from the west, with a separate attack at Bethlehem to the south. The Ottoman forces, cut off, dispirited and disorganized, put up little resistance and the city surrendered on 9 December. Four hundred years of Ottoman occupation had ended.

Two days later, Allenby himself entered the Holy City – on foot, in a deliberately understated demonstration that he came as a liberator, not a conqueror, and promising freedom of worship to all religions. It was a triumphant end to an autumn that had seen setbacks at Caporetto and Cambrai, in a year with other Allied disappointments and ructions. It is little wonder that Lloyd George promptly declared Jerusalem a "Christmas present for the British nation".

General Sir Edmund Allenby speeds towards Jerusalem in a Vauxhall staff car, flanked by cavalry, as crowds gather to witness his historic arrival. His actual entry into the city (11 December 1917) was on foot, a deliberate act of humility and respect.

79

LAWRENCE OF ARABIA'S RIFLE
T.E. LAWRENCE & THE ARAB REVOLT

1916 TO 1918

British withdrawal from Gallipoli in January 1916 changed the war in the Middle East. The Ottomans were now able to redeploy and reinforce their three main theatres of operations: fighting the Russians in the Caucasus, and the British in Sinai/Palestine and Mesopotamia (*see* Chapters 23 and 78). General Falkenhayn, arriving in Aleppo in early 1917 to direct Ottoman forces, knew that any British advance through Palestine into Syria risked severing the Ottomans' already fragile communications with the Mesopotamian Front 500 miles to the southeast.

At the same time, corruption and shortages were weakening the Ottoman Empire, and poor communications and lack of supplies were eroding the army's efficiency. Worse, the burden of Ottoman casualties was falling on ethnic Turks; other nationalities in the empire were openly hostile, and army desertions were up to 300,000 by December 1916. German influence and personnel were increasingly resented, too. Into this deteriorating situation came the Arab Revolt, beginning in summer 1916, and with it an extraordinary Englishman, who combined charisma, guile, diplomacy and guerrilla warfare in a cocktail that would create a legend.

> "I GAVE HIM A FREE HAND … HE WAS THE MAINSPRING OF THE ARAB MOVEMENT AND KNEW THEIR LANGUAGE, THEIR MANNERS AND THEIR MENTALITY."
>
> *General Sir Edmund Allenby, commanding the Egyptian Expeditionary Force on the Palestine Front*

The real T.E. Lawrence is often confused with the simpler romanticized character from David Lean's epic 1962 film *Lawrence of Arabia*. But Lawrence himself was a complex, mercurial individual – deeply committed to Arab independence, yet also intensely loyal to his own country, producing contradictions that in the end almost overwhelmed him. He was a visionary, understanding that Arab self-determination would only be possible if they moved north from the Hejaz desert to Syria itself; he understood guerrilla warfare, too, using a handful of men to pin down and intimidate much larger numbers of regular troops. He also appreciated that the Arabs had to protect the open flank of the Allied armies as they advanced through Palestine. From late 1916 until 1918, Lawrence served alongside Sherif Feisal, son of the Grand Sherif of Mecca. Feisal gave Lawrence this British rifle, which had been captured at Gallipoli and presented to him by the Ottoman authorities. Lawrence used it constantly and carved his initials and five notches on the stock to record the Turks he killed with it. After the war, Lawrence considered giving the gun to the Imperial War Museum, but in the end presented it to King George V. It was only after the king's death in 1936 that it arrived at the Museum, along with other royal wartime souvenirs. This well-used weapon, with its intriguing history, evokes both the complex, many-sided war in the Middle East and the continually fascinating personality of Lawrence of Arabia himself.

Although the Ottoman Empire had long claimed overlordship of the entire Arabian Peninsula, to all intents and purposes the central desert region (the "Nejd") was under the control of local Bedouins, who were largely neutral in the war. In the western Hejaz region, however, encompassing Medina and Mecca, the powerful Hashemite dynasty had ambitions to throw off the Ottomans and establish an Arab state centred on Damascus. Promoting these aspirations was Sir Henry McMahon, Egypt's High Commissioner. He had encouraged Hussein ibn Ali, the Sherif (overlord) of Mecca, to start a revolt against Ottoman rule by promising that Britain would guarantee an independent Arab kingdom after the war. On 10 June 1916, the Sherif called for a full rebellion. GHQ's special "Arab Bureau", based in Cairo, immediately offered Britain's support.

At the time, GHQ's staff in Cairo included a polyglot scholar and archaeologist working as a junior intelligence officer: T.E. Lawrence. In January 1916, he had analysed any Arab revolt as: "beneficial to us, because it marches with our immediate aims, the break up of the Islamic 'bloc' and the defeat and disruption of the Ottoman Empire, and because the states … set up to succeed the Turks would be … harmless to ourselves". In October 1916, Lawrence, with his local expertise and excellent Arabic, began his historic task with the British Military Mission, working with Hussein's forces. He was a good choice to act as liaison officer. He had already been an intermediary in Mesopotamia in spring 1916, trying to use a £1 million bribe to rescue the besieged British at Kut: an unusual responsibility for such a junior officer. When Lawrence met Emir Feisal, Hussein's third son (and warlord), the two men got on: it was Lawrence's initial job to identify which of the king's sons would make the best leader. The calculating and ambitious Lawrence reported that Feisal could be trusted to lead the Arab Revolt, urging Cairo not to send troops to the Arabs but rather advisors, weapons and money instead, with, naturally, himself in a leading role.

GHQ agreed and in January 1917 established a military mission to the Hejaz under Lieutenant Colonel S.F. Newcombe. He ordered Lawrence to attach himself to Feisal's ragged army of 7,000 Bedouins and encourage them to cut the Hejaz Railway, the vital Ottoman lifeline through Damascus and down to Medina. This strategy tied down large numbers of Ottoman troops defending and repairing the railway, while Feisal's roaming warriors could strike anywhere. For the next year, Lawrence fought a guerrilla war alongside Feisal and made him the principal beneficiary of British aid.

In July 1917, Lawrence persuaded the Arabs to make a surprise overland attack on Aqaba, the Ottomans' sole remaining port on the Red Sea. Its capture opened new supply lines from Egypt to the Arabs massing in the Sinai, allowing them to extend their operations northwards towards Palestine. When Lawrence reported to General Allenby, who was now commanding the Palestine Front, the general recognized the value of Lawrence's rag-tag guerrilla army harassing Ottoman supply lines and protecting his right flank; he quickly spotted Lawrence's Achilles' heel, too: vanity. Lawrence was promoted to major on Allenby's orders. With the commander-in-chief's personal backing, Lawrence was now in a much more powerful position. Through Aqaba he was able to funnel thousands of rifles and camels as well as artillery and armoured cars, but above all hundreds of thousands of gold sovereigns, to buy Feisal's Arabs.

On 24 October 1917, Lawrence and Feisal led the Arab forces on a 350-mile trek around the Turkish left flank to attack the Yarmuk Gorge, north of Jerusalem, in support of Allenby's renewed assault on Beersheba and Gaza. But this venture failed. Depressed and guilty over his failure, Lawrence made an ill-advised personal reconnaissance of the key Turkish railway junction at Der'aa and was captured. Although Lawrence's true identity was never discovered, he claimed he was sexually assaulted and beaten by his captors before escaping. Recovering in Palestine, he was invited to accompany Allenby's triumphal entry into Jerusalem on 11 December 1917.

> **"I WAS TIRED TO DEATH OF THESE ARABS; PETTY INCARNATE SEMITES WHO ATTAINED HEIGHTS AND DEPTHS BEYOND OUR REACH, THOUGH NOT BEYOND OUR SIGHT. THEY REALISED OUR ABSOLUTE IN THEIR UNRESTRAINED CAPACITY FOR GOOD OR EVIL; AND FOR TWO YEARS I HAD PROFITABLY SHAMMED TO BE THEIR COMPANION!"**
>
> *T. E. Lawrence, in his autobiographical* Seven Pillars of Wisdom, *1922*

At Tafilah, southeast of Amman, in January 1918 there was greater success when Lawrence's Arab forces routed a Turkish brigade sent to recapture the town, an action described in the *Official History* of the war as a "brilliant feat of arms". Lawrence was awarded the DSO and promoted lieutenant colonel. The Ottomans recognized his value, too, putting a price of £15,000 on his head, but still he evaded them. His Arab raiding campaign continued throughout the summer, in support of Allenby's continued advance northwards into Syria (*see* Chapter 89). On 1 October, Damascus fell and Lawrence helped to set up a provisional Arab government as the war drew to its close.

What happened next has remained in dispute ever since. A conference took place at Damascus between Allenby and Feisal, with Lawrence and the Australian General Chauvel present. Afterwards Allenby recorded that he merely emphasized his need to keep his victorious cavalry advancing north to push the fleeing Ottomans back. Chauvel, however, records a bitter dispute when Allenby told Feisal that he would have to accept French overlordship of the region under the terms of the Sykes–Picot agreement (*see* Chapter 89). Appalled at Britain's double dealing, Lawrence refused to work with the French after Feisal's humiliation and asked for long overdue leave. So ended the Arab Revolt. Lawrence returned to England a disillusioned man, tired of war, but determined to continue pressing the Arab cause in London.

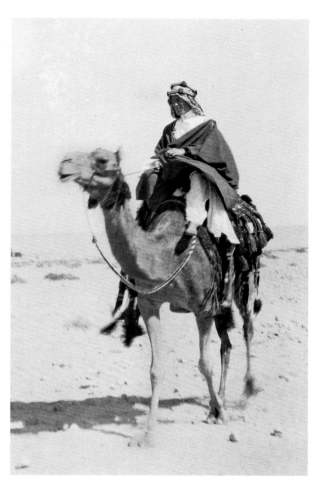

The classic image of T.E. Lawrence during his time as guerrilla leader with the Arab Revolt. Here he is at Aqaba. Despite the Bedouin trappings, Lawrence was caught between conflicting loyalties to his British superiors and the aspirations of the Hashemite Arabs of the Hejaz.

Much of Lawrence's heroic image is due to an American war correspondent, Lowell Thomas, who filmed him in the desert for two weeks in 1918. After the war, Thomas began a series of illustrated lectures, supported by dramatic pictures – of Lawrence in his Arab robes, of charging camels and of Bedouin warriors. Lawrence cooperated happily and Thomas's film, *With Allenby in Palestine and Lawrence in Arabia*, was shown around the world, making Lawrence a household name and Thomas rich. When Lawrence tried to distance himself from his growing celebrity, Thomas dryly observed that he "had a genius for backing into the limelight".

Lawrence's extraordinary postwar career reflected his complex and conflicted character. He attended the Paris Peace Conference in 1919 as an interpreter to the Arab delegation, only to see his promises to the Arabs betrayed. Election to All Souls College in Oxford, a literary autobiography of variable veracity (*Seven Pillars of Wisdom*), mysterious episodes of sado-masochism and service – under pseudonyms – as a ranker with the RAF and the Tank Corps all followed, before his death in a motorcycle accident in 1935. His legend was immortalized by the film biopic *Lawrence of Arabia* in the 1960s. Perhaps Lloyd George best summed up this strange and brilliant man: "a most elusive and un-assessable personality".

5

FROM NEAR-DEFEAT TO VICTORY

80

THE FOOD QUEUE
SHORTAGES & RATIONING IN BRITAIN

1917 TO 1918

By 1917 Germany's submarine war against Britain was beginning to bite deeply, and British civilians were having to come to terms with a new concept: queuing for food. In December 1917, the *Times* pointed out that: "Over a thousand people waited for margarine at a shop in New Broad Street in the heart of the city, and in the Walworth Road in the south-eastern side of London the queue was estimated to number about 3,000. Two hours later 1,000 of these were sent away unsupplied." Meat, sugar, tea and much else were running short. Like many features of the civilian experience of the First World War, queuing for food is nowadays largely seen as something that only happened in the Second World War. Yet it became a regular part of life in 1917–18.

The artist Christopher R.W. Nevinson began the war as an adherent of the Futurist school of art and ideas, with its embrace of modernity, technology and power. Before war's outbreak, he had believed the violent energy of conflict would offer a means of cleansing society. But his service as a civilian volunteer in the Friends' Ambulance Unit in Belgium, and then as a Royal Army Medical Corps orderly in London, changed his outlook. By 1916 his paintings reflected a starker, more brutal vision. In 1917, and by now commissioned as an official War Artist, he evoked the new realities of scarcity in this painting, *The Food Queue*, with its bedraggled civilians waiting in line. It was originally entitled "Squalor". Nevinson carefully contrasted the weary, run-down appearance of the queuers themselves with the colour and vibrancy of the shops behind, a disjunction that emphasized just how depressing life in Britain had become for ordinary people by 1918.

By the third year of the war, the British mood was one of grim endurance in a war that penetrated daily life ever deeper. For the majority of people, just getting by week to week was the important thing. As commodities went short people waited patiently in line in the hope of buying essentials – food, but also fuel. In April 1917, the *Observer* newspaper reported: "In south London trolleymen with coals were besieged by people who had requisitioned all types of receptacles including perambulators ... At a railway coal siding the would be purchasers assembled soon after seven o'clock in the morning and the queue of waiting women and children extended to a great length within a hour or so."

The most serious shortages remained those of food. U-boat sinkings – nearly 2 million tons of shipping by May 1917 (*see* Chapter 62) – had choked off the supply of wheat, meat, tea and sugar. Britain's flour stocks were down to just six weeks' supply. This was a serious crisis, as bread was the staple for the poor and for many

"A CUP OF HOT OXO AND A FEW BISCUITS MAKES A SUSTAINING LIGHT LUNCH AND CAN BE PREPARED IN A FEW MINUTES WITH THE MINIMUM CONSUMPTION OF FUEL"

From a "Let Oxo Help Out Your Meat Ration" advertisement, 1918

working families. A typical daily diet for a working-class family was recorded as a breakfast of bread, cheese and tea; lunch of meat, potatoes, bread and tea; and an evening meal of bread, dripping, jam and tea. If a man took his midday meal to work, then it would usually be bread and cheese.

The government's response was to push ahead with a major extension of state control. A two-pronged approach was already being considered in the final weeks of Asquith's time as prime minister. In the first month of Lloyd George's premiership, the Board of Agriculture, under R.E. Prothero, acquired a Food Production Department, which looked at means for putting farms under regional supervision to support Prothero's goal of trying to convert grazing land to arable use. That same month, a new Ministry of Food came into being, to handle the politically difficult areas of food consumption, distribution and pricing. It was headed by the Food Controller, Lord Devonport, a wealthy food retailer.

There were no quick fixes, though. In February 1917, Lord Devonport called for voluntary rationing, asking civilians to limit their consumption, and set guidelines such as 2.5 pounds of meat and 4 pounds of bread a week per person. They were widely ignored and, considering that an average worker probably went through about a dozen loaves a week, were totally unrealistic. By May 1917 high food prices and claims about profiteering were causing growing unrest, because although wages had risen sharply, the cost of food and other essentials had doubled. The situation was so serious that the government had a Royal Proclamation read out from the pulpit calling for the saving of grain. Devonport's position was now precarious: his calls for shops not to display exotic foodstuffs such as "sugared cakes" were met with derision, and he resigned, to be replaced by another of Lloyd George's inspired appointments, Lord Rhondda. Rhondda's aim was more overtly statist, within an economy ever more geared for "total war": to control the prices of essential foods via local Food Control Committees, which would enforce the ministry's regulations and identify and register retailers, and to oversee the distribution of sugar. He quickly secured Cabinet agreement for his plan, and from late summer 1917 food controls became increasingly effective. Sub-committees were set up with representatives of local trade associations to oversee other Government Food Orders, such as those regarding meat, flour and bread, potatoes and milk.

By October 1917 the first sugar ration cards were issued in parts of the country. Local inspectors with prosecution powers ensured that Food Orders were enforced. However, as the food crisis worsened controls grew stricter. Government "bread", with additives and high roughage content, became the only type bakers were allowed to make. It became a criminal offence to throw rice at weddings, feed stray dogs or even use starch in laundries.

Despite such measures, by Christmas 1917 things were getting worse, with long queues outside shops and shortages of butter, margarine and tea. Even potatoes were in short supply. Domestic food production that year remained below the pre-war levels, and the Board of Agriculture had to tussle with the demands of conscription to keep agricultural labourers on the land, leading to the development of the Women's Land Army and over 250,000 women working in agriculture by the end of 1917. People began to fear that the country was running out of food. Inevitably, this led to panic buying and shortages as shoppers cleared the shelves. The Ministry of Food now decided that control of all necessary foodstuffs should be introduced without delay – to guarantee supplies – and from January 1918 a programme of national rationing began, which deepened in the successive months. After sugar, meat was next, then butter and margarine. By July, there was nationwide rationing of them all. These new documents were a bureaucrat's dream and bore the instructions:

> To register for MEAT, BUTTER and SUGAR, fill up the counterfoils A B and C on the lower half of card, and give them to any Retailers you choose. The Retailers must write or stamp their names and addresses on these spaces. You will not be able to change your Retailer again without consent of the Food Office.

But they worked. The queues gradually disappeared. In March 1918, Wednesdays were fixed as meatless days and meat was rationed, with supplementary rations provided to adolescent boys and heavy workers. There were some unexpected benefits, too. Robert Roberts, whose family ran a shop in Salford, remembered: "Some of the poorest in the land started to prosper as never before. In spite of the war, slum grocers managed to get hold of different and better varieties of foodstuffs, of a kind sold before only in middle-class shops, and the once deprived began to savour strange delights." War changes lives, sometimes even for the better.

One result of shortages and rationing was the feeling that everyone was now really part of the war, suffering because of it. Politics drifted to the Left. At a special meeting of the Independent Labour Party and British Socialist Party in June 1917, delegates pointed to Russia's February Revolution, calling for soviet-style councils of workmen and soldiers, "the conscription of wealth" and highlighted the "inequality of sacrifice". A tone of increasing political militancy and class war was reflected by the trade unions as they flexed their muscle and demanded bigger wage settlements as prices rose. The mood of the country was becoming more sour and worried. The rich and established began to worry about "Bolshevism"; the middle classes felt economically squeezed by the war; and the organized working classes, on whom the war economy depended, were increasingly conscious of a new-found power and were demanding more. Charles Edmonds, back on leave, was unimpressed: "England was beastly in 1918. Envy, hatred, malice and all uncharitableness, fear and cruelty born of fear, seemed the dominant passions."

The war was changing the face of Britain, in some ways irrevocably.

81

A RATION OF EGGS
GERMANY UNDER THE BLOCKADE

1915 TO 1918

If German U-boats were, during 1917, playing havoc with British merchant shipping and British food stocks, then the long-standing British naval blockade of Germany was having a much deeper impact. One of the war's most successful and decisive campaigns, it contributed significantly to Germany's ultimate collapse and defeat. By 1918 Germans were literally starving.

Germany, like Britain, relied on imports to feed the population and supply the war industry. Much had come from the United States, but the Royal Navy's iron blockade stopped that. Added to Germany's overrigid bureaucratic controls, plus the military's misguided organization of the war economy, Germany faced inevitable economic doom the longer the war went on. The Central Powers' economies were shrinking. One business magnate, Albert Ballin, condemned "the dangerous notion of running the national economy and international trade from the parade ground".

A major problem was gaining access to vital cargoes, such as rubber, non-ferrous metals and phosphates for agriculture and explosives. Berlin turned to its neutral neighbours, the Netherlands and Scandinavia, but here the Allies were waging commercial warfare by offering higher prices for goods. A whole new front opened in European harbours as Allied commercial agents bought up cargoes.

With regard to food, despite the government's counterproductive centralization in so many areas, there was never an effective national rationing system. The early loss of millions of horses and thousands of agricultural labourers to the Front meant that manure and labour were soon in short supply. Millions of pigs were slaughtered in the 1915 "pig massacre" to save scarce grain and potatoes, resulting in an inevitable shortage of meat after the initial glut. By late 1916 food supplies to the cities were drying up, flower gardens became vegetable patches, as in Britain, and everyone kept rabbits for the pot. Real coffee disappeared, and *Kriegsbrot* – "war bread" – made out of potato flour became the staple. The availability of fish and eggs declined sharply. Even potatoes became difficult to obtain in the infamous "Turnip Winter" 1916–17, when the wet and cold destroyed crops and people had to fall back on eating turnips (along with the tasteless *Kohlrübe*), while shivering because of a parallel coal shortage. Life for all but the rich became, in the words of historian Lawrence Moyer, "a time of eating meals never entirely filling, living in unheated homes, wearing clothing that proved difficult to replace and walking with leaky shoes". Despite government soup kitchens in the streets, malnutrition affected many; one nutritionist stayed on the official ration for seven months and lost 42 pounds.

Bungling bureaucracy compounded the problem. The fixing of retail prices backfired, because the true (rising) wholesale prices were not passed on to the

"IT IS NECESSARY TO LOOK AT THE WAR AS A WHOLE; TO AVOID KEEPING OUR EYES ONLY ON THE GERMAN FLEET. WHAT WE HAVE TO DO IS STARVE AND CRIPPLE GERMANY."

Captain Herbert Richmond RN, after the Battle of Jutland, 1916

customer, so the official supply of essential goods dried up and a black market
flourished. The result of shortages was an increasingly *Ersatz* lifestyle: so much was
a poor substitute for something else (*see also* Chapter 90). By 1918 even the army
was reduced to using bandages made of paper.

Whereas in Britain formal, national rationing developed from January 1918,
in Germany the distribution of food and supplies was undertaken regionally.
Individual state governments and towns produced cards to control the supply
of many foodstuffs, including bread, meat, potatoes and eggs: this ornate *Eierkarte*
("egg card") was issued in Frankfurt. Lacking central control, German rationing
was unable to overcome the larger challenge to the country's widespread, chronic
shortages caused by naval blockade. Both in Germany and Austria-Hungary
people began to starve and, in the end, the blockade brought about as many
as 700,000 premature civilian deaths.

82

THE PRESIDENT'S FOURTEEN POINTS
U.S. PEACE FEELERS & RUSSIAN EXIT

NOVEMBER 1917 TO MARCH 1918

Russia's year of revolutions – 1917 (*see* Chapter 67) – saw Bolshevik leader Lenin, in November, sign a unilateral "Decree of Peace". In this way, Russia split herself from the Allies by guaranteeing a three-month cessation of hostilities and calling on "all the belligerent nations and their governments to start immediate negotiations for peace". Lenin's right-hand man, Leon Trotsky, was appointed Commissar for Foreign Affairs and soon began face-to-face peace talks with the representatives of the German government and the other Central Powers, which had started in December 1917 at Brest-Litovsk in Belorussia – "White Russia".

After preliminary discussions the talks were adjourned, supposedly so that Trotsky could issue invitations to the other Entente powers to attend – except that the Entente powers did not recognize the Bolshevik regime. Instead, Lenin found an unlikely ally in the shape of the United States' President Wilson. Sensing that the demise of Tsarist Russia and now the Bolshevik peace gambit offered an opportunity to make good on his call earlier in the year to "make the world safe for democracy" – and before any large-scale fighting involving American forces – Wilson saw a chance for a wider negotiated peace. The result was his celebrated "Fourteen Points".

> For over two years, Woodrow Wilson had struggled to keep the United States distant from the bitter, internecine struggle in Europe. But the war's nature as a global conflict, reaching out through direct military action and its economic tendrils, meant that the pressures were too great. In April 1917, the United States finally joined the Allies, but only as an "Associated Power". Large constituencies in the country remained sceptical about the purpose of the war and Wilson continued to work hard to draw out clear war aims from all the belligerents. With his Fourteen Points, he laid out the moral and political principles on which the American people had been prepared to take up arms and risk their lives. Speaking from these shorthand notes, he offered "justice to all peoples and nationalities". His opening remarks began by hoping that the current negotiations between Germany and the Russian Bolsheviks at Brest-Litovsk might extend into wider, global peace talks – the place name can be seen added to the second line of his notes. He went on to outline his specific Fourteen Points based on the values of transparency, fairness and self-determination. For him, they represented "the moral climax of this the culminating and final war for human liberty".

On 4 January 1918, Wilson and his emissary "Colonel" Edward M. House sat down in the White House to determine how best to capitalize on the Russian move.

"WHAT WE DEMAND IN THIS WAR, THEREFORE, IS NOTHING PECULIAR TO OURSELVES. IT IS THAT THE WORLD BE MADE FIT AND SAFE TO LIVE IN"

President Woodrow Wilson, "Fourteen Points speech" to US Congress, 8 January 1918

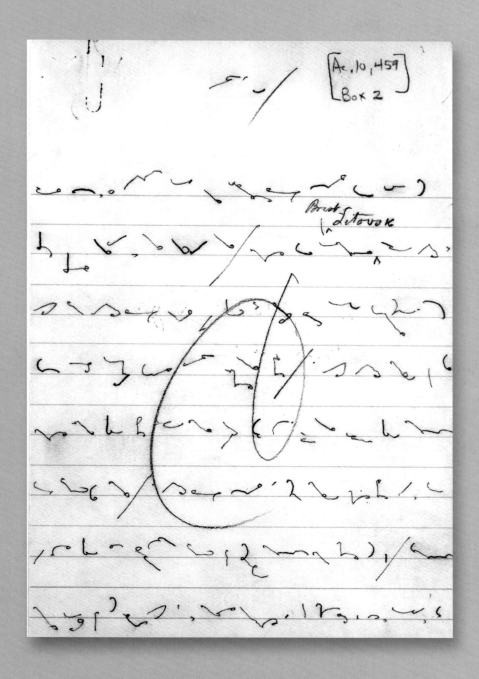

Brest Litovsk

In a few hours the two men hammered out a rough draft of what was to be the plan for any postwar world. Wilson then sent a hasty note to Lloyd George explaining that the United States had to make some response to any offer of peace talks and delicately warned the British prime minister not to try and delay or change Wilson's general line. Significantly, no note was sent to Clemenceau in Paris; Wilson had a shrewd idea that, after more than three years of war and with the Germans deep in French territory, the determined politician nicknamed "the Tiger" would not welcome any high-minded peace initiative.

Lloyd George's response to his ally's unilateral agenda was swift and has the hallmarks of diplomatic damage limitation and an attempt to get Britain's aims onto the table quickly. In a speech to the Trades Union Congress in London the very next day, Lloyd George spelled out Britain's equally lofty aims, stressing that Britain was not fighting a war of aggression and had invaded nobody, but that Germany would have to right the wrong done to Alsace and Lorraine and Belgium, and should lose her colonies, and that an independent Poland was an "urgent necessity". He added that only an international settlement could guarantee peace after the war. Domestically, Lloyd George felt under pressure to justify Britain's war aims, too, in an atmosphere of rising political tensions (stoked by Russian events), shortages and military disappointments on the Western Front.

Wilson was impressed with the prime minister's sentiments and declared himself delighted that London and Washington had similar aims. His subsequent speech to a joint session of Congress on 8 January 1918 outlined his Fourteen Points and his personal vision of a future world order. It also set out an informal international agenda to some of his fellow belligerents for any serious moves to end the war, despite having been made without prior coordination or consultation with his European allies.

Typically high-minded, Wilson's address was also intended to assure his fellow Americans that their war was really a moral crusade. The Fourteen Points speech was, in fact, based more on aspiration and hope than reality and experience, and was the logical extension of the cerebral former academic's understanding of international relations. Others were more sceptical. The cynical and world-weary Clemenceau – perhaps predictably – scoffed, pointing out sardonically that "even the Good Lord only had ten commandments". However, the Fourteen Points remained the only explicit statement of war aims by any of the nations fighting in the First World War and eventually was to serve as the basis for the discussions of peace. The essence of the points was:

1. A reliance on open diplomacy rather than secret agreements.
2. Freedom of the seas, in peacetime and in war.
3. Encouragement of freer international trade.
4. Disarmament.
5. Adjudication of colonial claims with respect for the sovereignty of the colonial peoples.
6. Assistance for Russia and restoration of Russian territory lost to the Central Powers.
7. Respect for the integrity of Belgium.
8. Restoration of French territories (including Alsace and Lorraine).
9. Adjustment of the border of Italy based on nationality.
10. Autonomy for the peoples of the Austro-Hungarian Empire.

Leon Trotsky (centre, in profile) arrives at the Brest-Litovsk peace negotiations in January 1918 with the Russian delegation, to be somewhat swamped by the Pickelhauben *of the German delegation. In the end, terms were virtually dictated by the Germans, who could exploit the Bolsheviks' urgent need to shore up their revolution at home.*

11. Guarantees for the independence of the various Balkan states.

12. Self-determination for the peoples of the Ottoman Empire and free passage through the Dardanelles.

13. Independence for Poland.

14. The formation of an international League of Nations to guarantee independence for all countries, large and small.

But Wilson's idealistic call quickly became a propaganda tool as well as a recipe for a negotiated peace. Some of his points were a direct response to revelations made by the Bolshevik government, which had sought to make mischief by revealing the secret treaties and deals that showed a certain *Realpolitik* among the Entente powers – for example, the backstairs deal to carve up Ottoman Syria and Palestine between France and Britain after the war (*see* Chapter 89). However, although Wilson's speech was widely disseminated in the German press and elsewhere, even left-wing German opinion remained unswayed and – for now – continued to back the Kaiser and the war. Moreover, Germany made it plain that she would brook no interference in what was effectively her bilateral negotiations with Russia.

These negotiations were about to come to a dramatic finale. On Lenin's instructions, Trotsky had been stalling and inventing excuses to prolong the Brest-Litovsk talks. The exasperated Germans finally ran out of patience and imposed their own tough terms and conditions on 3 March and, following an ultimatum, then proceeded to occupy Ukraine and the whole of European Russia virtually unopposed. Without a functioning army, Russia was forced to accept total defeat. Her war was over. Trotsky and the Bolsheviks fled back to Petrograd and were subsequently immersed in their own internal struggle to impose Bolshevism at home, as the country fractured into civil war (*see* Chapter 97).

With Russia definitively out of the war, and the United States not yet present in any force, the German military saw one last window of opportunity for knocking the British and French out of the war. It was an opportunity that was seized in the massive spring offensives from 21 March 1918 – the *Kaiserschlacht* (*see* Chapter 84) – so shattering any residual hopes harboured by Wilson that he might be able to inspire a peace conference and negotiated settlement. A disillusioned president told a conference in Baltimore on 6 April that it was now war to the bitter end against Germany's militaristic rulers. Force was now the only option and that "there can be no compromise".

83

DAZZLE CAMOUFLAGE FOR SHIPS
CONVOYS & "Q" SHIPS

1917 TO 1918

The British decision to reintroduce the age-old practice of convoys for her merchant shipping in April–May 1917 ranks as one of the decisive moments of the war. With hindsight, and with the knowledge of how vital the transatlantic convoys proved in the Second World War for sustaining Britain, the usefulness of convoys might seem self-evident. But it did not in 1917, at least not to all eyes including some at the very top of the Admiralty. Convoys transformed the U-boat war, along with the intriguing, counterintuitive form of camouflage that – to the uninitiated – appeared to make vessels shout their presence rather than hide it: "Dazzle Painting".

Although it was convoys that saved Britain's merchant fleet in 1917, they ran hand in glove with the development of the revolutionary form of disruptive camouflage known as "Dazzle", derived from the American slang phrase "Razzle Dazzle". It was the brainchild of a British marine artist, Norman Wilkinson, who had served in the Royal Naval Reserve both in the Dardanelles and along Britain's Channel coast. Wilkinson believed that if ships were painted in hard, angular patterns, it would create such visually confusing profiles that German U-boats would not be able to make out their size, shape or direction of travel. This uncertainty would then, he hoped, prevent a successful strike against the ship. Led by Wilkinson, in spring 1917 a Dazzle Section was established by the Admiralty at the Royal Academy in Burlington House. Wilkinson and his team had scale models of various ships made, painted them in carefully considered Dazzle shapes and then looked at them through a periscope to see how successful the patterns were at breaking up the appearance of the ship. This is the original model used to camouflage the liner RMS *Mauretania*, which was being used as a troopship in 1918. Once a Dazzle scheme was judged to be effective, scale drawings were sent to the ship's port so that it could be repainted. By summer 1918 over 2,300 British ships had been painted in this style, helping protect Britain's vital supplies.

At the start of the war, convoys for Dominion troop movements were routine, reflecting the threat from German surface ships around the globe, such as the *Emden* (*see* Chapter 22). On 3 October 1914, a highly secret convoy of 32 large passenger ships sailed across the Atlantic protected by a battlecruiser and a dozen warships, bringing the 32,000 men, 70 guns and 7,900 horses of the Canadian contingent to reinforce the BEF. A similar exercise attended the transportation of ANZAC troops to Egypt in November and December 1914, as it had the earlier conveyance of Indian troops to France. Convoys also protected the short cross-Channel routes. However, the Admiralty considered all these to be special cases, believing that modern steamships had rendered the idea of convoys essentially obsolete. Naval experts argued that it would take too much time to assemble ocean-going vessels regularly into convoy, and a convoy's speed would be limited to that of the slowest ship, rendering the other ships vulnerable. Moreover, naval officers felt that such a passive concentration of shipping would merely present easy targets for U-boats. In fact, the opposite was true; U-boats preferred single targets.

The first *routine* convoys during the war were organized by the neutral Swedes, who had lost a number of their iron-ore ships, and in April 1916 the German commander-in-chief in the Baltic approved regular escorts for German ships sailing to Sweden. The British also introduced convoys from July 1916 to cover the dangerous Holland–Harwich route: out of 1,861 sailings only 7 ships were ever lost to U-boats. Despite this, the British Admiralty remained stubbornly opposed to convoys as a routine naval operation.

It took the German renewal of unrestricted submarine warfare in February 1917 and the steep rise in merchant-shipping losses in spring 1917 to change naval policy (*see* Chapter 62). The Admiralty still believed that there were not enough Royal Navy escorts to make convoying viable, claiming that each merchant ship would need her own escort ship. Arguments were reiterated that merchant ships were not disciplined enough to sail in a convoy. But a worried Cabinet realized that at this rate the U-boats threatened to force Britain out of the war within months. Lloyd George was beginning to lose confidence in the senior commanders of what he later called his "palsied and muddle-headed" Admiralty. However, the Admiralty was already looking again at the statistics. Commander Reginald Henderson discovered that the Admiralty arguments were based on false assumptions and not supported by the evidence. Most of the losses to U-boats were among long-range ocean shipping, which only accounted for 10 per cent of maritime movements. Only a relatively small number of naval escorts would be needed for protection of Atlantic convoys. Maritime movement around Britain's coast was another problem, but protection could be provided by a mix of small escorts, armed trawlers, a few destroyers and aircraft patrols from the shore.

The Head of the Anti-Submarine Division at the Admiralty, Rear Admiral Duff, therefore recommended convoying on 26 April, and the policy was approved next day by the First Sea Lord, Sir John Jellicoe – unbeknown to Lloyd George, who, on 30 April, and armed with War Cabinet backing, strode into the Admiralty to insist on action.

Regular convoys thus began at the end of April, along the coastal route from the Shetlands and Orkneys south to the Humber, covered by airships from shore bases. Under the system, a large number of ships would gather in port, then all sail at the same time and at the same speed. The massed ships, including Royal Navy escorts, in fact made targeting more difficult for U-boats. Convoying also made U-boats rely on their limited numbers of torpedoes, since to surface and try to use gunfire would bring the warships' much heavier firepower down upon them.

The first deep-ocean convoy of merchant vessels left Gibraltar on 10 May 1917 and arrived off the South Downs on 22 May, having also been accompanied up the Channel by flying boats ahead of the convoy. No ships were lost and the convoy even arrived early. Air surveillance forced U-boats to dive, and once submerged they were slow and ineffective. Sinkings fell dramatically, to just 2 per cent of the previous independent-sailing casualties. The result was a gradual introduction of a widespread convoy system and a new construction programme for small escort vessels to back up the fleet destroyers.

Complementing convoying was the introduction of the "Dazzle" camouflage painting, across merchant ships and warships. To an extent, there was also a continued use of earlier the "Q" ships. First introduced in late 1914, Q ships were originally called "submarine decoy vessels" or "special service vessels" and intended to act as live bait for German U-boats, which preferred to attack smaller vessels using surface gunfire to save torpedoes. However, the Q ship – normally a coaster or old-looking tramp steamer – had a concealed armament, consisting of 4-inch and smaller guns, and a volunteer naval crew. The guns were concealed behind hinged superstructures and deck cargoes. The crew had a well-practised panic routine, which involved taking to the boats and abandoning ship. The U-boat would then close to sink the "helpless merchantman" with gunfire, at which point the Q ship would unmask her guns, hoist the White Ensign (required by international law) and open fire. The first success was on 24 July 1915, when the ex-coaster *Prince Charles* tackled and sank *U-36*. The month before, in a variation on the decoy theme, German submarine *U-40* was sunk by gunfire from the surfacing British submarine *C24*, which was being secretly towed by a former fishing vessel, *Taranaki*. Eventually, U-boat commanders became wise to the practice, and Q ship losses began to outnumber their successes, but they still had their place.

Convoying had come just in time. In May and June 1917, the U-boats sank another 600,000 and 700,000 tons of merchant shipping respectively. However, with convoying in place, the losses dropped off to a sustainable 300,000 a month. Confidence in the convoy system grew rapidly over the summer of 1917, especially when it was realized that the ratio of merchant vessels to warships could be increased. The size of convoys swelled, from 12 ships in June to 36 in October. By the end of the war almost all sea traffic in the war zones was convoyed.

The Germans had no answer to convoys. In the last 15 months of the war, convoy escorts sank over 150 U-boats. And in excess of a million Americans came safely over to France in heavily protected Atlantic convoys to tip the balance on the Western Front in 1918. The convoy system helped seal Germany's fate *on* the battlefield, too.

"CONVOYS FOR COMMERCE ARE WANTING."

Admirals' Report on British naval manoeuvres, 1888

"THE DAYS OF CONVOYS ARE PAST"

The Admiralty's response

84

FIELD MARSHAL HAIG'S SPECIAL ORDER
THE GERMAN SPRING OFFENSIVES –
KAISERSCHLACHT

21 MARCH TO 18 JULY 1918

By the autumn of 1917 General Ludendorff – now, with Hindenburg, wielding effective political control in Germany – knew he had to force a decision in the war before US divisions had a chance to make a decisive impact on the battlefield. Bolshevik Russia's unilateral truce in November gave Germany the opportunity to swing 40 divisions from the Eastern Front across to France: it happened at a rate of two divisions per week, from the end of 1917. But this fillip was balanced by growing internal problems on the German Home Front. Events emphasized what the German "Duo" of Hindenburg and Ludendorff knew too well: that time was running out. In 1918, Germany must either win or lose the war.

In the event, Germany made one last, massive attempt to win it. And it nearly succeeded, bringing Paris within artillery range and inspiring Field Marshal Haig to ask his men to "fight on to the end" whatever might come.

> The powerful offensive launched by the Germans east of the Somme on 21 March 1918 inflicted a serious defeat on the BEF. Sir Douglas Haig quickly concluded that its underlying purpose was to destroy the BEF and divide it from the French. Over the following days, Haig became deeply concerned, feeling that the French were not reacting fast enough and with sufficient urgency to the plight of their British allies. For the first time since becoming commander-in-chief in 1915, he appeared rattled. By early April Haig had recovered his equilibrium. But almost immediately his resolve was severely tested again when the Germans began another push against the British line in Flanders on 9 April. Possibly because he was facing a challenge to the integrity and cohesion of his army for the second time in less than a month, Haig issued this remarkable personal appeal to his troops. Reserved and taciturn, he generally avoided emotional expression. But on 11 April, he urged his men to remain firm and resolute: "With our backs to the wall and believing in the justice of our cause each one of us must fight on to the end." His words became famous among the troops, possibly because they were so uncharacteristic. This copy was posted up somewhere, as shown by its pin hole, and Haig later signed it in person. For a man usually lost for words, Haig's message encapsulated the anxiety but unbroken resolve that was felt by every man under his command.

The fateful decision was taken by Ludendorff at Mons on 11 November 1917, ironically a year to the day before the war's final Armistice. If Germany could divide and defeat France and Britain before the American armies arrived, Germany could

SPECIAL ORDER OF THE DAY
By FIELD-MARSHAL SIR DOUGLAS HAIG
K.T., G.C.B., G.C.V.O., K.C.I.E
Commander-in-Chief, British Armies in France.

D. Haig. F.M.

To ALL RANKS OF THE BRITISH ARMY IN FRANCE AND FLANDERS.

Three weeks ago to-day the enemy began his terrific attacks against us on a fifty-mile front. His objects are to separate us from the French, to take the Channel Ports and destroy the British Army.

In spite of throwing already 106 Divisions into the battle and enduring the most reckless sacrifice of human life, he has as yet made little progress towards his goals.

We owe this to the determined fighting and self-sacrifice of our troops. Words fail me to express the admiration which I feel for the splendid resistance offered by all ranks of our Army under the most trying circumstances.

Many amongst us now are tired. To those I would say that Victory will belong to the side which holds out the longest. The French Army is moving rapidly and in great force to our support.

There is no other course open to us but to fight it out. Every position must be held to the last man: there must be no retirement. With our backs to the wall and believing in the justice of our cause each one of us must fight on to the end. The safety of our homes and the Freedom of mankind alike depend upon the conduct of each one of us at this critical moment.

D. Haig. F.M.

Commander-in-Chief,
British Armies in France.

General Headquarters,
Thursday, April 11th, 1918.

PRINTED IN FRANCE BY ARMY PRINTING AND STATIONERY SERVICES.

PRESS A—4/18.

still win the war or at least be in a strong position to sue for peace. It was a legitimate strategic goal, but it failed to translate into a coherent series of steps. And therein lay the flaw of Germany's great last offensive.

The idea of a great final offensive was approved on 27 December, to include a number of separate attacks primarily aimed at hitting the British and the vulnerable seam between the Franco-British Allies on the Somme. Crown Prince Rupprecht, the overall Army Group commander, warned against the dissipation of effort that multiple axes would entail but was overruled; with 191 divisions against 178 Allied ones, Ludendorff felt strong enough to ignore the principle of concentration of force and pointed out that along the south of the British line, against the Fifth Army, he had mustered an overwhelming superiority of 76 divisions against 26 British.

Additionally, following the lessons of General Oskar von Hutier's attack on the Russians at Riga in September 1917, along with the victory at Caporetto (*see* Chapter 25) and counterattack at Cambrai (*see* Chapter 72), the Germans believed they had at last an answer to the tactical problem that had bedevilled trench warfare: how to break through. Their new offensive doctrine relied on three key elements: first, a short mass bombardment, without pre-registration of the guns, aimed at targets in the enemy's rear areas such as command and control, communications and artillery; second, "*Stosstruppen*", specialist stormtroop infantry – highly mobile and well-armed, using infiltration tactics to advance as deeply as possible and work around enemy strongpoints; and third, speed, surprise and sheer power.

The assault units – Germany's Second and Seventeenth armies, plus Hutier's Eighteenth Army – moved discreetly into position opposite Gough's Fifth and Byng's Third armies during February 1918. Lieutenant Colonel Georg Bruchmüller, the "artillery genius" who had developed the new artillery tactics on the Eastern Front, coordinated the overall German fire plan. German morale rocketed as fresh, well-trained troops flooded into the lines, and ammunition dumps were piled high.

By contrast, in March 1918, the BEF was at a low ebb. Haig had, in the course of three months, lost five divisions to the Italian Front, been forced to extend his line by 26 miles, and been ordered by the Cabinet to disband 141 battalions. To accommodate all this, he had to reorganize frontline divisions so that each of their three brigades was made up of three battalions, instead of the standard four. The prime minister's decision to hold back 100,000 men in Britain prompted Haig's description of Lloyd George as "shifty and unreliable"; it weakened the BEF just when it most needed reinforcement.

In the south of the new line, the severely overextended Fifth Army held 42 miles, but had taken over a badly underdeveloped system of trenches. Aware that a German offensive was likely, early in 1918 the BEF developed a new defensive doctrine after years of concentrating on the offensive. It called for a lightly held Forward Zone leading back to a main Battle Zone, where in theory a German attack would be stopped by redoubts and strongpoints long enough for a counterattack from the Reserve (or Corps) Line behind. But in many cases in Gough's sector, these had not been dug and the Reserve Line was merely marked out on the grass. There just wasn't enough time or enough manpower to dig all the trenches and lay all the wire. To make things worse, there was no general reserve of troops. Gough's own three reserve divisions were 20 miles back and effectively under GHQ control.

The blow fell on the morning of 21 March. "Operation Michael", the first phase of the German *Kaiserschlacht* (Emperor's Battle), got underway when 4,000 field and 2,500 heavy guns pounded the British with 1.5 million shells along a 40-mile

> "WE MUST STRIKE AT THE EARLIEST MOMENT BEFORE THE AMERICANS CAN THROW STRONG FORCES INTO THE SCALE. WE MUST BEAT THE BRITISH."
>
> *General Erich Ludendorff*

holocaust of destruction. Under Bruchmüller's five-hour *Feuerwalze* ("Fire Waltz"), headquarters were gassed, artillery lines hammered into ruin, ammunition dumps blown apart and frontline trenches and men pulverized. Then, masked by fog, the stormtroopers advanced, avoiding the surviving strongpoints like a tide foaming around the rocks. Isolated groups of defenders held out heroically, but the attackers were already moving a mile behind them. The Forward Zone collapsed quickly, but the British Battle Zone was also beginning to crumble. The British were hopelessly outnumbered. Communications failed as telephone wires were cut from frontline battalions as far back as divisional HQs, and commanders lost control, unsure where their units were and unable to influence the battle even as the German infantry arrived on their doorstep. Panic and disarray spread. Thousands of British soldiers – cut off, tired and leaderless – surrendered or retreated. By the end of 21 March, the British had lost 7,500 dead and 10,000 wounded, as well as over 21,000 captured, and the Germans had broken through in the south at several points. It was a disastrous defeat for the Fifth Army. The only saving grace was, that from a British perspective, this was the least crucial part of the line – so long as contact with the French could be maintained.

German Stosstruppen, *or shock troops, prepare for the beginning of the* Kaiserschlacht *in March 1918. Tactically, the German effort restored movement and manoeuvre to the Western Front battlefield, initially knocking the BEF for six.*

For the next two days, Gough's battered army retreated behind the River Somme. Those units left in the isolated frontline redoubts were surrounded and overwhelmed as the German follow-up units closed in for the kill with artillery pieces at point-blank range. To the north at Arras, the right wing of Byng's Third Army folded back to avoid being outflanked; in doing so it became separated from the retreating Fifth Army. A dangerous gap was opening between the two British armies and with the French to the south. Flushed with success, the Kaiser declared 24 March to be a national holiday. Many in Germany assumed that the war was all but over.

A total British disaster was avoided thanks to Ludendorff himself. On 23 March, he issued new orders. General von Below's Seventeenth Army was to attack north towards Arras and "push the British into the sea"; General Georg von der Marwitz's Second Army was to pursue the defeated British west up the valley of the Somme; and Hutier's triumphant Eighteenth Army was to attack the French now massing in the southwest. There can be few worse examples of dissipating attacking forces. Ludendorff reassured a sceptical Rupprecht: "We chop a hole. The rest follows." However, his enemy had other ideas. With no meaningful reserves left, and with the Germans now surging back across the old Somme battlefield, on 24 March, Haig turned to Pétain for help, but the French general, pessimistic as ever, talked instead of a rupture in the line. Haig for the first time appealed to "higher authority" for help.

At Doullens on 26 March a momentous decision was taken by politicians and generals. Lloyd George had been trying to establish political control over Haig, and now he got his way, although not quite in the manner he intended. An Allied Supreme Command would now be formed to coordinate the Western Front. General Ferdinand Foch was appointed effectively as the Allied *generalissimo*, with the power to issue orders to both armies.

Foch promptly insisted that Gough was sacked, and the imperturbable Rawlinson became the new commander of the Fifth Army. Better luck was about to attend the Allied defence now. Byng's forces around Arras stood firm, repelling a concerted attack by Below's Seventeenth Army on 28 March. On 4 April, Operation Michael finally ran out of steam, when an Australian-led counterattack at Villers-Bretonneux foiled the German thrust 10 miles short of the strategically important British railhead at Amiens. Although the Germans had advanced about 40 miles, captured 1,300 guns, and reduced the British Fifth Army from 14 divisions to a jumble of dispirited and confused soldiers, the failure to take Amiens was a serious one. The French were now pushing divisions into the Somme valley to reinforce their stricken ally, too. In addition, the Germans had outreached their supplies and their artillery – and, more worryingly, had lost around a quarter of a million men, many of them their irreplaceable stormtroopers.

Nevertheless, as a shaken BEF tried to catch its breath, Ludendorff struck again on 9 April, this time further north on a 12-mile front between La Bassée canal and Armentières, and then north of Armentières the next day. "Operation Georgette" was specifically aimed at cutting off the Ypres Salient from the south and capturing Hazebrouck, another important railway junction. Facing the Germans were primarily Horne's First Army in the south of the sector, with Plumer's Second Army north around Ypres. Part of the line heavily hit was held by two weak Portuguese

German stormtroopers practise infiltration techniques prior to the Kaiserschlacht. *The photograph captures the dynamism of the new tactics. Unfortunately for Ludendorff and his armies, the British and French soon adapted to the German methods and devised their own responses.*

divisions near Armentières. When Bruchmüller's hurricane bombardment struck, they broke and ran; the Germans penetrated about 3.5 miles west following the River Lys, recapturing Messines Ridge and reaching the commanding Mount Kemmel as the end of the month neared.

At the crisis of this Battle of the Lys, Haig made his only dramatic gesture of the war, publishing his Special Order of the Day appealing for his men to do their utmost. He need not have worried. The hard-pressed defenders fought the Germans to a standstill, and the furthest extent of the German advance was reached by 29 April. So far the offensives had cost the BEF about 235,000 casualties, many of them prisoners, and the French about 90,000, but the Germans had suffered as many as 350,000. For the attackers it was attrition in reverse.

Towards the River Aisne, in "Operation Blücher" on 27 May, Ludendorff struck again, between Soissons and Rheims, lured by the proximity of Paris. During the spring Krupp's monster long-range Paris Gun had been dropping shells on the city. The French commander, General Denis Auguste Duchêne, foolishly disregarded Foch and GQG's advice and packed his forward trenches, with the inevitable result that his soldiers were butchered by Bruchmüller's 5,000-odd guns. Stormtroopers – although not so many this time – surged through a 25-mile gap in the Allied lines and within six hours had crossed the Chemin des Dames Ridge and reached the Aisne. The Germans captured another 50,000 Allied soldiers and over 800 guns. By 3 June they were once again on the River Marne, only 35 miles from Paris. Only well-organized counterattacks by Pétain and the recently arrived Americans stopped them. Both sides had lost another 130,000 men, but there was one big difference as regards casualties: the Germans could not sustain such numbers; with the American Expeditionary Force (AEF) flooding into France at 250,000 men a month, the Allies could. Germany had lost nearly 800,000 men since the start of the year, while now having to man a frontline that had increased from 245 miles to 320.

At German High Command in Spa, Belgium, the Kaiser and his warlords reviewed their situation on 3 July. It was one of contrasts. Battlefield gains and the *coup de théâtre* of landing shells on Paris could not hide the increasingly severe shortages and unrest at home. The German leadership, however, confirmed that its terms for peace would remain annexation of Luxembourg and retention of the French iron and coal fields in Lorraine. And the attack would continue. So, on 15 July, Ludendorff launched his last offensive with 40 German divisions on either side of Rheims. He hoped to split the French, but this time he walked into an ambush. The tactical novelty of the German methods had worn thin. East of Rheims, General Henri Gouraud had pulled back nearly 3 miles. The attackers wasted their bombardment on empty space and were cut down when they advanced. To the west the German assault bridged the Marne and established a small bridgehead, but American and French counterattacks with strong air support stopped them within two days.

Pétain then launched his masterstroke. At Villers-Cotterêts on 18 July a major counterattack with 24 divisions, including two American divisions, supported by 300 tanks and aircraft, and led by the uncompromisingly aggressive General Charles Mangin cut into and overwhelmed the German right flank, inflicting severe casualties. The Germans retreated, a battered army.

The *Kaiserschlacht* that began on 21 March had burnt out. Ludendorff's gamble had failed, and a sense of impending crisis now began to grip him. There would inevitably be an Allied riposte, and the only question was: when?

85

A TOBY JUG FOR THE FIELD MARSHAL
GENERALSHIP IN THE WAR

1914 TO 1918

By and large the British generals of the First World War have received a bad press. Thanks to such bitter lines as Siegfried Sassoon's poem "The General" ("He's a cheery old card, grunted Harry to Jack, / As they slogged up to Arras with rifle and pack, / But he did for them both with his plan of attack"), they have been portrayed as murderous buffoons, or at least – along with their staffs – as hopelessly inefficient or mule-headedly stupid. It is true that in 1915–17 the gulf between frontline units and the General Staff was profound. Some of the criticisms are well-founded, some less so. But generalizations about generals can be misleading.

For a start, the war lasted four years. At the outset, few could properly envisage what this "total war" would entail – as the tactical and logistical failures in 1914 showed. By 1918 things were very different. The generals, just like the rank and file, were learning their trade, adapting to new technologies, experimenting tactically, adjusting to changing politics and personalities. The general of 1914 was, by and large, not the same as the general of 1918.

To modern sensibilities, Field Marshal Sir Douglas Haig, the BEF's commander-in-chief, embodies the idea of British generalship in the war and is a controversial figure. He is inextricably linked to the worst excesses of leadership – callous attrition, heavy casualties and unimaginative thinking. Much of this view originates in the sharp criticism of his command published after Haig's death by Lloyd George and Churchill, and it was a view that fed popular culture. From the 1960s' satirical revue (and film) *Oh, What a Lovely War!* to the television comedy series *Blackadder Goes Forth* (1989), Haig has regularly been portrayed as an incompetent, indifferent buffoon. But recently, scholars have unpicked this one-sided image, and many historians now recognize a calm, measured commander of vision and determination, who led the largest army Britain has ever placed in the field to its greatest series of victories in 1918. Nowadays, the wider perception of Haig probably lies somewhere between the two extremes. Perhaps the best clues, though, are found in evidence of how he was viewed at the time. In December 1917, London's new War Museum bought this Royal Staffordshire Pottery "toby jug" for its Children's Section. Resolute and imperturbable, Haig sits on the great new weapon of the war: the tank. A year later, a popular postcard showed a stolid-looking photograph of Haig on one side, with an explanation of who he was on the other. "He is at once trusted and loved by his own officers and men. His name will be handed down in History as one of the great leaders in the Great War for Freedom."

"IT SEEMS QUITE STRANGE TO ME, THAT I SIT HERE AT MY DESK AND MAP TABLE WHILE MY TROOPS FIGHT BETWEEN THE WARTHE AND THE VISTULA. SUCH, HOWEVER, IS THE CONDUCT OF MODERN WARFARE."

General August von Mackensen, 14 November 1914

Before the war, the great Prussian strategist Schlieffen had envisaged the generalship of the future: "There, in a comfortable chair before a wide table, the modern Alexander has before him the entire battlefield on a map." Herein, though, lies the essence of the complaints about wartime relationships between staff officers and the frontline: that staff officers were rarely seen in the trenches; that plans of attack frequently took no notice of realities on the frontline; and, as in every war, those who had to sleep in wet, dangerous holes in the ground found it hard not to resent those who enjoyed warm, dry beds. It all fed the idea of "château generals", well back from any danger or true understanding of the reality of the war.

It is perhaps surprising, therefore, that more British generals were killed in the First World War than in any other. No less than 78 British and Dominion generals died on active service, most as a result of shellfire and sniper fire, while 146 were wounded: a casualty rate of about 18 per cent. At the Battle of Loos in 1915, three of the nine commanders were killed in the frontlines, and the situation reached such an extent in 1916 that Haig had to issue a stern warning to his divisional commanders to stay at their desks. If generals were expected to devise strategies to win their battles, that was incompatible with exposing them to the same dangers as their frontline troops

But effective command and control was hampered by the inadequate communications with the frontlines (*see* Chapter 41). Many generals, particularly divisional commanders, chafed at the difficulties of commanding from positions far back while their men were in the line. Imbued with the regimental ideal of sharing their soldiers' discomforts, many were deeply uncomfortable at the feeling of impotence of having to command their units by telephone while their men risked their lives. Yet a visit to the frontline by a divisional major general, to see what things were like for himself, generally involved a trek of several miles through muddy trenches – with the knowledge that he then might be out of touch with his own headquarters in the case of any emergency. It must have been an intensely frustrating experience, and one that could certainly not be risked in the middle of a major battle.

A lingering criticism has been that generals stuck to a kind of bovine inflexibility and acclimatized themselves too much to the high casualty figures that the war unleashed. It is true that many of the old school felt that their duty lay in driving their men onwards, whatever the cost. One unnamed corps commander on the Somme supposedly said: "The men are much too keen on saving their own skins. They need to be taught that they are out here to do their job. Whether they survive or not is a matter of complete indifference."

The other great criticism was of generals' poor planning, particularly in the early years of the war. The problem was that all the regular generals had been trained on pre-war Napoleonic maxims – "the artillery blasts a hole, the infantry assaults and the cavalry exploits". The reality of trench warfare, the potency of modern artillery and machine guns, the novelty of gas and aircraft, and a host of other factors created a gulf between those maxims and what the generals actually had to deal with. It is hard to deny the historian Gary Sheffield's long-held assertion that for the BEF – as others – the First World War was "a long learning curve". But learning there was, and by 1918 the importance of the element of surprise, new infiltration tactics, the emergence of combined all-arms warfare, the discovery of how best to use tanks and much else showed it. Some lessons of both success and failure took long to sink in. But General Rawlinson's army that failed on the Somme in 1916 was a very different body to the Rawlinson army that defeated and drove the Germans back in 1918.

"IT MIGHT HAVE BEEN ... MORE ADVANTAGEOUS FOR ENGLAND IF THE BRITISH ARMY HAD NOT BEEN SO FULL OF MEN OF HIGH RANK WHO WERE SO READY FOR RESPONSIBILITY, SO UNFLINCHINGLY DEVOTED TO THEIR DUTY, SO UNMOVED IN THE FACE OF DIFFICULTIES, OF SUCH UNFALTERING COURAGE."

C.S. Forester, in his novel The General, *1936*

When it came to the standard staff work involved in procedures for fire plans, tactics and systems, the BEF also learned steadily. For example, the first day of the Somme took staff officers 115 days to plan and mount; by August 1918, the Battle of Amiens was mounted in just 26 days; and in the final days of the war, the BEF attack at Cambrai on 8 October 1918 took just 3 days. Senior officers understood better what they needed to do, and how to do it with the means available.

At the operational level, it is hard to see exactly what more the generals on the Western Front in the early years of the war could have done. A line of trenches and fortifications from the English Channel to Switzerland presented a wholly new sort of challenge. When Foch complained in 1914 that without flanks he could not manoeuvre, he was merely stating the truth. The generals on both sides were reduced to siege engineers. The years 1915–17 provided some tantalizing glimpses of potentially effective new tactics, but appreciation of them was easier in hindsight. Only after March 1918 did the Front break open and mobile warfare become a real possibility. Elsewhere, where generals had space to manoeuvre, they could demonstrate their skill: Hindenburg, Ludendorff and Brusilov on the Eastern Front, or Allenby's masterly swinging of his attacks from flank to flank in Palestine, for example.

Most of the First World War generals were far from stupid. On the Western Front, generals of *all* nations were faced by what seemed an insoluble problem: how to break what was effectively one long siege. They learned the hard way, albeit at terrible cost for those under their charge. German and French attacks ended with even longer casualty lists than the BEF's. But most who fought recognized the dreadful truth: there was no easy solution. At Haig's funeral in 1928 thousands of his old soldiers turned out to watch his cortège. Whatever the judgements of posterity, those who served with the stubborn Scot recognized Haig's achievement as "the general who won the war".

A visit to the trenches. Major General Gerald Cuthbert (foreground, left) and Brigadier General George Armytage, with staff officers, see things for themselves in a trench near Thiepval, on the Somme, 1916. But increasingly generals had to keep away from forward lines and trust to their often unreliable communications to keep abreast of events.

86

THE RED BARON'S BROKEN ENGINE
FIGHTER ACES & THE LATER AIR WAR

1917 TO 1918

From the summer of 1917, new and more effective aircraft were pouring from the factories to be committed in increasing numbers in the burgeoning air war. There was still room for a few of the older types; James McCudden, who took over Albert Ball VC's place in the elite 56 Squadron after Ball was killed in May 1917, sometimes flew his outdated Sopwith Pup in mid-1917. With its rotary engine and flimsy airframe it should have been mincemeat for the roving Albatrosses of the German air service. But the calculating, highly professional McCudden had worked out that with its light wing loading, at 17,000 feet his Pup could out-turn any aircraft in the German inventory; and he did, shooting down 57 enemy aircraft before his accidental death in July 1918, latterly flying the new SE5a.

McCudden was the first real British flying ace after Ball. But the whole culture of flying aces had really begun in Germany with the likes of Boelcke and Immelmann (*see* Chapter 68). Above the squalor of the trenches, the knights of the air achieved a fame granted to few soldiers on the ground. Fêted in their home countries, the aces and their exploits captured the public's imagination.

> Fighter aces like Albert Ball VC or France's Georges Guynemer became household names, and their deaths were widely mourned. But chief among them, the most enduring name, was German ace Baron (*Freiherr*) Manfred von Richthofen, or the "Red Baron". By mid-April 1918 he had been credited with 80 "kills". Richthofen had been promoted to command *Jagdgeschwader 1* (literally "Hunting Wing 1"), known as the "Flying Circus" because of the varied colours disguising its aircrafts' outlines as well as its peripatetic nature. He was piloting a red Fokker Dr.1 Triplane when, on 21 April 1918, he pursued a novice British pilot in a Sopwith Camel. A more experienced Canadian pilot, Roy Brown, swooped down and fired a burst that raked Richthofen's machine. Close to the ground, Richthofen was also hit by Australian machine gun fire. Whoever delivered the fatal bullets, he was mortally wounded and his plane then crashed. He was so famous that people clamoured for souvenirs. Pieces of canvas were cut from his aircraft, and his flying boots went to Australia. His Oberursel UR2 rotary engine from the crash-site, shown here, came to Britain as a trophy for the Royal Air Force, which passed it on to the new War Museum the following year. It remains a symbol of the man and machine that epitomized the era of the fighter ace.

After McCudden's death, his place within the RAF as the most highly respected combat pilot was taken by Major Edward "Mick" Mannock, who entered service over

the Western Front in 1917. From a shaky start – he was even suspected of cowardice – he screwed himself up for an extraordinary string of sorties, earning the Military Cross (and Bar), and then in May 1918 the DSO and two Bars (in other words, the DSO three times) for achieving 20 kills that month alone. He went on to become the highest-scoring British ace of the war, claiming 73 kills – the exact number is hard to verify.

But for the aces, as for all pilots, previous success was no guarantee as to future survival. Life expectancy was shockingly short for serving airmen. They inhabited a (literally) "live fast, die young" culture. Mannock lasted longer than most, but his end came on 26 July 1918, not from an enemy fighter but from ground fire as he crossed the lines at a low level. He was posthumously awarded the Victoria Cross, in 1919.

The days of the individual duel and the roving knight of the air were being challenged in other ways. The last 18 months of the war saw new and more powerful "in-line" engines, more professional operational techniques, better-trained pilots, new tactics and more experienced aircrew make their impact. If any one moment symbolizes the beginning of this shift it was the shooting down of Baron von Richthofen on 6 July 1917 by slow, cumbersome two-seater FE2s, whose defensive formation of flying in a circle like a wagon train, to cover each other's tails, paid off. Richthofen charged at this "merry go round" only to fall victim, as a British bullet grazed his skull. The unconscious ace's plane fell out of the sky, and he came round just in time to crash-land. It was a narrow escape.

The Richthofen who returned to the fray in October 1917 found a new and more challenging situation awaiting him. The Royal Flying Corps (RFC) was still taking casualties, but the combination of good fighting aircraft such as the new high-level Sopwith Dolphins, plus the increasingly numerous SE5s, Camels and Bristol fighters, as well as the fast, well-armed DH4 light bombers, were proving more than a match for the German air arm's increasingly outdated Albatrosses and Pfalzes.

In Britain, air power was now important enough to merit a completely new service, the Royal Air Force. The catalyst for the new service had been alarm about the seeming inability to prevent Gotha raids over Britain (see Chapter 28). Lloyd George ordered a wider inquiry into aerial warfare. A committee under Lieutenant General Jan Christian Smuts, in the War Cabinet from June 1917, recommended a single air service combining the RFC and the Royal Navy Air Service, under a new Air Ministry and Chief of the Air Staff, to undertake home defence, field operations and strategic bombing. The War Cabinet agreed, and there was a Parliamentary Bill in October 1917. But Lord Rothermere, the new Air Minister, and Sir Hugh Trenchard, the new Chief of the Air Staff, did not get on; Trenchard resigned, but remained in post until the foundation of the RAF on 1 April 1918; Rothermere fell soon after.

While these political battles were fought, on the real battlefront the German spring offensives of 1918 never achieved anything like air superiority. The large numbers of ground-attack planes assembled to bolster the offensive made little difference as the RAF fought back hard. British, French and growing numbers of American squadrons made life difficult for the advancing Germans by artillery spotting, reconnaissance and, increasingly, their own ground attack. The RFC/RAF's only real problem in spring 1918 was being forced to retreat from its frontline airfields before the advancing Germans. But in the air, large numbers of capable aircraft were fighting the Germans to a standstill.

As the German offensive pushed up the valley of the Somme, in April it claimed the life of the Red Baron himself. His Fokker half spun, stalled and crash-landed in a field, ending up on its nose near Corbie. A bullet had entered his right side and exited via his heart. No-one knows who fired the fatal shot. Germany's idol was gone, to be given a very public hero's funeral by the British – a good propaganda coup. Many British pilots noted Richthofen's death with respect and some sadness. But Mannock had a different view: "I hope he roasted the whole way down."

Richthofen's death symbolized the waning of German air power. The RFC took delivery of no less than 2,500 new aircraft in March 1918 alone, while Germany was suffering shortages of everything from oil to new pilots. Air supremacy was moving irrevocably to the Allies. Even the arrival of the superlative, dangerous Fokker D-VII fighter in June could not turn the tide. New aces like the Canadians' Billy Bishop and the Royal Navy's Raymond Collishaw began to rack up impressive scores of kills.

As the summer of 1918 wore on, the whole pattern of aerial warfare changed. Over the frontlines older fighters such as the Sopwith Camel were now used extensively for ground attack, shooting up and bombing the retreating Germans' positions. Above them, the artillery-observation two-seaters, now equipped with reliable and longer range radios, controlled artillery bombardments. Higher still were the massed fighters, including the new Sopwith Snipe: although, as the last of the rotary engine fighters, not a fast aircraft by the standards of its time, it was more than a good match for contemporary German fighters. Deep behind German lines, light bombers such as the excellent DH4 roamed day after day to attack railheads, headquarters and airfields, secure in the knowledge that the speedy (140mph) aircraft could outrun all its opponents, even the Fokker D-VII.

In June 1918, Trenchard became commander of the new Independent Air Force in France, and it began bombing military targets deep inside Germany. Bigger aircraft, carrying bigger bombloads, were rolling off the production lines. Even as news of the Armistice came through, the first of the four-engined Handley Page V/1500 aircraft were preparing to undertake bombing raids on Berlin. They didn't need to complete their flights. But if the First World War proved anything, it was that air power had come of age and that no future war could be successfully fought without it.

Oberleutnant Manfred von Richthofen poses (centre) with fellow pilots of his Jagdstaffel in April 1917. Their self-confidence perhaps reflects that this was the Royal Flying Corp's "Bloody April" of losses, many inflicted by Richthofen and his friends. The pilots here include Richthofen's brother, Leutnant Lothar von Richthofen (second from right).

87

A BRITISH MARK V TANK
THE BLACK DAY OF THE GERMAN ARMY

8 AUGUST 1918

The *Kaiserschlacht* (*see* Chapter 84) had been a calculated gamble by the German High Command. By July 1918, its failure now spelled disaster. It had cost Germany 800,000 men, and within weeks its consequences would cost Ludendorff a nervous breakdown – and eventually his job. On 20 July, Crown Prince Rupprecht gloomily noted of the fighting at Villers-Cotterêts: "we stand at the turning point of the war ... the necessity to go over to the defensive is now upon us, and in addition all the gains which we have made in the spring ... have been lost again". Summer 1918 saw the pendulum swing: now it would be the Allies' turn to strike back.

On 8 August 1918, the hammer blow came, spearheaded by Australians and Canadians – and using every operational tank the British had.

> On 8 August, British, Australian and Canadian forces delivered a mortal blow against the Germans, in a well-planned attack east of Amiens. It incorporated many of the tactics and technologies developed over the previous years: a devastating, surprise bombardment that evolved into a creeping barrage; ground-attack aircraft; and all 552 vehicles of the Tank Corps, including nearly 350 Mark V fighting tanks. The new Mark V, like this one preserved at the Imperial War Museum, was the most effective tank yet. Previous machines had required four crewmen just to drive them. But, with a new 150-horsepower Ricardo engine linked to an improved transmission system, the Mark V could be driven by just one man. The blueprint for Amiens had been tested in a sharp action on 4 July, when the village of Hamel was captured quickly by the Australian Corps using every element of the new all-arms battle, including Mark V tanks for the first time. The Australian commander, Lieutenant General John Monash, showed that he fully understood the nature of what war had become: "A perfect modern battle plan is like nothing so much as a score for an orchestral composition, where the various arms and units are the instruments, and the tasks they perform are their respective musical phrases." The modern general's role was to conduct the orchestra, and bring in all the sections at the correct time to deliver the symphony of battle.

Foch, as supreme commander, had concluded that the best strategy for retaliation was for the individual Allied armies to mount their own offensives – but, crucially, limited in space and time, and against achievable objectives. There was to be no single great breakthrough. The aim was to pull the German reserve divisions hither and thither, keeping their dwindling reserves always on the move.

"WITH HOPE FOR MANKIND AND WITH VISIONS OF A NEW WORLD A BLOW WILL BE STRUCK TOMORROW WHICH WILL DEFINITELY MARK THE TURN OF THE TIDE."

Lieutenant Hedley Goodyear MC, 102nd Canadian Battalion, letter to his mother, 7 August 1918. He was killed in action, 22 August.

Subsequently described by Ludendorff as the "Black Day of the German army", a surprise attack combining artillery, tanks, aircraft and new assault troops near Amiens revealed just how low German morale had sunk. The keys were speed, surprise and deception. Rawlinson, the very same general who had commanded on the disastrous first day on the Somme two years before, now planned and launched the first major *Blitzkrieg*-type all-arms operation in history. His Fourth Army (as the Fifth Army was now renamed), embracing the Canadians and Australians, smashed the German lines on a 15-mile front and advanced 8 miles in a day. It was a triumph for the BEF and its new methods.

Planning had started weeks before. Haig had accurately forecast the risks to Germany of any massive final attack as far back as January 1918, when he had agreed with his intelligence staff that "if Germany attacks and fails she will be ruined". The stalling of the German offensive short of Amiens in April 1918 not only dashed hopes of a German breakthrough on the Somme, but the new line gave Haig an ideal spot to counterattack across open ground. By 21 July Rawlinson had sold his battle plan to Haig with the enthusiastic support of his corps commanders – Monash for the Australians, Lieutenant General Sir Arthur Currie for the Canadians – plus the BEF's III Corps and the Cavalry Corps, backed by the senior artillery, air force and tank officers. When Foch was briefed a few days later he not only endorsed Rawlinson's plan strongly but placed the French First Army under Haig's command to join the fight.

One of the reasons for the confidence was that the plan was based on evidence. At Hamel, south of the Somme overlooking the road east from Amiens, on 4 July the Australians (with some Americans under their command) had demonstrated that combined all-arms tactics could not only break an enemy trench line but do so quickly and with minimum casualties. The attack had taken all its objectives in under two hours, using the combination of a surprise creeping barrage, supported by 60 tanks, and aircraft. The infantry effectively mopped up the shocked German survivors. The victory owed much to Monash's detailed staff planning, thorough preparation and the novel use of 12 supply tanks to bring forward vital stores such as ammunition, each tank ferrying as much ammunition and stores as 1,000 men could carry. Aircraft were used to para-drop medical supplies and ammunition to advanced troops, too. This successful employment of new tactics, combined with the battle-tested experience among the staff of the Fourth Army, now made the BEF a strong attacking machine.

Rawlinson's mission was to clear the Germans away from the railway link between Amiens and Paris. To do this he had four corps, plus the support of the French on his right. The Australian and the Canadian Corps were particularly formidable assault troops. The Dominion divisions were numerically stronger than the British divisions and, concentrated in their national armies, they had strong cohesiveness, too.

The attack would prove the model for the BEF's victorious advances for the rest of the war. Rawlinson's secret weapon was surprise. He went to great lengths to ensure security: the attack was called "The Raid"; soldiers' pay books had a slip pasted in with "Keep Your Mouth Shut"; all unusual movement was at night; *pavé* roads were sanded to reduce noise; and aircraft flew daily missions to check that nothing was visible from the air. Canadian signal units were sent to Ypres to broadcast a false Canadian presence there. The 550-odd British and French tanks that were to spearhead the assault, supported by over 2,000 guns, moved forward only when covered by the noise of aircraft engines. Crucially, there would be no preparatory bombardment.

Rawlinson struck at 04.20 on 8 August. The British tanks rolled forward accompanied by a hurricane bombardment modelled on Bruchmüller's "Fire Waltz" (*see* Chapter 84). Led by the Canadians and Australians, the Allied onslaught overwhelmed seven German divisions. On the right flank, the French started later but pushed the Germans back; and on the left, the British III Corps fought hard to evict the Germans from the wooded slopes north of the Somme. In the centre, five German divisions were swept away. By 11.00 the attackers had broken through along a 10-mile front and cavalry and light Whippet tanks were running amok, causing havoc in the German rear areas. Overhead the Royal Air Force bombed and strafed targets of opportunity. By the end of the day the attackers had punched a hole 8 miles deep, at its furthest, in the German lines and the new frontline was out of range even of the heavy guns. German sources admit to the loss of 28,000 men and 400 guns for the first day. Significantly, around 12,000 of the German losses had surrendered.

Two days later German reserves of troops and aircraft rushed to plug the gap. With the British objectives gained, and despite pressure from Foch to continue, Haig ordered the offensive stopped. With 13 infantry and 3 cavalry divisions, Rawlinson had routed 25 German divisions. German losses by the end were 70,000, almost 30,000 of them surrendering, and 1,300 guns. The battle had been a crushing riposte to Ludendorff's army, as he acknowledged.

"The Black Day of the German army" had a profound effect on the victors, too. Confidence and morale were restored to the BEF after the horrors of the March retreat. Haig and the BEF had made a key realization: strike hard, regroup, plan and then strike again at areas of weakness, rather than batter away relentlessly against stiffening resistance as German reserves arrived. British war correspondent Philip Gibbs detected a change "in the enemy's mind": "They no longer have even a dim hope of victory on this western front. All they hope for now is to defend themselves long enough to gain peace by negotiation."

He was right. Ludendorff and the Germans were now on the run.

> **"ON OUR SIDE THE ARMY SEEMS TO BE BUOYED UP WITH THE ENORMOUS HOPE OF GETTING ON WITH THIS BUSINESS QUICKLY"**
>
> *Philip Gibbs, official British war correspondent, 27 August 1918*

88

CAPTURED GERMAN SHOULDER STRAPS
THE LAST HUNDRED DAYS

JULY TO NOVEMBER 1918

With the British strike at Amiens on 8 August 1918 (*see* Chapter 87), what would later be called "The Last Hundred Days" was well and truly underway: a series of Allied attacks that kept the defeated German army on the run in the closing phase of the war. It is the story of the collapse of the German army on the Western Front, to the accompaniment of the psychological collapse of its master, General Erich Ludendorff.

In 1918, the war once again became one of dramatic movement. As August flowed into September, the Allies gained the ascendancy and began to drive the Germans relentlessly back. Influenced by Haig's incisive understanding of how events were unfolding, the Allied armies launched a series of attacks up and down the line. Instead of getting bogged down in protracted fighting, when the momentum of one attack waned the focus switched to another part of the line. The Germans were bewildered and unable to re-establish the kind of strong defensive positions they had held for four years. "It is very interesting in the front line just now," wrote Lieutenant Colonel Walter Vignoles, commanding the 9th Battalion, Northumberland Fusiliers, "continually chasing the Boche, moving forward every day, no billets, no shelters, everyone just sleeping under hedges or in shell holes. There is no doubt Fritz is in a great mess." German morale plummeted; masses of prisoners were taken. Between 21 August and the Armistice in November, V Corps (part of the British Third Army) moved steadily eastwards from the old 1916 Somme battlefields until on 11 November it was positioned around 8 miles south of Maubeuge, where the BEF had started the war in August 1914. V Corps captured thousands of prisoners, and as a record the shoulder straps of one man from each German regiment it encountered were mounted on three display boards at Corps HQ. These insignia provided intelligence as to the units being encountered, but more than that, the astonishing number and variety of them added up to a picture of a defeated army.

General Mangin's highly successful counterattack at Villers-Cotterêts on 18 July had already shaken the surprised Germans, who retreated almost as quickly as they had advanced. It also shook Ludendorff's nerve. Hindenburg suggested a counterattack north of Soissons, to which Ludendorff exploded: "Madness!" Even the core relationship of Germany's "Duo" was falling apart. By 20 July the defence expert Colonel Friedrich von Lossberg was calling for a complete withdrawal and defence behind the Hindenburg Line, to be dismissed by "a really agitated and nervous" Ludendorff. There was clearly no chance of going ahead with his next

planned offensive, Operation Hagen, against the British at Ypres. To do so would mean ignoring the French and Americans, who were now cutting deep into the south of the great German salient in the Champagne. The truth was that Germany, its great gamble of the *Kaiserschlacht* having failed (*see* Chapter 84), had run out of reserves, ideas and military options.

Sensing his adversary's weakness and indecision, on 24 July Foch, as Allied *generalissimo*, called a strategic conference of Allied commanders. They agreed on a strategic masterstroke against their weakened but still dangerous enemy: limited individual national offensives, which, crucially, would stop when each had achieved its objective. In effect, Foch planned to unleash a coordinated series of limited counterattacks, but switching from front to front as each one suceeded and ran out of steam. There was to be no single breakthrough, no surge to the Rhine; instead, the focus of attack would always move to another sector and divert the German reserves yet again.

The BEF's triumph at Amiens on 8 August conformed to this strategy. It also confirmed German weakness. So began a relentless pursuit of the whole German army as it withdrew under a succession of hammer blows. "The Hundred Days Offensive" would actually consist of no fewer that ten major Allied offensives, one after the other, all separated by space and time.

By now even Ludendorff could see the writing on the wall and offered to resign his responsibilities, only to be told by both Hindenburg and the Kaiser to stay at his post. At the German High Command, on 10 August, Ludendorff briefed the Kaiser in sombre terms, pointing out that "the war must be ended". The Kaiser's reaction to this apocalyptic analysis was, according to his personal liaison officer, one of surprise, well masked. After all, this was the general who only a month before had been briefing him that the war was as good as won.

A few days later, at the general conference at Spa on 13–14 August – the so-called *Kaiserkonferenz* – Ludendorff, despite fighting talk, admitted that Germany now had no alternative but to call for peace talks, with the Dutch acting as intermediaries. The political and social unrest back in Germany, combined with the disintegrating morale at the Front, left little alternative. Unrest in the German army on the Western Front was now widespread. Fresh drafts coming to the Front were being met by cries of "strike breakers, blacklegs" and accusations that they were "only prolonging the war for the capitalists and bosses". However, it was not surrender that Ludendorff was contemplating in August, but negotiation from Germany's current position: occupation of Belgium and parts of France.

Ludendorff's view was reinforced by the prospect of having to fight the American army in France, now moving into the line in the French sector west of Verdun; he realized it would be beyond the weakened German army's capabilities. He knew that his mistrustful, exhausted battalions, wracked by influenza, war weariness and a desire to go home, would be unlikely to stand up to the massive 28,000-strong divisions and the 1.5 million fresh troops of the oncoming steamroller that was the American Expeditionary Force – despite its inexperience.

A month later, on 12–16 September, Ludendorff's fears were realized. With the Americans now united under General Pershing, the US First Army launched its own offensive on the German salient at St Mihiel, southeast of Verdun. Twelve divisions, including two French, 2,900 guns, 1,100 aircraft and 273 tanks launched two deep strikes on converging axes into the salient to encircle the Germans. Although the defenders had been planning to abandon the sector, the American assault came as

"OCTOBER 1918 ... AT EXACTLY 4 O'CLOCK, ONE GUN FIRED – AND THEN ALL THE GUNS OPENED UP ALL THE WAY ALONG THE LINE, AND THERE WAS A CURTAIN OF FIRE FROM HORIZON TO HORIZON AS FAR AS THE EYE COULD SEE. IT REALLY WAS A MAGNIFICENT SIGHT."

Private W.G. Brown, 2/3rd Field Ambulance

In St Mihiel, in Lorraine, children enthusiastically swarm over a French officer's car, waving the Tricolore *in celebration of their liberation after four years of German occupation (13 September 1918). So rapid was the Allied advance in some areas during the "Hundred Days" that the only way of getting supplies to forward troops was by air-drop.*

a nasty shock. Taken by surprise in the middle of their withdrawal, the Germans surrendered in droves. By the end of the day Pershing's men had pinched out the whole salient, capturing 16,000 prisoners and over 440 guns, and shortening the Front by 16 miles. However, American courage and enthusiasm did not compensate for their lack of battle experience. The unskilled, half-trained "Doughboys" fought with a disregard for danger not seen since the opening campaigns of 1914.

This success augmented the other Allied actions of late August, which clearly exemplified Foch's strategy. By now, Haig was one of the few Allied commanders who could sniff victory, briefing a disbelieving Churchill (back in the Cabinet as Minister of Munitions since July 1917) that "we ought to do our utmost to get a decision this autumn". That same day, 21 August, the British Third Army attacked south of Arras; on 22 August, the British Fourth Army recaptured Albert; the next day, across a 33-mile front on the Somme, both armies attacked, supported by the US II Corps; and on 26 August, the British First Army launched itself out of Arras. All the old Somme positions of 1916 were won back; everywhere the German Front was breaking down.

On 31 August, the Australians of the Fourth Army added to Ludendorff's woes by beginning a masterly assault-crossing of the Somme, tearing apart the German lines between St Quentin and Péronne and pushing deeper into occupied territory: it was an action described by General Rawlinson as the greatest military achievement of the war. Three days later the Canadians struck to the north against the strong German defences between Drocourt and Quéant, to the east of Arras, driving the Germans back from this advance position of the Hindenburg Line on a 30-mile front. By mid-September, the BEF's advance in the Somme region was at least 25 miles, along a front of around 40 miles.

As the French closed in to the south, Ludendorff had no option but to pull his troops back to the apparent safety of the Hindenburg Line. It negated all the gains of the spring offensives. He ordered yet another withdrawal, this time to the Canal du Nord. German resistance remained strong, in places, but elsewhere morale was plummeting; increasingly, the withdrawing troops were relying on well-sited and determined teams of machine gunners to cover their backs.

Although American strength had not yet peaked on the Continent, Foch now realized that the Germans really were on the run and ordered a number of

The fog of war made manifest in this famous smoky battle scene, as machine gunners of the US 2nd Infantry Division blast away with their 37mm guns. It probably depicts the wasted woods of the Argonne, and shows the difficult terrain that American troops had to contend with in this, their most intensive contribution to the war.

simultaneous attacks, sometimes referred to as the "Final Grand Offensive", designed to cut into German communications from the flanks. It was a case of all hands on deck, or, in Foch's memorable phrase "*Tout le monde à la bataille*" – "Everyone to the battle!" And everyone came.

It unfolded in four steps. On 26 September, to the west of Verdun the Americans and French unleashed what would prove to be their final offensive, as over 25 divisions attacked the Germans in the forested Argonne region and up the Meuse in the greatest and bloodiest American battle of the war. In six weeks the Americans advanced 60 miles and lost over 26,000 killed and 95,000 wounded, but Pershing's men inflicted 130,000 casualties on the Germans as well as capturing 26,000 prisoners and over 870 guns.

No sooner had German reserves been ordered south to deal with this onslaught, when, at dawn on 27 September, four BEF divisions of the First and Third Armies attacked north and south of Cambrai before dawn, crossing the supposedly impassable Canal du Nord to approach the Hindenburg Line. The very next day, far to the north, the Flanders Army Group under the command of the King of the Belgians with 12 Belgian, 10 British and 6 French divisions, quickly penetrated the German defences beyond Ypres. They advanced up to 6 miles on the first day and only stopped 18 miles into the German lines when logistic support was unable to get any further forward across the all too numerous water obstacles.

On 29 September, the British Fourth Army north of St Quentin finally assaulted the Hindenburg Line itself along a 12-mile front, inaugurated the previous day by an extraordinarily ferocious bombardment. American and Australian divisions had heavy going against the defences, but the British 46th (North Midland) Division crossed the St Quentin canal in a brilliant *coup de main*, slicing through the Hindenburg's defences and capturing four-fifths of the enemy in the area.

Finally, Ludendorff's nerve snapped. On 28 September, he broke down in what was described as "a paranoid rage", blaming the Kaiser, the German people, the navy and civilian politicians in the *Reichstag* – anyone but himself – for Germany's impending defeat. That day, far from the Western Front, Bulgaria had broken ranks with the Central Powers and called for an armistice. So many shocks and reversals could not be withstood. The broken, frantic general went to see Hindenburg and told him that they now had no alternative but to seek a negotiated peace. The next day, as the Bulgarian Armistice was agreed, the Kaiser visited High Command at Spa to be told by the General Staff that the war could not be won.

But in the days and weeks to come, the Western Front Allies pushed on relentlessly, advancing and capturing. In the north, after a 10-mile advance in three days, bad weather caused a two-week delay, but by the third week of October a string of major towns and cities had been retaken – back in Allied hands for the first time since 1914, including Lille, Ostend, Douai and Zeebrugge. And they kept on.

In the centre, on 3 October, more of the Hindenburg Line was breached, and on 8 October, the British Third and Fourth armies, along with the French First Army, stormed the Hindenburg Line defences over a 17-mile front around Cambrai. The town itself fell on 9 October. A week later, and 4 miles further on, the retreating Germans were attacked along the River Selle.

To the south, the French and Americans were grinding their way through the difficult terrain of the Argonne Forest, but in mid-October they breached their section of the Hindenburg Line; once out of the Argonne, by the end of the month, they pushed on as far as Sedan.

The Germans were attempting a controlled retreat, and despite depleted numbers could still offer stiff resistance. But determined rearguards could only mask the completeness of defeat. The final offensive on the Western Front commenced on 4 November along a 30-mile front in the direction of Mauberge and Mons. The BEF was back where it had started the war. Haig threw his First, Third and Fourth armies at the German defenders, who lay behind a canalized stretch of the River Sambre and in the Forest of Mormal. The fighting was often intense, but the canal was bridged. To the south, the French First Army attacked, capturing Guise. Between them, the Allies broke through on a 40-mile front.

On 9 November, Foch prepared to administer the *coup de grâce*. He signalled each of the Allied armies:

> The enemy, disorganized by our repeated attacks, retreats along the entire front. It is important to coordinate and expedite our movements. I appeal to the energy and the initiative of the commanders-in-chief and of their armies to make decisive the results obtained.

In the end, his orders didn't need to be carried out. Within two days, the war was over.

These Hundred Days, for all their gains, were far from cheap. The victorious final advance had been as expensive as any other campaign of a very bloody war. The BEF lost over 350,000 men – at least as many as at Passchendaele on the Somme in 1916. However, the difference was that this time the BEF had advanced nearly 100 miles. Of course the victory was an *Allied* one, a coalition effort, but the figures show clearly that the BEF's contribution was both the costliest and the most decisive. Despite numbering less than a third of the Allied forces, the BEF suffered more casualties but also captured almost half the number of German prisoners taken (189,000) and around 40 per cent of the enemy guns. Haig's BEF had won Britain's greatest ever victory.

And all the time, as soldiers of all nationalities died in their thousands, a parallel series of events were shaping the final result. Germany was attempting to negotiate as advantageous as possible an armistice; but the Central Powers – and the German state itself – were imploding.

89

A WREATH FOR SALADIN
THE END OF THE PALESTINE CAMPAIGN

SEPTEMBER TO OCTOBER 1918

Following the success of the Egyptian Expeditionary Force (EEF) in capturing Jerusalem in December 1917 (*see* Chapter 78), General Allenby's Palestine campaign slowed as winter weather set in; before spring, troops were transferred to the Western Front to help resist the German offensives. After two EEF raids across the River Jordan were beaten back, Allenby then went on the defensive during the summer heat, while he incorporated his new Indian Army units and replacements. By late summer 1918, "The Bull" was ready to move again. In September, the EEF began its final offensive, this time against the strong defence lines of the Ottoman "Yilderim Army Group" with its 100,000 men, including 15,600 Germans and 500 guns. It would take Allenby – and T.E. Lawrence and the irregulars of Sherif Feisal – to Damascus, the symbolic heart of Arab aspirations, and beyond.

> On 23 October 1916, in a cool, shaded house at Wadi Safra in the Hejaz, T.E. Lawrence had his momentous first meeting with Sherif Feisal, whom he would go on to serve for the next two years. He deliberately invoked Damascus, noting that they were "far from" it: both men were already conscious of the need for the Arabs to liberate this historic city in distant Syria. Some weeks later, Feisal told his gathered tribesmen that when they arrived in Damascus they should "clean up the tomb" of Saladin, the renowned 12th-century Muslim warrior. To Feisal and many Arabs, Saladin's tomb had been defiled by Kaiser Wilhelm II when, following his state visit in 1898, he sent this ornate bronze wreath to be placed on it as a symbol of German–Ottoman friendship. On 1 October 1918, when the Arabs finally arrived in Damascus, Lawrence and a small group went to the tomb and cleansed it as Feisal had ordered. It was a highly symbolic act of political ascendancy, stripping away European influence from this venerated Islamic site. The wreath was given to Lawrence who, within days, returned to Britain to fight the Arab cause in London. On 8 November, he took it to the Imperial War Museum to hand it over for preservation, since, as he put it, "Saladin no longer required it."

Beginning on 19 September, Allenby smashed through the Ottoman defences in one of the war's most successful British and Imperial campaigns, dubbed the Battle of Megiddo (the Biblical Armageddon). Unlike his fellow generals on the Western Front, Allenby was able to use his infantry to break through the enemy lines and then send in his cavalry to exploit and attack the enemy rear.

He began by pretending to repeat his tactics at Gaza, by attacking on the right flank in the desert with the Camel Corps and cavalry, plus Arab irregulars, against

"I REMINDED THE AMIR FEISAL THAT THE ALLIES WERE IN HONOUR BOUND TO ENDEAVOUR TO REACH A SETTLEMENT IN ACCORDANCE WITH THE WISHES OF THE PEOPLES CONCERNED AND URGED HIM TO PLACE HIS TRUST WHOLE-HEARTEDLY IN THEIR GOOD FAITH."

General Sir Edmund Allenby, report to London, 18 October 1918

the Hejaz Railway. Rail communications between Damascus and the main Ottoman army were broken for a crucial week. The RAF gave close air support, strafing enemy columns and, more importantly, locating Ottoman positions. The Arab forces then continued their advance north up the railway towards Damascus. Meanwhile, Allenby switched his mobile cavalry across to his left flank and three days later launched an all-arms offensive against the Ottoman Seventh and Eighth armies dug in on the line from the Dead Sea to Jaffa on the coast. By mid-morning the infantry had broken through and Allenby's cavalry was pouring north up the coast road. The next day they had even reached the Ottoman GHQ at Nazareth, nearly capturing the German commander-in-chief himself, General Liman von Sanders, the man who had masterminded the Ottoman defence at Gallipoli.

The Ottoman forces were streaming back across the Front, and by 24 September the Seventh and Eighth armies had effectively ceased to exist. Thousands surrendered. On 25 September, Australians stormed the vital railway junction at Samakh, 50 miles to the north, and took it after hand-to-hand street fighting. The vital Ottoman railway, on which all their supplies depended, was lost for good.

While his main forces were pushing up the coast towards Haifa and Acre, Allenby now planned the final advance of his campaign, inland along the Jordan Valley. He switched his assault to a narrow thrust past the Sea of Galilee and Golan Heights towards Quneitra and then the road to Damascus, 70 miles to the northeast. By 28 September the leading elements were at Quneitra and, after a delay caused by German machine guns at Sa'sa the next day, pushed on to just 10 miles south of Damascus on the 30th.

Three cavalry divisions were now converging on the city. In ten days they had covered 150 miles, in a country with no food and little water, and destroyed two Ottoman armies. In Damascus, ammunition, petrol and military dumps were set ablaze, and the wireless mast for communication with Constantinople and Berlin was blown up. The Ottoman forces were on the run, many killed as an Australian brigade brought machine guns into action on the narrow road running west to Beirut, literally blocking a gorge with the dead bodies of transport animals and hundreds of men.

On 1 October 1918, the advance elements of General Chauvel's Desert Mounted Corps – the 10th Australian Light Horse – were the first Allied forces to enter Damascus, to a hero's welcome. But they moved on quickly having been ordered to avoid the limelight. The honour had to be seen to fall to Lawrence and the Arab irregulars, who, for political reasons, had to enter before the main part of Chauvel's force. The streets became alive with Arabs on horseback, firing in the air.

It remained for the last Ottoman resistance to be put down. On 8 October, the Indian contingents reached Beirut, and on 20 October Chauvel ordered his Desert Mounted Corps to halt their advance. Six days later, Aleppo fell to Major General H.J. MacAndrew. For the Ottomans in Palestine the war was over. In 38 days Allenby's EEF had advanced 350 miles and taken 75,000 prisoners, including 4,000 Germans, and 400 guns. It was a triumph for Allenby, and for his masterly handling of his forces. Using deception, concentration of force, surprise and the cavalry's mobility, he had shown himself to be one of the outstanding generals of the war.

Unfortunately, the clarity of the military triumph would give way to a muddied, bitter political legacy. British promises had been dangled in 1915–16 promising Arab independence as the reward for an Arab revolt against the Ottomans. But in May 1916, speaking for their respective governments, Sir Mark Sykes, an MP with knowledge

"WHEN A SOLDIER APPEARED IN THE STREETS OF DAMASCUS HE WAS SURROUNDED BY THE EXCITED AND DELIGHTED THRONG. THEY THREW OFF THEIR STOLID EXTERIOR, AND RECEIVED US WITH ECSTATIC JOY ... AND ACCLAIMED THE DAY AS THE GREATEST IN THE 4,000 YEARS OF THE HISTORY OF DAMASCUS."

Eyewitness to the liberation of Damascus, 1 October 1918

In October 1918, amid the celebrations of throwing off the Ottoman yoke, Damascus officially came under the control of an Arab administration, which now had to keep law and order. Here, members of the Hejaz Camel Corps impose discipline on Bedouin looters.

of the political problems of Mesopotamia and Syria, and François Georges-Picot, a former French consul in Beirut, came to an agreement: that after the war Britain would occupy Palestine, and France would occupy Syria (including modern Lebanon); they added some qualified statements about Arab self-rule. In May 1917, an uneasy Foreign Office warned: "French intentions in Syria are surely incompatible with the war aims of the Allies as defined . . . utterly incompatible with our ideas of liberating the Arab nation and of establishing a free and independent Arab State." To compound the problem, in a series of communications, culminating in Foreign Secretary Arthur Balfour's "declaration" – a letter to Lord Rothschild, leader of the British Jewish community – Britain appeared to be offering Jews a homeland in Palestine. In effect, there were now three conflicting promises for Arab land.

Lawrence communicated the gist of the Sykes–Picot discussions (if not all the details) to Feisal, but to Feisal there still appeared sufficient hope for Arab aspirations. If the Arabs could be seen as the liberators of Damascus, along with Homs, Hama and Aleppo, the agreement offered them some degree of independence. So, as soon as Ottoman forces evacuated Damascus, the Arabs proclaimed an Arab government over Syria and the surrounding region under King Hussein, Feisal's father. Thus, when Allenby entered Damascus, on 3 October, an Arab administration was already in being and the Arab flag was flying from government buildings. This was as Allenby had expected, and was consistent with the earlier British assurances. Feisal also arrived on 3 October, but it soon became clear to him and to Lawrence (*see* Chapter 79) just how unreliable any British assurances were, despite Allenby's continuing efforts to plead British good faith.

Allenby's victory left a hollow legacy, as the region was subsequently carved up between Britain and France (*see* Chapter 93). After Versailles, Syria was given to France, whose heavy-handed rule was, within two years, putting down Arab rebellion. There were consolation prizes: Feisal became the British client king of the new state of Iraq, while his brother Abdullah established the (continuing) royal dynasty of Trans-Jordan (now Jordan). Their father Sherif Hussein, though, remained in the Hejaz, his own kingdom taken over by the neighbouring Saudi dynasty in 1924. The victories of 1918 would bear bitter fruit and the politics of the Middle East have never recovered.

90

AN *ERSATZ* NIGHTDRESS
THE COLLAPSE OF THE CENTRAL POWERS

SEPTEMBER TO NOVEMBER 1918

It was inevitable, after the failure of the last German throw of the dice in the 1918 spring offensives (*see* Chapter 84), and the beginning of the Allied counteroffensives (*see* Chapters 87 and 88), that a disintegration of German morale at the Fighting Front would feed, and be fed by, the demoralization and confusion on the Home Front. In Germany, economic privations, social disruption and political agitation from all quarters were eating away the will to fight on. That so many German troops on the Western Front were surrendering was not only a testament to the Allies' overwhelming force and new tactics, but also the German rank and file, increasingly, had had enough.

In 1917–18, Germans had endured a severe winter of coal scarcities and a failed potato harvest. More generally, the country was plagued by lack of food, labour shortages, rising inflation and political radicalization. Resentment that the available supplies were still being prioritized for a war that clearly could not now be won was turning many Germans, whether in uniform or not, against the war and against the leadership and institutions behind the war effort. There was more than a whiff of revolution in the air.

Throughout the war, the Central Powers lacked the economic depth of Britain and France, which were able to fall back on the abundance of their empires and the considerable material support of the United States. By 1916 both Germany and Austria-Hungary had started to run short of many key resources. Over the next two years, the situation deteriorated rapidly. The British blockade successfully prevented the import of vital goods, ranging from chemicals to food, both directly into German ports and via the neutral northern European countries. To compensate, the Germans looked for substitute, or *Ersatz*, products. Never quite the same as the originals they were intended to replace, coffee was produced from roasted barley, tea from raspberry leaves and a variety of strange substances were billed as "meat". Textile staples such as cotton and wool were also hard to come by. Military uniforms took priority, and civilians had to find other ways of producing "cloth". Both paper and wood fibre were used to make clothes. Many were quite effective, but clearly they could not be washed or worn in the rain. This full-length white nightdress, complete with "lace" cuffs and collar, was made from lengths of woven paper string. It is one of several items obtained by the Imperial War Museum to show the extraordinary means by which German and Austro-Hungarian civilians kept themselves going during the war. But, despite this immense effort and all the ingenuity, by 1918 most citizens of both countries were tired, hungry, poorly clothed and fed up.

"THERE IS PRACTICALLY NO COAL TO BE HAD, AND I LIVE IN THE HOUSE IN MY OLD FUR COAT. THE GAS BURNS FROM 11 TO 1 IN THE MIDDLE OF THE DAY, FOR COOKING, AND FROM 4 TO 12 AT NIGHT – OTHERWISE IT IS CUT OFF."

A German resident, relating the privations of war

If Germany was beginning to disintegrate, her allies were even further along that road. On the Italian Front, whole Czech and Croat units of the Austro-Hungarian army were deserting and going over to the Allies, while the empire was crippled by strikes and shortages. The Habsburg Emperor Karl warned the Kaiser that Vienna could no longer fight on and had to seek peace if the dynasty were to survive. His foreign minister, Baron István (Stephen) von Burian, had proposed a joint proclamation calling on all sides to negotiate. This was too much for the Germans, whose officials at that time still believed Hindenburg and Ludendorff's assurances that the military position was strong. But on 1 September the Austro-Hungarian General Staff warned that "the army can no longer sustain the battle against the enemy" and any military collapse would lead to an internal revolution, Bolshevik-style. On 14th September, Vienna unilaterally called for peace talks in a neutral country, adding – much to Berlin's annoyance – that it was speaking on behalf of the other Central Powers: but the call was rebuffed anyway. To make things worse, Bulgaria was soon reeling under Franchet d'Espèrey's offensive out of Salonika (*see* Chapter 26). The Balkan front collapsed as his victorious forces flooded north into Bulgaria and Romania, even threatening Hungary. This was a direct blow to Germany too, threatening her vital supplies of grain and oil from Romania and the Ukraine, on which her tottering food supply and fuel for vehicles so much depended.

On the Western Front, thousands of German soldiers were deserting or not returning from leave that autumn and there were so many deserters hiding in the cellars and attics in Brussels that the German Military Police gave up making raids to arrest them. The military conference at High Command headquarters in Spa, on 28–29 September, confirmed Germany's, and the remaining Central Powers', need to seek an end to the fighting. In Ludendorff's own words, the capitulation of Bulgaria on 29 September "sealed the destiny of the Quadruple Alliance".

Despite this, and despite his own sudden breakdown at the end of September, Ludendorff, backed by Hindenburg, still planned for a fighting withdrawal from the German-occupied territories and proposed to "take up the battle on the German Frontier". The Duo thought that unilaterally they could better negotiate favourable peace terms with President Wilson, based on his Fourteen Points, from a position of relative strength. But they needed to demonstrate Germany's democratic credentials. Ludendorff reluctantly approved a visit by the recently appointed German Foreign Minister Paul von Hintze to Spa to hammer out a crucial deal between the military in the West and the politicians in Berlin. With the agreement of the Kaiser, a new chancellor would be appointed – the third since Bethmann Hollweg's resignation in July 1917 – replacing the elderly Count Georg Hertling. The new incumbent would then form a broadly based democratic government containing Social Democrats. This government would bring in political reforms and approach the United States, calling for peace on the basis of the Fourteen Points.

The new chancellor, officially appointed on 3 October, was Prince Max von Baden – a known liberal, despite his aristocratic breeding, and no admirer of Ludendorff. He formed a government of politicians from all parties and, to strengthen his hand, obtained a statement from the military that "there was no further chance of forcing a peace on the enemy", though this did allow the army to then distance itself from any subsequent peace moves. Prince Max, fully sensible of the potential catastrophe of an abject military surrender and defeat, and wary that an armistice request might sharpen the Allies teeth, nevertheless requested exactly that and asked to negotiate

A groundswell of protest. By autumn 1918, mass demonstrations, such as this one on Berlin's Zimmerstrasse, were common on the streets of the capital and other large German cities, as people reacted angrily to shortages and demanded political change. They would continue in 1919, reflecting factionalism, radicalism and German anger at the Treaty of Versailles.

on the basis of the Fourteen Points. But through October, in three separate formal replies, Wilson's tone increasingly stiffened in the light of his Allies' feelings, and he demanded as conditions the evacuation of all occupied territories and the cessation of all submarine attacks; he also insisted that the Allies could only negotiate with the government of a properly democratic state – that is, one without the Kaiser, or at the very least a constitutional monarchy. Among the Allies, Lloyd George was pressing the view that conditions for an armistice could not be fixed "until after consultation with the military experts", and a hardline Clemenceau played for time.

The last five weeks of war and haggling were agonizing: for the Germans; for the Allied politicians; but, above all for the troops who were still being wounded and killed, on all sides. Berlin begged the US president not to impose conditions "irreconcilable with the honour of the German people and the establishment of a just peace". But by the last week of October Wilson's hands were tied. The Allies had to speak with one voice and as their conditions hardened, so opposition grew in Germany to their proposals.

Ludendorff, back from his personal nadir, was feeling more bullish, suggesting Germany could still defend herself, that winter would slow the Allies and that holding out longer would bring better terms. But, having recovered his nerve if not his sense, he then made a fatal mistake. He attempted to rally the troops once more to fight on and ignore the civilian government's peace negotiations. On 24 October, he drafted a personal proclamation to the army saying that the politicians' plans for peace were "unacceptable to us as soldiers. [They] can thus be nothing … but a challenge to continue our resistance with all our strength".

The new chancellor was furious, as was the Kaiser. A draft copy of Ludendorff's (unissued) challenge to the political authority of Berlin was seen by a member of the Independent Socialist Party. The *Reichstag* erupted in rage and insisted that this "overmighty and insubordinate" general must go; and so, on 26 October Germany's "First Quartermaster General" was forced to submit his resignation personally to the Kaiser and dismissed without thanks, to be replaced by the more moderate, and more politically aware, General Wilhelm Groener. Prince Max of Baden reluctantly accepted all the Allied conditions. He had little choice. Germany was falling apart.

The game was already up for Austria-Hungary. Imperial authority collapsed on 16 October, when the emperor proclaimed a federation of nations. But it was already too late for many – Poles, Czechs and the Serbs and Croats were all busy forming provisional independent governments. Hungary was preparing to declare independence too. On 24 October, the rejuvenated Italians, with British and French help, stormed across the River Piave at Vittorio Veneto and put to flight those troops who had not deserted or come over to the Allies. Far off in the Aegean, on 30 October, the defeated Ottoman Empire signed an armistice at Mudros harbour, on the island of Lemnos. And by 1 November Vienna was anxiously suing for peace.

Germany was alone. The Kaiser had removed himself from Berlin to the High Command at Spa on 29 October. His beloved High Seas Fleet, idle in port for so long, was ordered by Admiral Scheer to steam out into the North Sea for one final confrontation with the Grand Fleet in order to go out in a blaze of glory and salvage Germany's honour – and, it was hoped, undermine the politicians' peace negotiations. The disgruntled, radicalized sailors were much less keen on what seemed a blatantly suicidal mission and, on 30 October, mutinied at Wilhelmshaven and Kiel. Sailors' soviets were proclaimed. At Kiel on 3 November the sailors joined striking workers in a mass revolt and raised the Red Flag. The German Revolution had begun, as insurrection spread to the streets of Berlin and half a dozen other major cities. Germany in 1918 was beginning to resemble Russia in 1917, with competing poles of power, and competing armed factions.

By now, after a series of military-political conferences, Marshal Foch had outlined his military terms for a ceasefire. The wording was harsh, harsher than Wilson anticipated, reflecting continued debate about interpretations of the Fourteen Points. Foch called for the liberation of all occupied territory including Alsace-Lorraine; reparations for all damage caused to France; and the occupation of the German Rhineland (which Lloyd George had contested). Haig demanded rolling stock, and Pershing surprised everyone by insisting on the immediate relinquishing of all U-boats – the freedom of the seas had always been an important issue for the United States. The final list also demanded the surrender of 5,000 heavy guns, 3,000 trench mortars, 36,000 machine guns, 2,000 aeroplanes (including the entire fleet of the latest Fokker D-VII fighter) and a big chunk of the High Seas Fleet in addition to the U-boats. This formidable list worried the Americans, and on 31 October "Colonel" House, on Wilson's behalf, asked Foch whether he believed that the war should continue or the Allies should seek an armistice? Foch replied: "I do not make war simply to make war ... the aim being achieved through an armistice ... no-one has the right to spill another drop of blood."

On 5 November, Wilson told the Germans that he was prepared to discuss an armistice, but that Foch would present the Allied terms. By then Germany was collapsing into anarchy. The Social Democratic Majority was warning two days later that they might pull out of the government, and that nationwide revolution threatened, unless the Kaiser went. On 9 November, Prince Max was forced to try and pacify popular opinion by announcing the Kaiser's abdication – slightly ahead of schedule.

On that day, as Foch was rallying Allied commanders for a possible final hammer blow, at Spa the Kaiser confronted his fate. Facing his generals, his belief that loyal troops would be despatched to quell the revolutionaries back home was rebuffed by Groener. German would fire on German: it could mean a civil war. But the generals were not even sure whether their weary and disgruntled army could be relied on. Groener told his master the unpalatable truth: he must abdicate. The incredulous "All Highest" stammered out: "but what about the soldiers' Blood Oath of loyalty?" Groener replied coldly: "The army no longer stands behind Your Majesty. The Blood Oath is only a form of words." Wilhelm II duly abdicated, fleeing the next day to Holland as Imperial Germany collapsed into a leaderless vacuum of competing states, politicians, soldiers, revolutionaries and starving citizens.

As revolutionaries across Germany tried to seize power, and in Munich the Independent Socialists under Kurt Eisner proclaimed a Bavarian Workers' Republic, the King of Bavaria abdicated, too. Prince Max stood down as chancellor to be replaced by the Majority Leader of the *Reichstag*, Friedrich Ebert, leader of the Social Democrats. To forestall a Bolshevik-style revolution, his colleague, Philipp Scheidemann, announced on the *Reichstag*'s steps the creation of a new workers' republic. Imperial Germany was no more.

One of Prince Max's last acts had been to choose the leader of the Centre Party, the Catholic Matthias Erzberger, to meet the Allies and get an immediate ceasefire. Erzberger was shocked by the General Staff now telling him to hurry with his mission, "as the Front could be broken from one minute to the next". By 7 November he was on his way to meet Foch face to face.

He travelled with Hindenburg's injunction ringing in his ears: "Go with God's blessing and try and obtain as much as you can for our homeland."

91

QUEEN MARY'S UNION JACK
THE ARMISTICE

11 NOVEMBER 1918

On 7 November 1918, a cavalcade of cars from German High Command headquarters at Spa, in eastern Belgium, rumbled through the night straight towards the enemy. As they neared the lines, a French bugler on the running board of the leading vehicle sounded a warning call to alert sentries not to shoot at the strange procession. It was carrying the German envoy Matthias Erzberger and his delegation, charged with procuring a ceasefire at all costs. It would take another four days, but an armistice there was. On 11 November the war ended, and the Allies had won a great victory.

> As news of the Armistice spread across London, people went wild. Big Ben chimed for the first time in years, having been silent during the war. Air-raid warning rockets burst overhead and Boy Scouts raced through the streets shouting out the news. Everywhere crowds thronged the streets. One woman officer worker in Kingsway remembered how "we tore out of the building. And we tore down the Strand. And the extraordinary thing was, before you could sneeze, there were thousands and thousands of tiny little Union Jacks everybody was holding. And we were carried right up to Oxford Circus in that crowd. It was quite terrifying." A mass of excited people gathered in front of Buckingham Palace, cheering for the king and the queen. It was, Queen Mary noted in her diary, "the greatest day in the world's history ... at 11 we went on to the balcony to greet the large crowd which had formed outside. At 12.30 we went out again & the massed bands of the Guards played the National Anthem." In the evening, after dinner, the royal couple went out for a third time and witnessed "another wonderful scene". During one of these appearances, the normally restrained queen waved this Union Jack at the crowd. For her and the king, as for all their peoples, the war had been a terrible ordeal. Now it was over, brought to an end by, in Queen Mary's words, "a day full of emotion & thankfulness – tinged with regret at the many lives who have fallen in this ghastly war".

Any notion that there was going to be much room for negotiation would soon evaporate. By 8 November the German delegation arrived at Tergnier, in Picardy, to be housed in a special train. The next day it moved to the Forest of Compiègne to arrive alongside Foch's command train hiding under the trees: Foch had deliberately chosen not to meet the Germans at his HQ at Senlis, because he felt it might be a target for a last-ditch bombing raid to scupper the talks. The Allied delegation of Foch and Admiral Sir Rosslyn Wemyss for Britain (there was no US representative) received the Germans coldly. Foch began by asking why they were present. After

"HISTORY HAS NO MORE GLORIOUS DAY THAN YESTERDAY, WHICH SAW THE END OF THE GREAT WORLD WAR AND THE TRIUMPH OF GREAT BRITAIN AND HER ALLIES. GERMANY, BEATEN IN THE FIELD, MENACED BY CERTAIN INVASION AND OVERWHELMED BY INTERNAL REVOLUTION, CAPITULATED TO THE ALLIES"

Daily Mirror, *12 November 1918*

some embarrassed cross-questioning, the Germans admitted that they sought an armistice. Foch brightened and told them that if they were here to "*ask for*" a ceasefire, then here were the Allies' conditions, take them or leave them. He was perfectly prepared to continue the war. Faced with this threat, a shocked Erzberger backed down. Germany could not carry on fighting.

Over the next 36 hours of wrangling he tried hard to obtain better terms, to little avail. An envoy was sent back to Spa (Foch refused to accept radio messages) with the final list of Allied demands. The German High Command argued hard for softer terms, stressing the dangers of a Bolshevik-style revolution throughout Europe, their need to retain some weapons to maintain order at home and the impossibility of feeding the German population in the face of the continuing Allied blockade, claiming that it was "unfair". Admiral Wemyss pointed out that Germany had engaged in her own "unfair" blockade using U-boats. Erzberger did, however, get an undertaking that the Allies would see that Germany was not reduced to famine. At 5 a.m. on the morning of 11 November an exhausted Erzberger signed for Germany. The final page was signed three hours later.

At 11 a.m. on the 11th day of the 11th month the guns fell silent. Despite some scattered last-minute fighting, this did indeed prove to be the end of the First World War. The BEF stopped its furthest advance at Mons – the very town where it had fought its first battle in August 1914. By a supreme irony two plaques now stand less than 100 yards apart near the Casteau crossroads there: the first commemorates the very first shot fired by the BEF in 1914; the second honours the very last member of the BEF to be killed in action (a Canadian) at 10.58 on 11 November 1918. Fittingly, Private George Lawrence Price is buried in the nearby St Symphorien cemetery alongside "old man" John Parr, the very first BEF soldier to be killed in far-off 1914.

News of the Armistice travelled fast. Foch immediately took the signed copy back to Paris for Clemenceau, to be read out in the Parliament at 16.00. The BEF sent flash signals to all units ordering "HOSTILITIES WILL CEASE AT 11.00". In the trenches the impact was immediate. British guns fired their last salvoes and stopped. Many batteries fired off all their ammunition to get rid of it. Men on both sides died in the last few hours. Many German machine guns, the scourge of the advancing BEF, kept firing until 11.00 on the dot. There are numerous reports of machine gunners firing one long last burst, standing up and just walking away. One group even walked over and shook hands with their former enemies. Another German was seen to stand up and make a theatrical bow, before disappearing over the hill.

As the artillery finally fell silent many soldiers could not take in the news. While behind the BEF lines celebrations and wild parties took place, for many others the news was greeted with stunned disbelief. The day was often remembered as a strangely quiet one. Soldiers in the trenches mostly sat quietly around campfires talking and remembering, or sleeping. Sentries were still posted. Officers still did their rounds, although they walked around in the open. For units in reserve there were rousing speeches by commanding officers, church services, impromptu football matches and a double issue of rum. The national anthem was sung. Further back, leave trains blew their whistles and soldiers cheered out of the windows as they rattled across northern France to the sound of church bells. At Folkestone leave boats sounded their sirens and foghorns, prompting puzzled soldiers to ask what all the noise was about.

Back in London news of the Armistice was greeted with rapture. Londoners exploded in a spontaneous celebration with drinking and dancing, and a happy

"TO ME THE MOST REMARKABLE FEATURE OF THAT DAY AND NIGHT WAS THE UNCANNY SILENCE THAT PREVAILED. NO RUMBLING OF GUNS, NO STACCATO OF MACHINE-GUNS, NOR DID THE ROAR OF EXPLODING DUMPS BREAK INTO THE NIGHT AS IT HAD SO OFTEN DONE."

Lieutenant Evans, Royal Welsh Fusiliers, diary entry for 11 November 1918

excitable crowd cheered the royal family as they drove through the West End and the City. Later, thousands surged to Buckingham Palace to roar out "God Save the King". In Paris similar celebrations took place. The church bells of Notre Dame boomed out; France had suffered grievously, and her citizens were relieved that their long nightmare appeared to be over. Americans, because of the time difference, awoke to victory at breakfast time. In Times Square, New York, huge emotional crowds rushed onto the street to sing, dance and cheer.

For many Germans, as for all the populations of the defeated Central Powers, the Armistice inevitably generated complex feelings. On the one hand there was relief. If the war really was ending, the nations' economies would no longer be enslaved to a war effort, the young men no longer dying for increasingly hollow-sounding reasons. But the Armistice raised new and disturbing questions for the vanquished. There would be no quick end to existing miseries and instabilities, especially with winter coming on and 1918's devastating influenza pandemic now entering a more deadly phase.

Of course, the Armistice was just a ceasefire – in theory, war could break out again at any moment. But as the peace held over the days and weeks to come, for the first time in many years the men in uniform could contemplate the future, now they actually *had* a future. The realization that they were going to live came as a surprise to many. For the tired and war-weary soldiers of all nations, from Scotland to Sarajevo where it all began, thoughts began to crystallize around one idea: demobilization. For the Allies, not everyone could be released – for example, 32,000 men of the BEF would be needed to occupy the Rhineland, and demobilization turned out to be slow. And the whole question of re-entry of millions of men back into a civilian society that had, itself, been irrevocably changed by war created new questions, new tensions.

But that was for the future. At least, on 11 November 1918, the Allied Home Fronts and Fighting Fronts could savour the moment.

Armistice Day witnessed explosions of a very different kind to those that typified the war – outpourings of joy, relief, celebration, patriotism, victory. Here, civilians occupy every possible surface on a London bus to cheer the news, and to entertain the passers-by. Some of the occupants of the buildings have also put out flags.

92

"HANG THE KAISER"
THE KHAKI ELECTION

DECEMBER 1918

It is common to talk of the First World War as the first "total war", in which all the human and material resources available to its belligerents were marshalled into a single overriding purpose: the "war effort". The Armistice of 11 November 1918 brought peace, and immediate elation – at least for the Allies. But the reality of peace also brought questions: what now? Would that wartime consensus hold?

From November 1918, the immediate problem was demobilization of the armed services. Impatient to get back to civilian life, and worried lest all the good jobs would be taken by those demobbed before them, the men of the British Army mounted more "strikes" and mutinies in the six months after the Armistice than there ever were during the war. Revolution may have already gripped Russia and Germany, but in Britain, too, emotions ran high, whether inspired by radicalism, wage demands, slow demobilization or the widespread desire to punish Germany. The General Election of 14–28 December 1918 allowed people to have their say for the first time in eight years – and significantly more people than ever before had a voice.

In December 1918, the General Election took place against the background of a completely transformed electoral landscape. The passing of the Representation of the People Act in February 1918 had almost tripled the number of people who could vote. Among them, many strongly believed that the Germans had caused the war and ought now to pay for it – with money and, in the case at least of the Kaiser, with lives. These two key questions, of reparations and responsibility, played a large part in the electioneering, as can be seen in this poster for the election of Captain Albert Martin. He was the Liberal Coalition candidate for Romford. Under the slogan "Trust Martin and help Lloyd George to put things straight", he won comfortably with a majority of over 5,000 votes.

In Britain, politicians had known for some time that women who had done so much on the Home Front (*see* Chapters 29 and 30), and men on the Home and Fighting fronts, must be allowed their say. Yet before February 1918 none of those women, and only those men who were property owners – about three-fifths – were allowed to vote. War highlighted these anomalies, and in the landmark February 1918 Representation of the People Act the franchise was extended to include men over 21 (plus soldiers over 19, on active service) and women over 30 (along with those married to, or a member of, the Local Government Register). In an additional reform, seats were redistributed to industrial towns. At a stroke, the electorate rose from 7.7 million in 1912 to 21.4 million in 1918. Women would not achieve *full* equality until 1928; nevertheless,

"I CANNOT THINK WHAT THESE MEN HAVE GONE THROUGH ... THERE ARE MILLIONS OF MEN WHO WILL COME BACK. LET US MAKE THIS A LAND FIT FOR SUCH MEN TO LIVE IN"

Prime Minister David Lloyd George, speech given in Wolverhampton, 23 November 1918

PARLIAMENTARY ELECTION
1918
ROMFORD DIVISION

VOTE FOR
MARTIN
MAKE GERMANY
PAY FOR THE WAR
AND
HANG THE KAISER

Printed & Published by A. HARVEY, (I. S.C.), 29, Sunningdale Avenue, Barking. and New Road, E.

the veteran campaigner Millicent Fawcett called the Act "the greatest moment in my life".

The election fought under the new Act was dubbed the "Khaki Election", reflecting its war-related issues and the flood back home of men in uniform. Lloyd George swept back to power at the head of a continued Liberal–Conservative Coalition government, on a platform promising a trial for the Kaiser, punishment for Germans who had committed atrocities and indemnities from Germany – and, in the words of his famous pre-election speech, "a fit country for heroes". Asquith was now in Opposition, heading a rump of Independent Liberals. He and the old Liberals would slowly fade into obscurity.

The election did not solve Britain's problems, as 1919 would show: 35 million strike days – a sevenfold increase – with even striking policemen threatening Whitehall, and in January 1919 the sailors on HMS *Kilbride* at Milford Haven hoisted the Red Flag. But, despite these alarms, a British revolution was averted.

Meanwhile, in Paris a new world order was being made.

6

A NEW EUROPEAN LANDSCAPE

93

SIR WILLIAM ORPEN'S *UNKNOWN BRITISH SOLDIER*
THE PARIS PEACE CONFERENCE

JANUARY TO JUNE 1919

The Armistice brought the ending of hostilities and a panoply of interim arrangements to move Europe from a climate of war to a climate of peace. But more was needed to move the Armistice on to the next stage – actual peace treaties. The years 1919 and 1920 saw the emergence of five separate treaties, dealing with all the defeated powers. Their fates were decided at the Paris Peace Conference, in the Palace of Versailles.

Thus, for the first six months of 1919 the leaders of the great powers descended on the French capital to hammer out an agreement to reshape their world and mould it in a new image. Empires were broken up and horse-traded over tea and biscuits in the Quai d'Orsay; new countries were debated and confirmed – or not. Royalty, politicians, journalists, economists, bankers, political advisors, not to mention the inevitable prostitutes and hangers on, poured into the "City of Light" to make their own unique contributions to building a new world order. Most of them had one overriding aim: to make sure that there could be no more wars on the calamitous scale of what they knew as "The Great War". But noble visions contrasted, as ever, with national interests and personal agendas.

The Imperial War Museum commissioned Sir William Orpen to paint three collective portraits of the proceedings at the Paris Peace Conference as an artistic record for the nation. Orpen had spent considerable time in France during the war, being particularly struck by the stoic resilience of the ordinary soldiers. As the negotiations continued, he became increasingly disenchanted by the politicians. He completed two works, portraying the leading figures in the architectural magnificence of Versailles. But when it came to the third, he found he could not continue. In his memoir he reflected: "The 'frocks' had won the war. The 'frocks' had signed the Peace! The Army was forgotten." From this painting, *To the Unknown British Soldier in France*, which shows the entrance to the Hall of Mirrors, he removed all the famous personalities he had already inserted and replaced them with the flag-draped coffin of the Unknown Warrior, flanked by two emaciated, half-dressed soldiers standing beneath a pair of hovering cherubs. Displayed at the Royal Academy in 1923, the painting was a popular success but a critical disaster. Perplexed, the Museum refused to accept it. Five years later, Orpen wrote to the Director General and offered to rework the image, removing the soldiers and the cherubs to leave behind only the image that exists today. The painting would be a gift, he explained, in memory of Earl (Sir Douglas) Haig who had died only a few weeks earlier, "one of the best friends I ever had".

> "WE WERE JOURNEYING TO PARIS, NOT MERELY TO LIQUIDATE THE WAR, BUT TO FOUND A NEW ORDER IN EUROPE ... FOR WE WERE BENT ON DOING GREAT PERMANENT AND NOBLE THINGS."
>
> *Harold Nicolson, a junior official at the Peace Conference, in his* Peacemaking 1919, *published in 1935*

An aeronautical graveyard. Aircraft of the now defunct German Luftstreitkräfte *("air forces") are broken up as demanded by the terms of the Treaty of Versailles in June 1919. The reduction of Germany's military capability to a small home-defence army, devoid of naval or air power, was an overt aim of the treaty.*

By the end of the war, the nations who had joined the Allies had mushroomed – they included Siam and Liberia, along with Brazil and a clutch of Central American countries. Over 30 national Members therefore got a place at the Peace Conference, with each of Britain's Dominions wanting – and gaining – separate representation. Nevertheless, it was the Big Three of President Wilson, Lloyd George and Clemenceau of France, with Prime Minister Vittorio Emanuele Orlando of Italy who would dominate the proceedings. Ostensibly, they came together to create a peace settlement that would not only formally end the Great War, but also usher in an era of permanent peace. In reality, they came determined to agree upon a settlement that would keep Germany down, albeit tempered by liberal-democratic ideals, and that would remove, or at least control, catalysts for future conflict. Wilson's call for a peace based on his Fourteen Points (*see* Chapter 82) and self-determination was widely supported – not least by the defeated Central Powers, as it seemed their best chance to salvage something. They were to be seriously disappointed.

Part of the problem lay in different agendas. Belgium and France had suffered grievously and wanted reparations – compensation for damage and loss suffered – and above all they wanted future security from any German threat. Britain had already achieved most of her war aims: the High Seas Fleet was in British hands (*see* Chapter 94); German economic competition was crushed for a generation; and German colonial ambitions were now a memory. Wilson insisted that there should be "peace without victory", believing that that if Germany were treated too harshly she might seek revenge and start another war. He insisted that the very first agenda item should be the formation of a League of Nations to keep the peace in future. In order to agree the many ideas being put forward, a Council of Ten – later called the "Supreme Council" – was set up, which by March had become the "Council of Four" (the same Big Three and Orlando). The Council met morning and afternoon to discuss key issues as they arose. The leaders soon realized that they needed a plenary session every week to ratify their decisions and to keep the journalists content. One early worry was the growing realization that the victorious Allied armies were shrinking rapidly and the option of invading Germany to enforce terms – should they ever need to – was fading by the day.

The personalities of the three key leaders were very different. Wilson came to Europe like some transatlantic Messiah, determined to show that American values and political ideas were applicable for the good of all mankind and driven by a pure motive of spreading democracy. Cynics – including Lloyd George and Clemenceau

– pointed out that these ideas, coming from a nation that controlled a Pacific empire from Hawaii to the Philippines and which had moved into Bolshevik Russia smartly enough, smacked of hypocrisy.

Lloyd George was very different. He was the energetic, pre-eminent British politician of his day, riding high after election victory at home, but also had a reputation as a slippery pragmatist of no fixed values; in "Colonel" House, the US advisor's, words, he was "a mischief-maker who changes his mind like a weather cock". Clemenceau's judgement of the slippery Welshman was harsher: "Lloyd George is a trickster … I don't like being double-crossed." Sandwiched between Lloyd George and Wilson was, Clemenceau was to growl, "like sitting between Napoleon and Jesus Christ".

Wilson's demand for a League of Nations to control his new world order was soon dealt with: Lloyd George went along to keep Wilson happy, as did Clemenceau, who believed that the League was theoretically a good idea but would never work (*see* Chapter 95). Diplomatic niceties such as the clash between the United States' so-called "Monroe Doctrine", which claimed South/Central America solely as a US sphere of influence, and the League's supposed powers were brushed under the carpet after Wilson burst out with an impassioned lecture about how "American values and principles of liberty and independence stood as a perpetual charter for the whole world". The startled delegates moved on rapidly to safer topics.

Russia presented a major problem: she was theoretically one of the victorious belligerents, despite the Treaty of Brest-Litovsk with Germany. But the Allies did not recognize the Bolshevik regime – indeed, the Western Allies were already intervening to protect their interests and support counter-revolutionaries (*see* Chapter 97). And anyway the Bolsheviks spurned such niceties as international diplomacy. The subversive international influence of Bolshevism, Lenin's flat refusal to pay Russia's debts, plus the murder of the former Tsar and his family in July 1918 sent a shiver down European politicians' spines. From his transatlantic perspective, Wilson took a loftier view, appearing to believe that the Bolshevik revolution just might be seen in the American revolutionary tradition, and that something akin to "the Swedish Social Democratic model" could emerge. The result was that the conference never really came to an agreed view about Lenin's Russia. Lloyd George worried that they "risked spreading Bolshevism by trying to stamp it out", and the powers opted to isolate Red Russia by blockade and provide dwindling support for the anti-Bolshevik Whites, while letting the locals sort it out for themselves.

The other big absentees were the Central Powers, and notably Germany. The Entente Allies were bitter. Their millions of dead stood as a mute reproach to any calls for leniency. The idea that the defeated should expect little mercy from their victors resonated strongly in France, and Clemenceau looked for victory with vengeance. His aims were clear: to punish Germany; to make the Germans pay for *all* the damage they had done to France and Belgium; to recover Alsace and Lorraine; and to restrict German military power to ensure that it was forever weaker than France. The Germans were not consulted – the treaty talks were never a *negotiation* with Germany, however much German politicians and generals had expected them to be. Like the other defeated countries, Germany was, in historian Norman Stone's dry comment, "just expected to sign on the dotted line". German protests that they had surrendered on the basis of Wilson's Fourteen Points and were now being cheated were dismissed by the Allies, pointing out with some justice that after Germany's own savage terms at Brest-Litovsk they must expect little better from their own conquerors.

"THE TREATY INCLUDES NO PROVISIONS FOR THE ECONOMIC REHABILITATION OF EUROPE – NOTHING TO MAKE THE DEFEATED CENTRAL EMPIRES INTO GOOD NEIGHBORS, NOTHING TO STABILIZE THE NEW STATES OF EUROPE, NOTHING TO RECLAIM RUSSIA."

John Maynard Keynes, in
The Economic Consequences
of the Peace, *1919*

Meanwhile, the peacemakers turned their attention to creating a new and supposedly more peaceful Europe. New countries sprang up in the Balkans – where the war had been sparked – from the now defunct Austro-Hungarian Empire: not only a separate Austria and Hungary, but a new Czechoslovakia and a "Kingdom of the Serbs, Croats and Slovenes" – Yugoslavia. Greece won the defeated Bulgaria's Thracian coast along the Aegean, and Bulgaria lost western border lands to the new Yugoslavia, too. Romania absorbed Transylvania.

An independent Poland was created and given a slice of Germany to provide it with a curious corridor to the Baltic, thus splitting the old Prussian states and isolating East Prussia – to create a serious international hostage to fortune. Danzig (modern Gdansk, in Poland) became an independent Free City, under the auspices of the new League of Nations. The Baltic states of Lithuania, Latvia and Estonia reappeared on the map, along with Finland. Italy was rewarded by northeastern frontiers now expanded to take in the Trentino, South Tyrol and Istria, from Austria.

At the edge of Europe, the Ottoman Empire was broken up, reduced to Anatolian Turkey, though retaining its small strip of mainland Europe beyond Constantinople. She lost control of the sea route from the Straits to the Black Sea to an international regime. The problem of the former Ottoman territories of the Middle East was solved by the device of "mandates", a legal method for transferring control of one country to another under a cloak of League of Nations' responsibility. (Many of these were agreed during Wilson's absence from the conference.) As a method of parcelling out the spoils of victory, mandates seemed to have much to recommend them. After a bitter squabble, the British failed to back the Arab claims for an independent kingdom with Damascus as its capital (*see* Chapter 89), so France came to acquire Syria (including modern Lebanon), while Britain got territory to the east ("Trans-Jordan"), much of Mesopotamia (to be renamed Iraq) and Palestine.

Five treaties emerged from the Paris Peace Conference during 1919–20, including the Treaty of St Germain (with Austria), Neuilly (with Bulgaria), Trianon (with Hungary) and Sèvres (with Ottoman Turkey – later superseded). But the main Treaty of Versailles was with Germany. When the details of the proposed terms were passed to Germany on 7 May, the immediate response was outrage at the nature of this "*diktat*" (as it was called) and a lengthy list of written complaints, most of which were simply ignored.

The final terms of the Treaty of Versailles were judged as harsh. The blame for the war was placed firmly on Germany. The "War Guilt Clause" (Article 231) in particular rankled. How could Germany be the only country to blame for the war, when it was sparked by a Serbian hothead assassinating an Austro-Hungarian archduke? Germans believed that they were being made the scapegoats for everything that had happened since. The detailed articles of the treaty deprived Germany of just over 13 per cent of her 1914 territory and 10 per cent of her population, around 7 million people. Part of East Prussia was handed over to Lithuania, and the ethnic German Sudetenland to Czechoslovakia; even Belgium and neutral Denmark got some of Germany. Germany's former colonies in Africa became mandates, passing to Britain, France and South Africa, while Australia, New Zealand and Japan retained the former German Pacific islands.

Germany was also ordered to pay reparations of around 226 billion gold marks by the Inter-Allied Reparations Commission – equivalent to about £284 billion in today's prices. The German army was reduced to a paltry 100,000 men; the navy

Georges Clemenceau (left), Woodrow Wilson (centre) and David Lloyd George (right) attend the Peace Conference at Versailles. Italy's prime minister, Vittorio Emanuele Orlando, was the fourth major Allied leader present, but in practice it was the other three who dominated proceedings.

to six warships and no submarines; and all military aircraft were to be destroyed. Heavy artillery, gas, tanks and military aircraft were banned. In addition there were to be no German soldiers or military equipment within 30 miles of the east bank of the Rhine. The former Kaiser and some German army officers were held guilty for "war-crimes" – although only about a dozen of them were later tried by the German courts and given light punishments, unlike the Kaiser who got to live out his retirement in the Netherlands.

The Allies also imposed a new form of government on Germany based on proportional representation. It was meant to prevent Germany from being taken over by a dictatorship; instead it would lead to more than 30 competing political parties, none of them big enough to form a government on its own, which did not help to stabilize the fragile new country.

The final act of Versailles was overshadowed by German refusals to sign. The government of Chancellor Philipp Scheidemann resigned: no politician was prepared to put his signature to what was seen as a dishonourable capitulation. Without a government there could be no treaty. The Allies refused to compromise, threatening to start Foch's armies marching again. But Germany's army was now, in Hindenburg's view, too weak to defend the country – renewed war was simply not an option – and Germany was still being blockaded. A new German coalition government was formed, and Germany was given just three weeks to accept the terms of the treaty, take it or leave it. With no alternative, republican Germany's National Assembly voted it through, and two German ministers headed to Versailles,

On 28 June 1919, in a glittering ceremony in the Hall of Mirrors at Versailles, the Treaty of Versailles was finally signed to end the First World War. The next day, the circus broke up as world leaders went home to sell their labours to dubious electorates. Paris rejoiced, *en fête*; in Germany the flags were at half-mast.

Some problems were solved at Versailles. A later generation would have to deal with those that remained – and with those that were *created* on 28 June 1919.

94

A GUN TO SHOOT SEAGULLS
THE END OF THE HIGH SEAS FLEET

NOVEMBER 1918 TO JUNE 1919

When it came to thrashing out the terms of the Versailles Treaty, one issue mattered to Britain above all else: the fate of the German High Seas Fleet. Prior to the war, Anglo-German tensions had revolved around an intense naval rivalry (*see* Chapter 4) and a naval arms race to rival anything seen later in the Cold War. But, despite the dreadnoughts, the war at sea eventually came down to a prolonged attempt by both navies to blockade and strangle the other's economy. By the time admirals of the Allied Armistice Commission and the German navy faced each other across the wardroom table on HMS *Hercules*, on 4 December 1918, the Royal Navy was merely putting the seal on what amounted to the greatest naval victory in its 500-year existence.

The Armistice of 11 November 1918 ordered the surrender of all German U-boats and, under Article XXIII, called for the internment in Allied or neutral ports of 74 named warships, their future to be determined at Versailles. The unvanquished German fleet might have expected better treatment than it received: to be turned over to its principal enemy, and to stagnate for seven months, while its restless, mutinous and hungry crews eked out an existence as virtual floating prisoners.

Only a fortnight after the signing of the Armistice, the 74 warships from the once proud and mighty High Seas Fleet sailed into their enemy's heartland and dropped anchor for the last time. Among the bleak surroundings of Scapa Flow, they resigned themselves to weeks of enervating internment. Technically, they had not surrendered, but few sailors could feel the difference. Slowly the bulk of the 20,000 men who had sailed the ships across the North Sea were returned to Germany until by early December fewer than 4,500 remained. Throughout the winter they remained on board their ships, bored and listless. The terms of the internment barred them from going ashore. Post from home was irregular and censored, even though they were not formal prisoners. But worst of all was the food. All rations came from Germany, which was still locked in the British blockade and enduring another wretched winter of extreme shortages. Supplies were sent twice a month. But the food was of poor quality and very monotonous. To supplement their diet, the men caught fish when they could and killed seagulls for meat. The crew of the destroyer *V125* improvised this gun to shoot at the gulls. A compressed spring inside the metal tube fired a sharp, solid bolt attached to a line that could then be hauled back in, with luck with a bird attached. Ingenious though this may have been, it showed how low the men had sunk, grubbing off the sea to solve their hunger and boredom.

> **"IT IS UNTHINKABLE TO SURRENDER DEFENCELESS SHIPS TO THE ENEMY. WE OFFICERS ARE BOUND BY OUR OATH AND DECISION OF THE ALL HIGHEST TO DESTROY THEM"**
>
> *Rear Admiral Ludwig von Reuter*

The designated warships – 50 destroyers, along with 8 light cruisers, 11 battleships and 5 battlecruisers – arrived off the Firth of Forth on 21 November, to be met by the massed ranks of the Grand Fleet under Admiral Beatty plus representatives of other navies. Led by the cruiser HMS *Cardiff*, two great lines of 44 battleships turned inwards to escort their prisoners north to internment at Scapa Flow. The massive British encirclement was not just a warning. It was also a victory parade at sea, intended to overawe the Germans with an overwhelming demonstration of naval power. At 03.57, Beatty ordered the German flag to be hauled down and not to be hoisted again.

Within days, the German fleet was in internment at Scapa Flow. For the next seven months the German ships rotted at anchor, their crew numbers reduced in December to around 4,500. Rear Admiral Ludwig von Reuter aboard the flagship *Friedrich der Grosse* had major problems. Despite his attempts to preserve the honour of the German navy he found his task humiliating. His sailors were angry at the internment, and at being confined on board their ships. Unlike the British, who lived on board when in port, the Germans had spent most of the war in comfortable naval barracks ashore. Instead, their food and drink was now curtailed and their conditions spartan. They also felt, with some justification, that they should have been interned in a neutral port and allowed ashore. The sailors made their point to their superiors by marching up and down all night on the deck above their admiral's cabin. A sleepless Reuter transferred his flag to the cruiser *Emden*, and had some troublemakers sent back to Germany. But officers increasingly found it difficult to maintain discipline. Many of the sailors had been involved in the Kiel mutinies of early November and were Bolshevik sympathizers. Sailors' councils were formed to be consulted and agree any orders from officers. Only the hope that the fleet would be allowed home after the peace talks kept the once proud German navy together.

As spring turned to summer, the talking at Versailles dragged on, and tensions rose. The fate of the German fleet was a potentially explosive issue. The British wanted to keep as many of the German ships as possible. The French, Italians and Americans wanted as many as they could get, too, but the British were notably wary of bolstering French naval power to potentially competitive levels. The Germans, however, were determined that the Allies would not get their hands on any of their ships. Meanwhile at Scapa, in June 1919, the ships' manpower was reduced further to mere skeleton crews: 75 per battlecruiser, 60 per battleship, 30 per cruiser and the bare minimum for the destroyers.

The crucial moment came when the news arrived that the German government was unwilling to sign the Versailles Treaty by the advertised deadline of 21 June: should the peace talks not succeed, then a state of war would break out again. What Rear Admiral Reuter did not know was that Germany had been granted an extension, and the signing was postponed to 28 June. Believing a crisis beckoned, Reuter resolved to scuttle his entire fleet rather than let the British seize it.

On the morning of 21 June, the British guardships of the 1st Battle Squadron left for exercises. Reuter, believing Germany's shame was imminent, signalled: "Paragraph eleven. Confirm" – the code for immediate scuttle. Below decks the Germans opened seacocks, cooling inlets and condensers. Bulkheads were torn down; watertight doors were jammed open. Crucial damage control equipment was sabotaged. Sea water flooded in, the ships began to settle and the skeleton crews took to the boats.

"AT DUSK AS THE SKY REDDENED OVER THE SCOTTISH HILLS, THE BUGLERS OF THE BRITISH FLEET SOUNDED THE CALL 'SUNSET', THE ENSIGNS OF THE IMPERIAL GERMAN NAVY FLUTTERED SLOWLY DOWN FOR THE LAST TIME. AND DARKNESS CLOSED LIKE A CURTAIN ON THE FINAL ACT OF THIS MIGHTY DRAMA AT SEA."

Rear Admiral W.S. Chalmers, on the German fleet steaming into captivity.

The principal witnesses to this extraordinary, unforgettable event were schoolchildren from Stromness on a boat trip. One of them, James Taylor, later wrote how "Suddenly without any warning and almost simultaneously these huge vessels began to list over to port or starboard." Another recalled "the marvellous display as the German ships sank all around us. In a way it was a very sad sight to see all these men getting into their boats, you really wondered what would happen to them. They had lost all their possessions ... The whole thing was done in such a peaceful way."

The only way to stop the ships from sinking was to tow them ashore. However, the only British warships present were the destroyers *Vespa* and *Vega* plus some auxiliary trawlers. They frantically signalled the 1st Battle Squadron to return at full speed. But, even as they watched, *Friedrich der Grösse* sank at noon, followed by the *Bayern*. Boatloads of German sailors could be seen landing on the islands around Scapa.

By 2 p.m. the British 1st Battle Squadron had arrived, in a desperate attempt to stop the débâcle. Armed Marines boarded the German ships, and nine Germans were shot dead, the last deaths of the war. The British managed to beach the *Baden* and the cruisers *Nürnberg*, *Emden* and *Frankfurt*. At 5 p.m. the last ship, the *Hindenburg*, went under. Over 400,000 tons of modern warships went beneath the waves, the largest ever loss of shipping in a single day.

Fifty-two German ships were sunk that day – out of sight until an intrepid scrap-metal dealer, Ernest Cox, salvaged most of them during the next decade and made himself rich. The few beached survivors, including destroyer *V125*, were later distributed among the Allied navies. In public the British professed themselves outraged by what they claimed was an act of war and a flagrant breach of the Armistice. The German crews were rounded up and thrown into PoW camps. However, a political problem had also gone away. Admiral Wemyss wrote: "I look upon this as a real blessing. It disposes of the thorny question of the distribution of the German ships."

The First World War at sea was finally over.

A deceptively tranquil scene shows the interned German High Seas Fleet, moored in the Orkney Islands setting of Scapa Flow. The quiet was rudely interrupted by Admiral von Reuter's decision to scuttle his ships en masse to prevent them falling into enemy hands.

95

A NEW STAMP FOR A NEW COUNTRY
THE BIRTH OF THE LEAGUE OF NATIONS

1919 TO 1920

Poland has had a long and chequered history. From a medieval commonwealth with Lithuania, to being carved up between Imperial Russia, Prussia and finally the Austrian Habsburgs in 1795, Poland's fortunes, and identity, have ebbed and flowed. After centuries of rule by her neighbours, a new independent Poland was just one of the countries brought into existence from the dismantled German, Austrian, Ottoman (and Russian) empires by the Paris Peace Conference (*see* Chapter 93). For their security they looked to another invention from the Paris deliberations and embraced in the Treaty of Versailles: the League of Nations.

Postage stamps are a symbol of national identity. Only *real* countries need stamps. A few weeks into the Arab Revolt, while still in Egypt, T.E. Lawrence designed a set of stamps for Sherif Hussein to confirm and declare the independence of the Hejaz. Lawrence was determined that the look and appearance of the stamps would show they were "an entirely new and independent national issue which had not moulded itself on that of any other Government". They were a statement of arrival, a new badge for a new nation. This "20 marka" postage stamp is from the issue of 1921, which performed the same role for Poland. Before the war, the territory of modern Poland had been split, with part being German, most Russian and the rest Austro-Hungarian. The border between the Central Powers and Russia ran down the middle. For three years, fighting swept over these territories, with ethnic Poles serving on both sides. By 1917, a distinct Polish nation had begun to emerge, strengthened by a specific reference to an independent Poland in President Wilson's Fourteen Points. Fighting between Poland and her neighbours continued long after the war, and it was not until 1921 that the country's borders achieved some stability. It had been a long, tiring struggle to bring Poland back to life. In a neat, understated way, the intensity of this effort was reflected in this stamp. A man, who has cast off his sword, sows the seeds of peace under a rainbow that offers the promise of calm after the storm.

The last of Wilson's Fourteen Points (*see* Chapter 82) had called for the establishment of "a general association of nations" to be formed "for the purpose of affording mutual guarantees of political independence and territorial integrity to great and small states alike". The League had two basic aims: the first was to prevent war by collective action, disarmament and settling international disputes through negotiation and arbitration by the League's Council, and if that failed, to impose economic, then military, sanctions. The second was to promote international

> "IT [A LEAGUE OF NATIONS] WILL ONLY RESULT IN FAILURE … IT WILL PUT A VERY STRONG LEVER INTO THE HANDS OF THE WELL-MEANING IDEALISTS WHO ARE TO BE FOUND IN ALMOST EVERY GOVERNMENT, WHO DEPRECATE EXPENDITURE ON ARMAMENTS"

Sir Maurice Hankey, Secretary to the Cabinet, 1919

cooperation in economic, social and legal affairs such as labour conditions, arms trading, global health and protection of minorities.

It was all easier said than done. These typically ambitious Wilsonian objectives depended on the Great Powers acting as enforcement agents because, crucially, the League lacked any hard power – no armed forces or police to serve in its name and impose its will. Not for nothing had the 17th-century philosopher Thomas Hobbes pointed out that "covenants without swords are but words and of no strength to secure a man at all". Nevertheless, ever since Immanuel Kant's *Perpetual Peace* of 1795, calling for a "league of nations" that would control conflict and establish a peaceful world community, the idea had attracted many. In 1919, the founders of the League of Nations were determined to build a better world and desperate to avoid a repetition of the horrors of the Great War – a goal reflected in the League's Covenant, which referred to "open, just and honourable relations between nations, by the firm establishment of the understandings of international law as the actual rule of conduct among Governments, and by the maintenance of justice and a scrupulous respect for all treaty obligations in the dealings of organised peoples with one another".

The League originally consisted of 42 countries, 26 of which were non-European. At its largest, 57 countries were members. But there were three major absentees at the start: Germany, which was at first not allowed to join; Bolshevik Russia, which refused to join; and the country whose president had actually proposed the birth of the League – the United States. Germany's absence, as a defeated power, was initially no problem for the organization, and Russia was absorbed in her post-revolutionary civil war. Both countries were later admitted. But the American absence was a serious setback.

The US failure to join the League was part politics, part bad luck and partly reflective of how Americans viewed themselves. Many Americans now wanted to extricate themselves from Europe. They were only too conscious of the war's casualties, small though they were compared with Europe's dreadful losses. Isolationism was resurgent, and there was fear that a League would embroil the country in future conflicts. There were worries that the League would interfere with the ability to pursue trade and commerce freely, as well as a lingering suspicion of kow-towing to the Old World empires of Britain and France. Wilson strenuously sought to counter these views, but (literally) a stroke of bad luck intervened. While travelling by train on his hectic nationwide tour to sell the Treaty of Versailles and the League, he suffered a stroke on 2 October 1919. He was then unable to influence the national debate.

In Washington, the politics typified the perpetual struggle between the White House and Congress over the control of foreign policy. Republican opposition to the terms of the treaty and the Covenant's Articles, which defined the League, was led by the powerful Henry Cabot Lodge, Republican Senate Leader and Chairman of the Foreign Relations Committee. Over summer and autumn 1919 Wilson refused to compromise, urging Congressional Democrats to vote down Republican changes. In November 1919, the Senate rejected both Lodge's amended treaty and the full treaty. In March 1920, the now bedridden president tried to get it through again – and met another Senate defeat, by 49 votes to 35.

The nail in the coffin was the looming presidential election in 1920, on the back of an economy that was beginning to slide into recession. Wilson was too ill to stand, and while his Democratic replacement backed the League, the Republican candidate, Warren G. Harding, espoused an anti-League "return to normalcy" – and was elected in a landslide. It effectively killed the issue. The United States went into her own version of "splendid isolation".

Thus, even before its first meeting of delegates in November 1920, the League of Nations had suffered what turned out to be a crippling handicap. Without US membership and with Britain and France too impoverished by the war – militarily, economically and spiritually – to provide firm leadership, the organization was compromised from the start. There were successes, such as the plebiscite that divided Silesia between Poland and Germany, and the arbitrations – between Sweden and Finland over the Aaland Islands in 1921, with Turkey over her claim to Iraqi Mosul in 1924, and in the 1934 war between Colombia and Peru. And the League used the power of moral condemnation in 1925 to stop the Greeks invading Bulgaria.

But the League could not stop wars and grabs by determined belligerents, especially if they were large states. It was ineffective regarding Poland's invasion of western Russia in 1920 or Greece's ill-fated attempt to seize Western Anatolia the same year, which ended with the sack of Smyrna (Izmir) in 1922 and the birth of Atatürk's new Turkey. And in German eyes, since the League was created by the Treaty of Versailles, and in turn was supposed to uphold the treaty, the body remained suspect.

In 1933, the weakness of the League in an era of resurgent nationalism and arms races was clearly demonstrated when, faced with comprehensive condemnation of her invasion of Manchuria, Japan simply walked out, followed by Germany. By 1935 Mussolini's invasion of Abyssinia could only provoke toothless sanctions, and in 1937 Italy left, in the wake of Germany and Spain's departure. Hitler's final seizure of Czechoslovakia and onslaught on Poland in 1939, along with the Soviet Union's invasion of Finland, finally exposed the League's impotence in the face of unabashed aggression.

The League was founded as a response to a world war. It closed its doors for ever in 1946 having failed in its primary purpose: to prevent another one.

Delegates at the inaugural session of the League of Nations, in Geneva, turn to the camera for a photo opportunity (15 November 1920). At this stage, 42 nations had ratified their membership, with the notable – and permanent – exception of the United States. Deeply flawed though the international body was, it provided lessons for the future.

96

THE OLD KAISER'S CROWN
GERMANY IN TURMOIL

NOVEMBER 1918 TO MARCH 1919

The Armistice saved the German army from having to fight a last-ditch battle on Germany's borders to defend the homeland. But while a hostile invasion from the Allies was averted, that did not mean that there would be no foreign soldiers on German soil. It was a condition of the Armistice that the German military should vacate miles of German land not only west of the Rhine, but also east of it, so that Allied contingents could enter and established occupation zones. Cold and hungry Rhinelanders watched with astonishment as the glossy horses and gleaming guns of the BEF's 29th Division clattered across the Cologne Bridge in the first week of December 1918 to set up the "British Army of the Rhine".

British troops were to remain in possession of Cologne for over ten years. It was, and remains, one of Germany's most important cities. A century-old centre for commerce and trade, goods flowed through it, via its major river port but also on the railway. By the 1890s, Cologne's original central station was bursting at the seams and a new *Hauptbahnhof* was built, fronted by a grand new facade and imposing ticket hall. Kaiser Wilhelm II even had his own separate waiting room, adorned with the symbols of Hohenzollern majesty, including a throne. Being a significant link in Cologne's chain of communications, the station was controlled by the British occupying forces, one of whom, Captain A.H. Cooper, was involved in overseeing its administration. He set up his office in the former Royal Waiting Room. Conscious of the revolutionary tides that were sweeping over Germany, Cooper, as he later explained, carefully removed this large, imposing mahogany crown from the canopy over Wilhelm's throne only just in time: hours later, a German gang arrived to strip the room of "all emblems of the old Imperial regime". It was all change in the new Germany.

The British occupied an area roughly between Düsseldorf and Siegburg; to the south, around Koblenz, was the American zone, and to their south the French were based around Mainz. While everyday administration was still in the hands of local authorities, the Allied presence imposed an overarching order. Elsewhere in Germany, things were taking a very different course.

In the febrile atmosphere leading up to the Armistice, the Social Democratic Party (*Sozialdemokratische Partei Deutschlands*, or SPD), which led the *Reichstag*, and the revolutionaries outside it both manoeuvred for advantage. Gustav Noske, a Social Democrat, headed for Kiel to try and harness the sailors' revolt to the Social Democrat cause. But as mass protests and strikes swept the country, mutinous sailors

> "ONLY ONE WEEK AGO, THERE WAS STILL A MILITARY AND CIVIL ADMINISTRATION SO DEEPLY ROOTED THAT IT SEEMED TO HAVE SECURED ITS DOMINION BEYOND THE CHANGE OF TIMES ... YESTERDAY AFTERNOON IT WAS ALL GONE."

Berliner Tageblatt *(newspaper),* *10 November 1918*

were heading home, spreading revolution as they scattered. Around 3,000 went to Berlin to join the Bolshevik-inspired revolutionaries, taking over the Imperial Palace and Stables, and calling themselves "the People's Naval Division". As the Kaiser and his last chancellor fell on 9 November, the SPD in the *Reichstag* tried to head off the radical Left by immediately announcing the foundation of a new German republic, before rapturous crowds.

Friedrich Ebert, the SPD leader, now faced the unenviable task of securing the Armistice, keeping order on the streets and trying to keep the country running as the soldiers came home in their millions. The SPD were mostly moderate socialists, committed to Parliamentary rule. To their left were the Independent Socialists

(USPD), many of whom began to capitalize on the unrest on the streets; some even seized the Berlin police HQ, their leader making himself police chief. In Bavaria, Independent Socialists under Kurt Eisner had effected a coup (though were later to hold elections). Even further to the left were the revolutionary Marxists of the Spartacist League, who drew their support from the slums of Berlin's eastern quarters and demanded nothing less than a full-blown Bolshevik revolution.

The army's generals had stood back from propping up the Kaiser with force. But now, with the streets in ferment, the army intervened. Troops loyal to the government surrounded the Chancellery and arrested prominent Independent Socialists and revolutionaries. Shots were fired and soldiers opened fire on a Spartacist demonstration, killing 16. By 11 December 1918 no fewer than nine army divisions had returned to Berlin, and a civil war appeared inevitable – except that most of the soldiers voted with their feet and deserted to get home for Christmas.

The revolutionary People's Naval Division now flexed its muscle by demanding money to disband and marched to the Chancellery to blockade the building. Ebert begged the army's High Command for loyal troops, and a regiment of Guards entered Berlin, blocked the sailors' retreat and an armed standoff ensued. Ebert now panicked and asked the army leadership to withdraw. But General Groener refused: "[We] are determined to hold to the plan of liquidation of the Naval Division, and we shall see to it that it is carried out."

At 7.40 a.m. on Christmas Eve 1918 the army opened fire, blasting the naval mutineers and seized the Imperial Palace and Stables. The sailors raised a white flag. The army then made a fatal mistake by agreeing to the truce, and thousands of protesters sympathetic to the rebels poured onto the streets. Surrounded by civilians, the troops held their fire and army commanders ordered a retreat. Ebert and the SPD government were appalled at the loss of control; conversely, the Spartacists now saw their chance for outright revolution before new elections (to be held in January could

Pro-government forces on the streets of Berlin, the day after the Kaiser abdicated (10 November 1918), anticipating trouble. A fragile power-sharing Cabinet of the SPD and USPD soon fractured, and by December the revolutionary Spartacists and their allies were strong enough to mount a challenge on the streets. Brute force would play a large role in determining events.

give Ebert a democratic mandate. At the end of 1918, the extreme Left formed the German Communist Party (*Kommunistische Partei Deutschlands*, or KPD) and prepared for revolution.

Matters came to a head when the militants and trade unions called a general strike, for 5 January 1919. However, they had not reckoned on the SPD's new enforcers, the *Freikorps*. These were military veterans, hand-picked for their reliability, many of whom had served as stormtroopers on the Western Front but who were now estranged from civilian life and smarting from Germany's defeat. The *Freikorps* phenomenon, with its deep historical roots as a volunteer militia, came to the fore as ex-soldiers banded together, with the army's tacit support, to take the law into their own hands. They were well armed and determined to restore order.

By 6 January 1919, following government attempts to dislodge the USPD police chief, the political situation was spiralling out of control in Berlin with huge protests and a growing expectancy of full-scale revolution. But now the *Freikorps* mobilized. On 11 January, Major Franz von Stephani of the Potsdam *Freikorps* called on the Spartacists to surrender. They refused and opened fire. The superior firepower of the ex-regulars then battered the rebels with artillery, mortars and machine guns. Spartacists who surrendered were executed.

The next day – led by Noske himself, now Defence Minister – other *Freikorps* units moved in to assault the rebel stronghold in the police headquarters. No quarter was given as the *Freikorps* stormed the building. On 13 January, the government unleashed its full repertoire of measures: massive searches, roadblocks, the breaking up of protest meetings by force, a civilian curfew, street shootings and the arrest of suspected revolutionaries. The two Spartacist leaders Karl Liebknecht and Rosa Luxemburg were captured and executed out of hand, achieving lasting fame as revolutionary martyrs. By 15 January the general strike was called off and the Bolshevik-Spartacist revolution collapsed.

The promised elections went ahead, on 19 January, and the SPD won with 40 per cent of the vote. A new National Assembly gathered at Weimar, well away from the revolutionary ferment of Berlin. But uprisings continued to flare up across the country, though the *Freikorps* was there to crush each insurgency.

In March 1919, the Spartacists once again tried to seize control, calling for another general strike. *Freikorps* units entered Berlin on 4 March, along with infantry and even a tank, and for a week Berlin was rocked by civil war. The People's Naval Division joined the demonstrators, to be chased into the suburb of Lichtenberg, where 10,000 armed revolutionaries barricaded themselves in for the final showdown. The government issued the notorious order: "Any individual bearing arms against government troops will be summarily shot", and for the next four days the *Freikorps* ran riot in the barricaded slum tenements of East Berlin, with atrocities all round. The Spartacists and rebel sailors were crushed. The casualties were high, but one-sided: up to 1,500 revolutionaries and civilians were dead and roughly 12,000 wounded. The *Freikorps'* losses were negligible. But the results were profound.

The general picture of Germany's politics for the "Weimar Era" was emerging. In the middle stood a fragile democracy, with a myriad of competing parties, whose leaders were unable to prevent the humiliation of the Treaty of Versailles later that year; to the left stood the determined KPD, with which the USPD merged in 1920; to the right stood equally determined ultra-nationalists, the *Freikorps* – and the new German Workers' Party. It would become better known by a later, shorthand name: the Nazi Party.

97

AUGUSTUS AGAR'S BOAT
THE ALLIES VERSUS THE BOLSHEVIKS

1918 TO 1920

The Bolsheviks' unilateral ceasefire in winter 1917, followed by the humiliating Treaty of Brest-Litovsk to which the Germans subjected Russia in March 1918 (*see* Chapters 67 and 82), threw the Western Allies into confusion. Their instincts, mostly, were to help topple the upstart Bolshevik regime and aid the Tsarist ("White Russian") and other local "Green" counter-revolutionary peasant forces, with the aim of restoring Russia as a fighting ally; at the very least, they wanted to secure the war supplies they had sent for the Tsar's army. After the Armistice, they were more interested in destabilizing a regime whose revolutionary ideology was proving too attractive to the discontented across Europe, and already causing havoc in the defeated Central Powers, notably Germany (*see* Chapter 96). In the end, 14 Allied nations sent troops into Russia, including Britain.

Late in 1918, Lieutenant Augustus Agar RN was asked by "C", the head of Britain's Secret Intelligence Service, to undertake a dangerous and clandestine mission in the Baltic as part of the Allied intervention in the Russian Civil War. Secretly, Agar was to take two fast, shallow draught Coastal Motor Boats (CMBs) and from a covert base in newly independent Finland, only 13 miles from Petrograd, he was to land and recover British agents working deep under cover inside Bolshevik Russia. Agar was a career naval officer who had learned independent thought and initiative. He became deeply concerned at the sight of defenceless White Russian soldiers inside the fortress of Krasnya Gorka being shelled by Red Russian warships. Agar decided to act. Armed with an unofficially obtained torpedo, on the night of 17 June 1919 he took this boat, *Coastal Motor Boat 4*, and under cover of darkness penetrated the Bolshevik destroyer screen surrounding the Russian cruiser *Oleg*. Throwing caution to the wind, Agar launched his strike, then raced away as fast as possible. All the Russians guns immediately leapt into action. But it was too late. The torpedo hit home and the *Oleg* exploded. Turning and twisting, Agar escaped unscathed and returned in triumph to his secret headquarters. It had been an intrepid and audacious act, in keeping with the finest traditions of the Royal Navy. But it was part of a secret war. Agar's deeds could not at first be publicly acknowledged. Instead, he simply became known as "the mystery VC".

Murmansk, on the Barents Sea, had been built as an ice-free port to accept (mainly British) supplies during the war, and an 800-mile railway connected it with the interior. Over 160,000 tons of war stores lay on the docks by mid-1918 and the British naval squadron based there could do little to prevent the Bolsheviks removing the *matériel*, without payment, to Moscow, which Lenin had proclaimed as Russia's new capital. In June 1918, British, French and US forces – along with Canadians, Italians and Serbs – landed at Murmansk, and in August at Archangel, on the White Sea inlet. Apart from trying to secure the *matériel*, a rather more strategic goal was to send forces south to try and link up with elements of the Czech Legion, considered the most powerful Allied asset in the country (*see below*). The British force headed south by rail to check the line and encountered a train-load of Red Guards heading north. Fighting broke out and soon British, American and French contingents were digging in to protect the ports, with the cooperation of local anti-Bolshevik groups, against the encircling Reds. An American-led advance south along the River Dvina ran into heavy fighting until the winter of 1918–19 forced both sides into a series of isolated skirmishes in sub-zero temperatures. With the spring of 1919 came the decision to withdraw, and by October 1919 the last of the Allied forces left Archangel, to be followed by the evacuation of Murmansk.

Meanwhile, the Royal Navy attempted to support the firmly anti-Bolshevik forces of the soon to be independent Baltic states of Latvia, Lithuania and Estonia, by way of a Baltic blockade that encompassed the Russian naval base at Kronstadt, near Petrograd. It was conducted by the British Baltic squadron (1st Light Cruiser Squadron), commanded by Rear Admiral Sir Walter Cowan, and used Coastal Motor Boats (CMBs) – some weeks after Lieutenant Agar's unofficial action had shown the way – to torpedo several Russian warships in Kronstadt's harbour, sinking a cruiser and damaging two battleships.

The first act of Allied intervention was, however, in the Far East, when in December 1917 Japanese troops landed, sensing an opportunity to move into eastern Russia and control Vladivostok – to the initial alarm of the United States. There were at least half a million tons of Allied war supplies lying on the dockside and – initially – no Bolsheviks in sight. Also heading towards Vladivostok from the west, by May 1918, were as many as 60,000 men of the so-called "Czech Legion" – Czech and Slovak nationalists, who had been fighting with the Russian Imperial Army. When Red Guards attempted to disarm them, at the behest of the Germans in the aftermath of Brest-Litovsk, a battle ensued, and the legion began an extraordinary fighting trek eastwards along the Trans-Siberian Railway, which it eventually controlled east of the Volga.

With the aim of evacuating the legion, along with Austro-Hungarian PoWs in Siberia whose nationalist tendencies made them potential Allied recruits, a multinational force including 7,000 Americans landed at Vladivostok in August 1918. By September 1918 the Czechs, strung out along the railway corridor, had steamrollered in their armoured trains as far as Lake Baikal, pausing to fight ad-hoc naval actions there against Bolshevik patrol boats, and even capturing a hoard of imperial gold. They reached Vladivostok, but after the Armistice, Czechoslovakia's president ordered those remaining Czechs to support (with the British and French) the White Russian campaign led by Admiral Alexander Kolchak in Siberia.

American forces were more cautious, though they helped the Czechs guard the Trans-Siberian Railway, which they did for much of 1919. The British contingent in Siberia, after an initial battle with Red Guards, moved west to Omsk for the winter of 1918–19. There they supported Kolchak, who had taken over the "Supreme Leadership" of the anti-Bolsheviks and had set up a White Russian government in Irkutsk. All civil wars tend to be merciless, but Kolchak's rule specialized in a brutal oppression, one of his orders reading: "Those villages whose population meets troops with arms, burn down the villages and shoot the adult males without exception. If hostages are taken in cases of resistance to government troops, shoot the hostages without mercy." Not surprisingly, his methods drove the infuriated peasantry of Siberia into the Bolsheviks' camp.

In December 1918, the British and French began to back the equally unsavoury White General Anton Denikin in southern Russia and the Crimea, despite his series of pogroms based on a conviction that the Bolsheviks were "the evil force which lives in the hearts of Jew-Communists". British and French ships supported actions by Denikin and General Peter Wrangel along the Black Sea coast from 1919, but in 1920 were having to evacuate defeated White Russians from the region.

The Western Allies, and even the Germans postwar, continued to try and undermine the Bolshevik regime. Germans left in Finland helped defend that country, while the French supported newly independent Poland in her 1919–21 war with Russia. But Allied policy regarding the Bolsheviks, as shown during the Paris Peace Conference, was inconsistent, and their forces in Russia were never big enough to sway the outcome; their main support was supplying arms and ammunition to Kolchak

A young Bolshevik volunteer, pictured c.1919, is armed for action with hand grenades and a bolt-action rifle. A mixture of idealism, terror, superior organization and sheer numbers came together to create, in the Red Army, a force coherent enough to see off the challenges of White Russian armies, Allied intervention forces and other opponents.

and the other Whites. But the White forces were vastly outnumbered by the millions of soldiers in Trotsky's new and potent Red Army, who advanced, picking off and defeating their rivals piecemeal, from the invading Poles at the gates of Petrograd to the Don Cossacks of the south.

By the end of 1919 the Bolsheviks were even advancing east against Vladivostok, and their opponents were falling apart from desertion, lack of food, typhus and a general collapse of hope and morale. By 1920 most of the Allies in Siberia had left, including the last of the Czech Legion, having swapped its gold for a truce with the Bolsheviks. On 25 October 1922, Vladivostok fell to the Red Army – and the last anti-Bolshevik government was extinguished.

The Russian Civil War had been a bloody affair. But it did have a clear result: Communist Russia – the Soviet Union. The Allies' failure to strangle it at birth would have dramatic consequences for the course of the 20th century.

98

THE FAMOUS NÉRY GUN
THE CREATION OF THE IMPERIAL WAR MUSEUM

1917 TO 1920

In 1914, the widespread recruitment of "Kitchener volunteers" and the Pals battalions in particular (*see* Chapters 8 and 9) created direct connections between many British villages, towns and cities and the events of the war. The legacy of that connection continues to this day. That early flood of volunteers reflected the widespread civic pride felt by communities large and small, as their men marched off to war. Come 1916, as the casualties among these volunteers on the Somme sank in, individual communities became increasingly conscious of the sacrifices that were being made.

The breadth and depth of this feeling could not be compared to Britain's colonial wars, even one as large as the Anglo-Boer War. It was like no event that people had experienced before. Its scale and its nature needed to be made sense of. A widespread desire built up to make sure that the men of this unprecedented war, and the dead in particular, be remembered, and that their actions be recorded and understood for generations to come.

The direct result was the establishment of the Imperial War Museum in London.

As a mist-filled dawn broke on 1 September 1914, from positions beyond the French village of Néry, the British 1st Cavalry Brigade suddenly came under intense and accurate German fire. Three 13-pounder field guns of "L" Battery, Royal Horse Artillery, turned to engage the invisible enemy, but two were instantly knocked out. The third continued to fire. Its officer, Captain Bradbury, was mortally wounded, but Sergeant Nelson carried on working the gun. Soon Battery Sergeant Major Dorrell arrived, and between them they kept shooting until all the shells had gone. As the mist cleared, an infantry counterattack brought the action to an end. "The Affair at Néry" became one of the most celebrated episodes of the opening months of the war. The British were outnumbered and overwhelmed, but pluck and tenacity won out. The Germans were beaten, and three men received the Victoria Cross. Out of the battery's six guns, only this one was fit to be driven away. It was returned to Britain, and in 1919 the famous "Néry gun" was among the first artillery pieces to arrive at the Imperial War Museum. It became one of the focal points of the displays in the Museum's first exhibition at the Crystal Palace. Every year on 1 September a large laurel wreath was reverently placed on the gun to commemorate the battery's gallant stand and heavy losses, a practice that continued until the 1950s. Battle-scarred and broken, the gun's physical presence provides a tangible, evocative link with the terror of that day. A hundred years on, it remains one of most powerful objects in the Museum's collection.

"TO US IT STANDS, NOT FOR A GROUP OF TROPHIES WON
FROM A BEATEN ENEMY, NOT FOR THE SYMBOL OF THE PRIDE
OF VICTORY, BUT AS AN EMBODIMENT AND A LASTING
MEMORIAL OF COMMON EFFORT AND COMMON SACRIFICE"

*King George V, at the opening of the first Imperial War Museum at the Crystal Palace, South London,
9 June 1920*

In March 1917, Sir Alfred Mond MP outlined to the Cabinet an ambitious plan to establish a National War Museum. The museum would be broad-based and reflect all levels of society. It would not just be about leading figures, or political or military events, but would cut across class boundaries to ensure the widest possible experience was recorded. It would be about everyone's war.

For Lloyd George, this was an attractive proposition. Heavy casualties, air raids, food shortages and conscription were all straining the nation. The cost of the war seemed high; the return felt low. The new prime minister saw an opportunity to lift morale. The sacrifices of ordinary people would be more tolerable if they were publicly recognized. This new national institution could ensure that future generations understood what the men and women had gone through on their behalf, and reassure contemporaries that their efforts would not be overlooked or forgotten.

Events moved quickly. A steering committee, chaired by Mond, was soon established, with the curator of the Tower Armouries, Charles ffoulkes, appointed Museum Secretary and the Slade Professor of Art at Cambridge, Sir Martin Conway, as Director General. A series of sub-committees were formed to record the work being undertaken by women (*see* Chapters 29 and 30), and the role of the Dominions and of the air services. Charles ffoulkes appealed directly to fighting units for trophies (*see* Chapter 26) and was keen to ensure there would be much in the Museum's eventual displays that old soldiers would recognize. To highlight the efforts of individuals, he appealed in newspapers like the *Daily Mail* for details of soldiers' services to be sent to the Museum together with photographs. A steady stream of responses began to flow in.

A Canadian officer, Major Henry Beckles Willson, was appointed the Museum's field agent. Beckles Willson believed that the collections should reflect the detail of battle and the involvement of ordinary soldiers at ground level. From late spring 1917, he set about his task with great enthusiasm and energy, meeting both soldiers and French civilians, and observing and collecting wherever he could (*see* Chapter 66).

Inevitably, much of the first material he acquired related to the Somme, including the steel helmet worn by Private William Short VC (*see* Chapter 48).

While these initiatives were underway, ffoulkes, Conway and Mond also began to think in more detail about what role the new Museum should fulfil. All wanted to see the Museum take on a more overt role as a national memorial. But the Cabinet was not impressed, remaining sceptical about the suitability of a museum to act as a memorial. They agreed only to establish a ministerial committee under Lord Crawford to examine the proposals in greater depth.

The following month another important development took place. The Dominions sub-committee suggested that, as so many soldiers from Canada, Australia, New Zealand and South Africa were fighting with the British armies, it should not be a National War Museum, but an Imperial War Museum. This apparently small change, adopted in January 1918, ultimately amounted to a fundamental recasting of the Museum's purpose, giving it a very special status. Instead of being concerned solely with Britain and Ireland, the new Imperial War Museum would concern itself equally with the wider contribution of the other nations of the British Empire (*see* Chapter 69), embracing a wider common wealth (in the literal sense) of history.

A week before the great crisis of the German spring offensives began in March 1918, Lord Crawford's committee finally delivered its verdict. It did not agree with the idea that the Museum should also be a national memorial, which naturally disappointed the Museum. But Conway clung to the hope that the Cabinet might still come round. As it was, soon the people themselves made their voices heard and answered the questions of how, and where, the nation should remember its dead: a temporary Cenotaph in Whitehall soon gave way to a permanent structure and the Tomb of the Unknown Warrior allowed over a million pilgrims to pay their respects within a week and lay their ghosts to rest (*see* Chapter 100).

So quickly and firmly were the Cenotaph and the Unknown Warrior established as the rightful symbols for the national memory of the "Great War", that no possibility remained of this function being carried out by the Imperial War Museum. Instead, the Museum turned to fulfilling the two key tasks that only it could undertake: creating a place of learning and scholarship, where the war could be studied and more closely understood; and, above all, providing a living exhibition, constantly reconfigured to record and interpret for changing generations the events and experiences that had made the First World War a unique global event.

Early in 1920 it was agreed that the Museum's first galleries would open in the Crystal Palace, Sir Joseph Paxton's celebrated glass and cast-iron exhibition hall then in Sydenham, South London, though originally adorning Hyde Park for the Great Exhibition of 1851. Displays were put together in just six weeks; over 400 tons of material were installed, from a collection already estimated at more than 136,000 items. Prominent among them was "Mother", the first 9.2-inch howitzer (*see* Chapter 35), and the naval gun that fired the first British shell of the war (*see* Chapter 10).

Initial visitor numbers were high – 2.5 million in the first year. But what did the future hold? What role would the Museum continue to play as the generation of 1914–18 faded away? King George V gave some insight, when he opened the Museum on 9 June 1920. He explained that the museum was not about "trophies won from a beaten enemy", nor about "the pride of victory", but rather "a lasting memorial of common effort and common sacrifice" and a record of the impact of war upon ordinary people's lives. And so it continues to be.

99

GUNNER MILLER'S CROSS
WAR GRAVES & REMEMBRANCE

FROM 1918

After the First World War, something like a collective case of Post-Traumatic Stress Disorder set in. The realization that something enormous had happened overwhelmed the combatant countries. The sheer magnitude of loss sank in as millions of individual deaths combined to become huge, almost incomprehensible, numbers. Individual families grieved over their sons, brothers, husbands and fathers; factories, schools, colleges, villages, towns – all kinds of communities – tallied up their losses. The results were unprecedented manifestations of commemoration – indeed, the creation of the modern concept of war remembrance – expressed in everything from the names carved in a school's roll of lost alumni to the grand monuments on the Western Front. But first there was the urgent matter of burying the dead.

Reginald Miller was a 19-year-old gunner in "B" Battery, 190th Brigade, Royal Field Artillery. In March 1918, the brigade arrived back on the Western Front after four months in Italy, going straight into the line with the rest of the 41st Division, northeast of the old 1916 Somme battlefields. But on 21 March the Germans struck, and everyone retreated. Soon the British were back where they had been in February 1917. The exhausted 41st was ordered north to Flanders to recover. On 2 April, its infantry boarded buses at Bienvillers, but the gunners stayed behind. It made no difference to Reginald Miller: on that day, he was killed and buried nearby. Bienvillers Military Cemetery was first used from September 1915 to March 1917. In March 1918, it was reopened and used again for six months. It was here that Reginald Miller came to rest, 200 miles from his home in South London. This, his original grave marker, was apparently made from fence posts. In the middle of the hand-painted details, the Graves Registration Unit placed one of its regular zinc strips to confirm his name and details. After the war the Imperial (now Commonwealth) War Graves Commission rebuilt the cemetery at Bienvillers and replaced the original crosses with headstones. As with many grieving families, Miller's parents had his wooden cross sent back so that it could act, as it still does, as a poignant reminder of just one of the hundreds of thousands of British and Commonwealth soldiers who were killed on the Western Front.

Between 1914 and 1918 Britain lost over three-quarters of a million dead; France 1.4 million; Germany 2 million; Canada 65,000 and Australia 62,000; even little New Zealand lost 18,000 men, a proportion comparable to Britain's. Russia's losses have never been accurately assessed but are accounted as at least 5 million. Overall, the war had cost over 16 million dead, of whom about 10 million were military and the

> **"THESE MEN, BE THEY OFFICERS OR RANK AND FILE, WHO FELL, DIED WITH THE SAME COURAGE AND THE SAME DEVOTION AND FOR THE SAME CAUSE, AND THEY SHOULD HAVE THEIR NAMES AND THEIR SERVICES PERPETUATED BY THE SAME MEMORIAL."**

Herbert Asquith, debating in Parliament whether war graves should have a uniform design, 4 May 1920. As Asquith noted, "There are some of us, of whom I am one, who have a direct and personal interest in this matter": his own son was a war casualty.

rest civilians. Another 20 million men had been wounded. The horrific "butcher's bill" was the worst in recorded history – up to that time.

So much death, meted out on chaotic battlefields, made for an immediate problem in the days after the Armistice. Hundreds of thousands of bodies remained unburied, while others lay in temporary or shallow graves. Among the debris of war, skeletons and rotting body parts had to be buried – and quickly. In the chaos of the Eastern Front, mass graves were dug, although many of the dead just lay where they had fallen. However, on the Western Front a huge effort was made to observe the decencies.

Germany had left many of her sons in the earth of France and Flanders. But after the war reluctant French and Belgian farmers gave up the smallest plots of land they could get away with and shovelled German corpses into mass graves as quickly as possible. The German War Graves Commission (*Volksbund Deutsche Kriegsgräberfürsorge*), founded under the Treaty of Versailles, became responsible for the discovery and upkeep of the German war dead, and by 1925 began consolidating remains from the thousands of scattered Flanders graves into 128 cemeteries. In 1954, these were concentrated into just three large cemeteries – at Langemarck-Nord, Vladslo and Menin – along with 25,000 unnamed dead reburied under the huge concrete slab of the "Comrades Grave" (*Kameradengrab*) at Langemarck. Vladslo contains 25,662 bodies, plus a mother's powerful tribute to her dead son in the shape of Käthe Kollwitz's world-famous statues *The Parents*, showing two kneeling figures wracked by grief. But the largest German military cemetery on the old Western Front is in France at Neuville Saint Vaast, near Arras. Like the others it is a "concentration cemetery", with many soldiers buried four to a grave, and contains the remains of 44,833 German soldiers, 8,040 of them unidentified and buried in a common grave.

France also has some very large cemeteries and, in the French tradition, a number of ossuaries, of which Verdun's is the biggest. Perched high on the ridge overlooking Fort Douaumont, Verdun's Monument contains the bones of 130,000 unknown French and German soldiers who fell on the battlefields there. Bleached skulls stare out, sightlessly, over this French National Cemetery with its 15,000 graves of French soldiers, "*mort pour la patrie*". As in other French cemeteries each grave is marked by a simple white cross with a name plate. French Muslim soldiers from North Africa are buried beneath a suitable gravestone facing towards Mecca.

Further north in Artois is the largest French National Cemetery and Memorial anywhere, covering wars from 1914 to the Algerian War. Its imposing chapel and monument of Notre Dame de Lorette, with its basilica and the remains of 39,985 French soldiers, commemorates the sacrifices made to seize Vimy Ridge in 1915 and the attack on Notre Dame de Lorette itself. Four mass graves contain the unidentified remains of thousands more. Yet, even those buried here represent only 2.5 per cent of the French war dead of 1914–18. At its dedication in 1922, the Bishop of Arras used words that embrace the loss of all the nations: "she must become the voice which weeps for her youth cut down in its flower, the voice which prays for the eternal rest of their souls, the voice which talks of hope to the widows, fiancées, parents".

The United States suffered under 117,000 casualties, but made sure the dead were laid to rest with fine monuments. The largest war cemetery appropriately enough is at Meuse-Argonne, with its 14,246 graves in over 130 acres of ground. Unexpected nationalities are represented elsewhere. There is a Russian war cemetery at St Hilaire le Grand, on the Marne, with 1,000 graves of the Imperial Russian Special

"THE SACRIFICE OF THE INDIVIDUAL IS A GREAT IDEA AND WORTHY OF COMMEMORATION; BUT THE COMMUNITY OF SACRIFICE, THE SERVICE OF A COMMON CAUSE ... THESE ARE GREATER IDEAS, WHICH SHOULD BE COMMEMORATED IN THOSE CEMETERIES WHERE THEY LIE TOGETHER"

Lieutenant Colonel Sir Frederick Kenyon, War Graves, *report for the Imperial War Graves Commission on the design and purpose of military cemeteries, November 1918*

Edward, Prince of Wales, leads 11,000 British Legion "War Pilgrims" on a march to the Menin Gate (8 August 1928), in Ypres, for a ceremony of remembrance. The very large number of "missing" servicemen – one of the truly shocking aspects of the war – created a need for major communal monuments to honour their collective contribution.

Force, which fought – and then mutinied – on the Western Front from 1917. There is even a cemetery for Czech and Polish volunteers, who fought with the French Foreign Legion, in Artois.

In previous wars, British soldiers who died on campaign were usually buried anonymously in mass graves. Occasionally, individual monuments were erected to officers. By early 1915 it was becoming clear that – as with so much else in this unparalleled war – something different was required. But the BEF was simply not prepared for the scale of its losses and had no effective organization for dealing with them. In October 1914, a British Red Cross Mobile Ambulance Unit under the leadership of a volunteer called Fabian Ware began to plot the known burial sites (*see also* Chapter 59). This was difficult, because individual units buried their own dead, and his unit was soon overwhelmed by the work. The BEF eventually formalized the unit as the Graves Registration Commission in March 1915, and it became the Directorate of Graves Registration & Enquiries (DGR&E) in February 1916. Its Military Graves Registration Units became responsible for recording the burial of the dead and plotting the location of military cemeteries. The ground for permanent graves was confirmed by a French law in December 1915, which granted land to be maintained as a *sépulture perpétuelle* for British war dead.

The actual work of burying the bodies was often given to battalions "resting" out of the line. It was not a popular task. The 1/19th Battalion, London Regiment, cleared the battlefield after the successful assault on High Wood on 15 September 1916. The divisional chaplain noted: "Many men who have stood it all, cannot stand this clearing of the battlefield ... no words can tell you all I feel, nor can words tell you of the horrors of clearing a battlefield ... several men went off with shell-shock ... caused not just by the explosion of a shell nearby, but by the sights and smell and horror of the battlefield in general."

The BEF worried about the strain this work put on morale. In early 1917 the Adjutant-General noted: "the necessity of provision of some special organisation to undertake burials". He also pointed out: "It is doubtful policy, from the point of view of morale, to use as burial parties troops as may be called upon to fight later."

Ware, by now promoted an acting temporary major general, was also concerned about the problems of military morale and, more important, public perception, writing in June 1917: "We are on the verge over here of serious trouble about the number of bodies lying out still unburied on the Somme battlefields. The soldiers returning wounded or in leave to England are complaining bitterly about it and the War Office has already received letters on the matter." In response to what was a growing problem, the Imperial War Graves Commission (IWGC) came into being by Royal Charter in May 1917, with Ware as its leader, tasked with identifying and interring all the British Empire's war dead.

At the end of the war it was plain that clearing the battlefields of equipment, ammunition, debris and bodies was going to be a major task. Over 160,000 individual graves had to be concentrated and over half a million missing men had to be located and identified. By early 1919, with 587,000 graves identified, a political row blew up over the problem of how to treat the dead. For logistical reasons, repatriation was impossible, but there was heated debate on whether the planned cemeteries abroad should reflect individual families' wishes, with different kinds of memorials and headstones, or whether there should be uniformity. The previous year, a report for the IWGC made the case for uniform designs to prevent any discrimination over rank or class. It also made a distinction between the private family memorial in local parishes, reflecting individual loss, and the sense of communal sacrifice on the battlefields. Eventually, the report's principles won through, and leading architects were engaged for the new cemeteries.

The exhumation of the bodies was a major undertaking. Volunteers were recruited with extra pay of 2 shillings and sixpence per day, with Chinese Labour Corps workers and PoWs drafted in to help. By mid-1919 there were 20,000 men working on the old Western Front. Exhumation Companies had squads of 32 men, who gathered up what they found and carried them away on stretchers soaked with creosol, a coal-tar-based disinfectant.

Not all the work was so grisly: one exhumer reported that: "It's jolly hard work. But it 'as its better side. Some fellers the other day came on a dug-out with three officers in it, and they picked up five thousand francs between 'em." Identification was the most important task. Relatives needed the truth. The workers had to search pockets, the neck, wrists and braces for "dog tags" or any other means of identification. Many of the earlier fibreboard ones had rotted: hence today's metal tags. Most of the corpses were

Remembrance, French style. An early photograph of the ossuary (in the background) and cemetery at Douaumont, Verdun. The cloister, containing the bones of 130,000 French and German dead, and the tower, offering panoramic views, were designed by Léon Azéma, Max Edrei and Jacques Hardy. Opened in 1932, they provided a fitting memorial to what both sides called the "hell of Verdun".

identified by identity discs; about 30 per cent by other methods, such as a name on a cigarette case, or half-rotted letters; and about a quarter were unidentifiable.

By 1921 the first IWGC cemeteries were being built. They had uniform headstones of Portland stone engraved with the man's name, rank, dates, his regimental badge and a maximum number of characters of text chosen by the family. VCs, uniquely, had the medal carved into their headstone. The model chosen was the tranquil cemetery at Forceville, where designer Gertrude Jekyll had created a walled English rose garden. Depending on the size of the cemetery, a Cross of Sacrifice with a bronze crusader's cross of varying sizes, as designed by Sir Reginald Blomfield, stood as a marker; in the bigger cemeteries there was an altar-like stone of remembrance, designed by Sir Edwin Lutyens, engraved with words from the Book of Leviticus chosen by Rudyard Kipling: "their name liveth for evermore". Over the next ten years hundreds of cemeteries were constructed in France, Belgium, Italy, Egypt, Palestine, Macedonia, Mesopotamia and at Gallipoli.

The known, identified dead were one thing, but the war generated millions of "missing" (*see also* Chapter 59), whose last remains were lost or unidentified. The IWGC took a policy decision that they, too, should have permanent places of remembrance, and large memorials were built up and down the Western Front to give recognition to them. Grandest among them were Lutyens' imposing arch at Thiepval, on the Somme, which was unveiled in 1932; and Blomfield's Menin Gate at Ypres, at whose dedication in 1927 General Lord Plumer memorably said: "they are not missing – they are here". At Thiepval, over 72,000 men from Britain, Ireland and South Africa are remembered, while at the Menin Gate almost 55,000 Commonwealth names are recorded.

The imposing cemeteries and memorials in Flanders and France were echoed, in miniature, across the home nations, in thousands of local war memorials – expressions of grief and loss, but also of local and civic pride, which act as reminders of how the war's tendrils crept into all corners of Britain and her empire. It remains a sobering experience to chance upon a small village's war memorial and register the unlikely number of names etched into it. Remembrance seeped into the culture in other ways, too. The London Brighton and South Coast Railway even named one of its tank engines "Remembrance" and the London North Western Railway built a Claughton express engine with the number "1914" in memory of its dead employees.

Inevitably, not all the spirit of remembrance was reverential or uncritical. Perhaps the complexity of it all is best summed up in Kipling, poet of empire, patriot and a stalwart of the war effort, whose chosen inscriptions adorn the Menin Gate, yet also the father who helped his medically unfit son "Jack" get a commission that led to Jack's death at the Battle of Loos, and who afterwards wrote so unsparingly of his own generation's shortcomings. In one of his *Epitaphs* (1919), "A Dead Statesman" goes to meet his maker:

> Now all my lies are proved untrue
> And I must face the men I slew.
> What tale shall serve me here among
> Mine angry and defrauded young?

As demonstrated by the discovery in 2007 of the remains of hundreds more bodies (mainly Australian) near Fromelles, the "young" continue to be found.

"TWO PAIRS OF RUBBER GLOVES, TWO SHOVELS, STAKES TO MARK THE LOCATION OF GRAVES FOUND, CANVAS AND ROPE TO TIE UP REMAINS, STRETCHERS, CREOSOL AND WIRE CUTTERS."

The typical equipment of a British Exhumation Company after the war

100

A SKETCH FOR THE CENOTAPH
ENDURING SYMBOLS OF THE GREAT WAR

1919 AND BEYOND

When the war was over, a new set of pressing problems and concerns presented themselves. Life went on. For Germans, it was everything that went with defeat and a revolution: *vae victis* (*see* Chapter 96). For returning soldiers of all nations, it was coming to terms with civilians and family life again, followed by the imperative to find work to replace soldiering. In Britain, and elsewhere, generals were concerned with the welfare of their ex-soldiers. Politicians and leaders in all spheres of life had to reshape their countries from a war footing back to "regular life", while internationally they tried to carve a new world order that – they hoped – would ensure that the Great War remained a unique, unrepeatable, phenomenon.

The war had touched nearly everyone. Beatrice Webb wrote after the Armistice: "Every day one meets saddened women with haggard faces ... and one dare not ask after husband or son." There was, accordingly, a universal need to find some meaning for what soldiers and civilians alike had endured and to try and comfort those who had lost loved ones. The public mood demanded an immediate recognition of this huge national trauma. The result was the creation of some enduring rituals and symbols that, in time, came to memorialize not only the First World War but every conflict since.

"Cenotaph." Today it is such a familiar word that it is hard to remember that in 1919 few would have known what one was. Early in July 1919 the British government learned that the French were planning to place a catafalque, or symbolic grave, at the heart of France's parade to mark the signing of the Treaty at Versailles. The Cabinet felt Britain should have one, too, for its own parade the following week. The architect Sir Edwin Lutyens had already been informally asked to design something, and now he proposed to Lloyd George not a catafalque but a "cenotaph", or empty tomb, a quieter, more elegiac structure. This is one of Lutyens' first drawings, dated 4 June, already showing the clean, straight lines and freedom from religious or nationalistic adornment that would invest the memorial with such universal power and meaning. It was simply about remembering "The Glorious Dead". Quickly approved, the first Cenotaph was built in five days from plaster and wood for the Peace Parade of 19 July. It brilliantly captured the public mood and a campaign immediately began to retain it where it stood in Whitehall. The Cabinet agreed. A new stone structure was built and unveiled on 11 November 1920, as part of the funeral of the Unknown Warrior. Its simplicity and elegance allowed each grieving relative – mother, widow, father, son – to invest it with their own emotions. Within a week, more than a million people had filed past and a carpet of flowers covered its base, 10 feet deep.

> "ALL THAT THEY HAD THEY GAVE – THEY GAVE; AND THEY SHALL NOT RETURN, / FOR THESE ARE THOSE THAT HAVE NO GRAVE WHERE ANY HEART MAY MOURN."
>
> *Rudyard Kipling, from "The King's Pilgrimage", 1922*

It was King George V who suggested that on the first anniversary of the Armistice, 11 November 1919, the nation should remember the fallen. That first two-minute silence was described by the Manchester *Guardian*:

The first stroke of eleven produced a magical effect. The tram cars glided into stillness ... Someone took off his hat ... An elderly woman, not far away, wiped her eyes ... Everyone stood very still ... the hush deepened. It had spread over the whole city ... It was a silence which was almost pain ... And the spirit of memory brooded over it all.

Armistice Day has become one of the enduring symbols of the war, its powerful *tableau vivant* in Whitehall matched by similar ceremonies across the world. In the United States and the old Dominions, even still in Chinese Hong Kong, the ceremony lives on. In France the anniversary of the Armistice remains one the most important national days, remembered with blue cornflowers. After the war, memorials to the dead sprang up everywhere, their symbolism ranging from the Christian cross to iron crosses in Germany, while in France weeping Madonnas, triumphant *poilus* and many a proud cockerel can be seen in every French town and village as its memorial dedicated to those who fell in the conflict – a situation paralleled in Britain.

Some permanent, physical focal point – a national memorial – was clearly needed and for Armistice Day November 1920 Sir Edwin Lutyens' permanent version of his Cenotaph was unveiled by the king. The Whitehall Cenotaph was followed by other permanent and imposing memorials elsewhere: in Flanders, the Menin Gate (*see* Chapter 99), where since 1928 "The Last Post" is played every evening; the Australian War Memorial at Villers-Bretonneux and the towering Canadian memorial atop Vimy Ridge. In 1960, Turkey completed a striking memorial, the Çanakkale Martyrs' Memorial, to "253,000 immortals" at Gallipoli. Long after the Armistice, the Memorial Park to the Heroes of the First World War was finally dedicated in Moscow in 2005.

The 1920 ceremonies surrounding the Cenotaph included the burial of Britain's "Unknown Warrior" at Westminster Abbey. The idea to inter an anonymous soldier with national honours came from an army chaplain, who remembered seeing a rough grave with a pencilled inscription: "An Unknown Soldier of the Black Watch". The Dean of Westminster Abbey approached the government, which backed the idea. Six unidentified bodies were disinterred, one each from the battlefields of the Marne, Aisne, Ypres, Somme, Arras and Cambrai. They were placed on stretchers in the Chapel of St Pol and a brigadier, blindfolded, touched one of the flag-covered bodies, which was sent by ambulance to Boulogne. There it was transferred to a coffin, made of wood from Hampton Court, with a cast of a crusader's sword from the Tower of London, and guarded by French soldiers for its last night on French soil. The next morning the sealed coffin set sail, along with barrels of soil from Ypres, aboard the destroyer HMS *Verdun* for Dover.

On 11 November, at the Cenotaph the king laid his wreath on the coffin, then followed the gun carriage to Westminster Abbey, where the coffin passed through two rows of Victoria Cross holders. At the end of the service King George sprinkled earth from the battlefields into the grave and buglers sounded "The Last Post" and "The Rouse". By 27 November as many as 1.5 million people had filed past the grave.

**"FOR KING AND COUNTRY /
FOR LOVED ONES HOME AND EMPIRE /
FOR THE SACRED CAUSE OF JUSTICE AND /
THE FREEDOM OF THE WORLD"**

From the inscription on the grave of the Unknown Warrior, Westminster Abbey, London

Recognition of Field Marshal Haig himself eventually came in the form of an earldom, and, from Parliament in March 1919, a vote of thanks and £100,000. Haig was very conscious that while the dead needed remembering, the living needed help, and he called for government aid for demobilized soldiers. By the early 1920s the big cities were awash with unemployed ex-soldiers. Even former officers were begging or selling matches in the street. For the rest of his life Haig – the man whose unenviable job it had been to send men to face death – devoted himself to raising money for ex-servicemen in need, irrespective of rank. It is in the context of helping the living while simultaneously remembering the dead that the potent symbol of the poppy emerged.

Poppies grow quickly on disturbed earth. In 1915, at the dressing station at Essex Farm, near Ypres, after a long day's surgery, the Canadian doctor John McCrae came and found poppies and other wild flowers covering the broken soil. They inspired his famous lines of verse beginning: "In Flanders' fields the poppies grow, / Between the crosses, row on row". The poem rapidly became synonymous with the soldiers who died. Nevertheless, it was the American Legion that first used the poppy as a symbol of remembrance, in 1919. One American teacher, Moina Bell Michael, was so moved by McCrae's poem that she sold poppies to raise funds for US ex-servicemen. Anna Guérin, a Frenchwoman present at the American Legion's convention in September 1920, took up the idea and popularized the selling of artificial poppies as a way to raise funds for ex-servicemen. In 1921, millions were sold throughout the United States.

A Remembrance Day poster from 1923 urges people to wear a poppy on 11 November and support Earl Haig's charitable fund and the British Legion. Along with the Imperial (Commonwealth) War Graves Commission, the Royal British Legion, as it is now called, has proved a permanent legacy of the war.

As part of Guérin's efforts, she persuaded Haig to adopt the poppy. Thus, for Remembrance Day in 1921, he set up the Earl Haig Poppy Fund with the first Poppy Appeal, in order to raise money for the newly established British Legion – which brought together the previously disparate veterans' organizations – so that it could help disabled and needy ex-servicemen. In Britain, the factory to make and sell poppies was set up in 1922 by Major George Howson, founder of the Disabled Society, with five ex-servicemen. He suggested to the British Legion that the artificial flowers should be designed so that someone who had lost the use of a hand could assemble them. Within a few months the factory was providing work and an income for 50 disabled veterans. To this day, it still makes millions of poppies – the most visible, most portable, most ubiquitous and enduring reminder of the calamitous First World War.

To say that the conflict still affects us today is no exaggeration: the shadow of that grim conflict between 1914–18 has shaped our modern world. The millions who died or were maimed a century ago stand as grim testimony to political failure and the horrors of modern war … "lest we forget".

EUROPE IN 1914
& WARTIME ALLIES

Allied Powers

Central Powers

Neutral countries

NORWAY

Christiana (Oslo)

SW

NORTH SEA

DENMARK

Copenha

Berli

Potsda

GERMAN

BRITISH
ISLES

Dublin

NETHERLANDS

The Hague

London

Brussels
BELGIUM

LUX.

Paris

LORRAINE

ALSACE

FRANCE

Berne
SWITZERLAND

TYROL

TRENTINO

STRIA

ITALY

Rome

PORTUGAL

Madrid

SPAIN

Lisbon

M E D I T E R

Tunis

Gibraltar

Algiers

TUNISIA
(France)

ATLANTIC
OCEAN

Casablanca

ALGERIA
(France)

Tripol

MOROCCO
(France)

FINLAND

St Petersburg (Petrograd)

BALTIC SEA

ESTONIA

LIVONIA

LATVIA

COURLAND

LITHUANIA

Moscow

USSIA

Warsaw

POLAND

GALICIA

RUSSIA

Kiev

Kharkov

enna

Budapest

AUSTRIA-
HUNGARY

U K R A I N E

SNIA-
ajevo
EGOVINA

Belgrade

ROMANIA

Odessa

CRIMEA

SERBIA

Bucharest

Sebastopol

NTENEGRO

BULGARIA

BLACK SEA

ALBANIA

Sofia

GREECE

Constantinople

Athens

OTTOMAN

E M P I R E

PERSIA

N E A N   S E A

CYPRUS
(Britain)

PALESTINE

Baghdad

LIBYA
(Italy)

EGYPT (Britain)

Jerusalem

CENTRAL ARABIA
(NEJD)

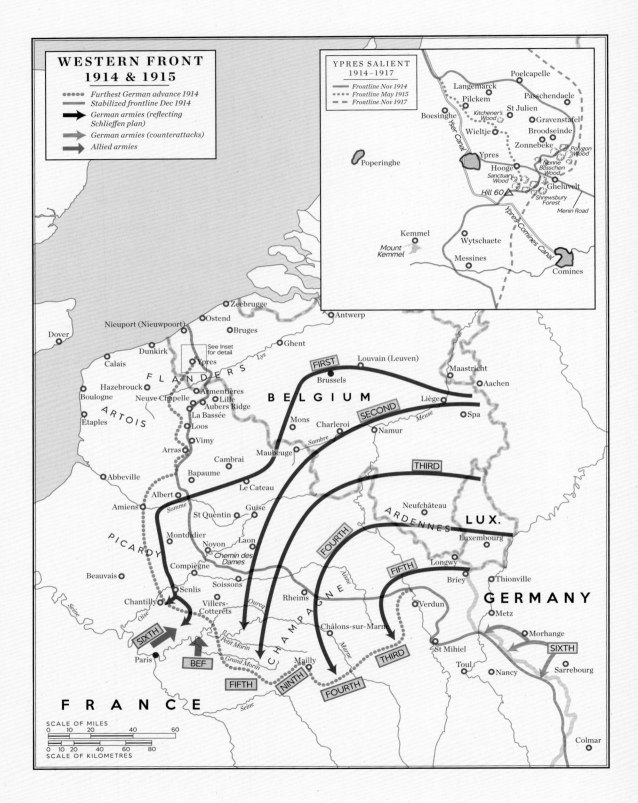

WESTERN FRONT 1914 & 1915

- •••• Furthest German advance 1914
- —— Stabilized frontline Dec 1914
- ➜ German armies (reflecting Schlieffen plan)
- ➜ German armies (counterattacks)
- ➜ Allied armies

YPRES SALIENT 1914–1917

- —— Frontline Nov 1914
- •••• Frontline May 1915
- – – – Frontline Nov 1917

Poelcapelle
Langemarck
Pilckem
Passchendaele
St Julien
Boesinghe
Kitchener's Wood
Gravenstafel
Wieltje
Broodseinde
Zonnebeke
Polygon Wood
Ypres
Nonne Bosschen Wood
Poperinghe
Hooge
Gheluvelt
Sanctuary Wood
Shrewsbury Forest
Hill 60
Menin Road
Kemmel
Wytschaete
Mount Kemmel
Messines
Comines
Ypres Comines Canal
Yser Canal

Zeebrugge
Ostend
Antwerp
Dover
Nieuport (Nieuwpoort)
Bruges
Ghent
Calais
Dunkirk
See Inset for detail
Ypres
Lys
Louvain (Leuven)
FIRST
Brussels
Maastricht
Hazebrouck
Boulogne
FLANDERS
Armentières
Lille
BELGIUM
Liège
Aachen
Neuve Chapelle
Aubers Ridge
Mons
Charleroi
SECOND
Spa
ARTOIS
La Bassée
Loos
Namur
Meuse
Étaples
Vimy
Maubeuge
Sambre
Arras
Cambrai
THIRD
Abbeville
Bapaume
Le Cateau
Neufchâteau
ARDENNES
LUX.
Amiens
Albert
Somme
St Quentin
Guise
Luxembourg
PICARDY
Montdidier
Noyon
Laon
FOURTH
Beauvais
Compiègne
Chemin des Dames
FIFTH
Longwy
Briey
Thionville
Senlis
Soissons
Rheims
Aisne
Verdun
GERMANY
Chantilly
Villers-Cotterêts
Oise
Ourcq
Metz
SIXTH
Petit Morin
Châlons-sur-Marne
St Mihiel
Morhange
BEF
Grand Morin
CHAMPAGNE
Marne
THIRD
SIXTH
Paris
FIFTH
NINTH
Mailly
FOURTH
Toul
Nancy
Sarrebourg
FRANCE
Seine
Verdun
Colmar
Seine

SCALE OF MILES
0 10 20   40   60
0 10 20 40   60   80
SCALE OF KILOMETRES

EASTERN FRONT
1914–1918

———— Frontline end Sept 1914
•••••••• Frontline Armistice 1917
– – – – Brest-Litovsk Treaty Line

SCALE OF MILES
0   50   100   150   200

SCALE OF KILOMETRES
0   50 100 150   250

ESTONIA

LATVIA

St Petersburg (Petrograd)

Tsarskoe Selo

Pskov

Riga

COURLAND

Dvina

R U S S I A

BALTIC SEA

Dvinsk

Moscow

LITHUANIA

Memel

Kovno
(Kaunas)

Lake Naroch

Smolensk

Königsberg

Gumbinnen

Neris (Viliya)

Vilna (Vilnius)

Danzig

EAST
PRUSSIA

Mogilev

*Masurian
Lakes*

Grodno

Minsk

Tannenberg

Neman

Bialystock

Thorn

Posen

Warsaw

Bug

Brest-Litovsk

Lublin

Vistula

Lodz

Breslau

P O L A N D

Krasnik

Kovel

Oder

SILESIA

Komarov

Lutsk

Kiev

Vistula

Jaroslav

Cracow

Tarnow

Lvov (Lemberg)

Ternopil

Limanova-Lipanov

Gorlice

Przemysl

San

Dnieper

Vienna

Danube

C A R P A T H I A N   M O U N T A I N S

Dniester

U K R A I N E

Rostov

Budapest

A U S T R I A - H U N G A R Y

Odessa

Theiss

ROMANIA

BLACK SEA

BOSNIA-
HERZ.

SERBIA

BULGARIA

MONTENEGRO

ALBANIA

Constantinople

GREECE

O T T O M A N
E M P I R E

GERMANY

SALONIKA & GALLIPOLI

— Salonika frontline Nov 1916
····· Salonika frontline Oct 1918

THE DARDANELLES 1915

Maximum Allied area held in summer 1915

HUNGARY

ROMANIA

Bucharest

BOSNIA-HERZEGOVINA

Sarajevo

Belgrade

Cor

Kolubara

Morava

Ibr

Danube

Nish

SERBIA

Sofia

BULGARIA

MONTENEGRO

Cetinje

Scutari

ALBANIA

KOSOVO

Vardar

Doiran

Monastir

Struma

Marica

MACEDONIA

Salonika

Valona

ITALY

ADRIATIC SEA

GREECE

Lemnos

AEGEAN SEA

Athens

Constantinople

Bosphorus

SEA OF MARMARA

See Inset for detail

OTTOMAN EMPIRE

Izmir (Smyrna)

Suvla Bay
Anzac Cove
Gaba Tepe
Gallipoli Peninsula

Chanak

Cape Helles
Krithia

Dardanelles Straits

Kum Kale

SCALE OF MILES
0   50   100   150

SCALE OF KILOMETRES
0   50   100   150   200

ITALIAN FRONT

— Frontline May 1916
····· Frontline Jan 1918
– – – Frontline 4 Nov 1918

AUSTRIA-HUNGARY

SWITZERLAND

CARPATHIA

Adige

Tolmezzo

Caporetto

TRENTINO

Trento

Piave

Belluno

VENETIAN ALPS

Udine

BAINSIZZA PLATEAU

Ljubljana

Gorizia

Isonzo

Monte Grappa

Asiago

Vittorio Veneto

Tagliamento

KARST PLATEAU

Bassano

Livenza

Piave

Trieste

Lake Garda

VENETO

Vicenza

Venice

Verona

Padua

Adige

Po

ADRIATIC SEA

ISTRIA

Fiume

Pola (Pula)

SCALE OF MILES
0   10   20   40   60

SCALE OF KILOMETRES
0   10   20   40   60   80

THE MIDDLE EAST
1914–1918

- – – – Frontline 1914–1916
- ·········· Frontline Aug 1916
- ▪ ▪ ▪ ▪ Frontline Mar 1917
- ●●●●● Frontline Jan 1918
- —— Frontline 30 Oct 1918

RUSSIA

CAUCASUS MTS.

BLACK SEA

CASPIAN SEA

GEORGIA

Trebizond

OTTOMAN EMPIRE

ARMENIA

AZERBAIJAN

PERSIA

Aleppo

Mosul

Hama

Homs

Euphrates

Tigris

Tripoli

SYRIA

MESOPOTAMIA

Beirut

LEBANON

Damascus

Baghdad

Ctesiphon

Acre

Haifa

Der'aa

Kut-al-Amara

Megiddo

Jordan

Abadan oilfields

Jaffa

Amman

Suez Canal

Jerusalem

Gaza

PALESTINE

Basra

Beersheba

Tafilah

PERSIAN GULF

Maan

Aqaba

SINAI

A R A B I A

Hejaz Railway

RED SEA

HEJAZ

E G Y P T

Medina

Yenbo

SCALE OF MILES
0   100   200   300

SCALE OF KILOMETRES
0   100   200   300   400

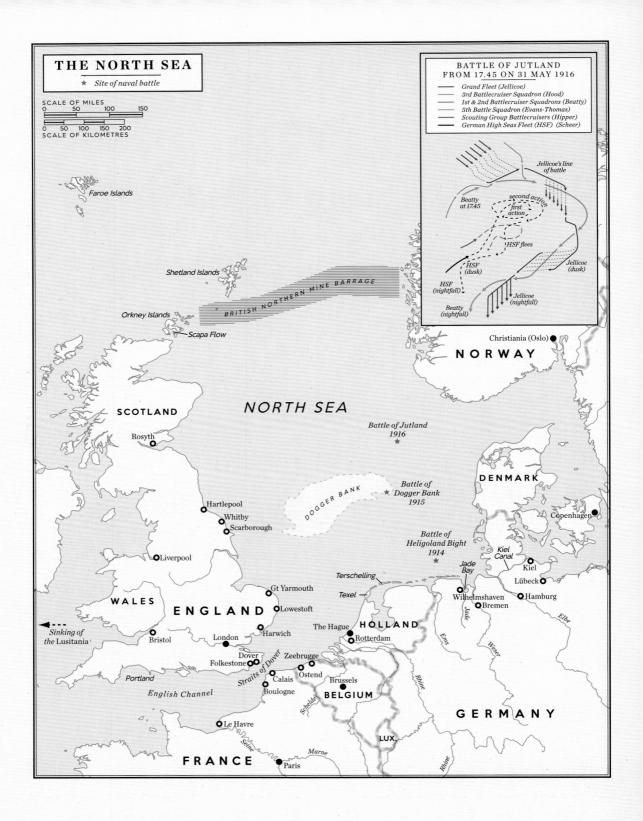

THE NORTH SEA

★ *Site of naval battle*

SCALE OF MILES
0   50   100   150

SCALE OF KILOMETRES
0   50   100   150   200

BATTLE OF JUTLAND
FROM 17.45 ON 31 MAY 1916

—— Grand Fleet (Jellicoe)
—— 3rd Battlecruiser Squadron (Hood)
—— 1st & 2nd Battlecruiser Squadrons (Beatty)
—— 5th Battle Squadron (Evans-Thomas)
—— Scouting Group Battlecruisers (Hipper)
—— German High Seas Fleet (HSF) (Scheer)

Jellicoe's line of battle

Beatty at 17.45

second action

first action

HSF flees

HSF (dusk)

Jellicoe (dusk)

HSF (nightfall)

Beatty (nightfall)

Jellicoe (nightfall)

Faroe Islands

Shetland Islands

BRITISH NORTHERN MINE BARRAGE

Orkney Islands
Scapa Flow

Christiania (Oslo)

NORWAY

NORTH SEA

SCOTLAND

Rosyth

Battle of Jutland
1916
★

DENMARK

Copenhagen

Hartlepool
Whitby
Scarborough

DOGGER BANK

Battle of
Dogger Bank
1915

Battle of
Heligoland Bight
1914
★

Kiel
Canal

Kiel

Liverpool

Jade
Bay

Lübeck

Terschelling

Wilhelmshaven
Bremen

Hamburg

WALES

ENGLAND

Gt Yarmouth

Lowestoft

Texel

Jade

Ems

Weser

Elbe

Sinking of
the Lusitania

Bristol

London

Harwich

The Hague
Rotterdam

HOLLAND

Dover
Folkestone

Zeebrugge
Ostend

Straits of Dover

Calais

Boulogne

Brussels

BELGIUM

Rhine

GERMANY

Portland

English Channel

Schelde

LUX.

Le Havre

Seine

Marne

Rhine

FRANCE   Paris

WESTERN FRONT
1916–1917

Frontline Jan 1916
Hindenburg Line 1917

Battle of Verdun, Feb–Dec 1916

Battle of the Somme, July–Nov 1916

Third Battle of Ypres 1917
for detail see Ypres Salient map, p.430

SOMME CAMPAIGN
JULY–NOV 1916

Frontline 1 July 1916
Frontline 19 Nov 1916

Serre
Beaumont-Hamel
Beaucourt
Hamel
Thiepval
Ovillers
La Boisselle
Albert
Fricourt
Bray

Bazentin Wood
High Wood
Delville Wood
Bapaume
Courcelette   Flers
Pozières
Bazentin   Ginchy
Montauban   Longueval
Mametz   Hardecourt
Carnoy   Maurepas
Mametz Wood   Cléry
Frise   St Quentin
Morval
Péronne
Flacourt

Ancre
Somme

Dover
Calais
Boulogne
Étaples
Dunkirk
Bruges
Ghent

FLANDERS
Passchendaele
Ypres
Lys

ARTOIS
Hazebrouck
Lille

BELGIUM
Mons

Meuse

Abbeville
Somme
Amiens
Vimy
Arras
Bullecourt
Serre   Bapaume
Thiepval   Flers
Albert   Cambrai
Péronne

See Inset
for detail

Montdidier
Noyon

PICARDY

Compiègne
Oise
Chantilly

Malmaison
Soissons
Rheims

Sedan

ARDENNES

Longwy
Briey

Côte 304
Verdun
Fort Douaumont
Fort Vaux
St Mihiel

Toul

Marne
Petit Morin
Grand Morin
Seine

Paris

FRANCE

Seine

SCALE OF MILES
0 10 20   40   60

0 10 20   40   60   80
SCALE OF KILOMETRES

WESTERN FRONT
1918

Frontline beginning of 1918
Furthest extent of German offensive from 21 Mar
Main lines of Allied counterthrusts
Line at Armistice 11 Nov 1918
Postwar Rhineland demilitarized zone

Dover

Zeebrugge

Ostend   Bruges   Antwerp

Ghent

BELG.

Dunkirk   Passchendaele

Calais   Ypres

Cassel   F L A N D E R S   Lys   Brussels

Hazebrouck   BELG/BEF   B E L G

Lille

A R T O I S   Drocourt   Mons   Charleroi

Vimy   Sambre

Arras   BEF   Maubeuge

Quéant   Cambrai

Abbeville   Bapaume   Flesquières   Le Cateau

Somme   Albert   Busigny

Amiens   Péronne   Guise

Villers-Bretonneux   Hamel   St Quentin   FRENCH

FRENCH   Méz

P I C A R D Y   La Fère   Aisne

Montdidier   Noyon   Malmaison   FRENCH

Beauvais   Compiègne   Soissons   Rheims

Oise   Senlis   Villers-Cotterêts   FRENCH

Seine   Chantilly   Marne

Château-Thierry   Châl

Paris   Petit Morin

Grand Morin

F R A N C E

Seine

SCALE OF MILES
0   10   20   40   60

0   10   20   40   60   80
SCALE OF KILOMETRES

NETHERLANDS

M

Liège

Meuse

Spa

ARDENNES

LUXEMBOURG

dan

Longwy

Briey

Verdun

US

St Mihiel

US

Toul

Nancy

LORRAINE

Düsseldorf

BRITISH OCCUPATION ZONE 1919

Cologne

Siegburg

Rhine

AMERICAN OCCUPATION ZONE 1919

Koblenz

Frankfurt

FRENCH OCCUPATION ZONE 1919

Mainz

GERMANY

Moselle

Mannheim

Metz

SAAR

Karlsruhe

Rhine

ALSACE

EUROPE AFTER THE PEACE TREATIES 1919–1925

Areas of dispute or League of Nations control

NORWAY
Christiana (Oslo) ●

SWED

NORTH SEA

DENMARK
Copenhag ●

GREAT BRITAIN

Dublin ●
IRISH FREE STATE (1922)

NETHERLANDS

London ●

BELGIUM

Rhineland occupied /
demilitarized zone

GERMAN
Berlin ●

LUX.

Weimar ●
Pr

Saar, to Germany
in plebiscite 1935

LORRAINE

Paris ●

FRANCE

ALSACE

Berne ●
SWITZERLAND

AUST

Klagenfurt,
to Austria
in plebiscite
1921

Fiume Free
1920–2

ITALY

ATLANTIC OCEAN

Corsica (Fr.)

● Rome

Madrid ●

Sardinia (It.)

SPAIN

PORTUGAL

Lisbon ●

M E D I T E R

Tunis ●

**TUNISIA
(France)**

Algiers ●

Casablanca ●

**ALGERIA
(France)**

Trip

**MOROCCO
(France)**

FINLAND

Helsinki

○ Leningrad (Petrograd)

Tallinn

ESTONIA

BALTIC SEA

Riga

LATVIA

Memel ○ Occupied by Lithuania, 1923

LITHUANIA

●Moscow

ree City of Danzig

Kovno

Vilna (Vilnius) ○

EAST PRUSSIA

POLISH CORRIDOR

Central Lithuanian Republic, 1920–22

ned by Germany
lebiscite 1920 ● Warsaw

**R U S S I A /
S O V I E T   U N I O N**

POLAND

Upper Silesia to Germany and Poland in plebiscite 1921

GALICIA

○ Kiev

ECHOSLOVAKIA

●Budapest

TRANSYLVANIA

BESSARABIA

HUNGARY

R O M A N I A

GOSLAVIA

●Belgrade

Bucharest

SNIA-
EGOVINA   SERBIA

DOBRUDJA

BLACK SEA

ALBANIA

Sofia ● BULGARIA

THRACE

Constantinople (Istanbul) ●

GREECE

●Ankara (capital from 1923)

T U R K E Y

Athens

PERSIA

N E A N   S E A

CYPRUS (Britain)

SYRIA (France)

Beirut ●
● Damascus

IRAQ (MESOPOTAMIA) (Britain)

PALESTINE (Br.)   Amman ●

Baghdad ●

LIBYA (Italy)

Jerusalem ●

TRANS-JORDAN (Br.)

EGYPT (Britain)

ARABIA

FURTHER READING

Asprey, Robert, *The German High Command at War: Hindenburg and Ludendorff and the First World War* (New York, 1991)

Bainton, Roy, *A Brief History of 1917: Russia's Year of Revolution* (London, 2005)

Banks, Arthur, *A Military Atlas of the First World War* (London, 2001)

Barker, Ralph, *A Brief History of the Royal Flying Corps in World War I* (London, 2002)

Barnett, Correlli, *The Swordbearers: Supreme Command in the First World War* (London, 1963)

Bennett, Geoffrey, *Naval Battles of the First World War* (London, 1968)

Blaxland, Gregory, *Amiens, 1918* (London, 1968)

Brook-Shepherd, Gordon, *November 1918: The Last Act of the Great War* (London, 1981)

Brown, Malcolm, *Tommy Goes to War* (London, 1978)

Brown, Malcolm, *The Imperial War Museum Book of the Western Front* (London, 1993)

Cecil, Hugh and Peter Liddle, *Facing Armageddon: The First World War Experience* (London, 1996)

Churchill, Winston, *The World Crisis 1911–1918* (London, 1923; new edition 2005)

Clayton, Anthony, *Paths of Glory: The French Army 1914–18* (London, 2003)

Coogan, Tim Pat, *1916: The Easter Rising* (London, 2001)

Cooksey, Jon, *The Barnsley Pals: The 13th and 14th Battalions, York & Lancaster Regiment* (Barnsley, 2008)

Cooper, Bryan, *The Ironclads of Cambrai* (London, 1970)

Cooper, Jilly, *Animals in War* (London, 1984)

Corns, Cathryn and John Hughes-Wilson, *Blindfold and Alone: British Military Executions in the Great War* (London, 2001)

Corrigan, Gordon, *Mud, Blood and Poppycock* (London, 2003)

Creveld, Martin van, *Supplying War: Logistics from Wallenstein to Patton* (Cambridge, 1977)

Creveld, Martin van, *Command in War* (Cambridge, MA, 1987)

De Leeuw, Adele, *Edith Cavell: Nurse, Spy, Heroine* (London, 1968)

Dunn, J.C., *The War the Infantry Knew, 1914–1919: A Chronicle of Service in France and Belgium* (London, 1938; reprinted 1989)

Fromkin, David, *A Peace to End All Peace: The Fall of the Ottoman Empire and the Creation of the Modern Middle East* (New York, 2001)

Fromkin, David, *Europe's Last Summer: Who Started the Great War in 1914?* (New York, 2004)

Fussell, Paul, *The Great War and Modern Memory* (Oxford, 1975)

Gordon, Andrew, *The Rules of the Game: Jutland and British Naval Command* (London, 1996)

Griffith, Paddy, *British Fighting Methods in the Great War* (London, 1998)

Hay, Ian, *The First Hundred Thousand* (London, 1916)

Haythornthwaite, Philip J., *The World War One Source Book* (London, 1992)

Hayward, James, *Myths and Legends of the First World War* (London, 2002)

Holmes, Richard, *The Western Front* (London, 1999)

Holmes, Richard, *Tommy: The British Soldier on the Western Front 1914–1918* (London, 2004)

Horne, Alistair, *The Price of Glory: Verdun 1916* (New York, 1994)

Horne, John and Alan Kramer, *German Atrocities, 1914: A History of Denial* (London, 2001)

Hough, Richard, *The Great War at Sea: 1914–18* (Oxford, 1986)

Hughes-Wilson, John, *The Puppet Masters: Spies, Traitors and the Real Forces Behind World Events* (London, 2002)

Keegan, John, *The First World War* (London, 1998)

Kennedy, Ross A., *The Will to Believe: Woodrow Wilson, World War I, and America's Strategy for Peace and Security* (Kent, OH, 2009)

MacDonald, Lyn, *1914: The Days of Hope* (London, 1987)

MacDonald, Lyn, *1915: The Death of Innocence* (London, 1993)

Macmillan, Margaret, *Peacemakers: The Paris Conference of 1919 and Its Attempt to End War* (London, 2002)

Marwick, Arthur, *The Deluge: British Society and the First World War* (London, 1965)

Massie, Robert K., *Castles of Steel: Britain, Germany and the Winning of the Great War at Sea* (New York, 2003)

Middlebrook, Martin, *The Kaiser's Battle* (Barnsley, 2007)

Millar, Ronald, *Kut: The Death of an Army* (London, 1969)

Morris, Captain Joseph, *The German Air Raids on Great Britain, 1914–1918* (London, 1925; reprinted 2001)

Mosley, Leonard, *Duel for Kilimanjaro: An Account of the East African Campaign, 1914–1918* (London, 1963)

Murphy, David, *The Arab Revolt 1916–18: Lawrence Sets Arabia Ablaze* (Oxford, 2008)

Nutting, Anthony, *Lawrence of Arabia: The Man and the Motive* (London, 1966)

Palmer, Alan, *The Gardeners of Salonika: An Account of the Campaign in Macedonia, 1915–1918* (London, 1965)

Philpott, William, *Bloody Victory: The Sacrifice on the Somme and the Making of the Twentieth Century* (London, 2009)

Pipes, Richard, *The Russian Revolution* (New York, 1990)

Prior, Robin and Trevor Wilson, *Passchendaele: The Untold Story* (New Haven, CT, 1996)

Purnell (publishers), *History of the First World War*, partwork series of 128 issues in 8 vols (London, 1969–71)

Ramsay, David, *Lusitania: Saga and Myth* (London, 2001)

Richards, Frank, *Old Soldiers Never Die* (London, 1933)

Ritter, Gerhard, *The Schlieffen Plan: Critique of a Myth*, translated by A. Wilson and E. Wilson (London, 1958)

Ritter, Gerhard, *The Sword and the Sceptre: The Problem of Militarism in Germany*, translated by Heinz Norden, 4 vols (London, 1971–3)

Salandra, Antonio, *Italy and the Great War: From Neutrality to Intervention* (London, 1932)

Sheffield, Gary, *Forgotten Victory: The First World War – Myths and Realities* (London, 2001)

Showalter, Dennis E., *Tannenberg: Clash of Empires, 1914* (Hamden, CT, 1991)

Simpson, Andy, *Hot Blood and Cold Steel: Life and Death in the Trenches of the First World War* (London, 1993)

Steel, Nigel and Peter Hart, *Defeat at Gallipoli* (London, 1994)

Stevenson, David, *1914–1918: The History of the First World War* (London, 2004)

Stone, Norman, *The Eastern Front 1914–17* (London, 1975)

Stone, Norman, *World War One: A Short History* (London, 2007)

Strachan, Hew, *The First World War: A New Illustrated History* (London, 2003; paperback edition, without subtitle, 2006)

Taylor, A.J.P., *The Struggle for Mastery in Europe: 1848–1918* (Oxford, 1954)

Terraine, John, *White Heat: The New Warfare 1914–18* (London, 1982)

Tolson, Roger, *Art from the First World War* (London, 2008)

Travers, Tim, *The Killing Ground: The British Army, the Western Front and the Emergence of Modern Warfare, 1900–1918* (London, 1987)

Tuchman, Barbara W., *The Zimmermann Telegram* (London, 1958)

Tuchman, Barbara W., *The Guns of August* (London, 1962)

Warner, Philip, *The Battle of Loos* (London, 1976)

Wheeler-Bennett, John W., *Brest-Litovsk: The Forgotten Peace – March 1918* (London, 1938)

Wilson, Trevor, *The Myriad Faces of War: Britain and the Great War, 1914–1918* (Cambridge, 1986)

Winter, Denis, *Death's Men: Soldiers of the Great War* (London, 1978)

Woodward, E.L., *Great Britain and the German Navy* (London, 1964)

Woollacott, Angela, *On Her Their Lives Depend: Munitions Workers in the Great War* (Berkeley, CA, 1994)

INDEX

OBJECT SOURCE REFERENCES

01 Imperial crown
(Royal Collection)

02 Ulster pen
(Ulster Museum)

03 *Pickelhaube*
(IWM UNI 12198)

04 Recruitment sign
(IWM FEQ 144)

05 European map
(IWM PST 6964)

06 Archduke's tunic
(Heeresgeschichtliches Museum,
Vienna)

07 Paper money
(IWM CUR 12700 and CUR 12701)

08 Kitchener artwork
(IWM PST 2735)

09 Newcastle Commercials' Drum
(IWM EPH 3122)

10 HMS *Lance* gun
(IWM ORD 114)

11 Marching boots
(IWM UNI 12643)

12 *Pantalons rouges*
(IWM UNI 12209)

13 Atrocity poster
(IWM PST 13606)

14 Web equipment
(IWM EQU 714)

15 London bus
(IWM 4017.5.1)

16 Mock Iron Cross
(IWM EPH 2171)

17 Christmas Truce button
(IWM DOCS E Rowden)

18 Commemorative ribbons
(IWM EPHEM 00488 and IWM
EPHEM 00505)

19 Barnardiston's sword
(IWM WEA 1272/1)

20 African eagle
(IWM EPH 9011)

21 Souchon's medals
(IWM OMD 6240-
6250)

22 Tirpitz the pig
(IWM EPH 9032)

23 Anderson's stick
(IWM UNI 12252)

24 Australian flag
(IWM FLA 2038)

25 Italian helmet
(IWM UNI 12281)

26 Bulgarian maxim
(IWM FIR 9205)

27 *Lusitania* passenger's camisole
(IWM UNI 11978)

28 Zeppelin ammunition box
(IWM FIR 11621)

29 Ticket collector's hat
(IWM UNI 9694)

30 First heavy shell
(IWM MUN 3281)

31 Kaiser Bill toilet roll
(IWM EPH 5245)

32 Cavell's diary
(IWM DOCS Edith Cavell)

33 Fryatt's watch
(IWM EPH 10292)

34 NCF membership card
(IWM DOCS W Harrison)

35 "Mother" 9.2" Howitzer
(IWM ORD 108)

36 Vickers machine gun
(IWM FIR 8100)

37 Message streamer
(IWM FLA 394)

38 Trench shovel
(IWM FEQ 5255)

39 Petrified glove
(IWM EPH 4377)

40 Jackson's prayer book
(IWM DOCS 2nd Lieutenant
E C Jackson)

41 Fullerphone
(IWM COM 176)

42 Deceptive tree
(IWM FEQ 854)

43 Geophone
(IWM FEQ 874)

44 Escape aids
(IWM EPH 810)

45 Dog collar
(IWM COM 1068)

46 Chisholm's decorations
(IWM OMD 2623–2629)

47 Bérenger's helmet
(IWM UNI 8199)

48 Short VC's helmet
(IWM UNI 11312)

49 Startin's cudgel
(WEA 2160)

50 French 75mm gun
(IWM ORD 125)

51 Eastern Front postcard
(IWM EPH 947)

52 Nevill's football
(Museum of the Queen's (RWS)
Regiment)

53 Cope's jacket
(IWM UNI 10830)

54 Film programme
(IWM K 93/1572)

55 Army rations (IWM EPH 4379
and EPH 7442)

56 Douglas the dummy
(IWM EPH 3863)

57 Phrase book
(IWM K 76194)

58 Clayton's chalice
(Toc H, Poperinghe)

59 Body Density Map
(IWM 57c edition 2 M.5/761)

60 Bairnsfather cartoon
(Nigel Steel)

61 Remnant of HMS *Indefatigable*
(IWM MAR 72)

62 U-boat wireless receiver
(IWM COM 78)

63 Thomas's last words
(National Library of Wales)

64 Surrender document
(IWM DOCS Special Misc X)

65 Model prime ministers
(IWM EPH 3255 and EPH 9361)

66 Stars and stripes
(IWM FLA 5468)

67 Bolshevik banner
(IWM FLA 2055)

68 Culley's Sopwith Camel
(IWM 2010.275.1)

69 Vimy trench mortar
(IWM ORD 52)

70 Toy *poilu*
(IWM 6282)

71 German officer's cap
(IWM UNI 9414)

72 Hassell's tank mask
(IWM EQU 1654)

73 Simplex locomotive
(IWM 4109.71.1)

74 Aerial camera
(IWM PHO 26)

75 Highgate's charge sheet
(The National Archives)

76 Sassoon's revolver
(IWM FIR 11852)

77 Singer Sargent's *Gassed*
(IWM ART 1460)

78 Hanukkah lamp
(IWM EPH 6879)

79 Lawrence's rifle
(IWM FIR 8255, loan from Royal
Collection)

80 Nevinson's *The Food Queue*
(IWM ART 840)

81 Egg ration card
(IWM K12/1278)

82 President's 14 Points (Library
of Congress, Washington DC)

83 Dazzle ship model
(IWM MOD 2474)

84 Haig's order
(IWM K11670/130 EPH. C. PERS
– Rare B)

85 Haig's toby jug
(IWM EPH 8727)

86 Richthofen's engine
(IWM 2020.165.1)

87 Mark V tank
(IWM 4100.90.1)

88 German shoulder straps
(IWM EPH 9319)

89 Saladin's wreath
(IWM EPH 4338)

90 *Ersatz* nightdress
(IWM UNI 11991)

91 Queen Mary's flag
(FLA 5409, loan from Royal
Collection)

92 Election poster
(IWM PST 12171)

93 Orpen's To the *Unknown
British Soldier*
(IWM ART 4438)

94 Seagull gun
(FIR 11624)

95 A new stamp
(Mark Hawkins-Dady)

96 Kaiser's crown
(IWM EPH 9457)

97 Agar's boat
(IWM MAR 563)

98 Néry gun
(IWM ORD 102)

99 Miller's cross
(IWM EPH 8612)

100 Lutyens' Cenotaph sketch
(IWM ART 3991 b)

A HISTORY OF THE FIRST WORLD WAR IN 100 OBJECTS

In association with Imperial War Museums
www.iwm.org.uk

An Hachette UK Company
www.hachette.co.uk

First published in Great Britain in 2014
by Cassell, a division of
Octopus Publishing Group Ltd,
Carmelite House,
50 Victoria Embankment,
London EC4Y 0DZ
www.octopusbooks.co.uk

First published in paperback in 2016

ISBN 978-1-84403-918-0

A CIP record for this book is available from the British Library

Set in Chronicle Deck and Keep Calm

Printed and bound in China

Group Publishing Director: Denise Bates
Senior Managing Editor: Clare Churly
Managing Editor: Mark Hawkins-Dady
Art Director: Jonathan Christie
Designer: David Rowley
Map illustrations: Nick Rowland
Picture Researcher: Jennifer Veall
Assistant Production Manager: Caroline Alberti

PICTURE ACKNOWLEDGEMENTS

akg-images Erich Lessing 33. **Alamy** The Print Collector 115. By permission of **The National Library of Wales** 263. **Corbis** 152, 165, 303, 345, 8; Bettmann 31, 35, 53, 281, 353; dpa/dpa 36; Museum of Flight 285; STR/Keystone 405. **Getty Images** Alinari via Getty Images 381; Apic 204; A. R. Coster/Topical Press Agency/Hulton Archive 315; Bob Thomas/Popperfoto 427; Central Press/Hulton Archive 47, 264; De Agostini 382; Fotosearch 101; Gamma-Keystone via Getty Images 390; General Photographic Agency/Hulton Archive 290; Henry Guttmann/Hulton Archive 22, 348; Hulton Archive 15, 27, 83, 128, 149, 329, 397, 408; John Warwick Brooke 298; London Expressa/Hulton Archive 43; Mondadori via Getty Images 116, 277; Oesterreichsches Volkshochschularchiv/Imagno 84; P. Otsup/Slava Katamidze Collection 413; Popperfoto 269, 322, 401; Roger Viollet 422; Three Lions 394; Time & Life Pictures 2 background, 372; Topical Press Agency 19, 38; Topical Press Agency/Hulton Archive 272, 338, 387; UIG via Getty Images 371; Universal History Archive 141. **Imperial War Museums** 3 (UNI 11312), 10 (Q 81771), 21 (UNI 12198), 25 (FEQ 144), 29 (PST 6964), 41 above (CUR 12701), 41 below (CUR 12700), 45 (PST 2735), 49 (EPH 3122), 51 (ORD 114), 55 (UNI 12643), 59 (UNI 12209), 63 (PST 13606), 64 (Q 53271), 67 (EQU 714), 69 (Q 51200), 71 (4107.5.1), 73 (Q 57328), 75 (EPH 2171), 77 (Q 22687), 79 (DOCS E Rowden), 81 (EPHEM 00488 and EPHEM 00505), 87 (WEA 1272/1), 89 (EPH 9011), 91 (Q 67818), 93 (OMD 6240-6250), 95 (Q 23732), 96 (Q 13622), 99 (EPH 9032), 103 (UNI 12252), 104 (Q 24191), 107 (FLA 2038), 109 (HU 53360), 111 (Q 13622), 113 (UNI 12281), 118 (FIR 9205/3), 121 (Q 31865), 123 (UNI 11978), 125 (Q 20220), 126 (FIR 11621), 131 (UNI 9694), 133 (Q 27854), 135 (MUN 3281), 137 (Q 30011), 138 (EPH 5245), 143 (DOCS Edith Cavell), 145 (EPH 10292), 147 (DOCS W Harrison), 151 (ORD 108), 155 (FIR 8100), 157 (Q 3987), 159 (FLA 394), 161 (Q 67057), 163 (FEQ 5255), 167 (EPH 4377), 169 (Q 48951), 171 (DOCS 2ND LIEUTENANT E C JACKSON), 172 (HU 63277B), 175 (COM 176), 177 (Q 2750), 179 (FEQ 854), 181 (FEQ 874), 182 (E(AUS) 1681), 185 (EPH 810), 187 (Q 1598), 189 (COM 1068), 190 (E(AUS) 668), 192 (OMD 2623-2629), 195 (Q 9221), 196 (Q 1071), 199 (UNI 8199), 201 (Q 1778), 203 (UNI 11312), 207 (WEA 2160), 211 (ORD 125), 213 (Q 23760), 214 (ART 4415), 217 (EPH 947), 223 (Q 79501), 225 (UNI 10830), 226 (Q 70164), 229 (K 93/1572), 231 (Q 5575), 233 LEFT (EPH 7442), 233 RIGHT (EPH 4379), 235 (EPH 3863), 237 (CO 2013), 239 (K 76194), 243 (Q 1152), 245 (57C EDITION 2 M.5/761), 247 (Q 721), 250 (Q 30515), 253 (MAR 72), 255 (SP 1592), 256 (SP 1708), 259 (COM 78), 267 (DOCS Special Misc X), 271 (left, EPH 9361; right, EPH 3255), 275 (FLA 5468), 279 (FLA 2055), 283 (2010.275.1), 287 (ORD 52), 292 (EPH 6282), 295 (UNI 9414), 297 (Q 2901), 301 (EQU 1654), 305 (4109.71.1.3), 306 (E(AUS) 844), 309 (PHO 26), 311 (Q 26945), 317 (FIR 11852), 320 (ART 1460), 325 (Q 1464), 327 (EPH 6879), 330 (FIR 8255), 333 (Q 60212), 334 (Q 65857), 337 (ART 840), 341 (K12/1278), 346 (MOD 2474), 351 (K11670/130 EPH. C. PERS - Rare B), 354 (Q 47997), 357 (EPH 8727), 359 (Q 1065), 361(2020.165.1), 363 (Q 42284), 365 (4100.90.1), 369 (EPH 9319), 375 (EPH 4338), 379 (UNI 11991), 385 (FLA 5409), 389 (PST 12171), 393 (ART 4438), 399 (FIR 11624), 405 (EPH 9457), 410 (MAR 563), 414 (ORD 102), 416 (Q 20539), 419 (EPH 8612), 421 (Q 47901), 425 (ART 3991b). **Library of Congress** 343. **Mark Hawkins-Dady** 403. **Mary Evans Picture Library** Epic/Tallandier 56; Pump Park Photography 209, 319; Robert Hunt Collection 61; Robert Hunt Collection/Imperial War Museum 366. **National Museums Northern Ireland Collection, Ulster Museum** 16. **Nick Pope** 221. **Nigel Steel** 249. **Royal Collection Trust, ©Her Majesty Queen Elizabeth II 2013** 13. **©Talbot House** 241. **The National Archives** WO71/387/1 313. **TopFoto** 289, 377; ullsteinbild 219, 261.